FAIRY TAIL

34

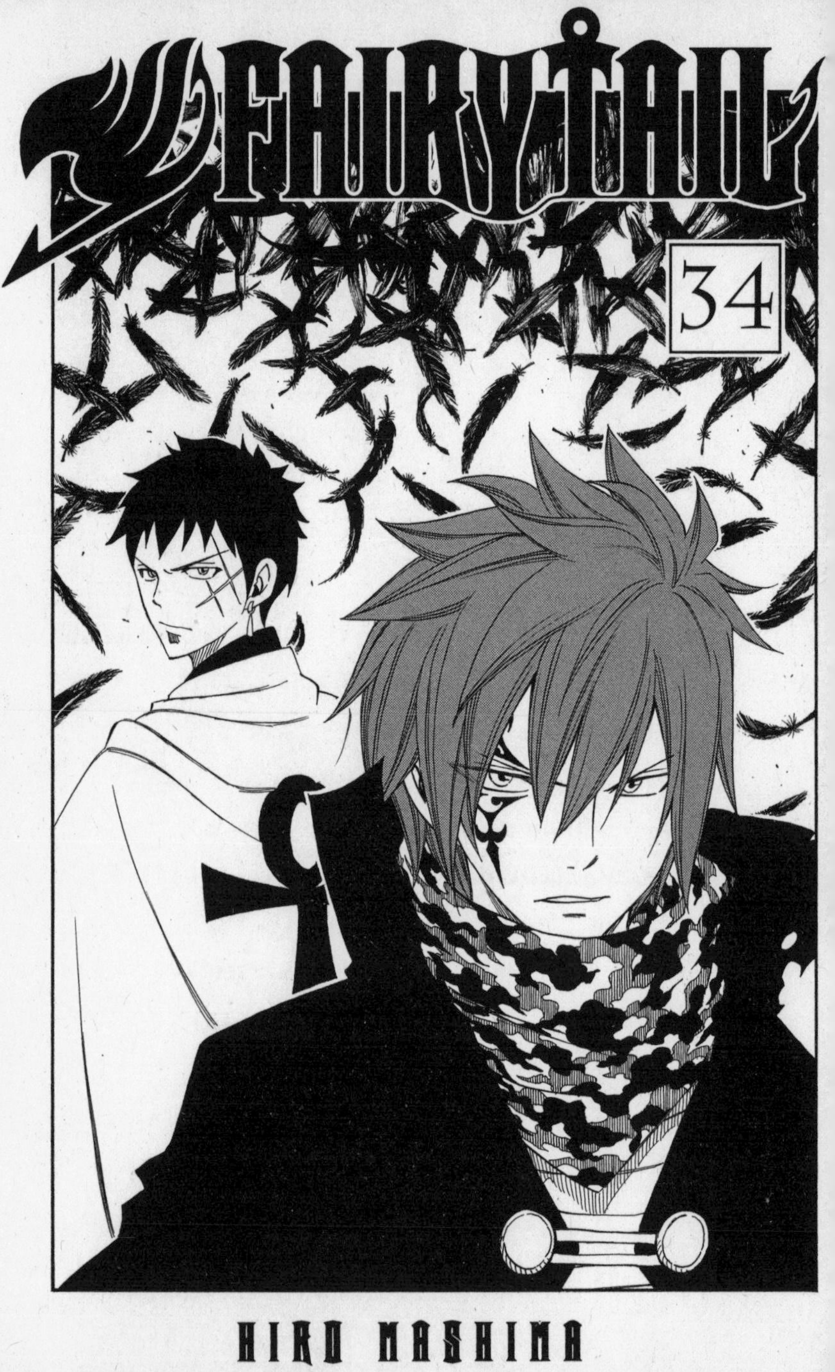

HIRO MASHIMA

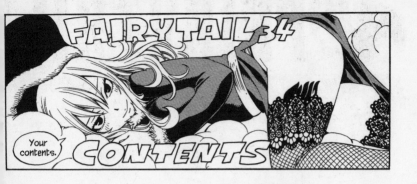

FAIRY TAIL 34

Your contents.

CONTENTS

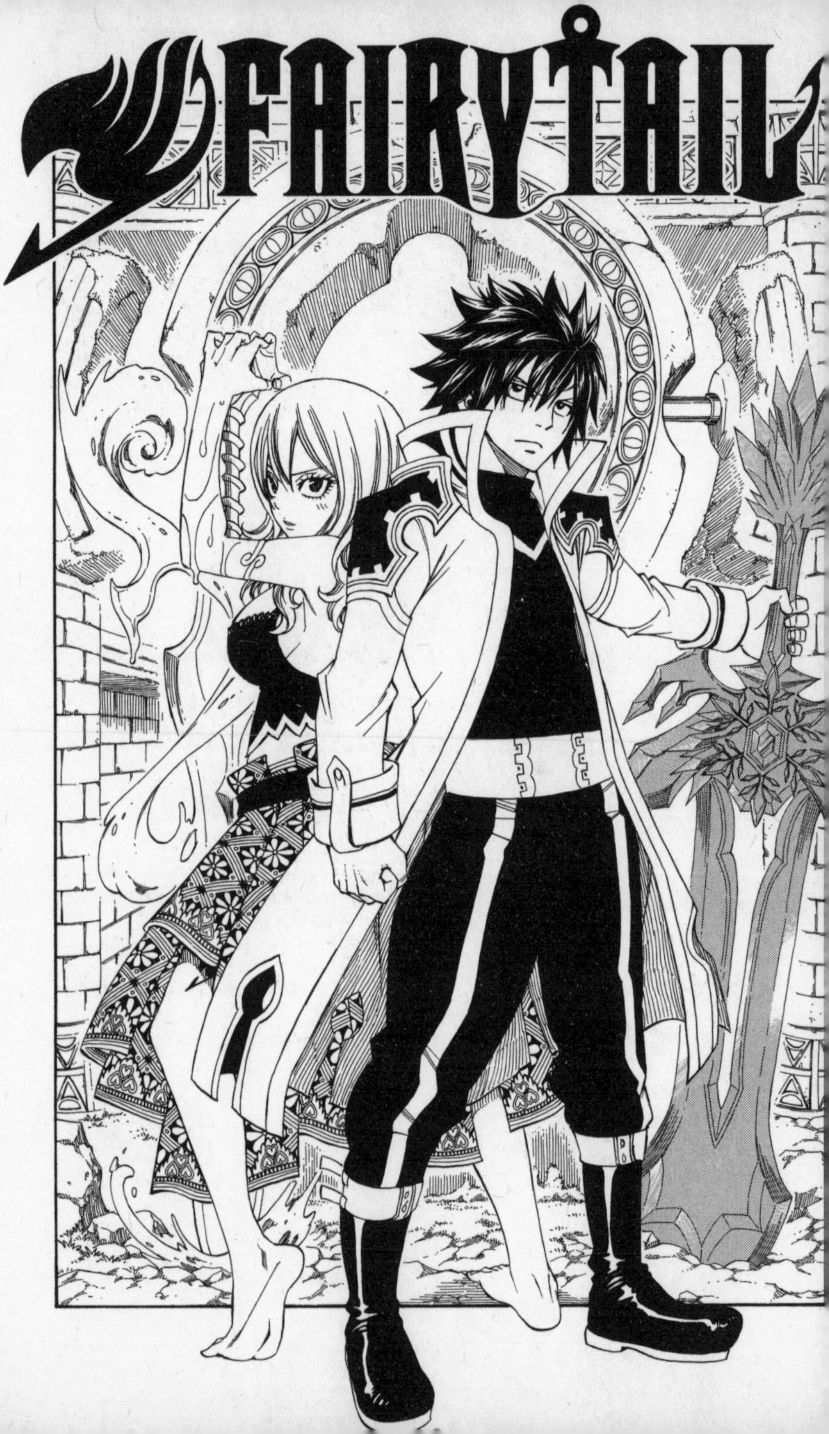
FAIRY TAIL

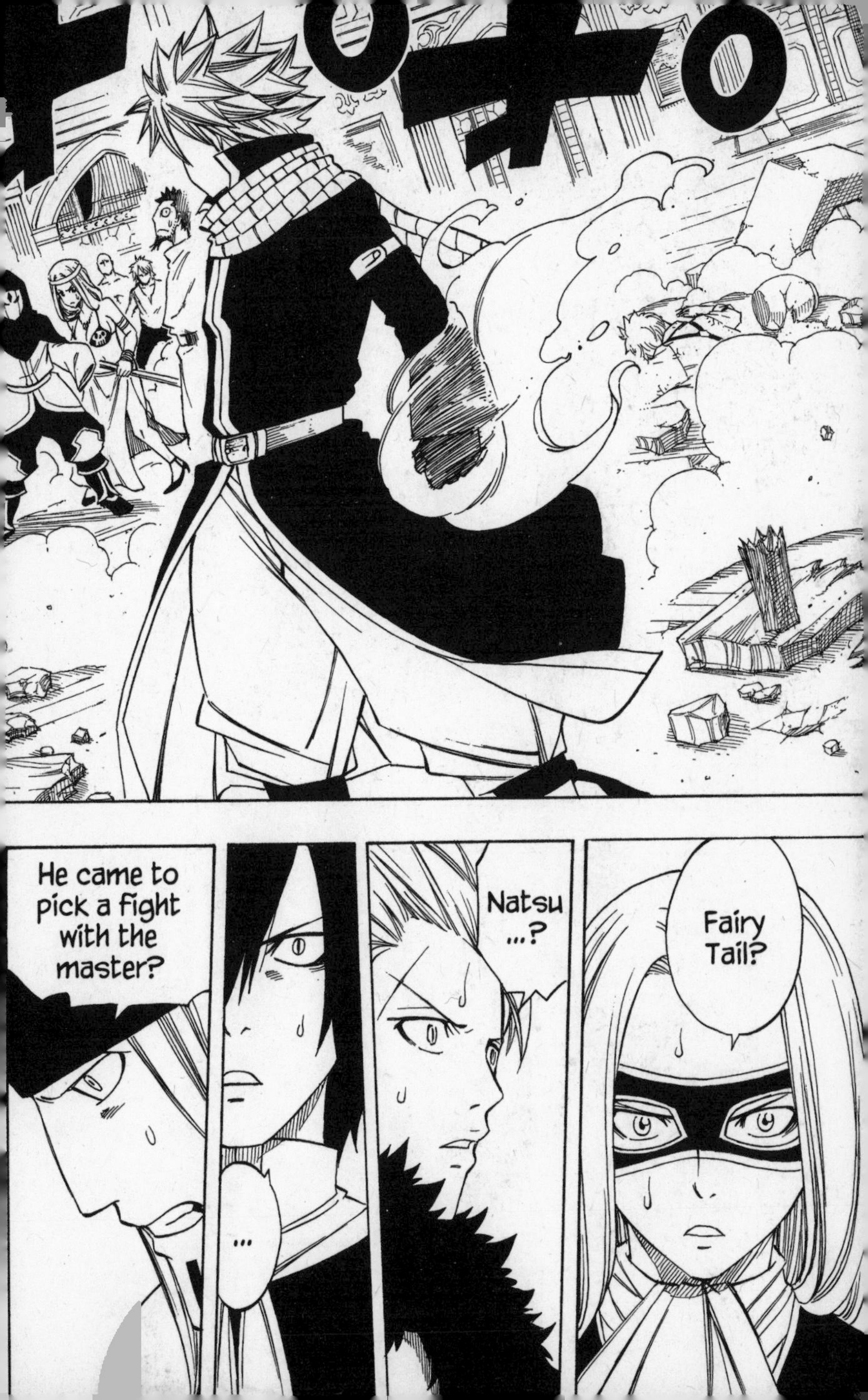
Fairy Tail?
Natsu ...?
...
He came to pick a fight with the master?

Chapter 283: Natsu vs. Saber Tooth

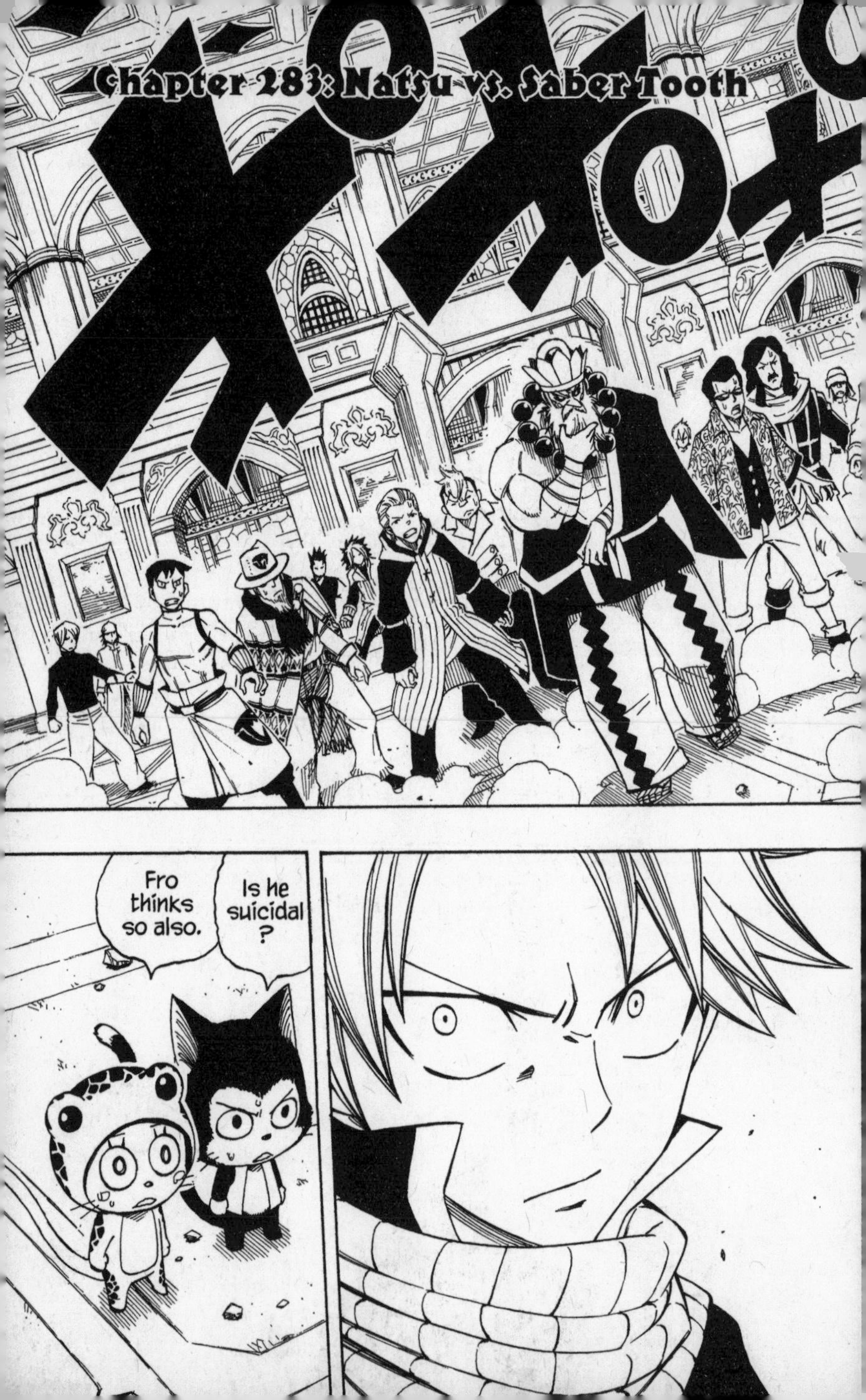
Is he suicidal?
Fro thinks so also.

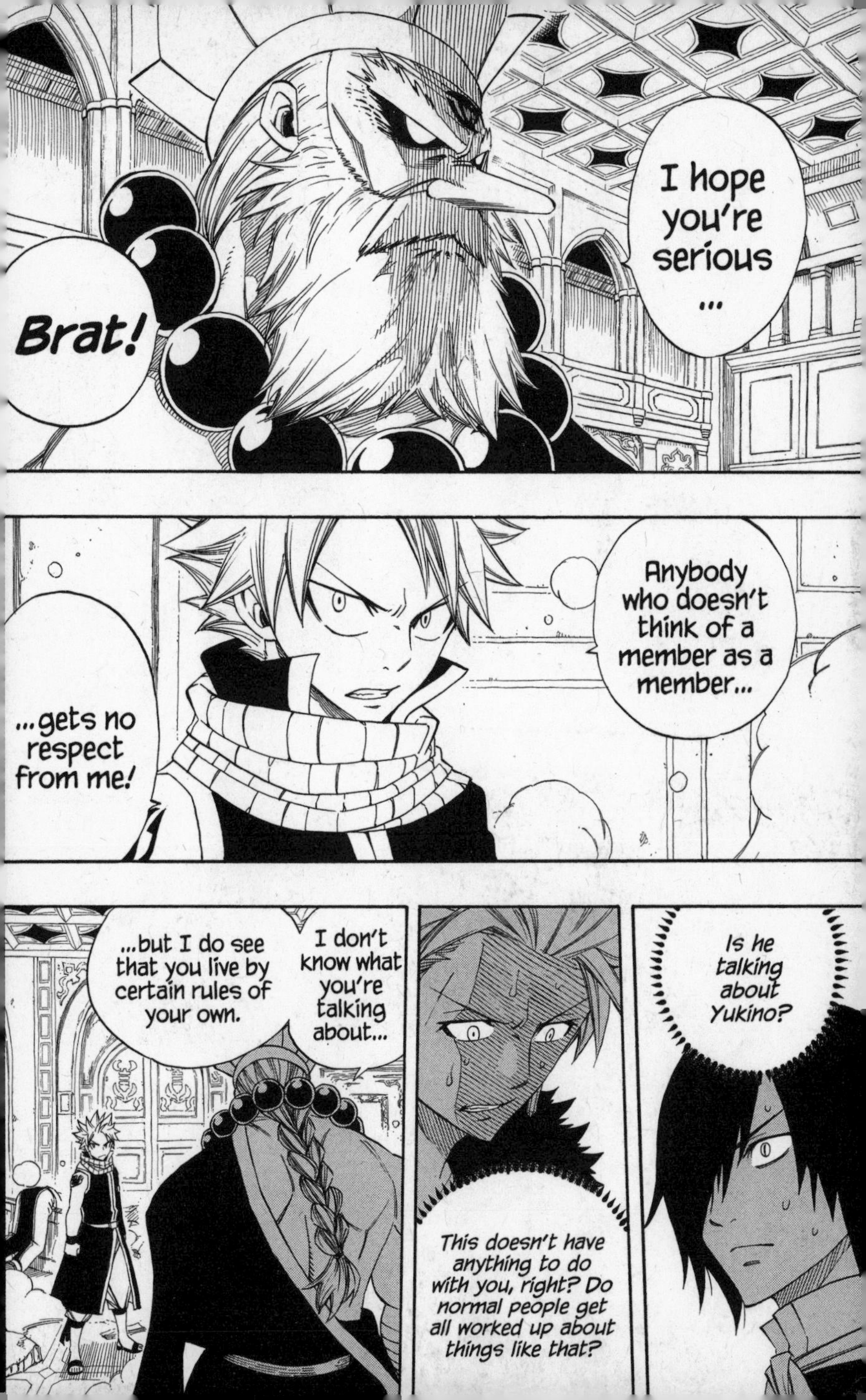
I hope you're serious ...
Brat!
Anybody who doesn't think of a member as a member...
...gets no respect from me!
Is he talking about Yukino?
This doesn't have anything to do with you, right? Do normal people get all worked up about things like that?
I don't know what you're talking about...
...but I do see that you live by certain rules of your own.

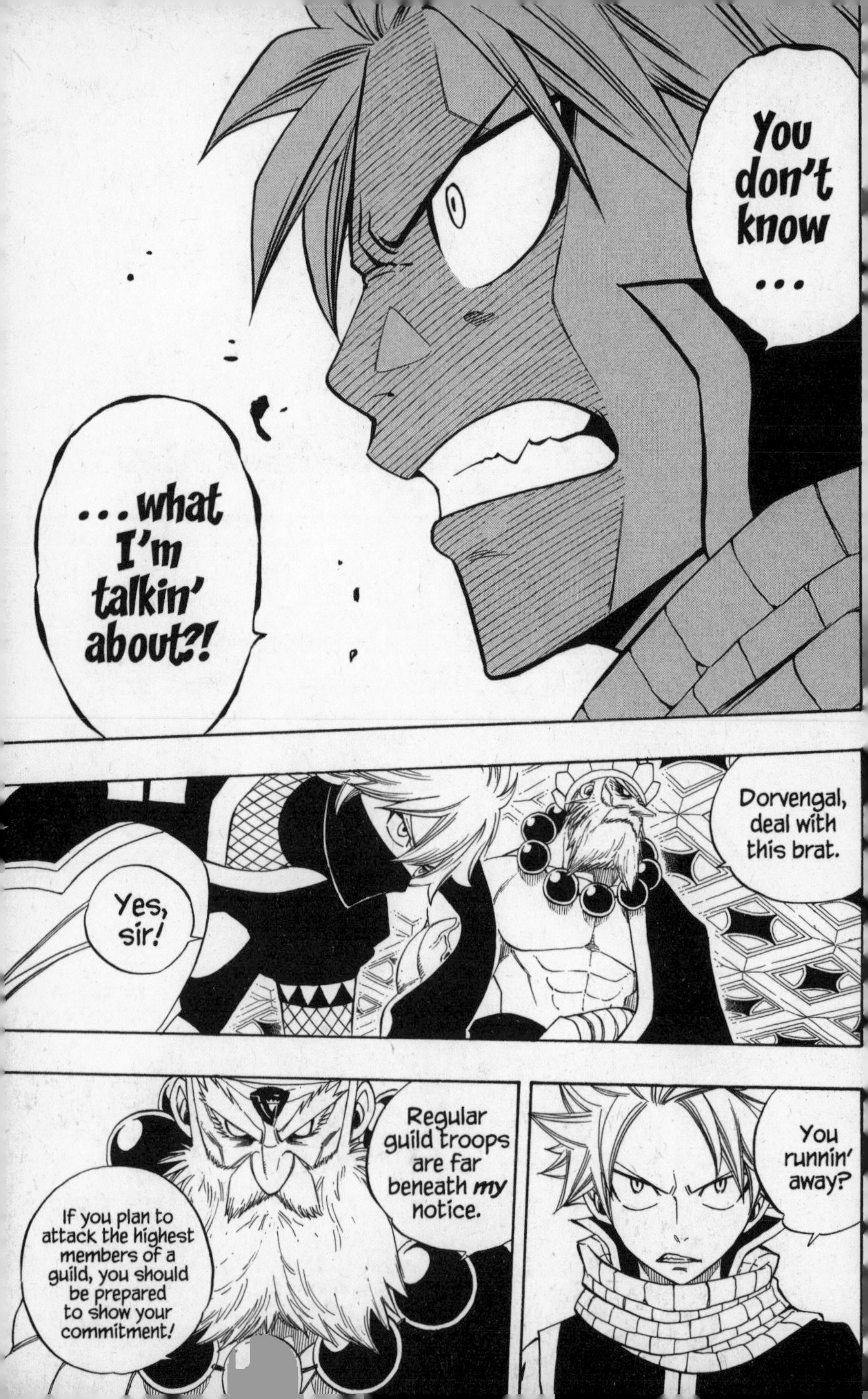
You don't know ...
...what I'm talkin' about?!
Dorvengal, deal with this brat.
Yes, sir!
You runnin' away?
Regular guild troops are far beneath *my* notice.
If you plan to attack the highest members of a guild, you should be prepared to show your commitment!

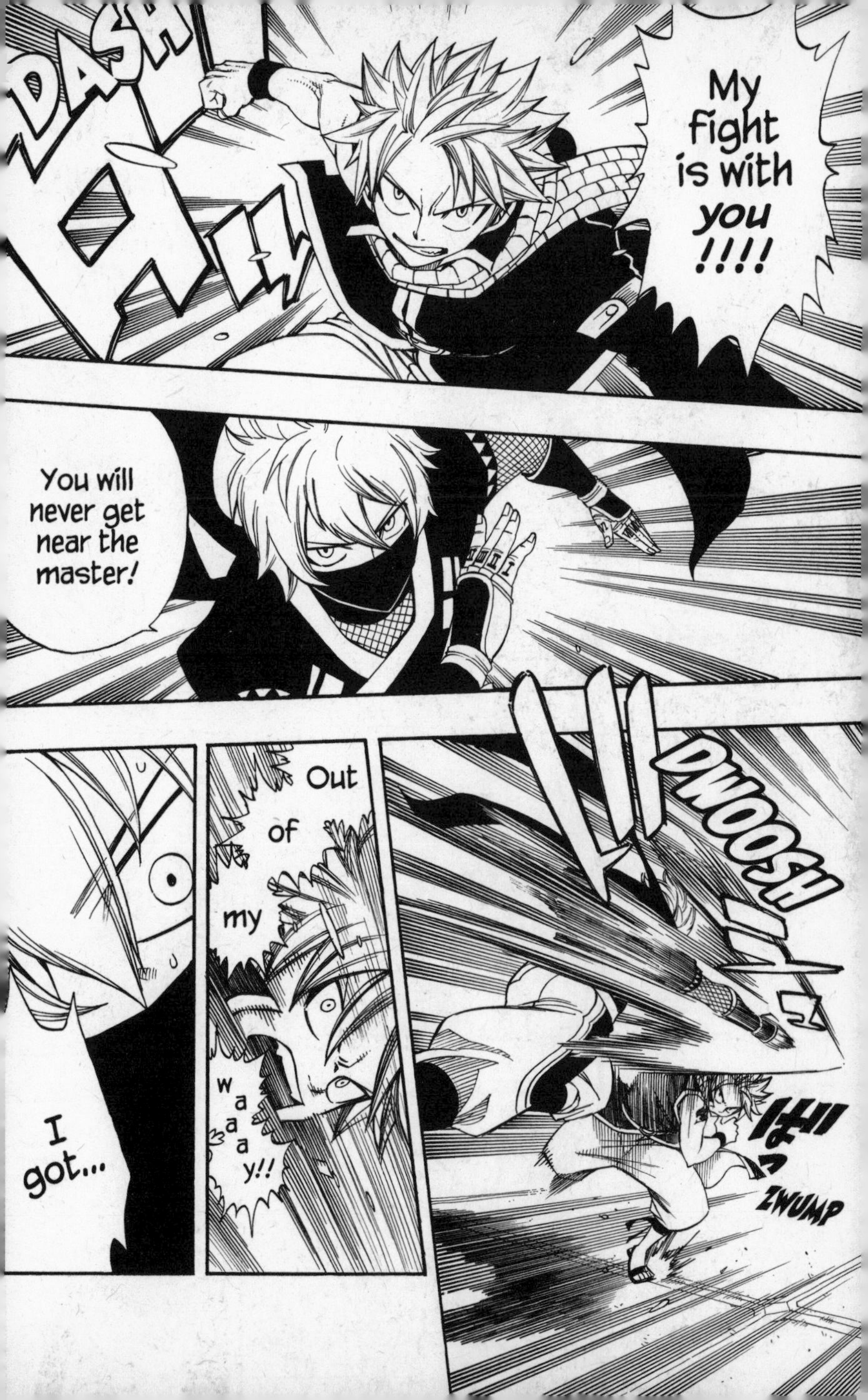
My fight is with you!!!!
DASH
You will never get near the master!
DWOOSH
はっ
ZWUMP
Out of my waaaay!!
I got...

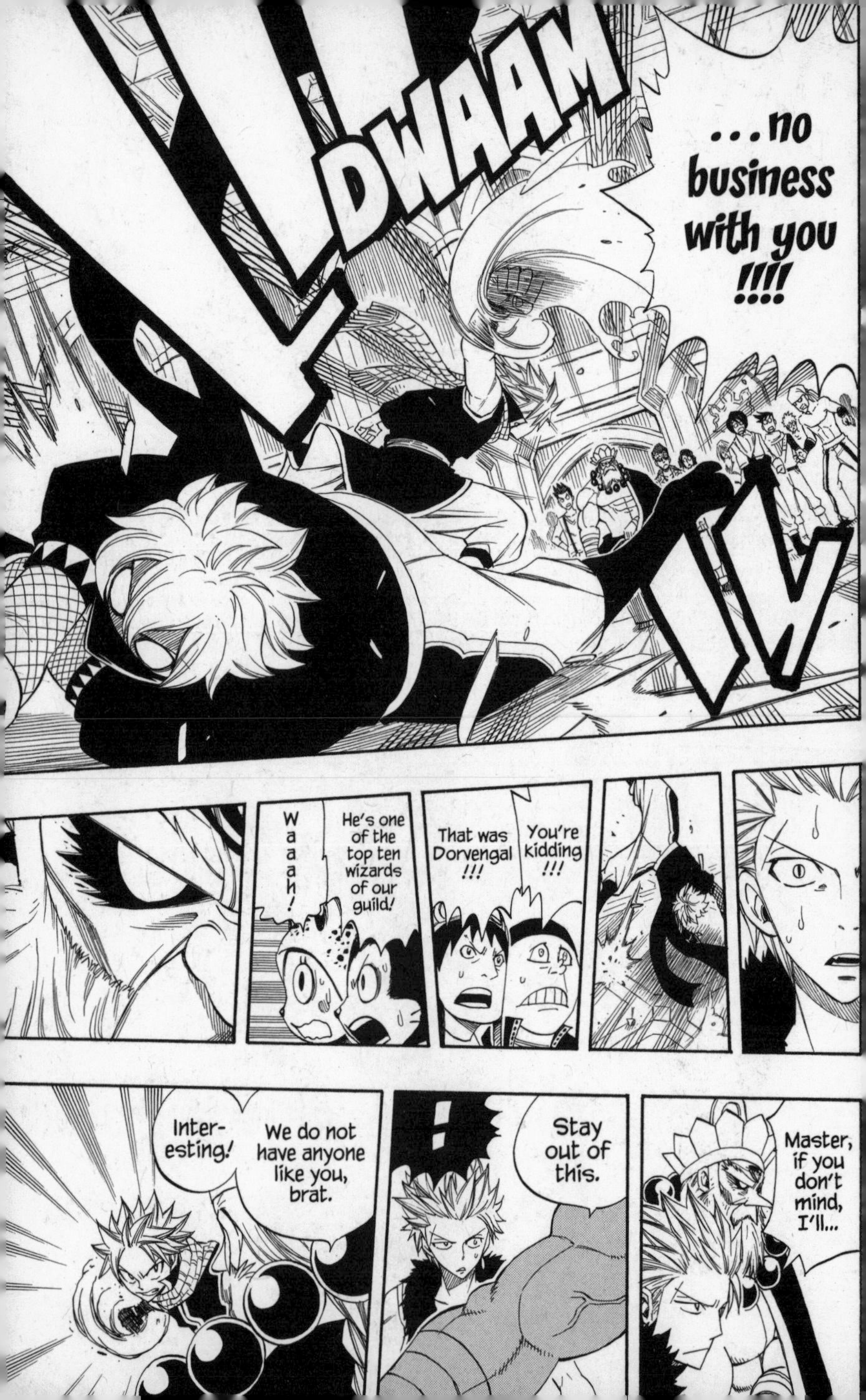
...no business with you !!!!
DWAAM
You're kidding !!!
That was Dorvengal !!!
He's one of the top ten wizards of our guild!
Waaah!
Master, if you don't mind, I'll...
Stay out of this.
!
We do not have anyone like you, brat.
Inter-esting!

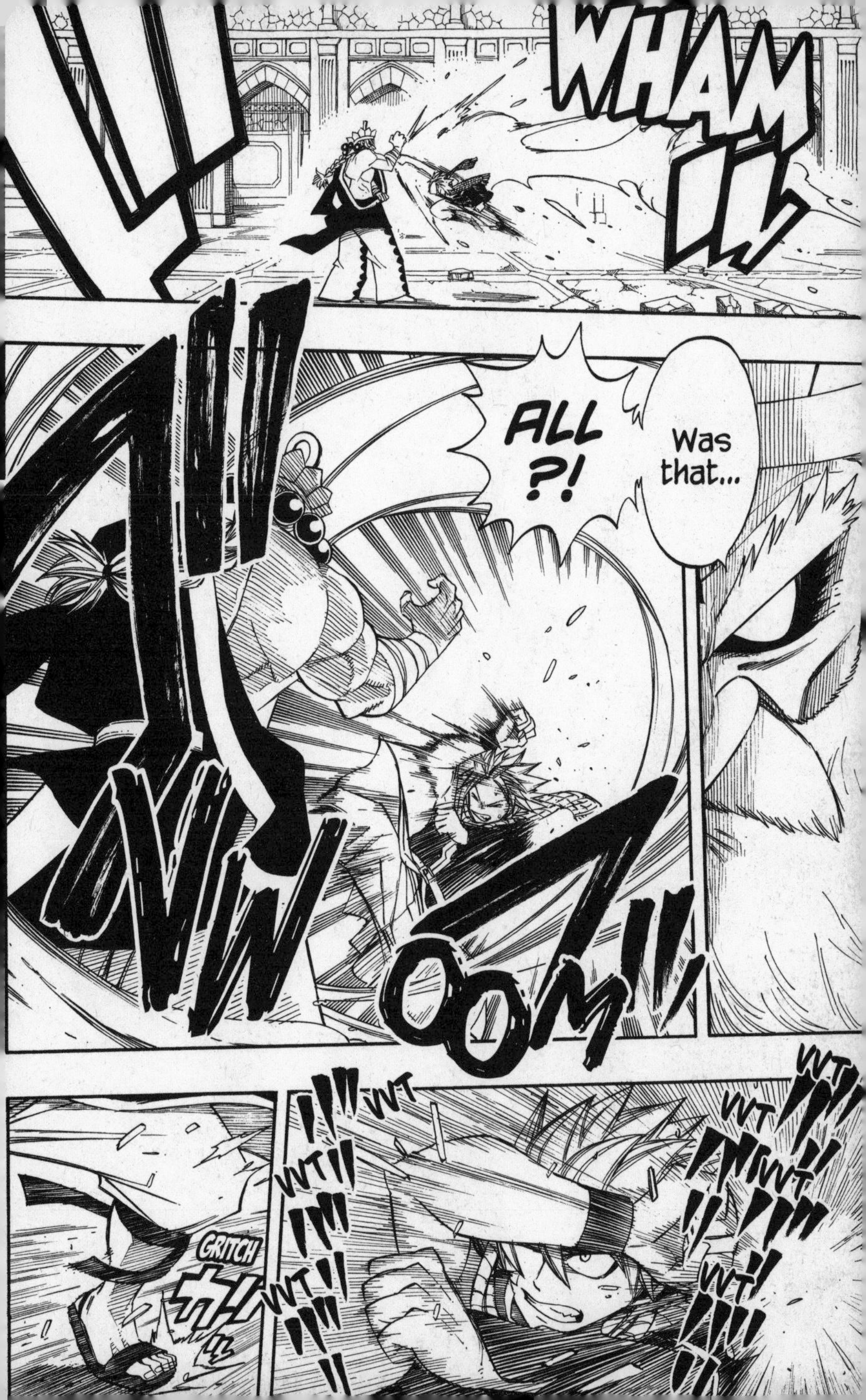
WHAM!!
Was that...
ALL?!
VWOOM!!
VVT
VVT
VVT
VVT
VVT
VVT
VVT
GRITCH

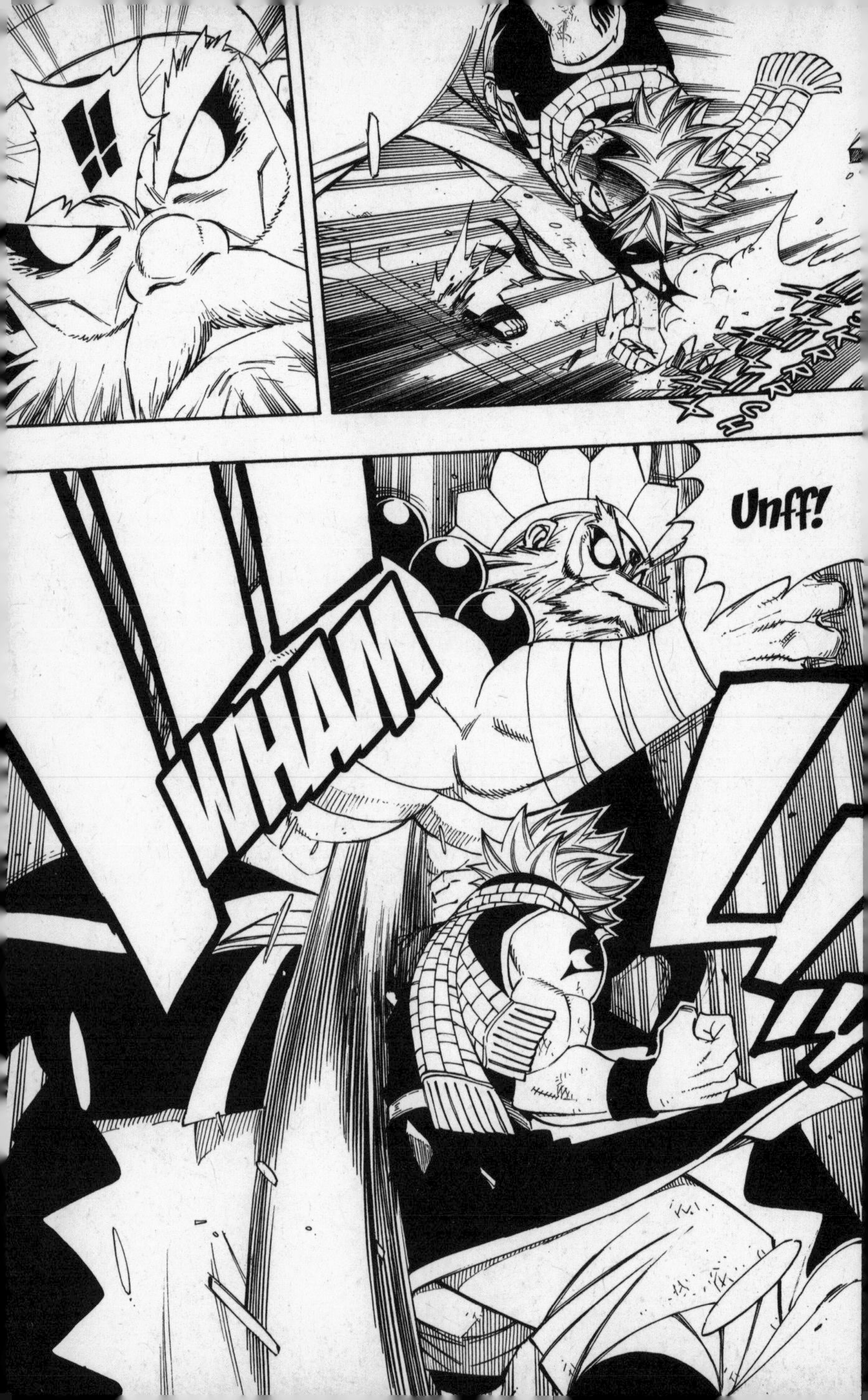
SKRRRCH
!!
Unff!
WHAM

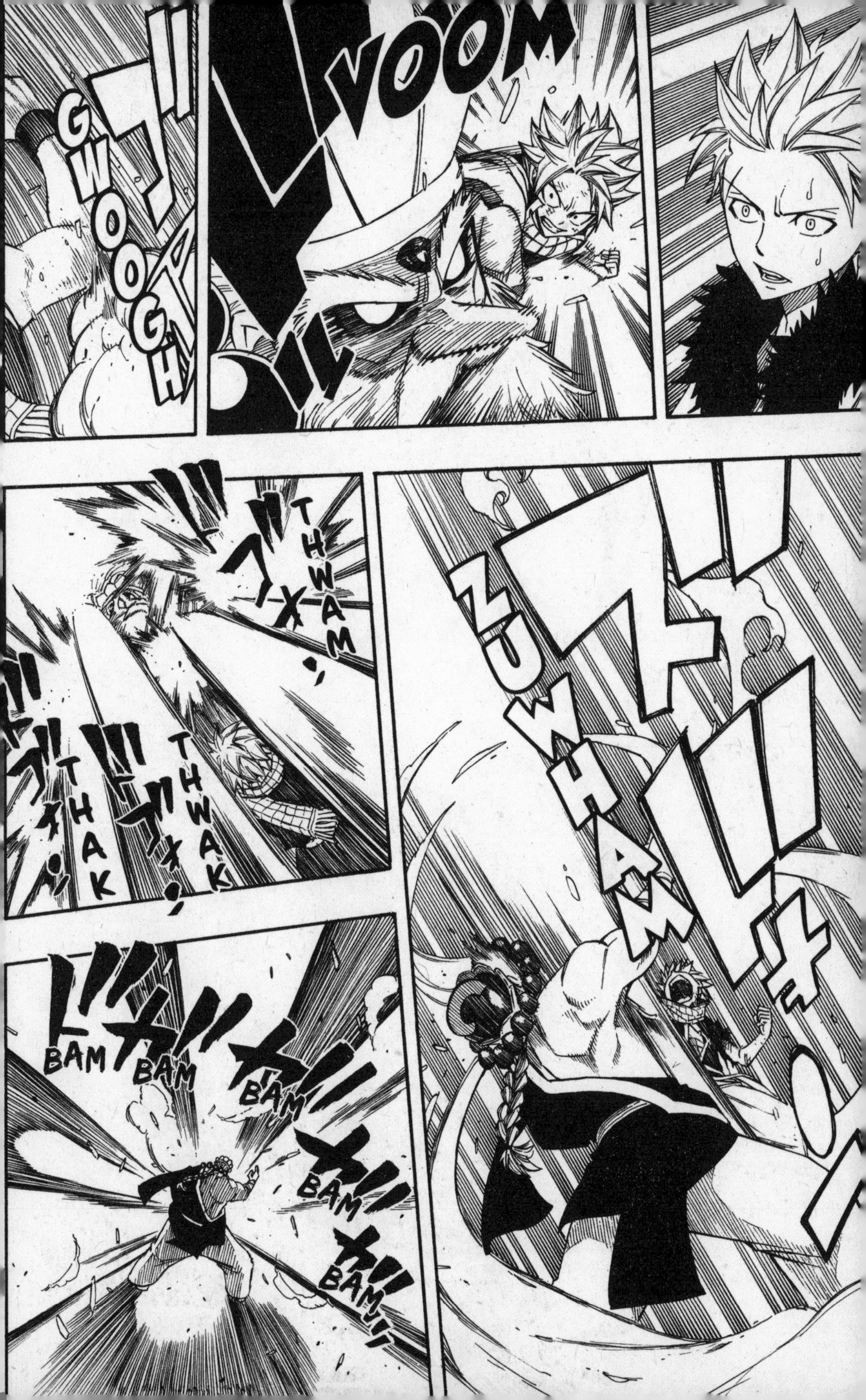
VOOM
GWOOOGH
ZUWHAM
THWAM
THWAK
THWAK
BAM
BAM
BAM
BAM
BAM
BAM

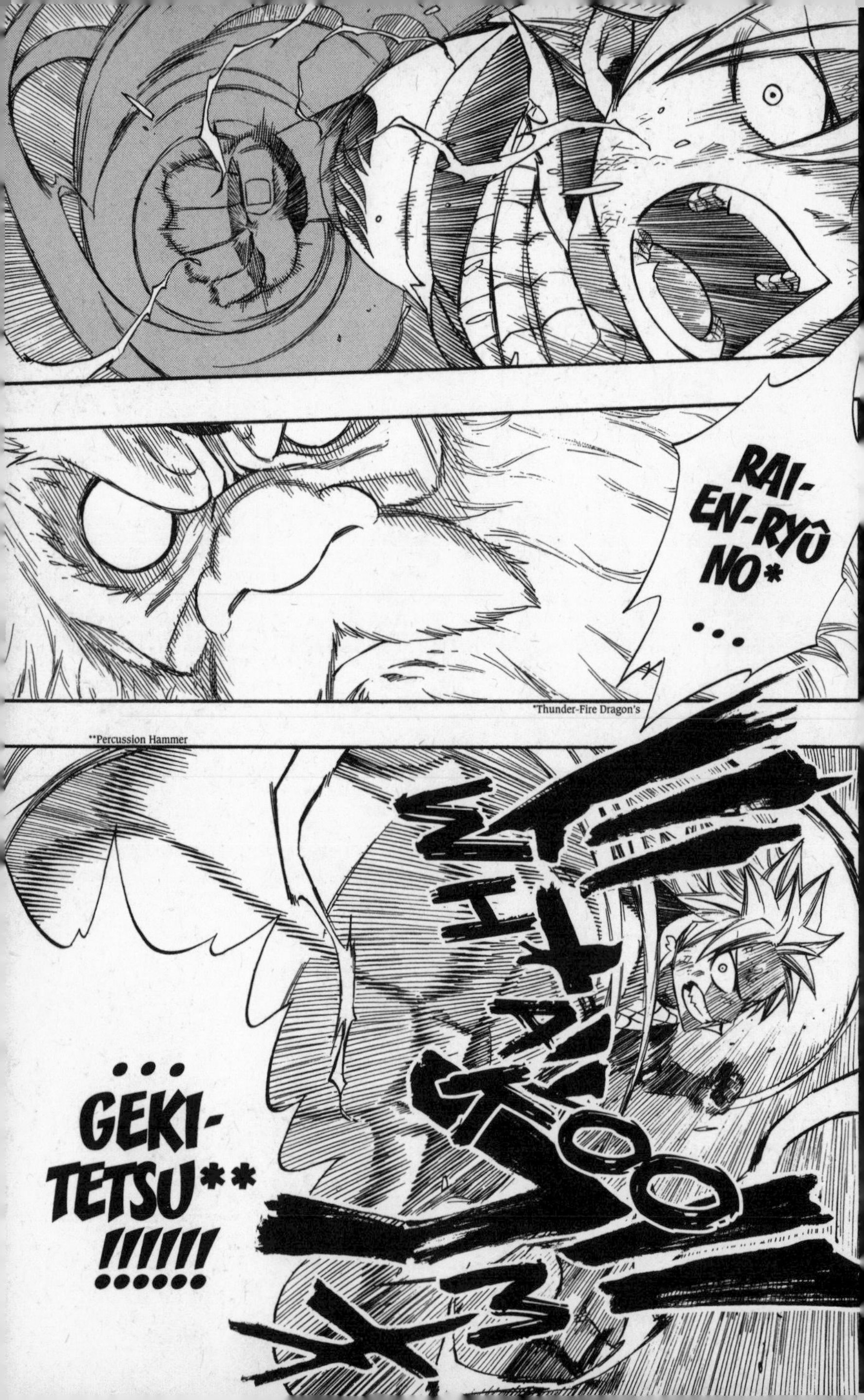
RAI-EN-RYÛ NO* ...
*Thunder-Fire Dragon's
**Percussion Hammer
...GEKI-TETSU** !!!!!!

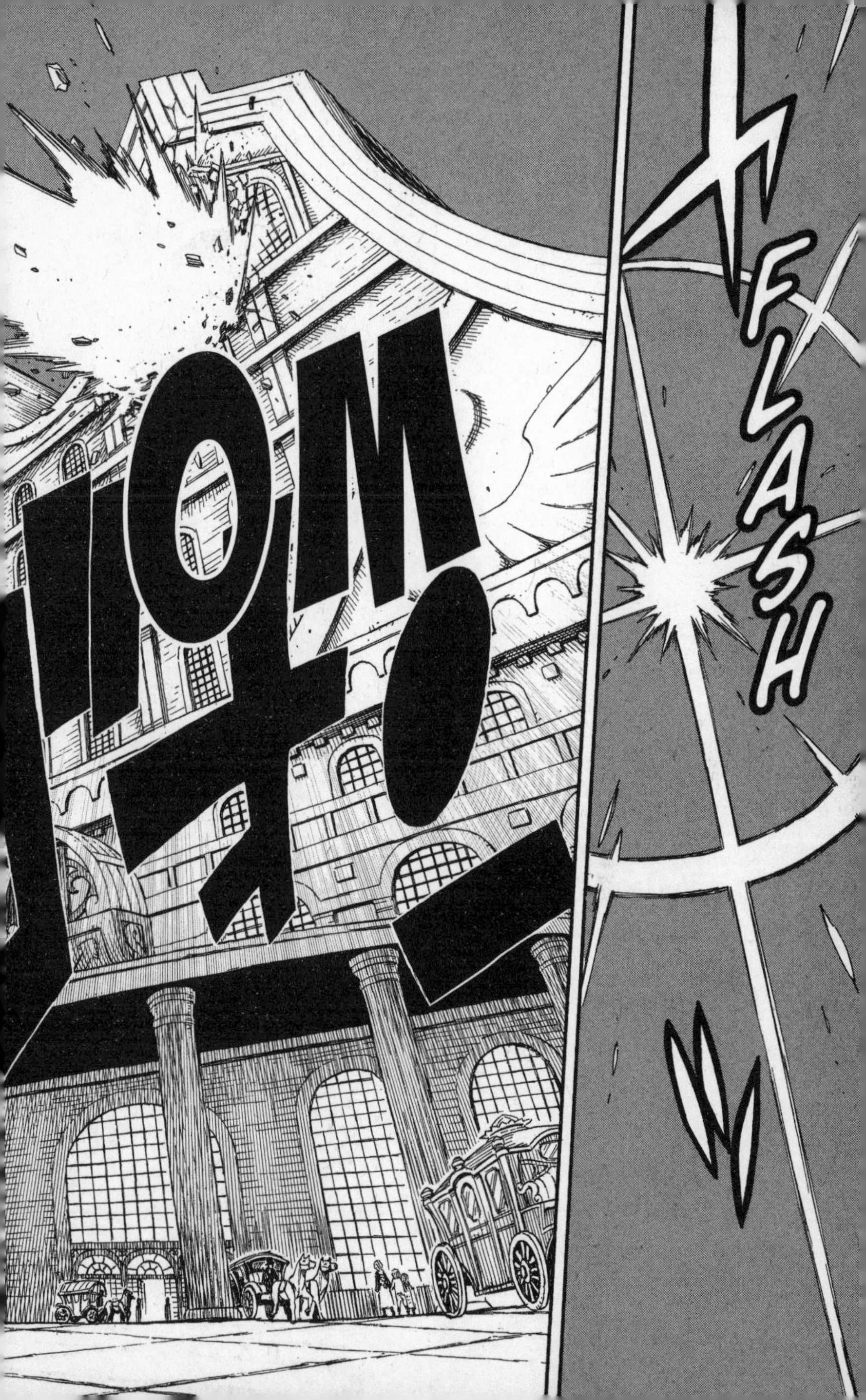
FLASH

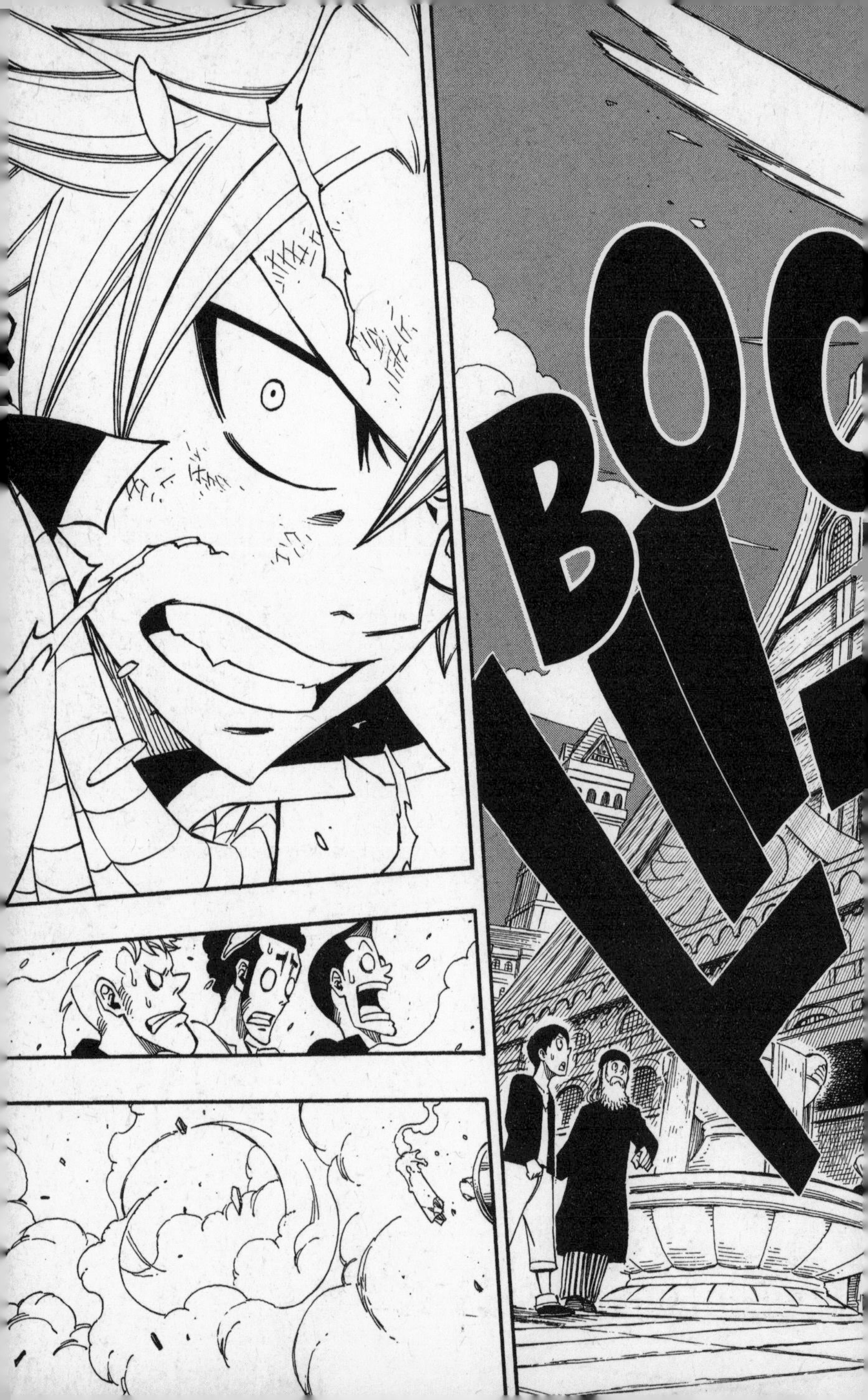
BOO

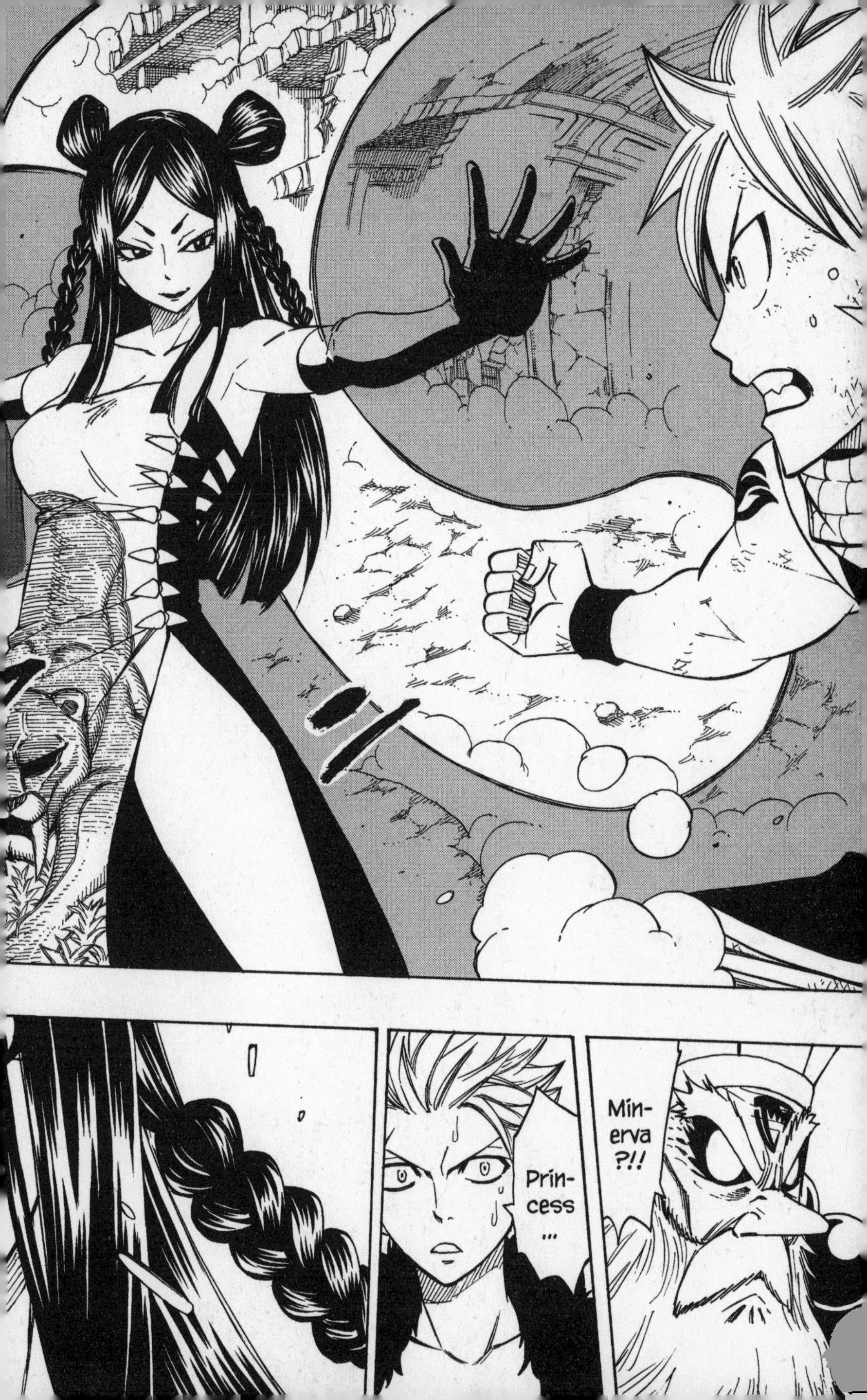
Minerva?!!
Princess...

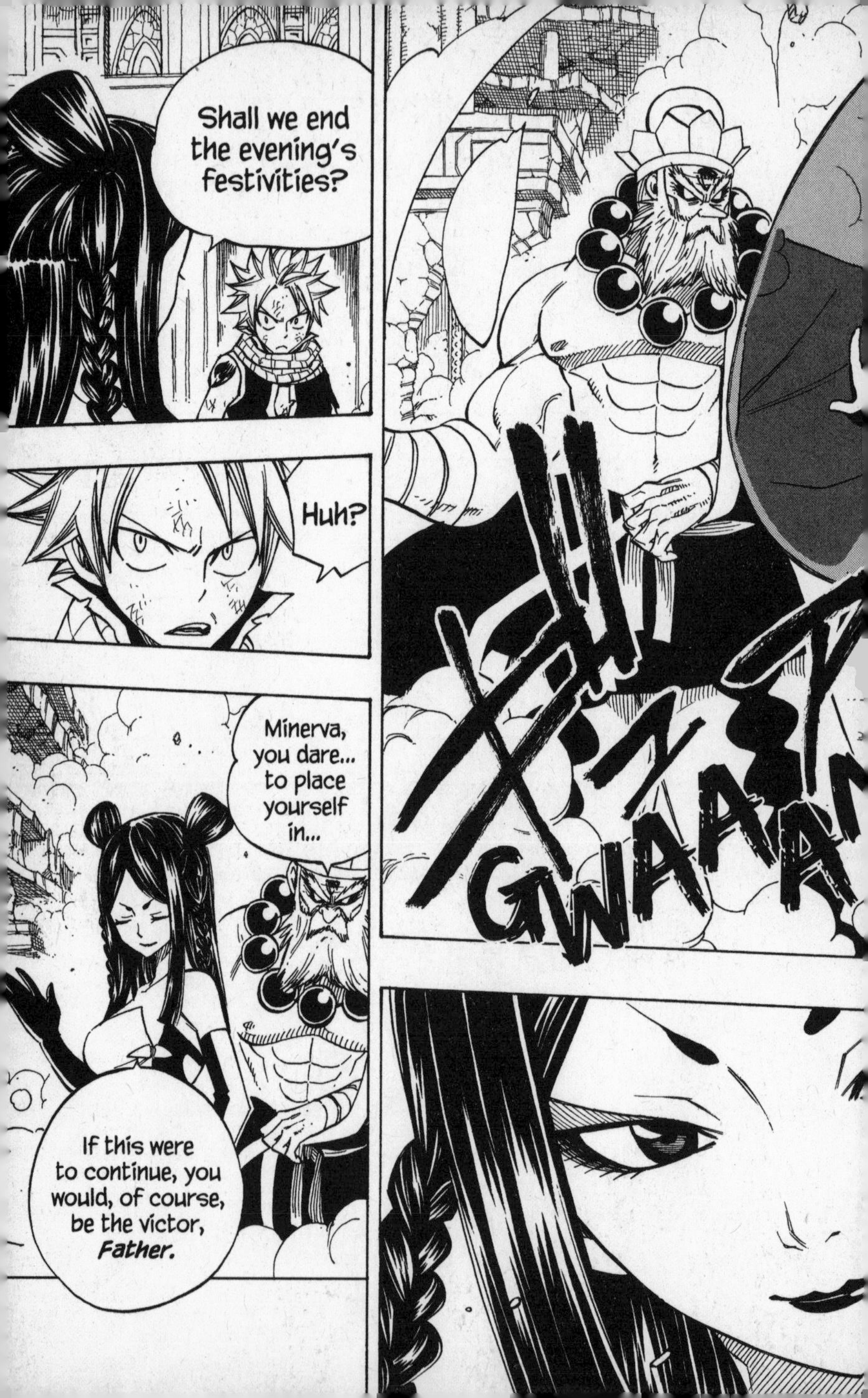
GWAAA
Shall we end the evening's festivities?
Huh?
Minerva, you dare... to place yourself in...
If this were to continue, you would, of course, be the victor, *Father.*

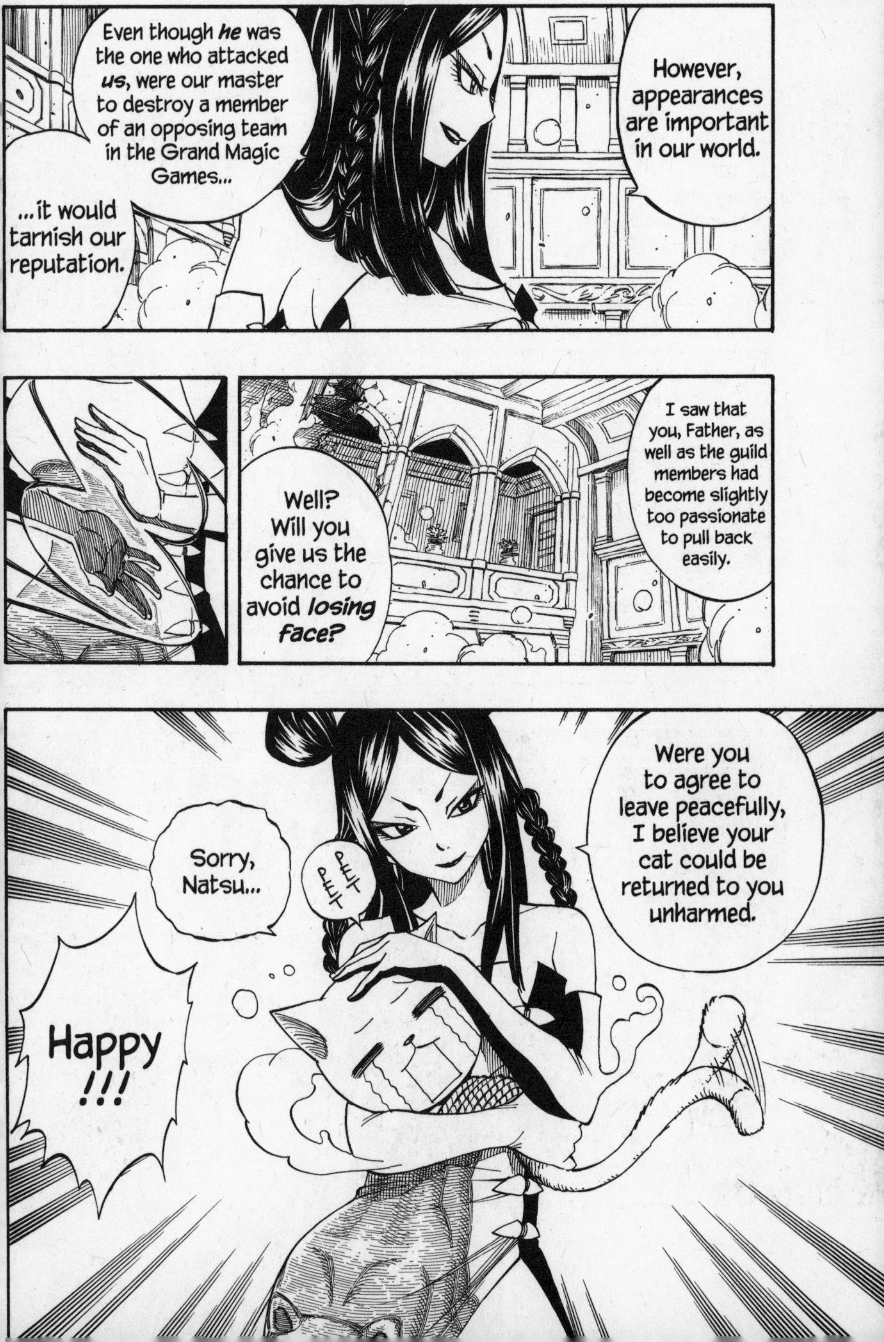
However, appearances are important in our world.
Even though *he* was the one who attacked *us*, were our master to destroy a member of an opposing team in the Grand Magic Games...
...it would tarnish our reputation.
I saw that you, Father, as well as the guild members had become slightly too passionate to pull back easily.
Well? Will you give us the chance to avoid *losing face?*
Were you to agree to leave peacefully, I believe your cat could be returned to you unharmed.
PET PET
Sorry, Natsu...
Happy !!!

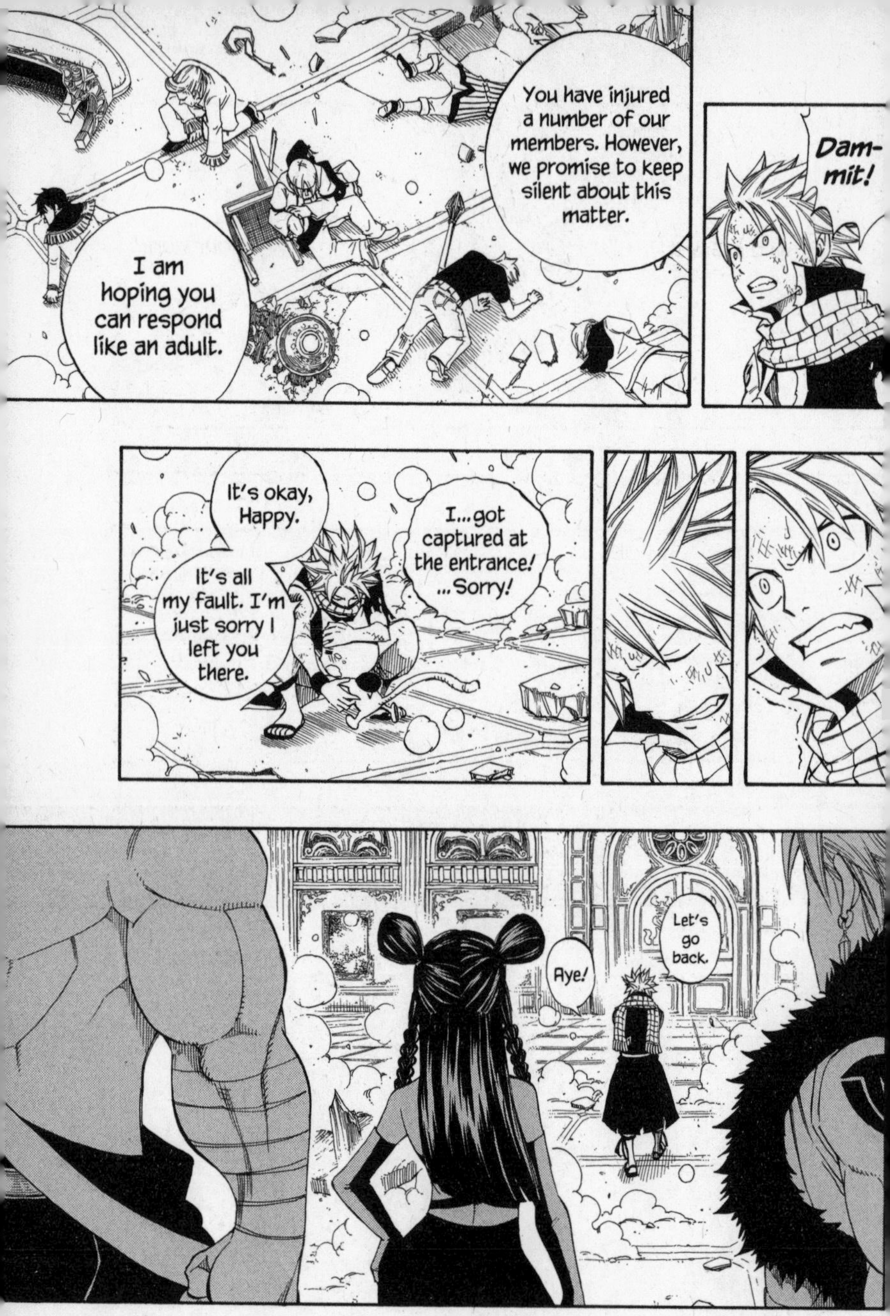
Dam-mit!
You have injured a number of our members. However, we promise to keep silent about this matter.
I am hoping you can respond like an adult.
I...got captured at the entrance! ...Sorry!
It's okay, Happy.
It's all my fault. I'm just sorry I left you there.
Let's go back.
Aye!

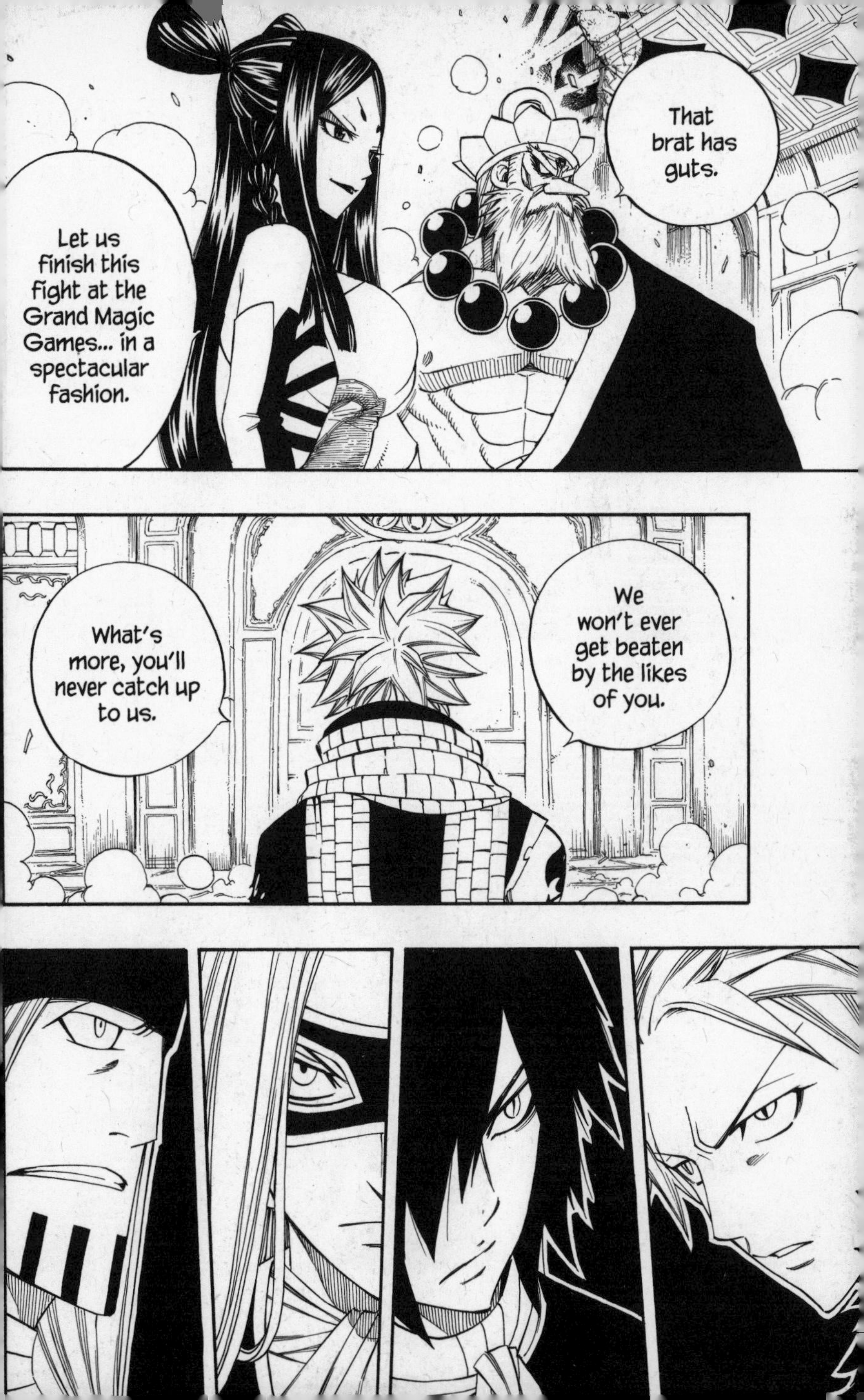
That brat has guts.
Let us finish this fight at the Grand Magic Games... in a spectacular fashion.
We won't ever get beaten by the likes of you.
What's more, you'll never catch up to us.

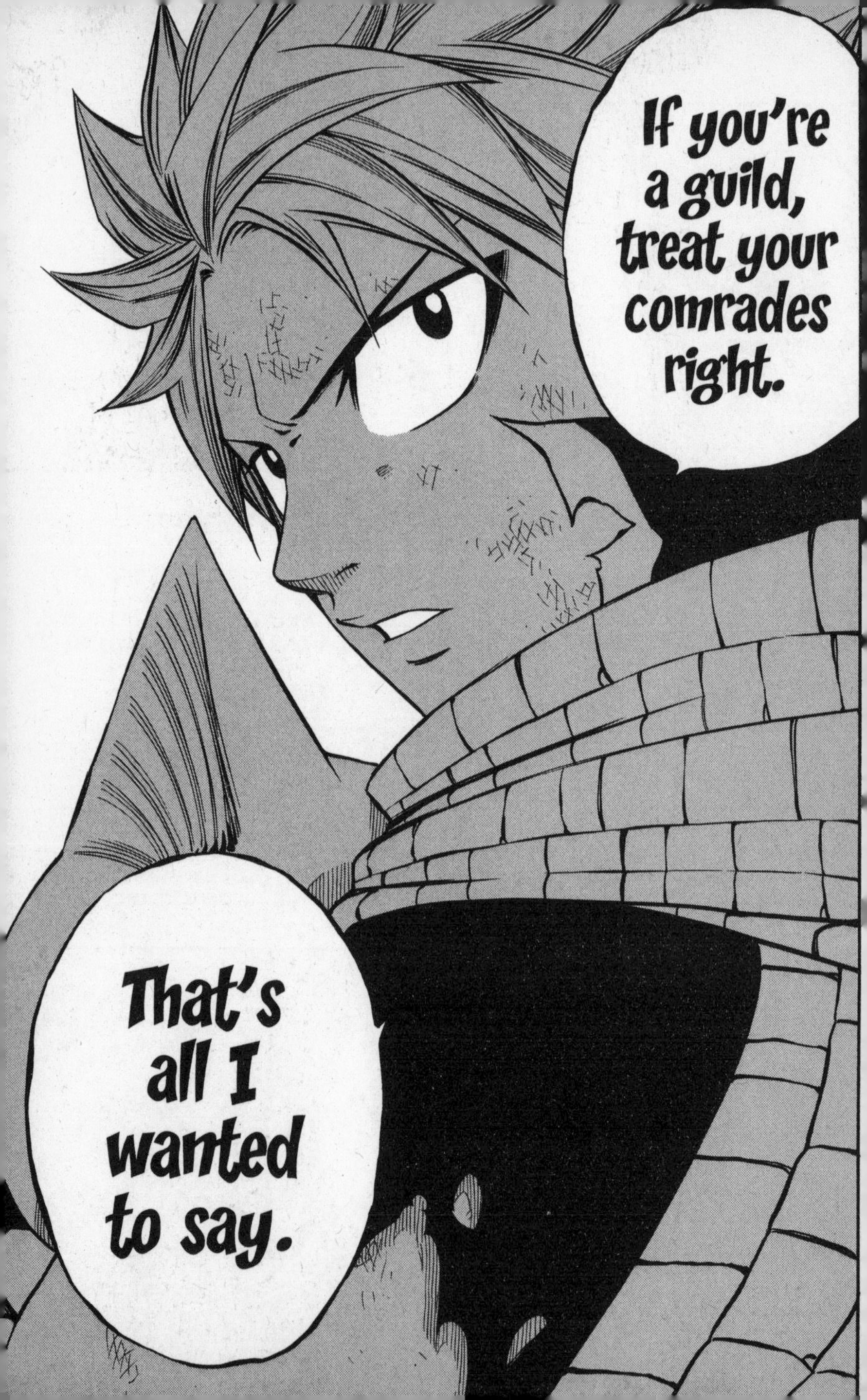
If you're a guild, treat your comrades right.
That's all I wanted to say.

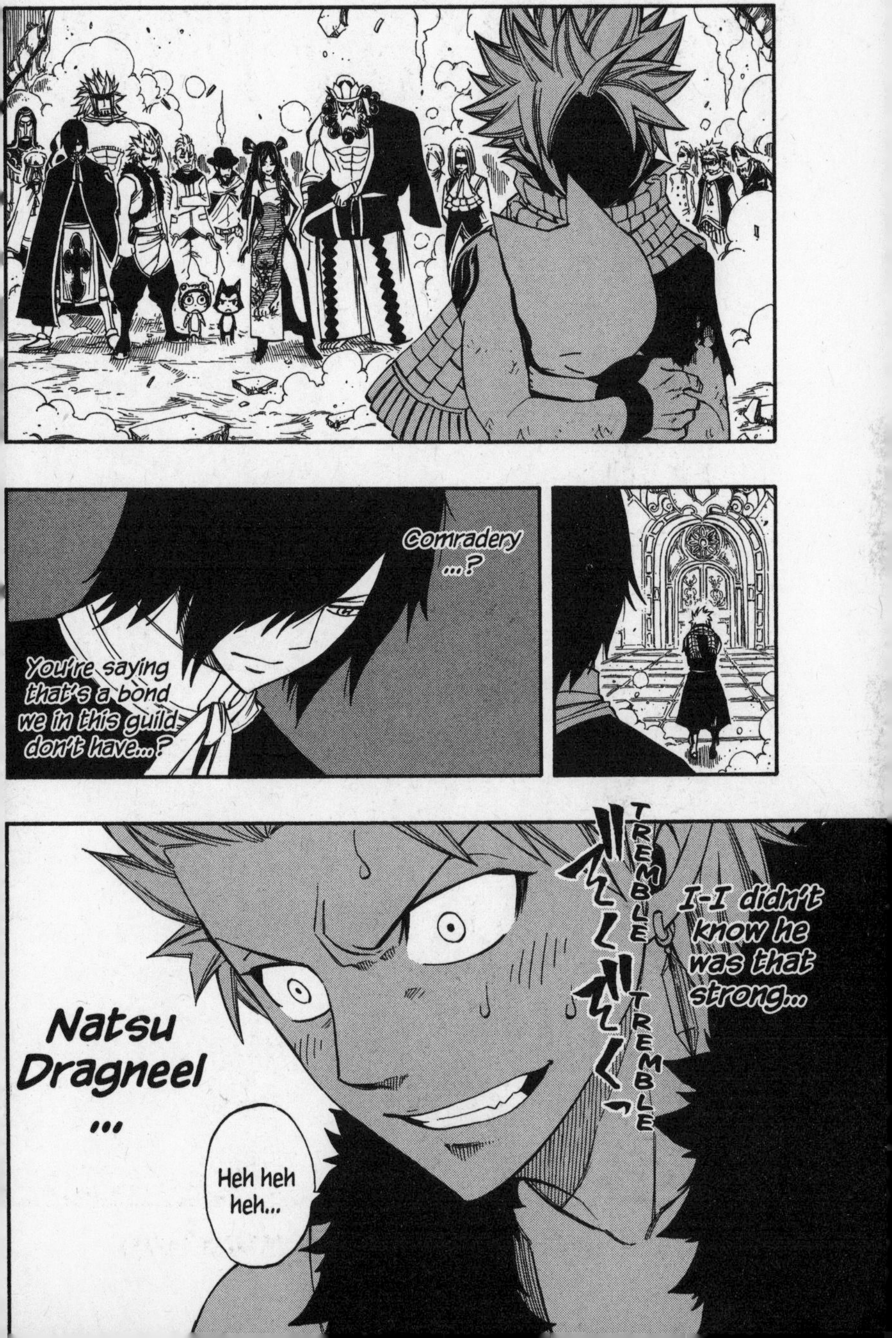
Comradery ...?
You're saying that's a bond we in this guild don't have...?
I-I didn't know he was that strong...
TREMBLE TREMBLE
Natsu Dragneel ...
Heh heh heh...

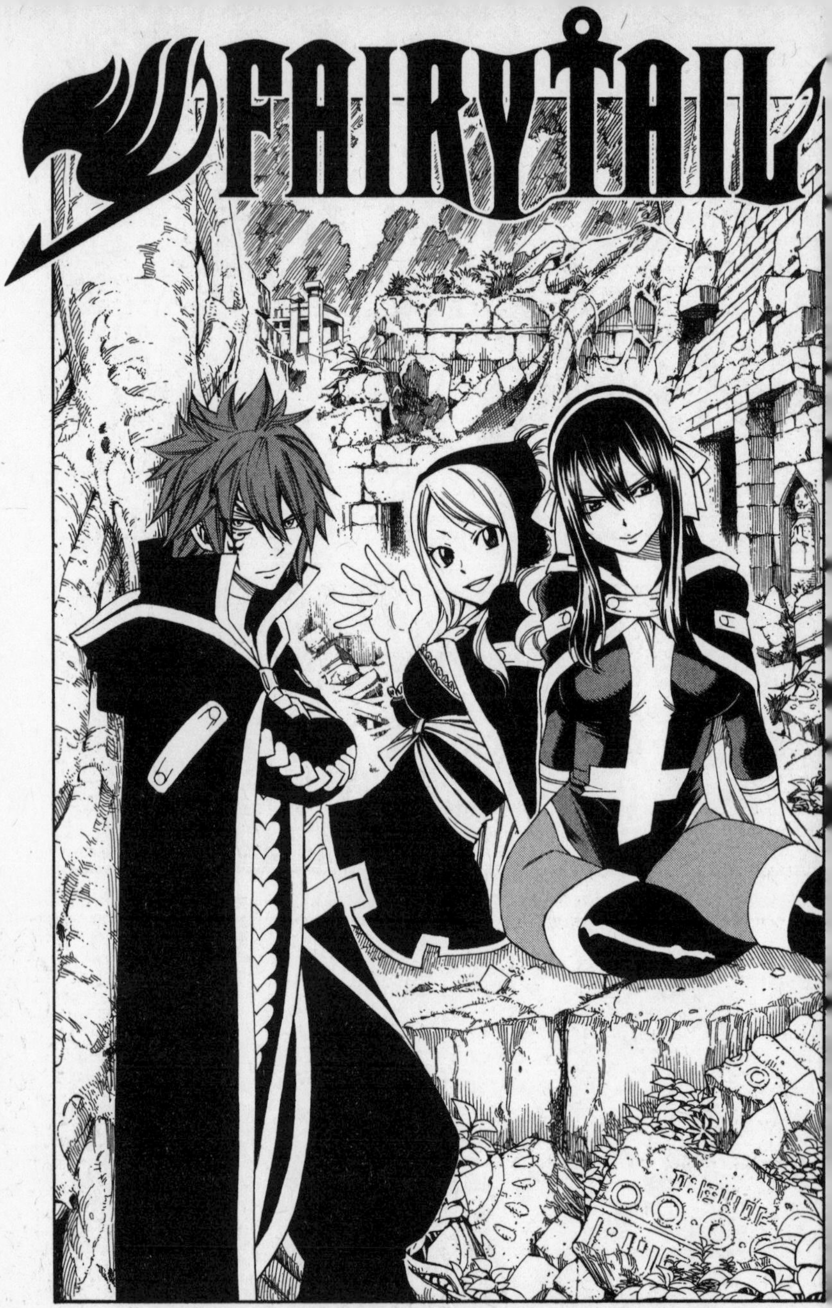
FAIRY TAIL

Chapter 284: Pandemonium

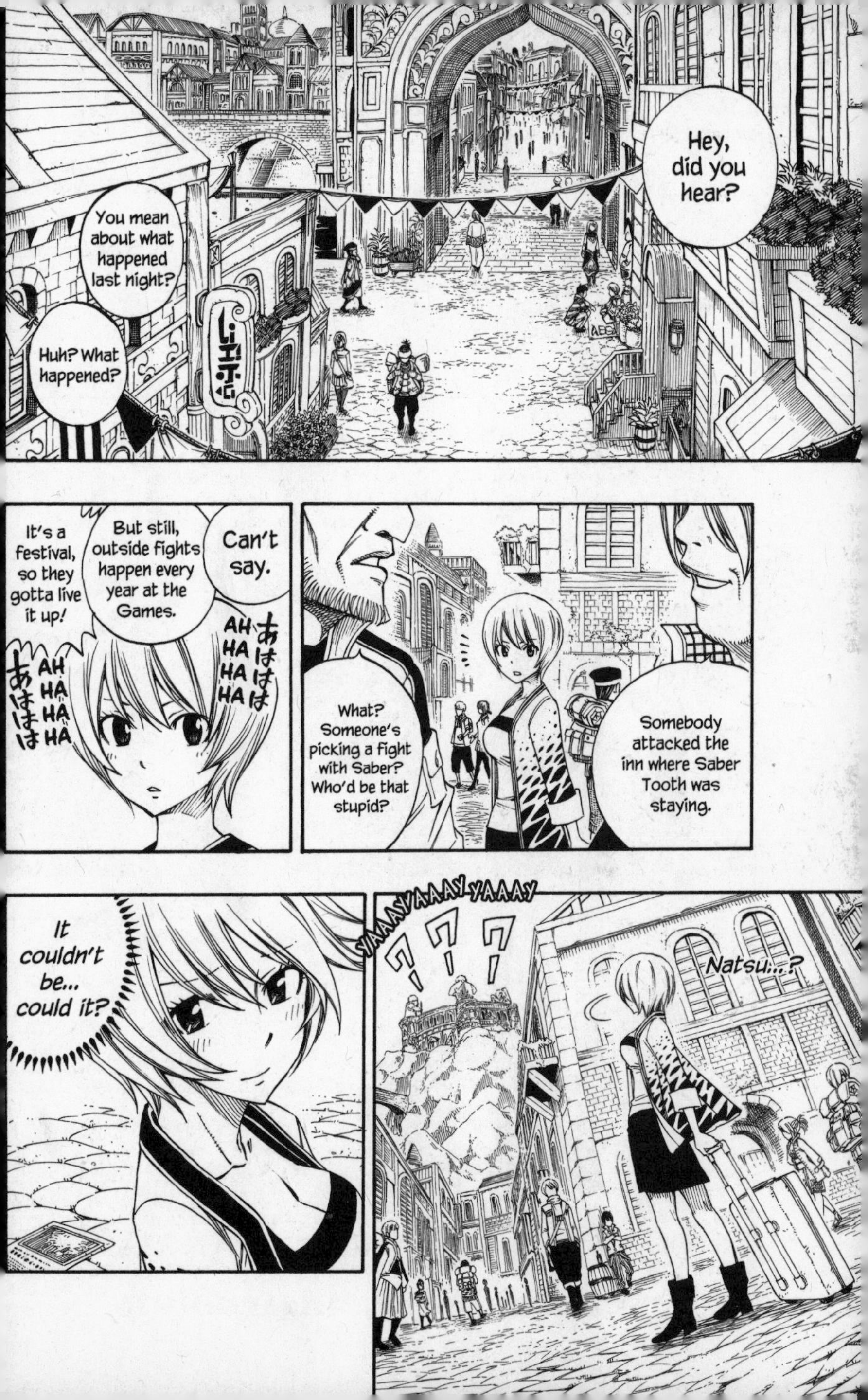
Hey, did you hear?
You mean about what happened last night?
Huh? What happened?
Somebody attacked the inn where Saber Tooth was staying.
What? Someone's picking a fight with Saber? Who'd be that stupid?
Can't say.
But still, outside fights happen every year at the Games.
It's a festival, so they gotta live it up!
AH HA HA HA あははは
AH HA HA HA あははは
YAAAY YAAAY YAAAY
? ? ?
Natsu...?
It couldn't be... could it?

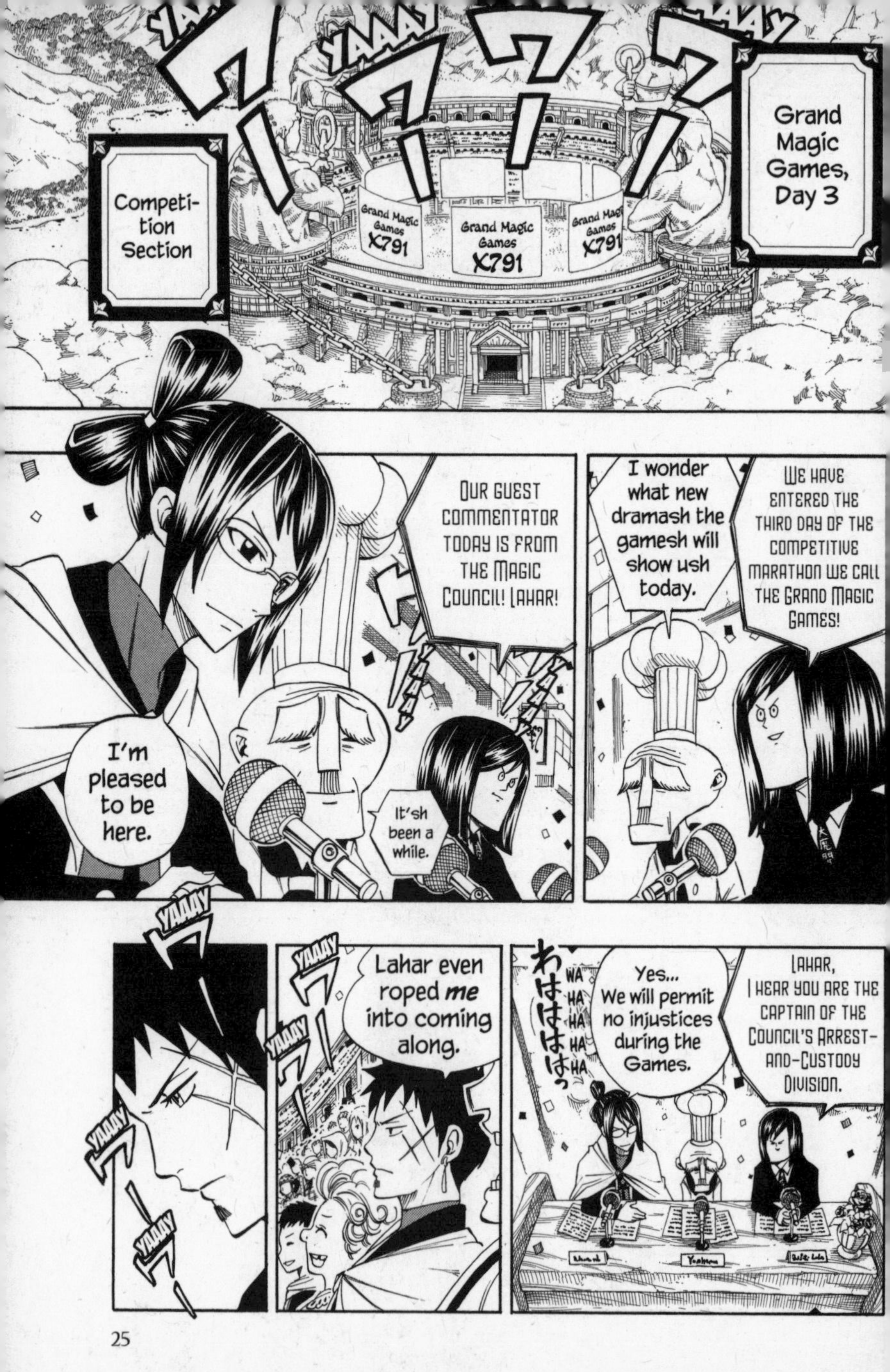
YAAAY
YAAAY
Grand Magic Games, Day 3
Competition Section
Grand Magic Games X791
Grand Magic Games X791
Grand Magic Games X791
WE HAVE ENTERED THE THIRD DAY OF THE COMPETITIVE MARATHON WE CALL THE GRAND MAGIC GAMES!
I wonder what new dramash the gamesh will show ush today.
OUR GUEST COMMENTATOR TODAY IS FROM THE MAGIC COUNCIL! LAHAR!
It'sh been a while.
I'm pleased to be here.
LAHAR, I HEAR YOU ARE THE CAPTAIN OF THE COUNCIL'S ARREST-AND-CUSTODY DIVISION.
Yes... We will permit no injustices during the Games.
わはははっ
WA HA HA HA HA
Lahar even roped *me* into coming along.
YAAAY
YAAAY
YAAAY
YAAAY

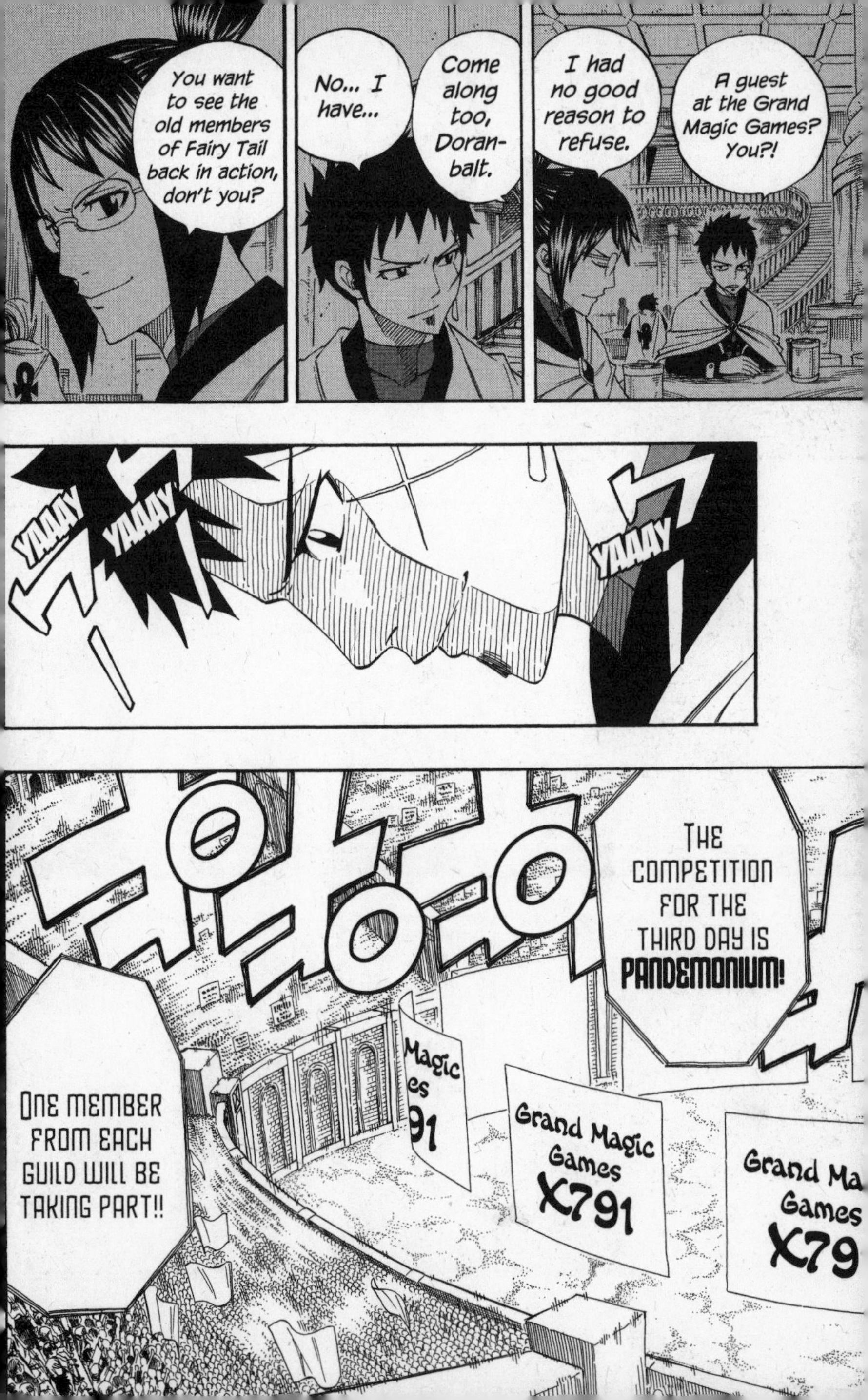

A guest at the Grand Magic Games? You?!
I had no good reason to refuse.
Come along too, Doranbalt.
No... I have...
You want to see the old members of Fairy Tail back in action, don't you?
YAAAY
YAAAY
YAAAY
THE COMPETITION FOR THE THIRD DAY IS PANDEMONIUM!
Grand Magic Games X791
ONE MEMBER FROM EACH GUILD WILL BE TAKING PART!!

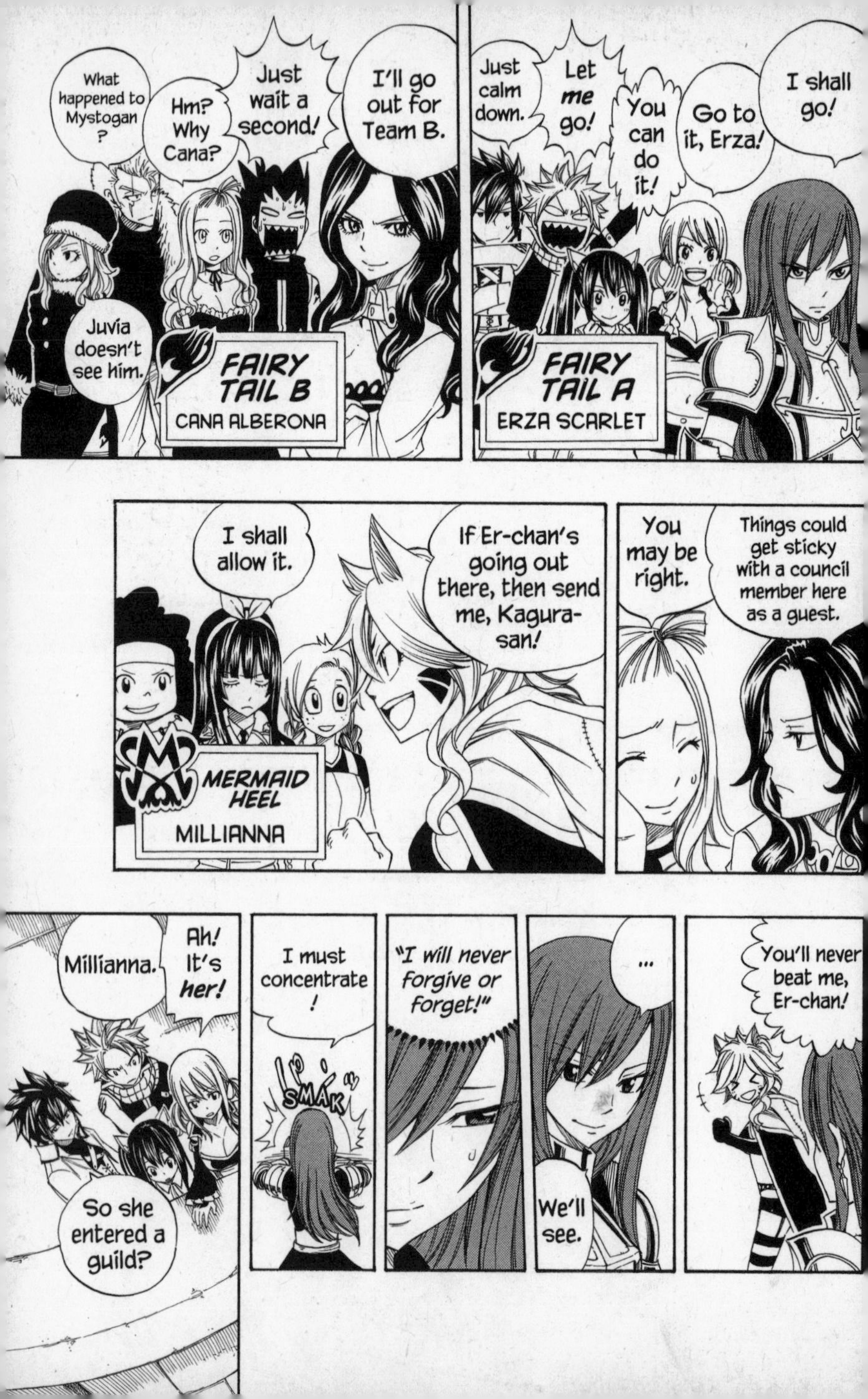
I shall go!
Go to it, Erza!
You can do it!
Let *me* go!
Just calm down.
FAIRY TAIL A
ERZA SCARLET
I'll go out for Team B.
Just wait a second!
Hm? Why Cana?
What happened to Mystogan?
Juvia doesn't see him.
FAIRY TAIL B
CANA ALBERONA
Things could get sticky with a council member here as a guest.
You may be right.
If Er-chan's going out there, then send me, Kagura-san!
I shall allow it.
MERMAID HEEL
MILLIANNA
You'll never beat me, Er-chan!
...
We'll see.
"I will never forgive or forget!"
I must concentrate!
SMAK
Ah! It's *her!*
Millianna.
So she entered a guild?

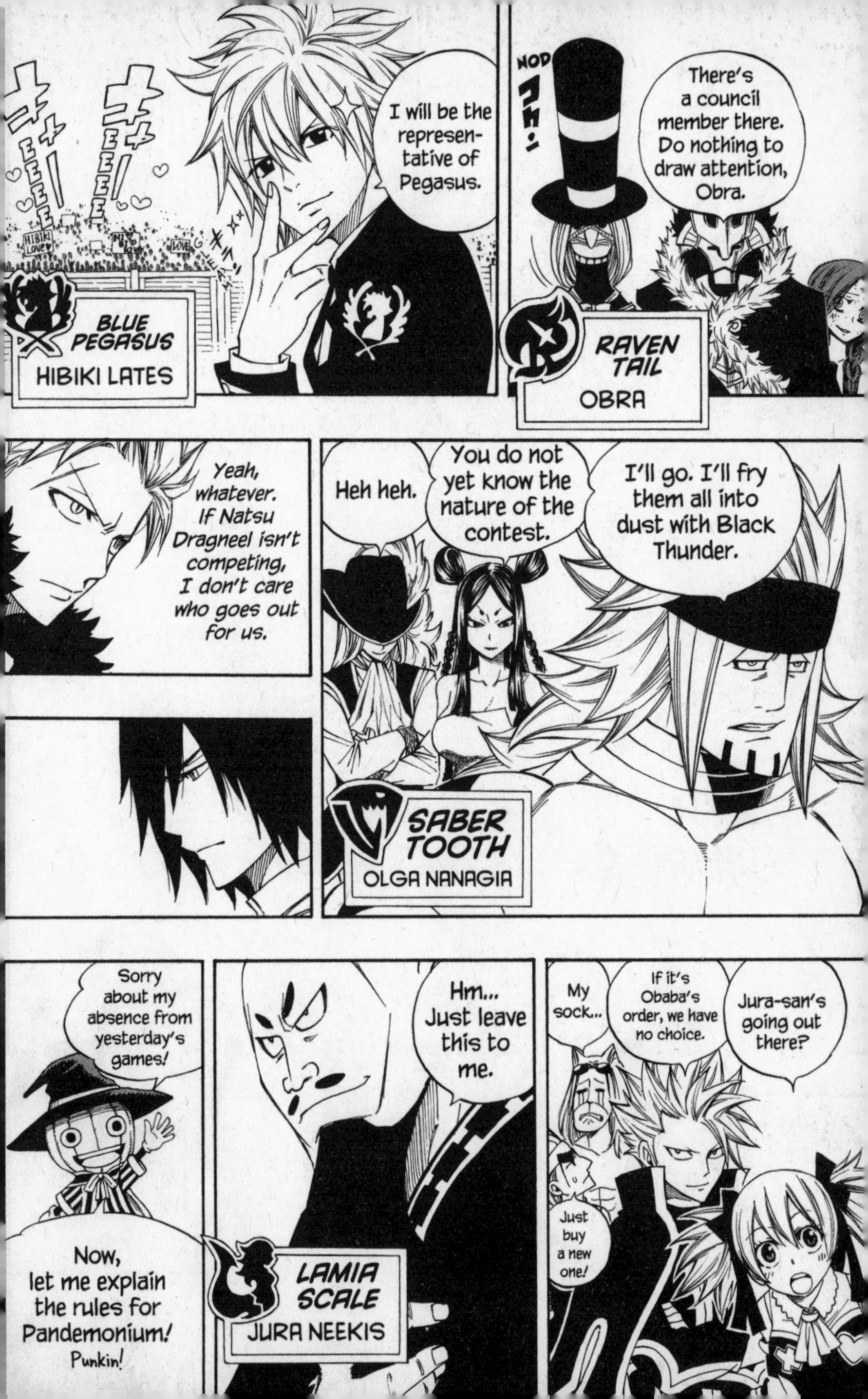

NOD
There's a council member there. Do nothing to draw attention, Obra.
RAVEN TAIL
OBRA
I will be the representative of Pegasus.
HIBIKI LOVE
LOVE
GLEAM
BLUE PEGASUS
HIBIKI LATES
I'll go. I'll fry them all into dust with Black Thunder.
You do not yet know the nature of the contest.
Heh heh.
SABER TOOTH
OLGA NANAGIA
Yeah, whatever. If Natsu Dragneel isn't competing, I don't care who goes out for us.
Jura-san's going out there?
If it's Obaba's order, we have no choice.
My sock...
Just buy a new one!
Hm... Just leave this to me.
LAMIA SCALE
JURA NEEKIS
Sorry about my absence from yesterday's games!
Now, let me explain the rules for Pandemonium!
Punkin!

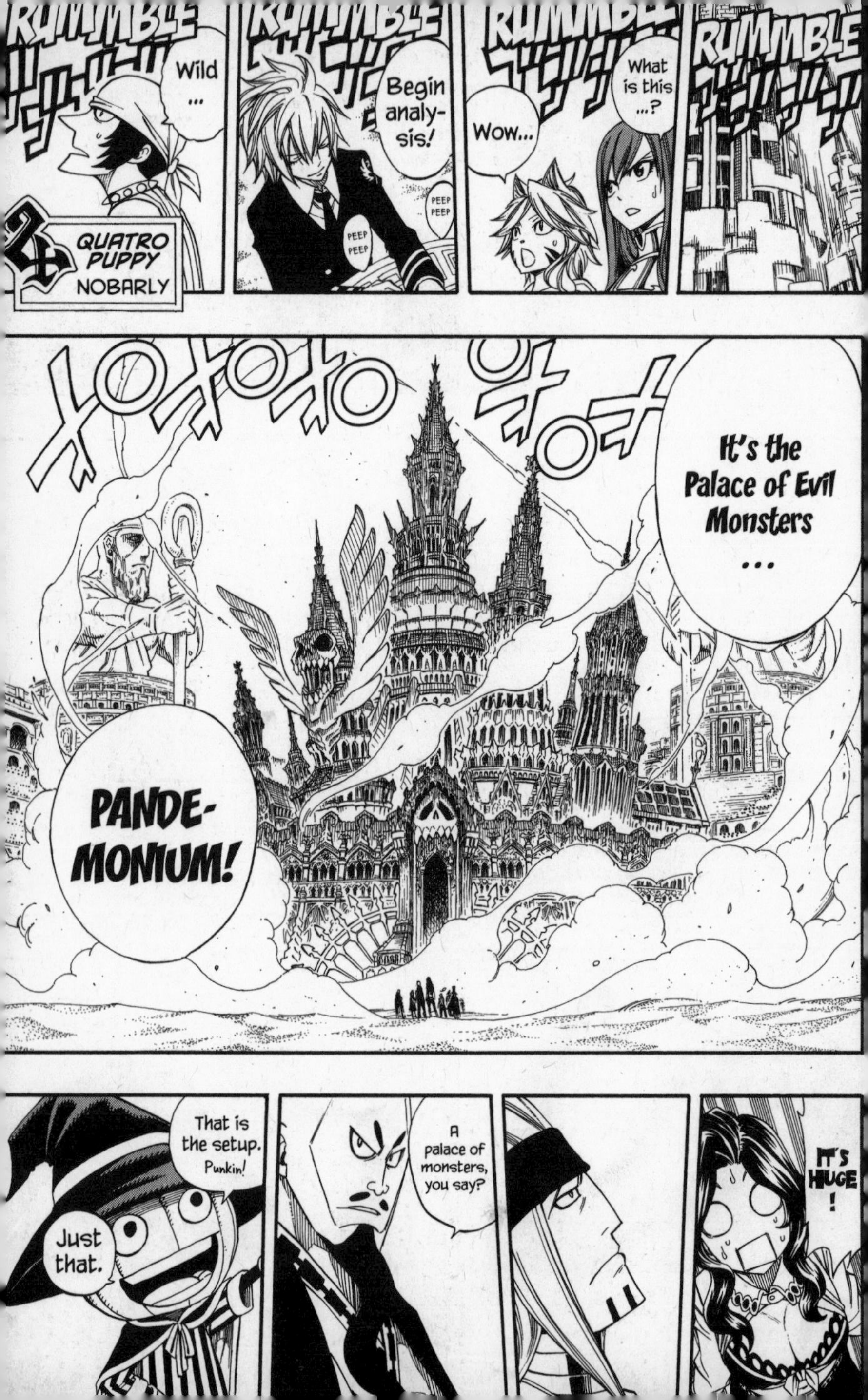
RUMMBLE
What is this ...?
Wow...
RUMMBLE
Begin analy-sis!
PEEP PEEP
PEEP PEEP
RUMMBLE
RUMMBLE
Wild ...
QUATRO PUPPY
NOBARLY
It's the Palace of Evil Monsters ...
PANDE-MONIUM!
IT'S HUGE!
A palace of monsters, you say?
That is the setup. Punkin!
Just that.

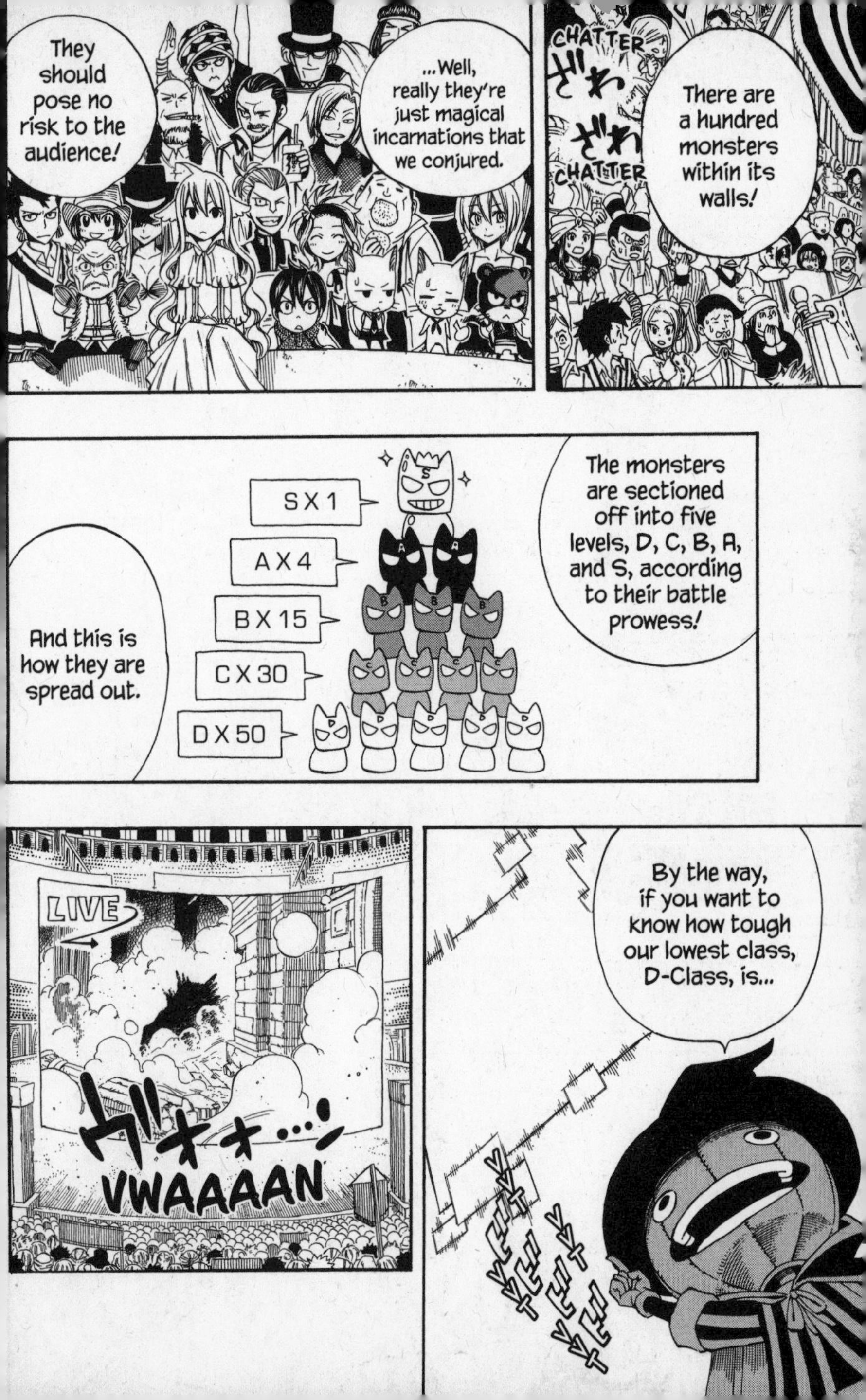
CHATTER
ざわ
ざわ
CHATTER
There are a hundred monsters within its walls!
...Well, really they're just magical incarnations that we conjured.
They should pose no risk to the audience!
The monsters are sectioned off into five levels, D, C, B, A, and S, according to their battle prowess!
S X 1
A X 4
B X 15
C X 30
D X 50
And this is how they are spread out.
By the way, if you want to know how tough our lowest class, D-Class, is...
LIVE
VWAAAAN

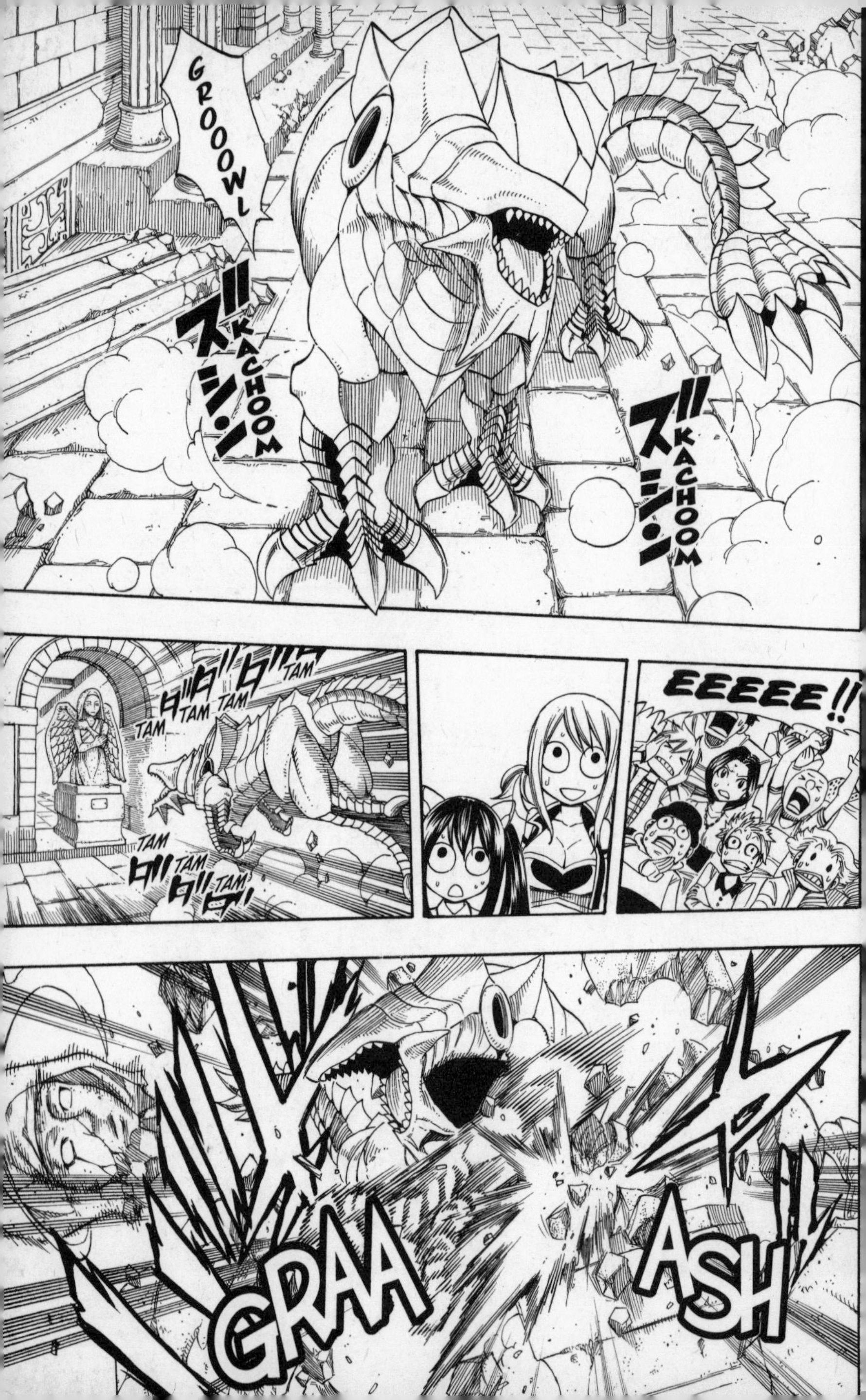
GROOOWL
KACHOOM
KACHOOM
EEEEEE!!
TAM TAM TAM TAM
TAM TAM TAM
GRAA
ASH

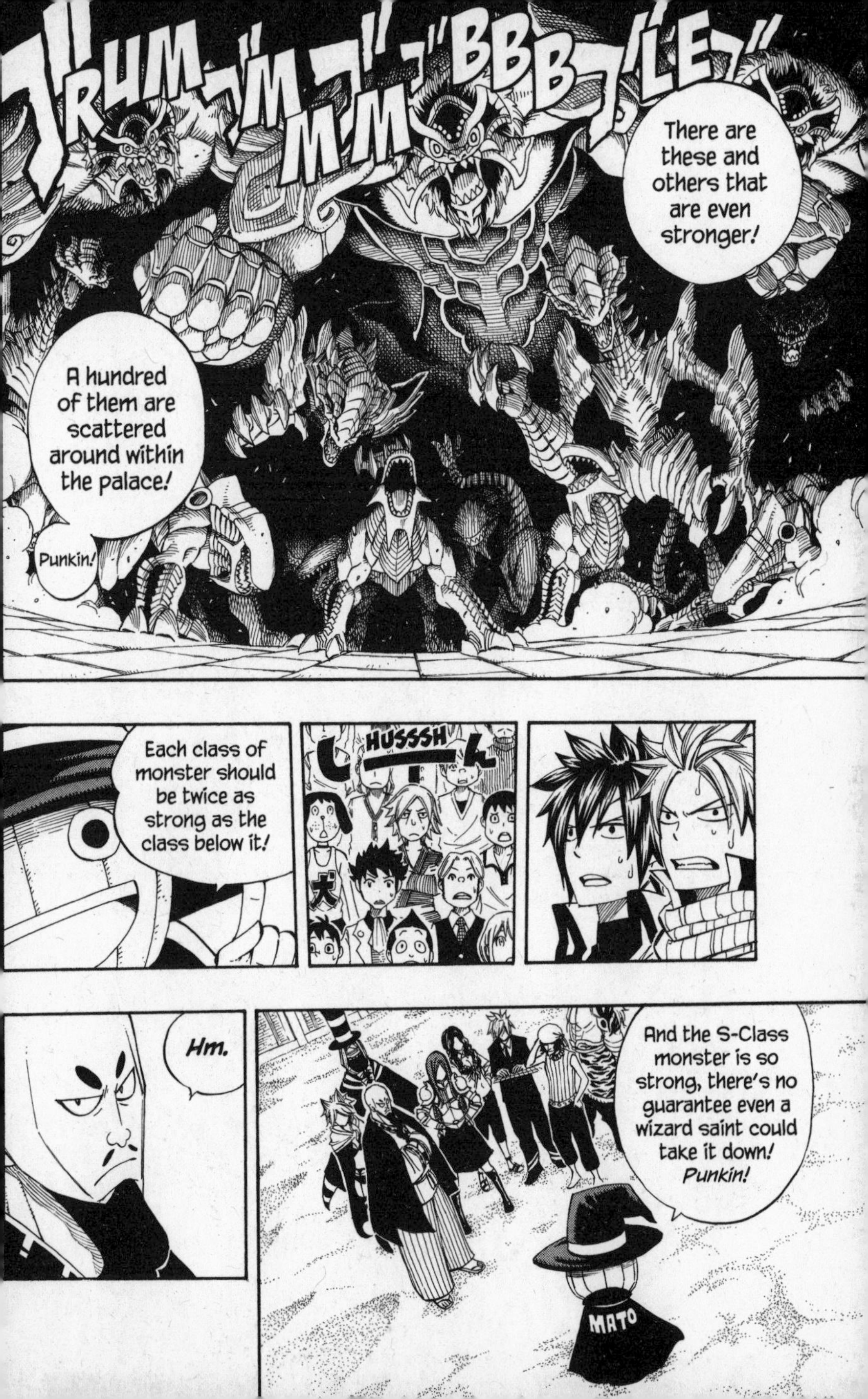
RUMMMMBBBLE
There are these and others that are even stronger!
A hundred of them are scattered around within the palace!
Punkin!
HUSSSH
Each class of monster should be twice as strong as the class below it!
And the S-Class monster is so strong, there's no guarantee even a wizard saint could take it down! Punkin!
MATO
Hm.

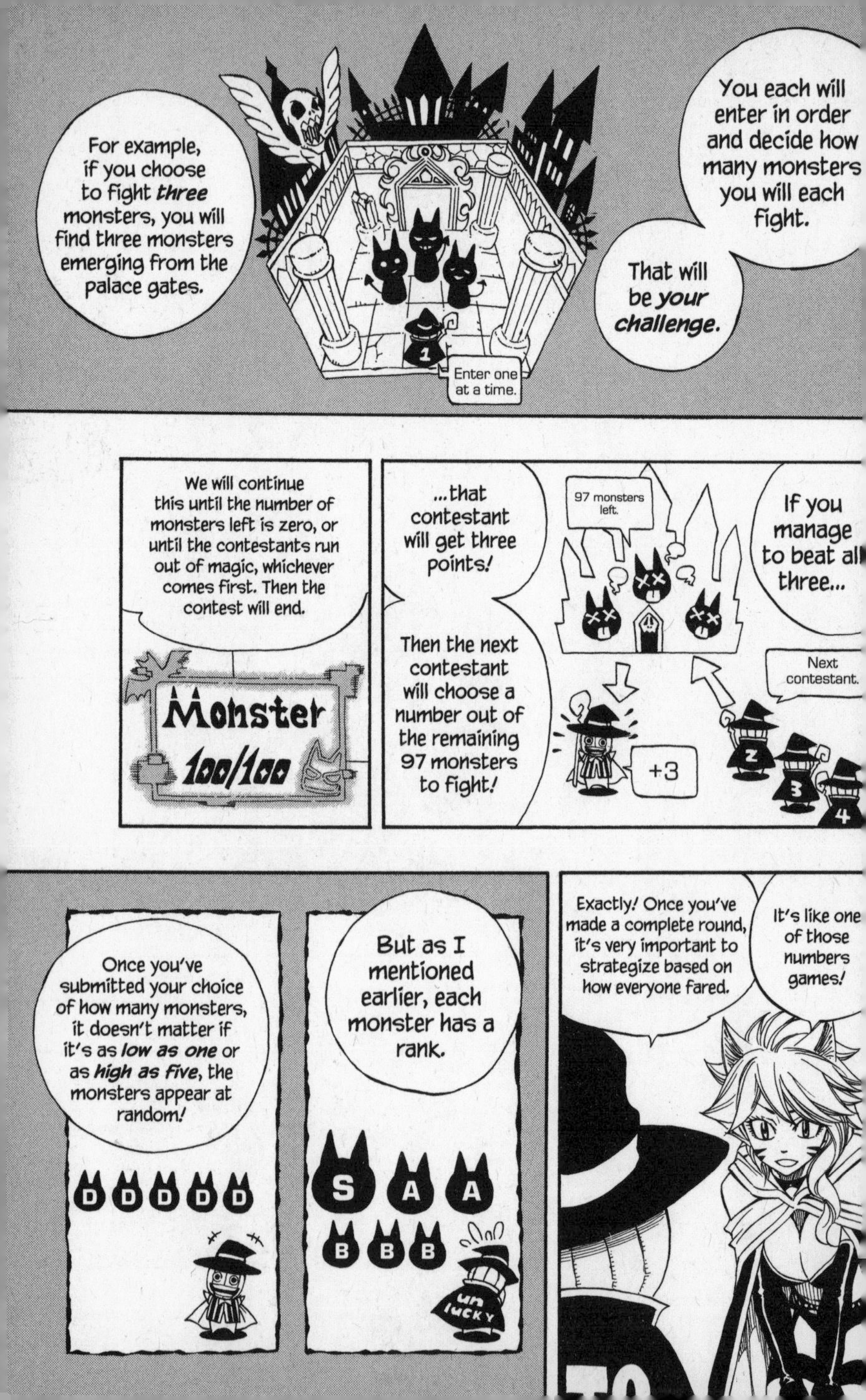
You each will enter in order and decide how many monsters you will each fight.
That will be your challenge.
For example, if you choose to fight three monsters, you will find three monsters emerging from the palace gates.
1
Enter one at a time.
If you manage to beat all three...
97 monsters left.
Next contestant.
2
3
4
+3
...that contestant will get three points!
Then the next contestant will choose a number out of the remaining 97 monsters to fight!
We will continue this until the number of monsters left is zero, or until the contestants run out of magic, whichever comes first. Then the contest will end.
Monster
100/100
It's like one of those numbers games!
Exactly! Once you've made a complete round, it's very important to strategize based on how everyone fared.
But as I mentioned earlier, each monster has a rank.
S
A
A
B
B
B
un LUCKY
Once you've submitted your choice of how many monsters, it doesn't matter if it's as low as one or as high as five, the monsters appear at random!
D
D
D
D
D

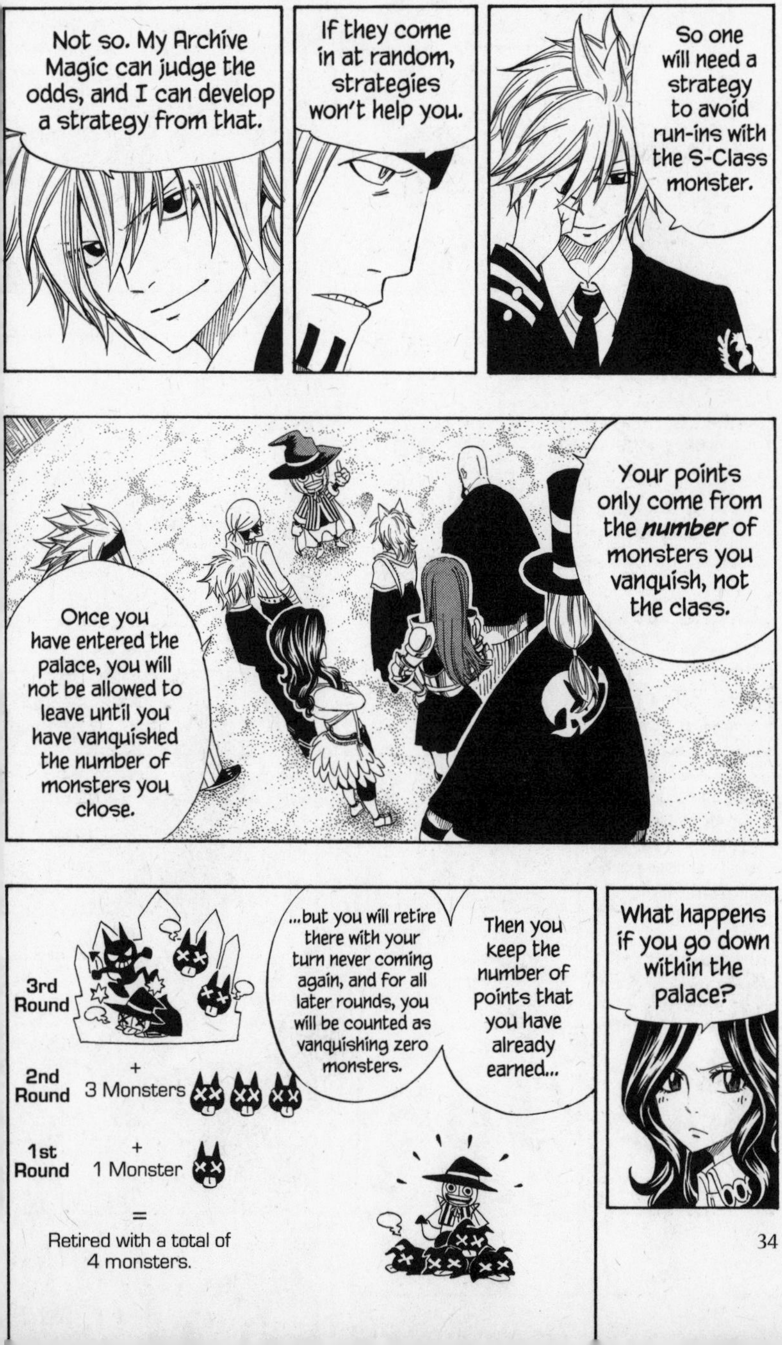
So one will need a strategy to avoid run-ins with the S-Class monster.
If they come in at random, strategies won't help you.
Not so. My Archive Magic can judge the odds, and I can develop a strategy from that.
Your points only come from the *number* of monsters you vanquish, not the class.
Once you have entered the palace, you will not be allowed to leave until you have vanquished the number of monsters you chose.
What happens if you go down within the palace?
Then you keep the number of points that you have already earned...
...but you will retire there with your turn never coming again, and for all later rounds, you will be counted as vanquishing zero monsters.
3rd Round
2nd Round
+
3 Monsters
1st Round
+
1 Monster
=
Retired with a total of 4 monsters.

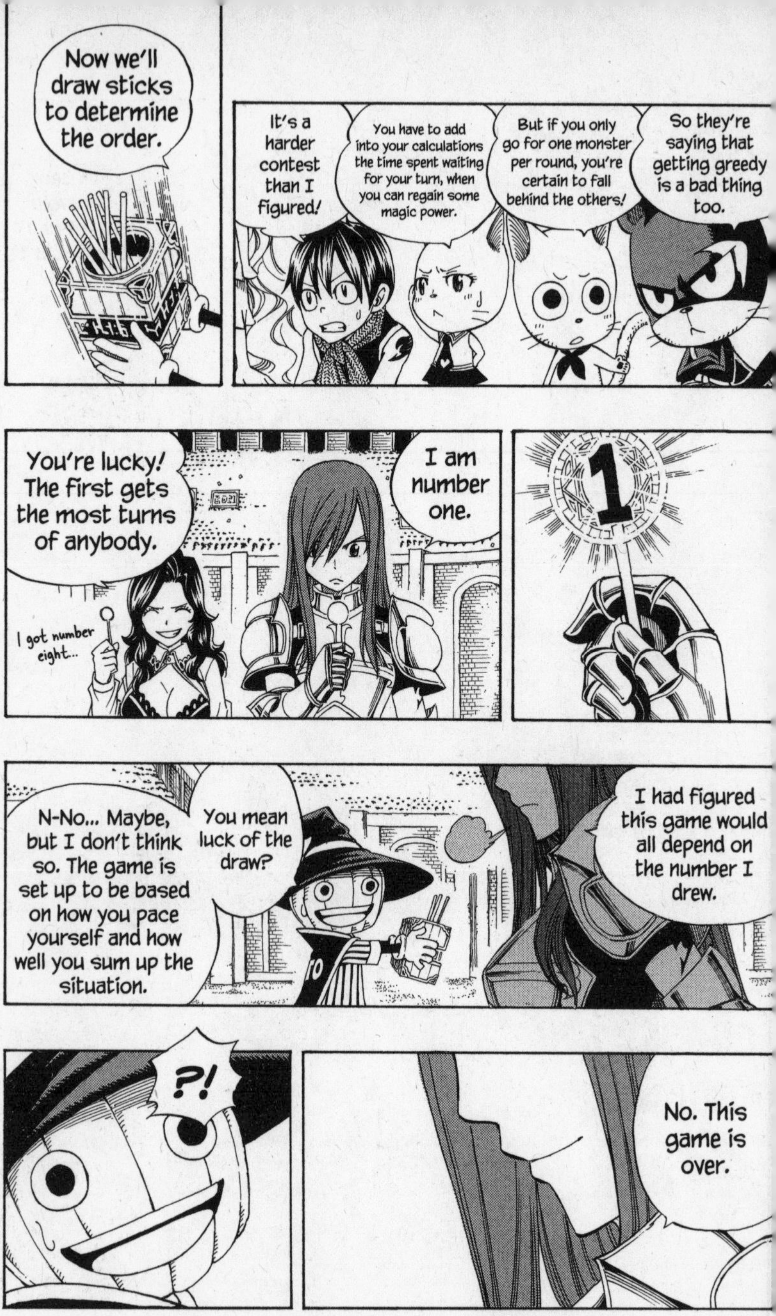
So they're saying that getting greedy is a bad thing too.
But if you only go for one monster per round, you're certain to fall behind the others!
You have to add into your calculations the time spent waiting for your turn, when you can regain some magic power.
It's a harder contest than I figured!
Now we'll draw sticks to determine the order.
1
I am number one.
You're lucky! The first gets the most turns of anybody.
I got number eight...
I had figured this game would all depend on the number I drew.
You mean luck of the draw?
N-No... Maybe, but I don't think so. The game is set up to be based on how you pace yourself and how well you sum up the situation.
No. This game is over.
?!

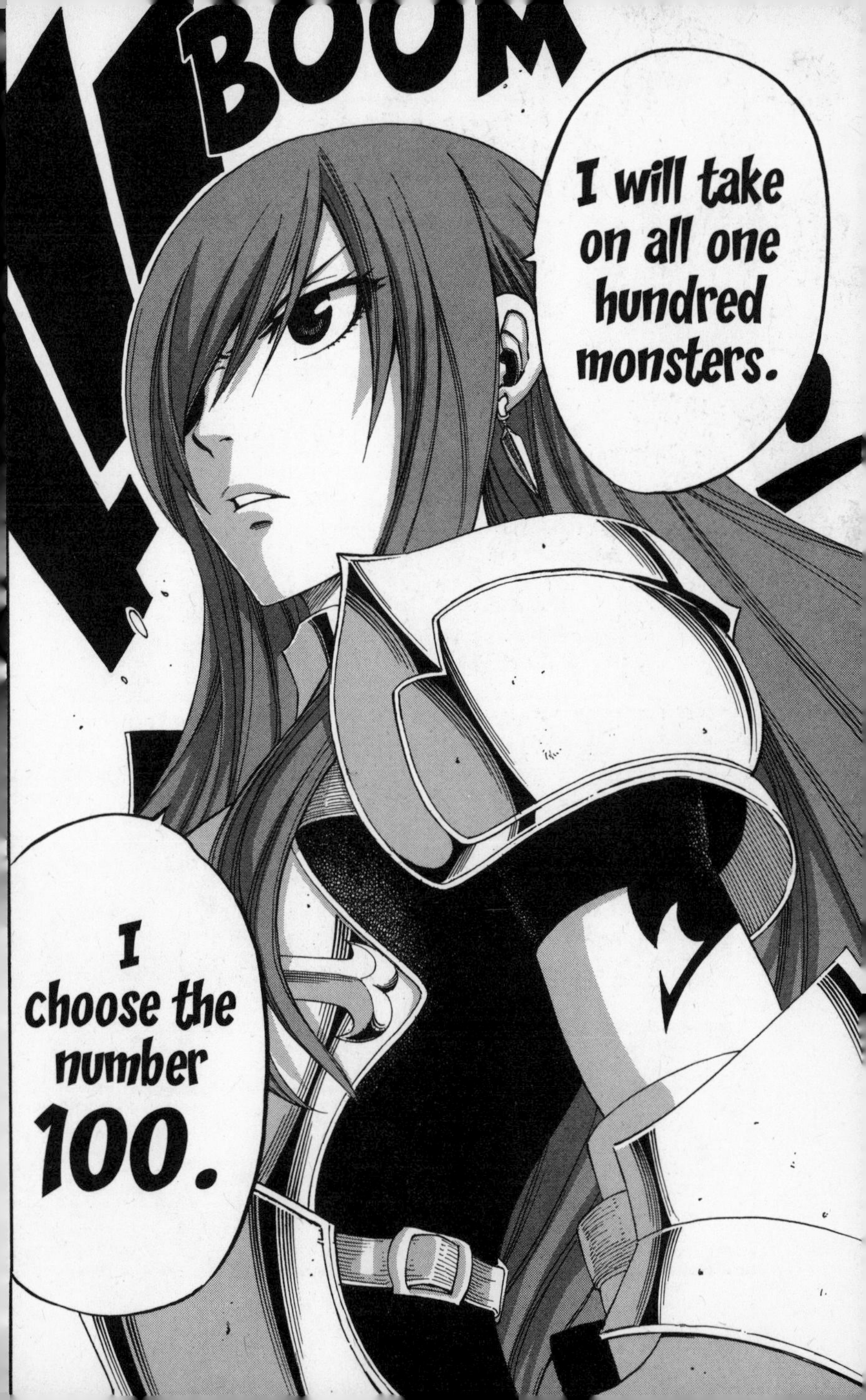
BOOM
I will take on all one hundred monsters.
I choose the number 100.

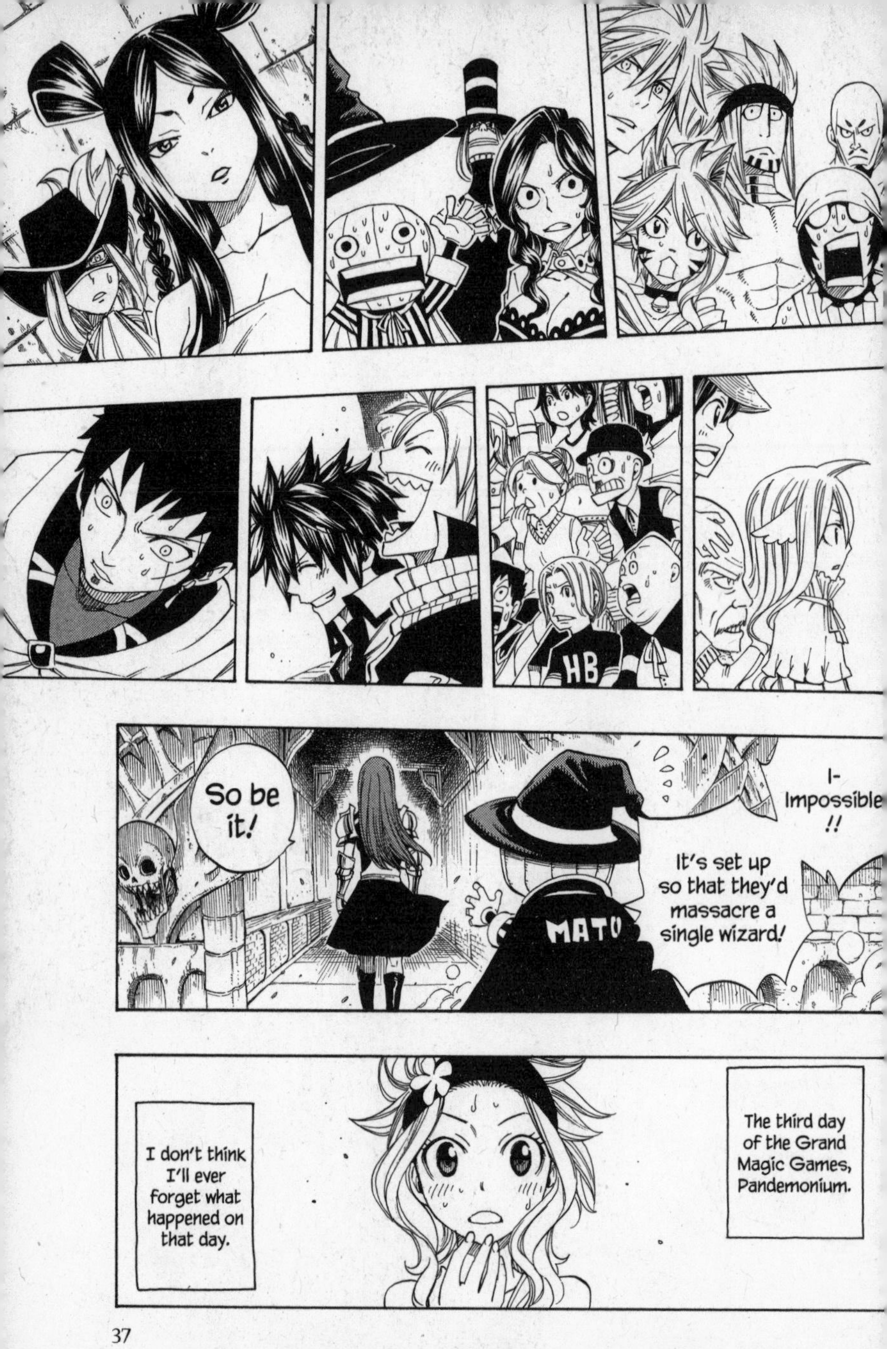
I- Impossible !!
It's set up so that they'd massacre a single wizard!
So be it!
The third day of the Grand Magic Games, Pandemonium.
I don't think I'll ever forget what happened on that day.

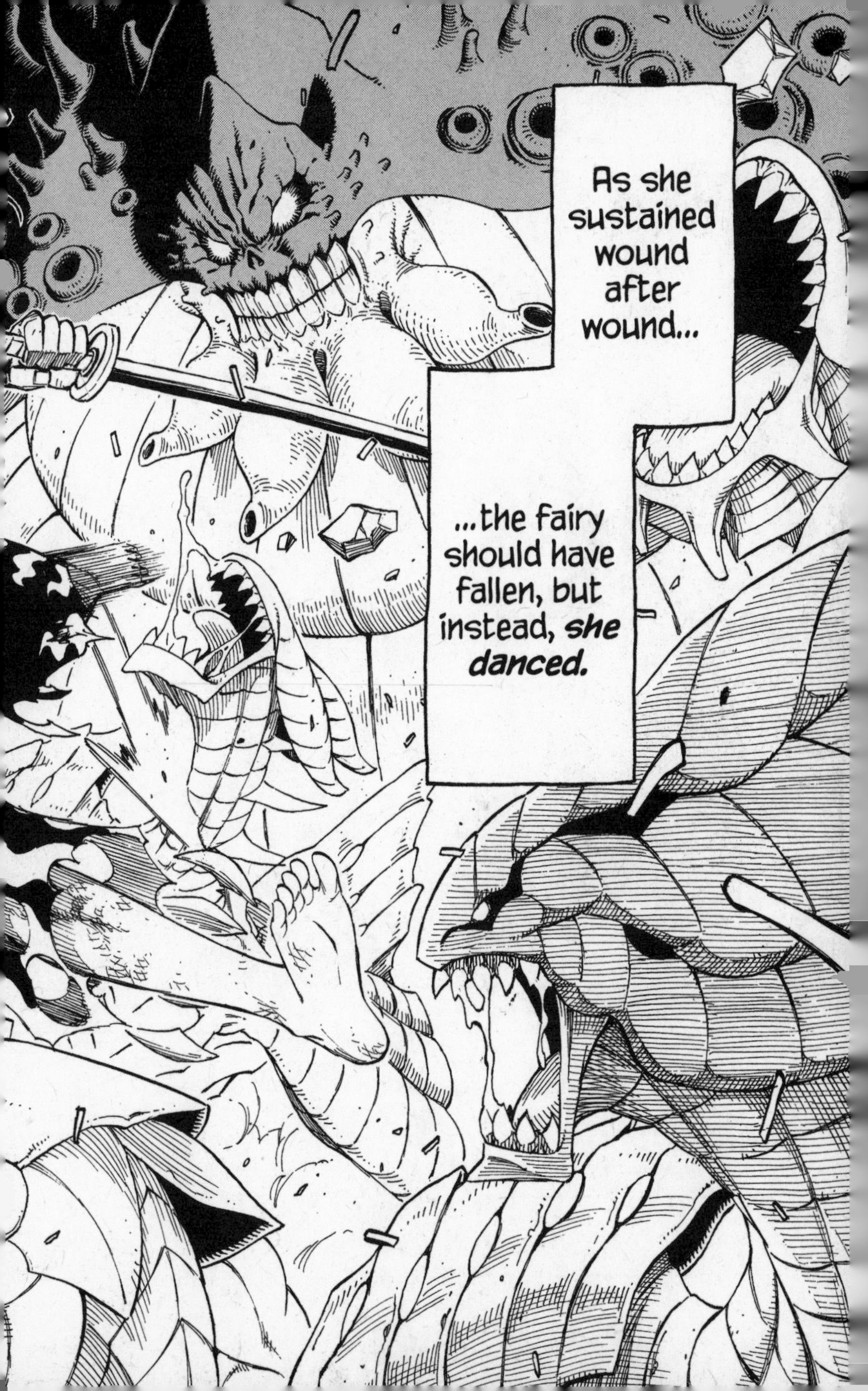
As she sustained wound after wound...
...the fairy should have fallen, but instead, *she danced.*

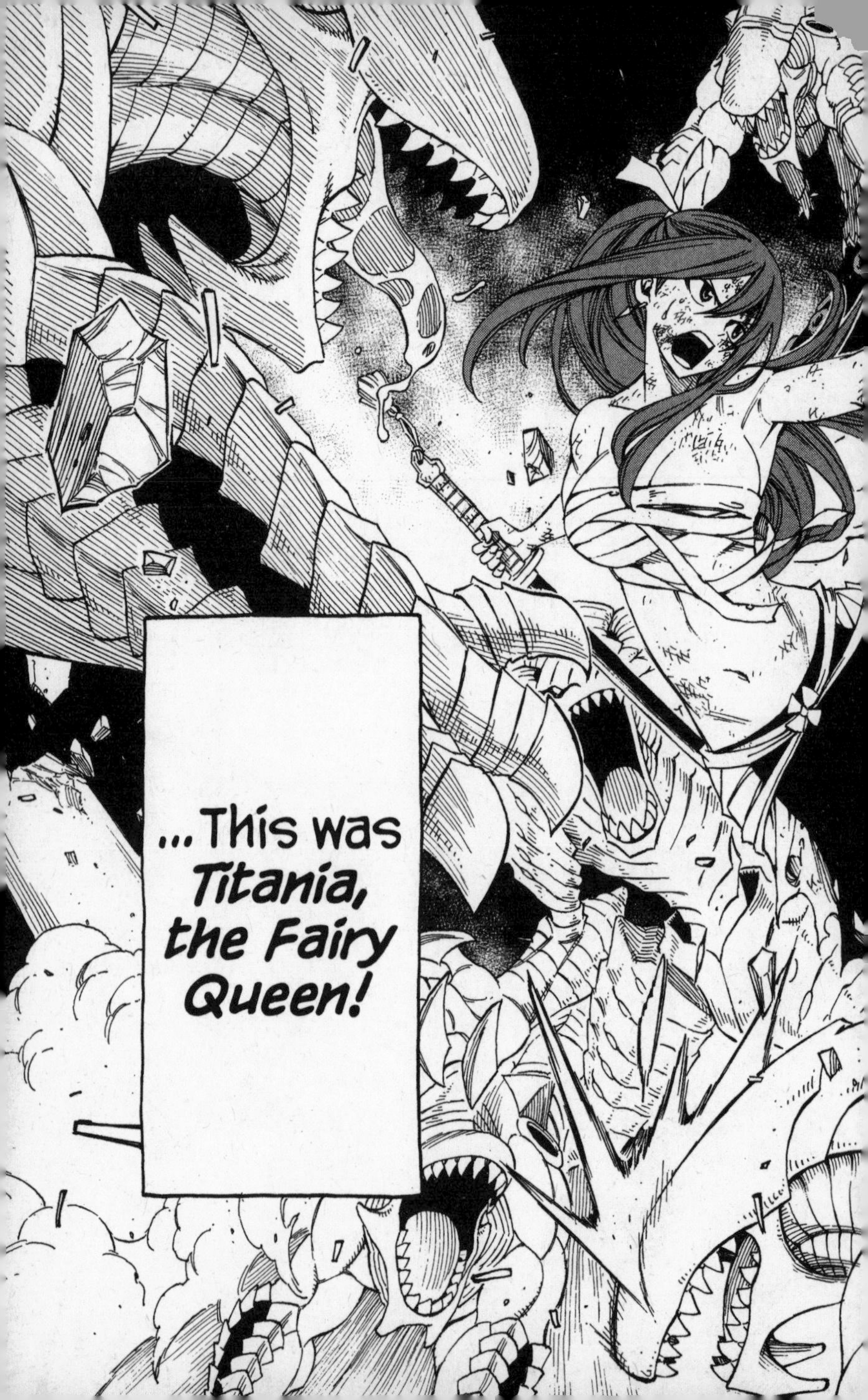
...This was *Titania, the Fairy Queen!*

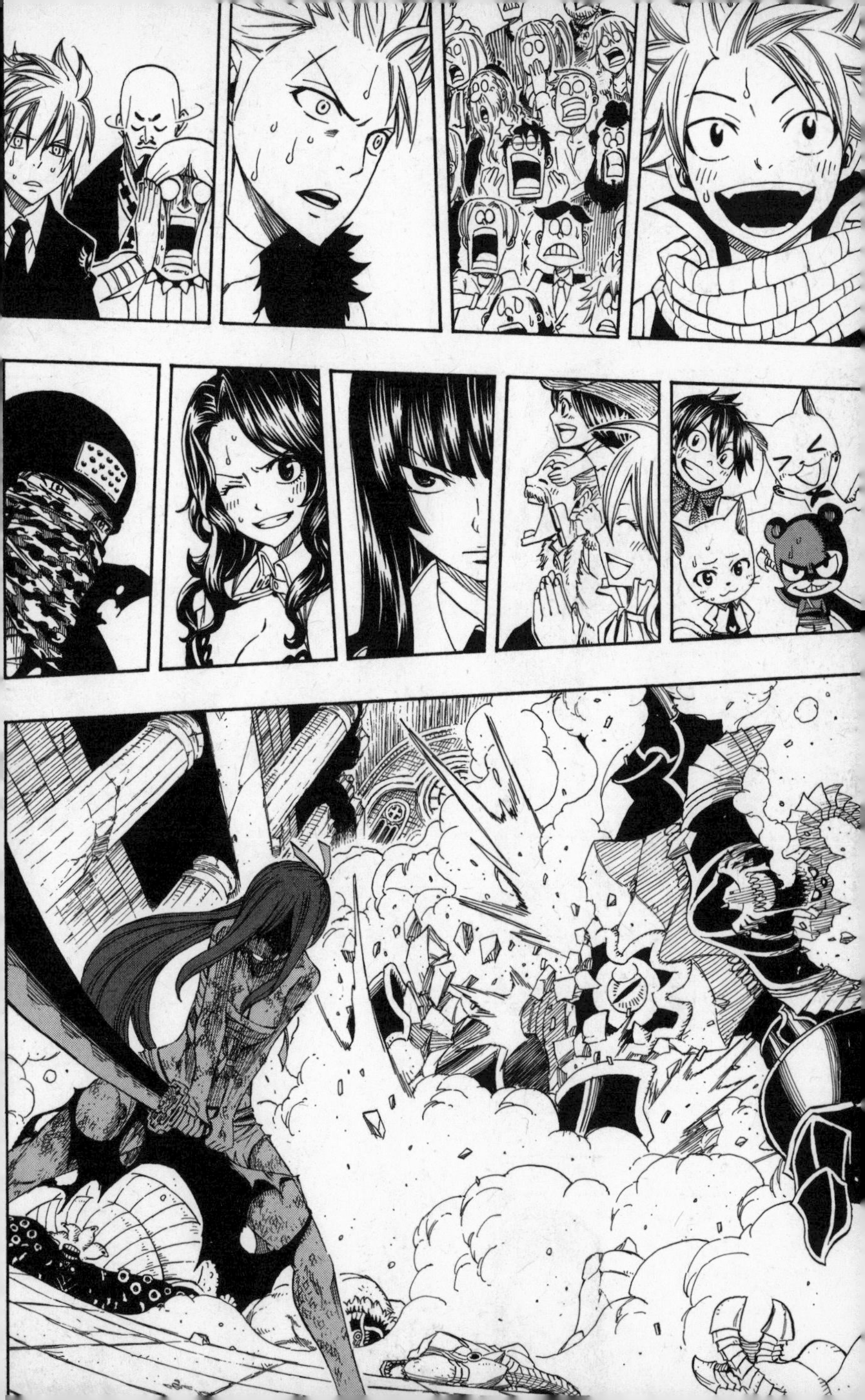

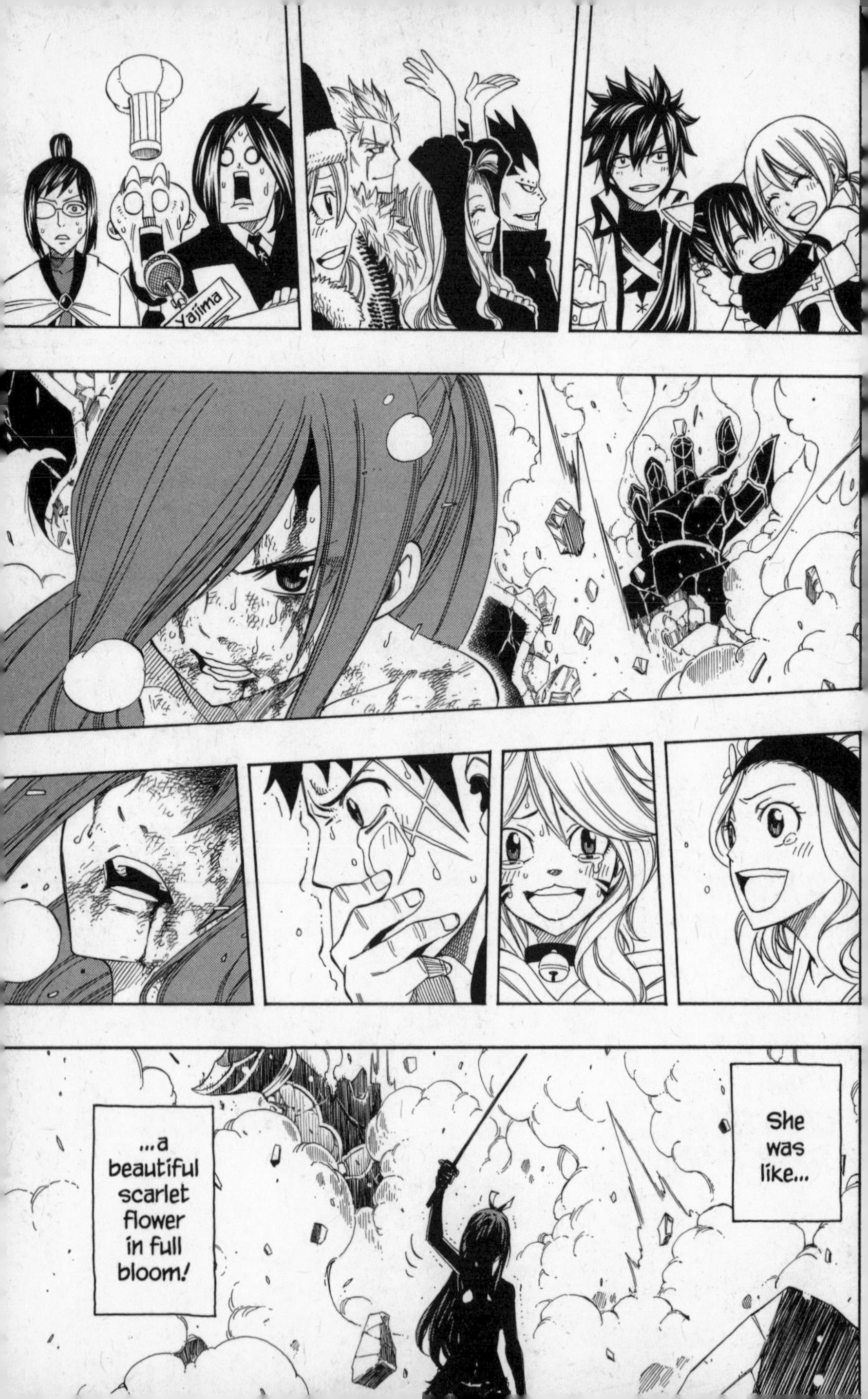
Yajima
She was like...
...a beautiful scarlet flower in full bloom!

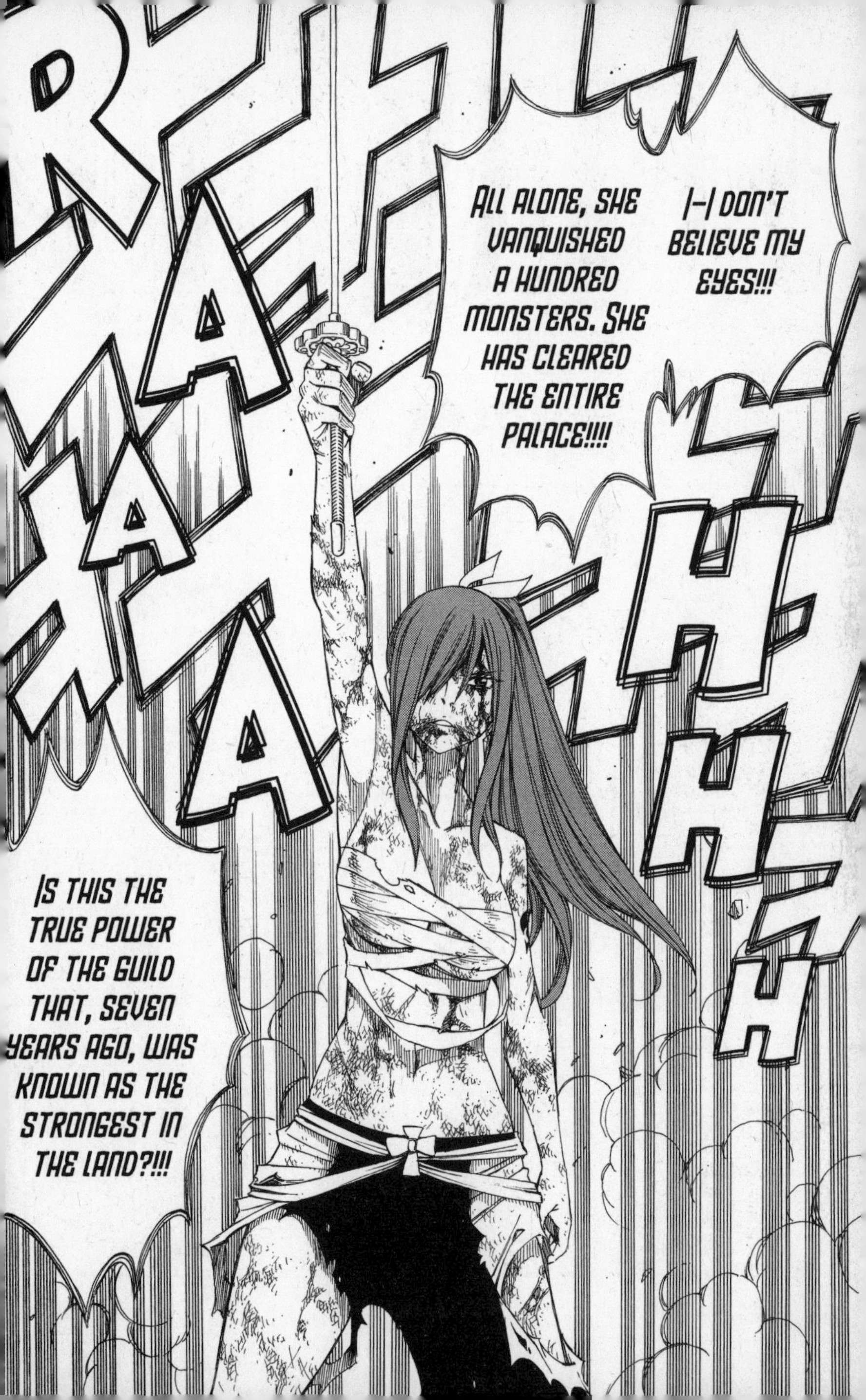
I–I DON'T BELIEVE MY EYES!!!
ALL ALONE, SHE VANQUISHED A HUNDRED MONSTERS. SHE HAS CLEARED THE ENTIRE PALACE!!!!
IS THIS THE TRUE POWER OF THE GUILD THAT, SEVEN YEARS AGO, WAS KNOWN AS THE STRONGEST IN THE LAND?!!!

FAIRY TAIL
フェアリーテイル

Chapter 285: MPF

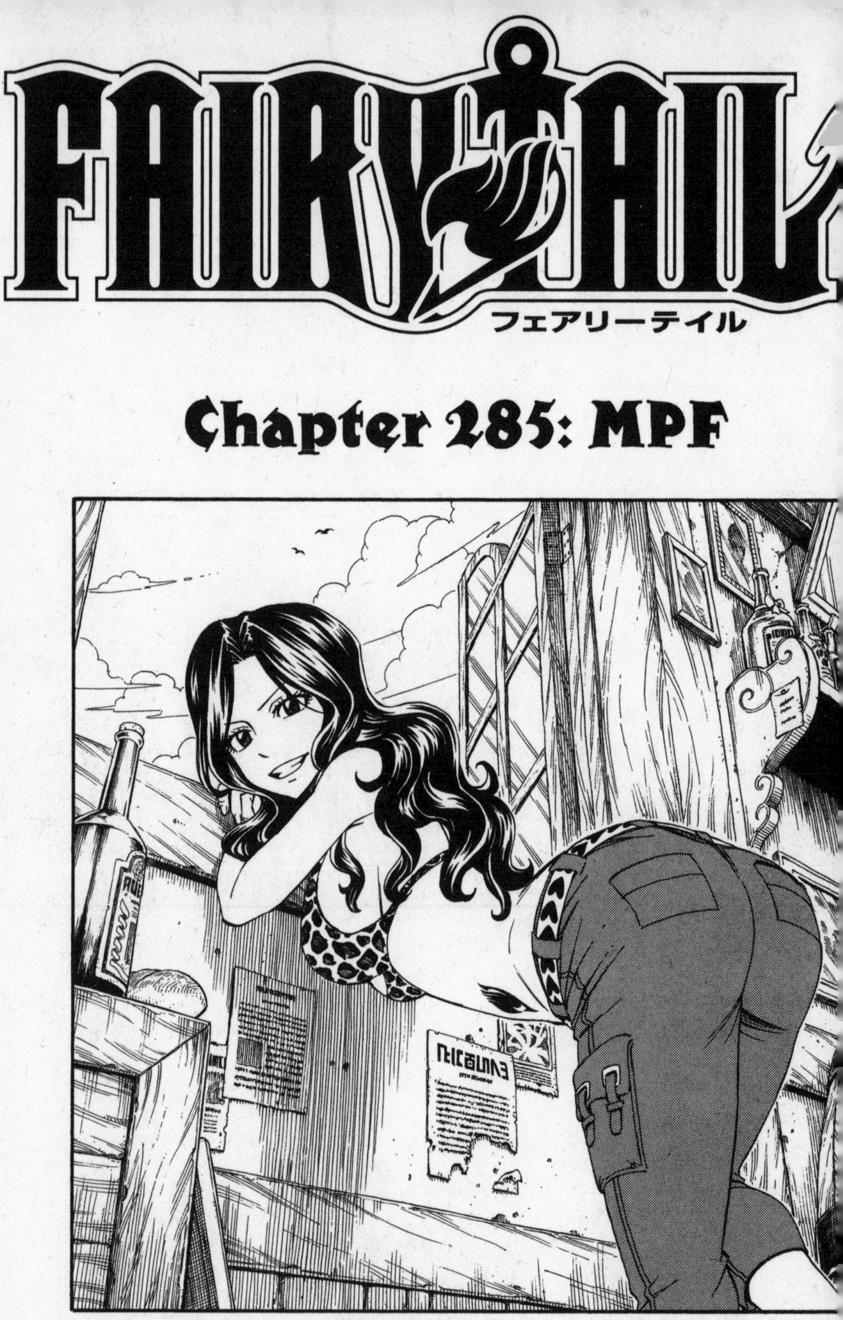

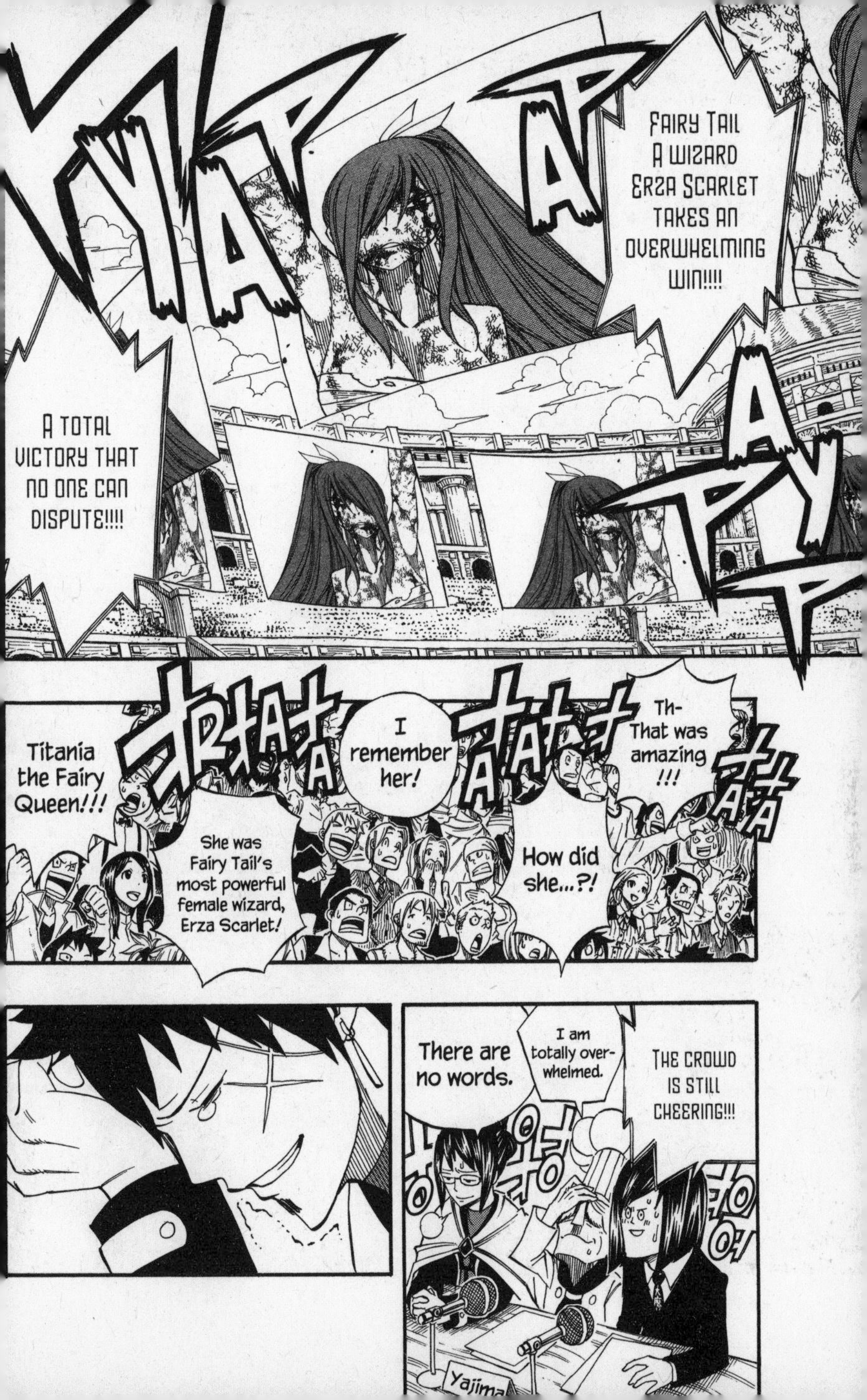
Fairy Tail A wizard Erza Scarlet takes an overwhelming win!!!!
A total victory that no one can dispute!!!!
Th- That was amazing!!!
How did she...?!
I remember her!
She was Fairy Tail's most powerful female wizard, Erza Scarlet!
Titania the Fairy Queen!!!
The crowd is still cheering!!!
I am totally over-whelmed.
There are no words.
Yajima

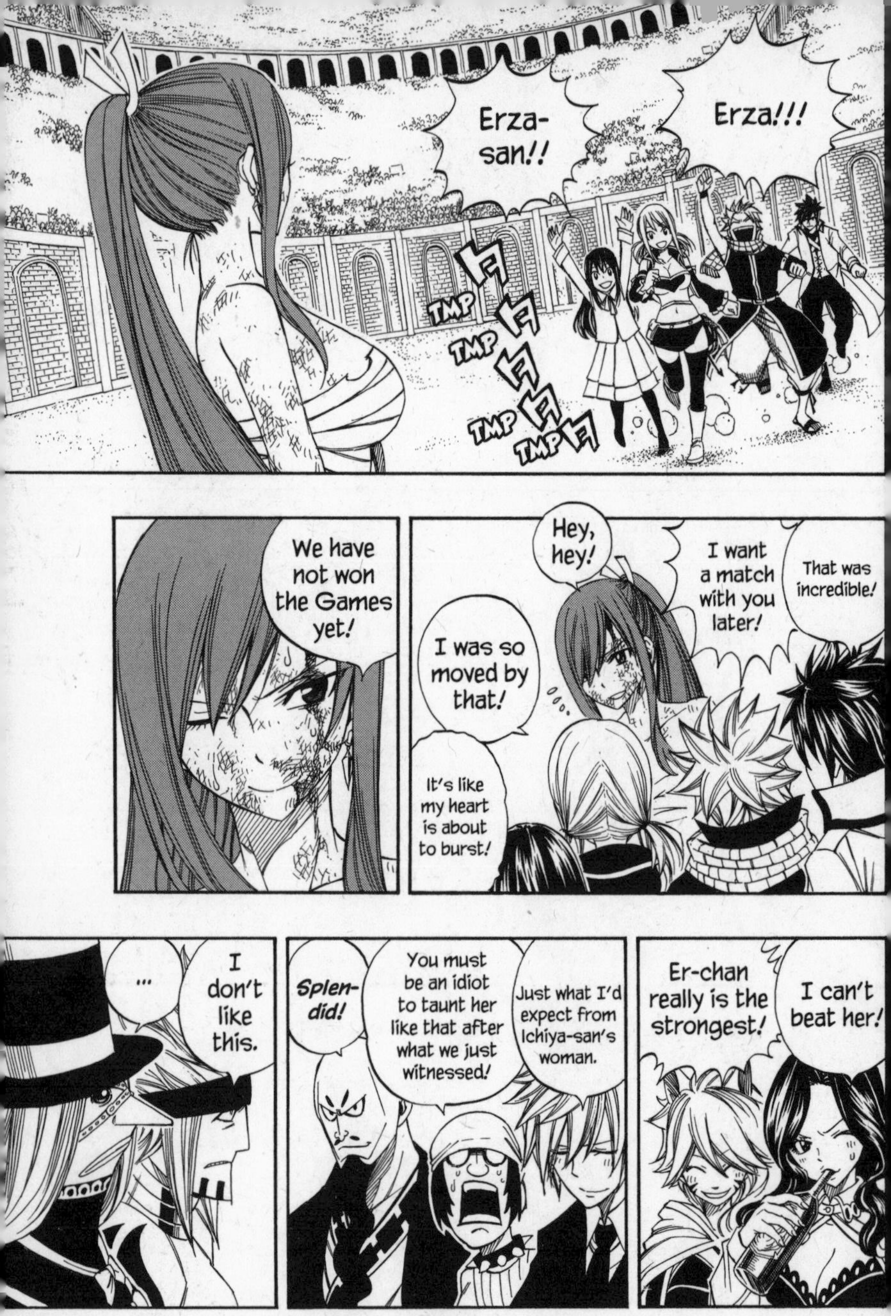
Erza!!!
Erza-san!!
TMP TMP TMP TMP
That was incredible!
I want a match with you later!
Hey, hey!
I was so moved by that!
It's like my heart is about to burst!
We have not won the Games yet!
I can't beat her!
Er-chan really is the strongest!
Just what I'd expect from Ichiya-san's woman.
You must be an idiot to taunt her like that after what we just witnessed!
Splendid!
I don't like this.
...

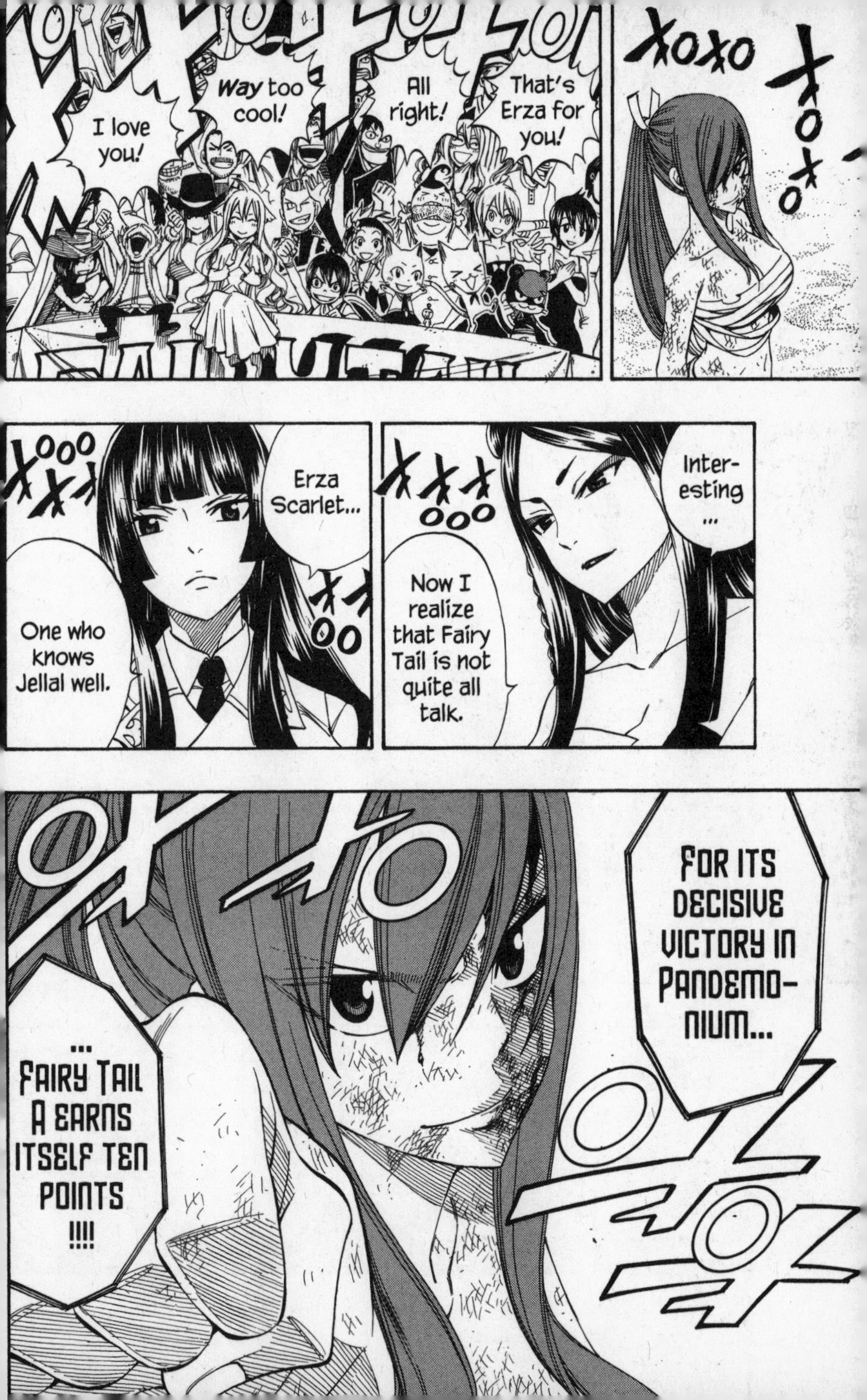
That's Erza for you!
All right!
Way too cool!
I love you!
Inter-esting...
Now I realize that Fairy Tail is not quite all talk.
Erza Scarlet...
One who knows Jellal well.
For its decisive victory in Pandemo-nium...
...Fairy Tail A earns itself ten points!!!!

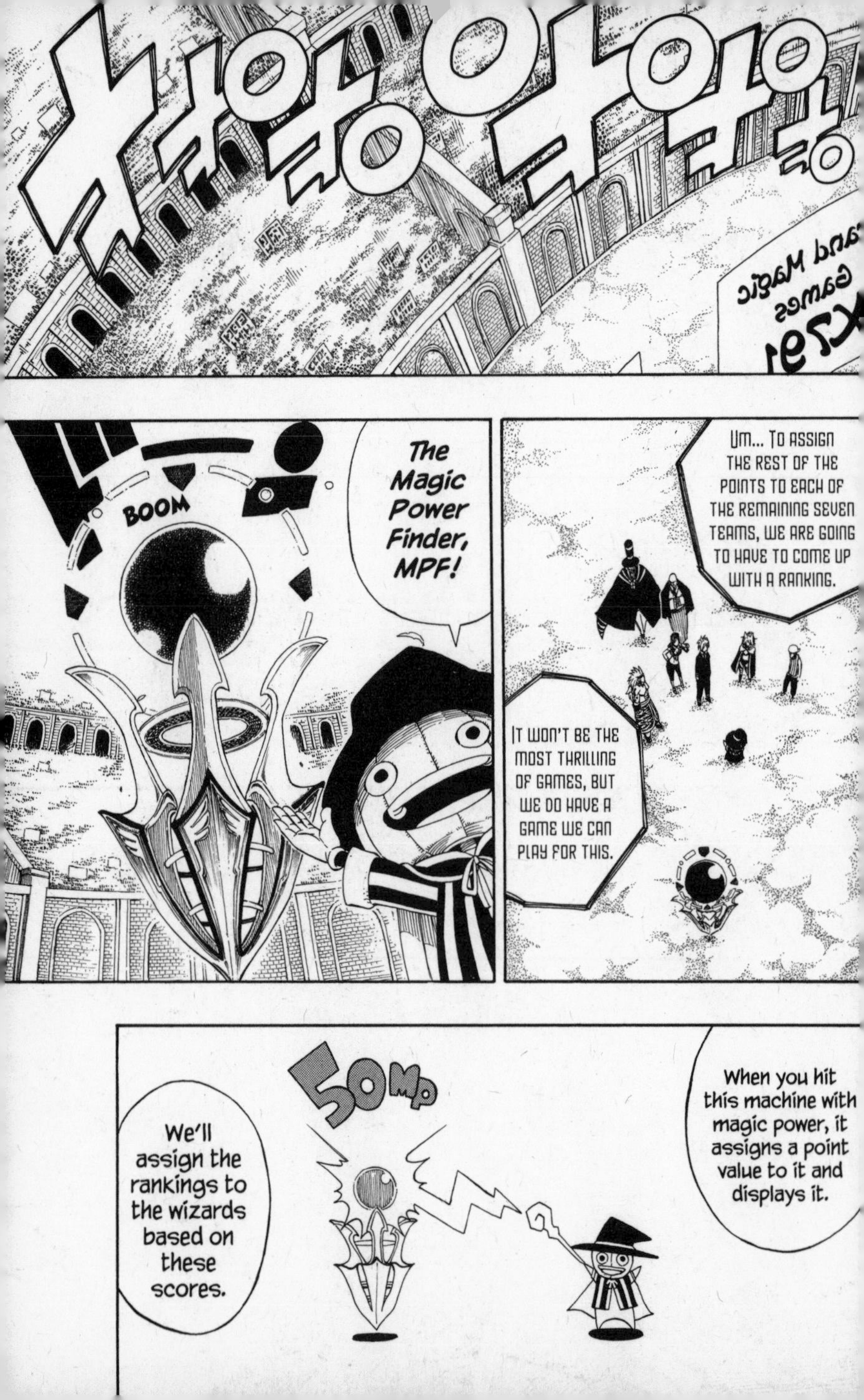
Um... To assign the rest of the points to each of the remaining seven teams, we are going to have to come up with a ranking.
It won't be the most thrilling of games, but we do have a game we can play for this.
The Magic Power Finder, MPF!
BOOM
When you hit this machine with magic power, it assigns a point value to it and displays it.
50 MP
We'll assign the rankings to the wizards based on these scores.

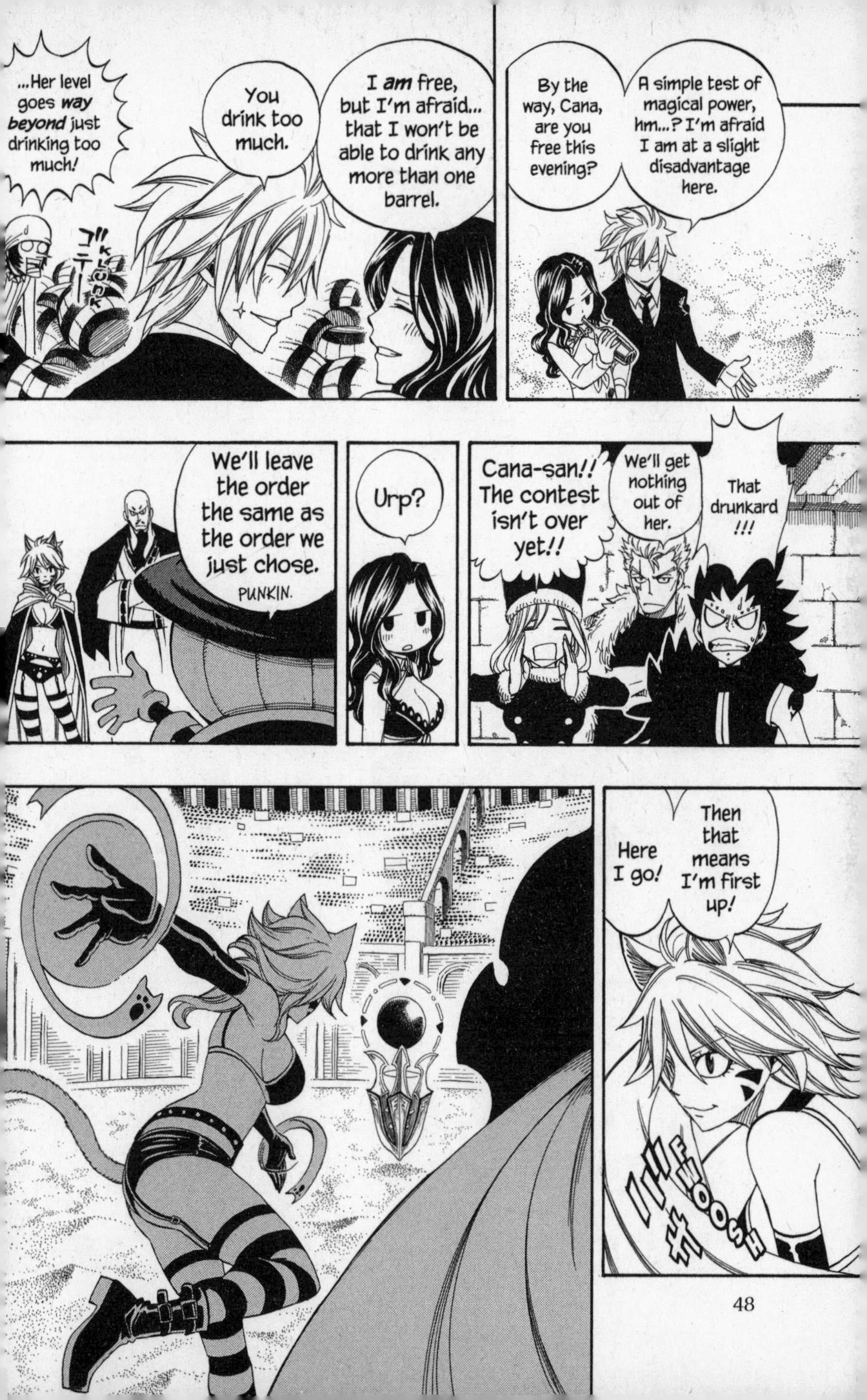
A simple test of magical power, hm...? I'm afraid I am at a slight disadvantage here.
By the way, Cana, are you free this evening?
I **am** free, but I'm afraid... that I won't be able to drink any more than one barrel.
You drink too much.
...Her level goes **way beyond** just drinking too much!
That drunkard!!!
We'll get nothing out of her.
Cana-san!! The contest isn't over yet!!
Urp?
We'll leave the order the same as the order we just chose.
PUNKIN.
Then that means I'm first up!
Here I go!
FWOOSH

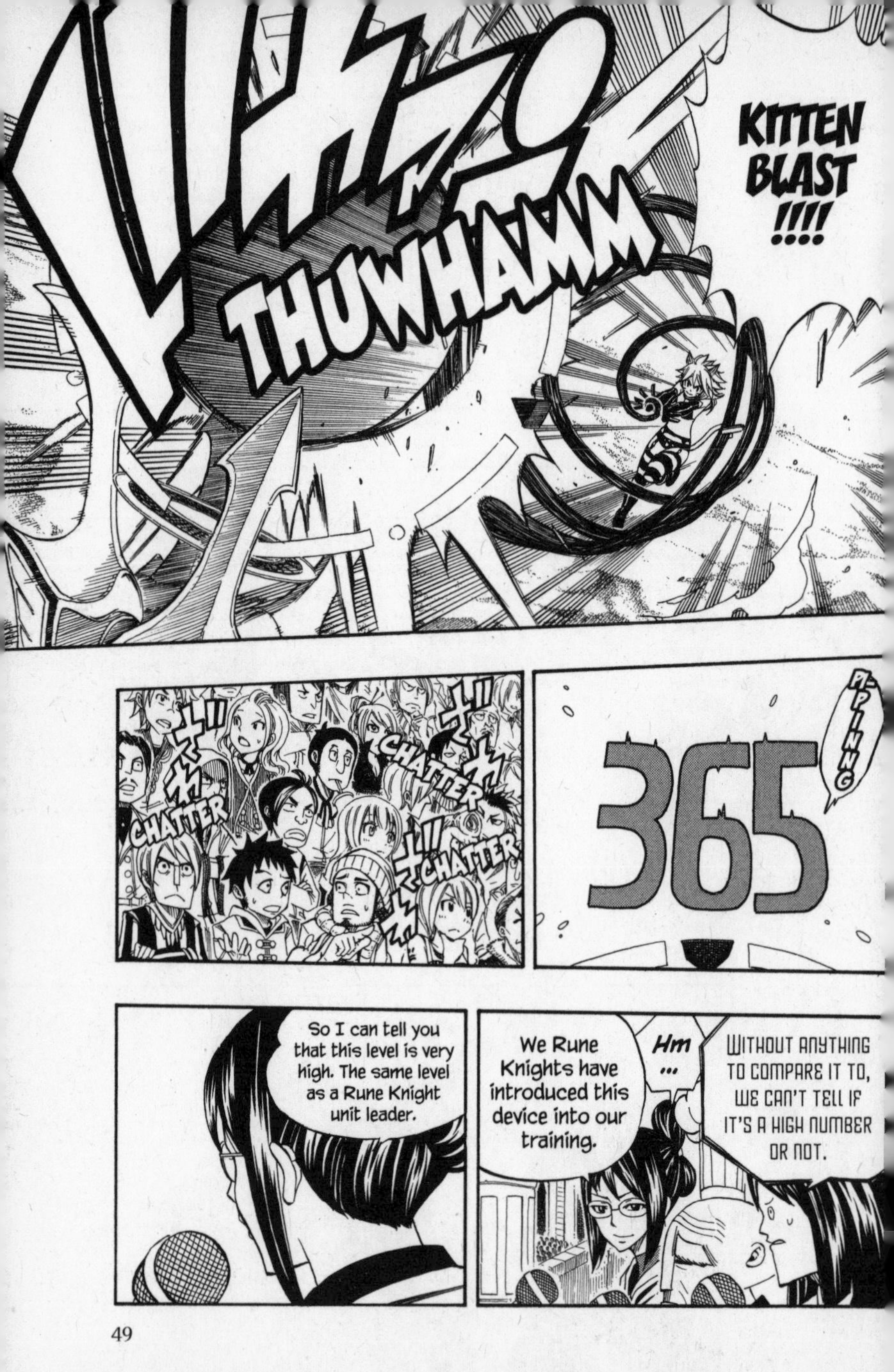
KITTEN BLAST !!!!
THUWHAMM
P-PINNG
365
CHATTER
CHATTER
CHATTER
WITHOUT ANYTHING TO COMPARE IT TO, WE CAN'T TELL IF IT'S A HIGH NUMBER OR NOT.
Hm ...
We Rune Knights have introduced this device into our training.
So I can tell you that this level is very high. The same level as a Rune Knight unit leader.

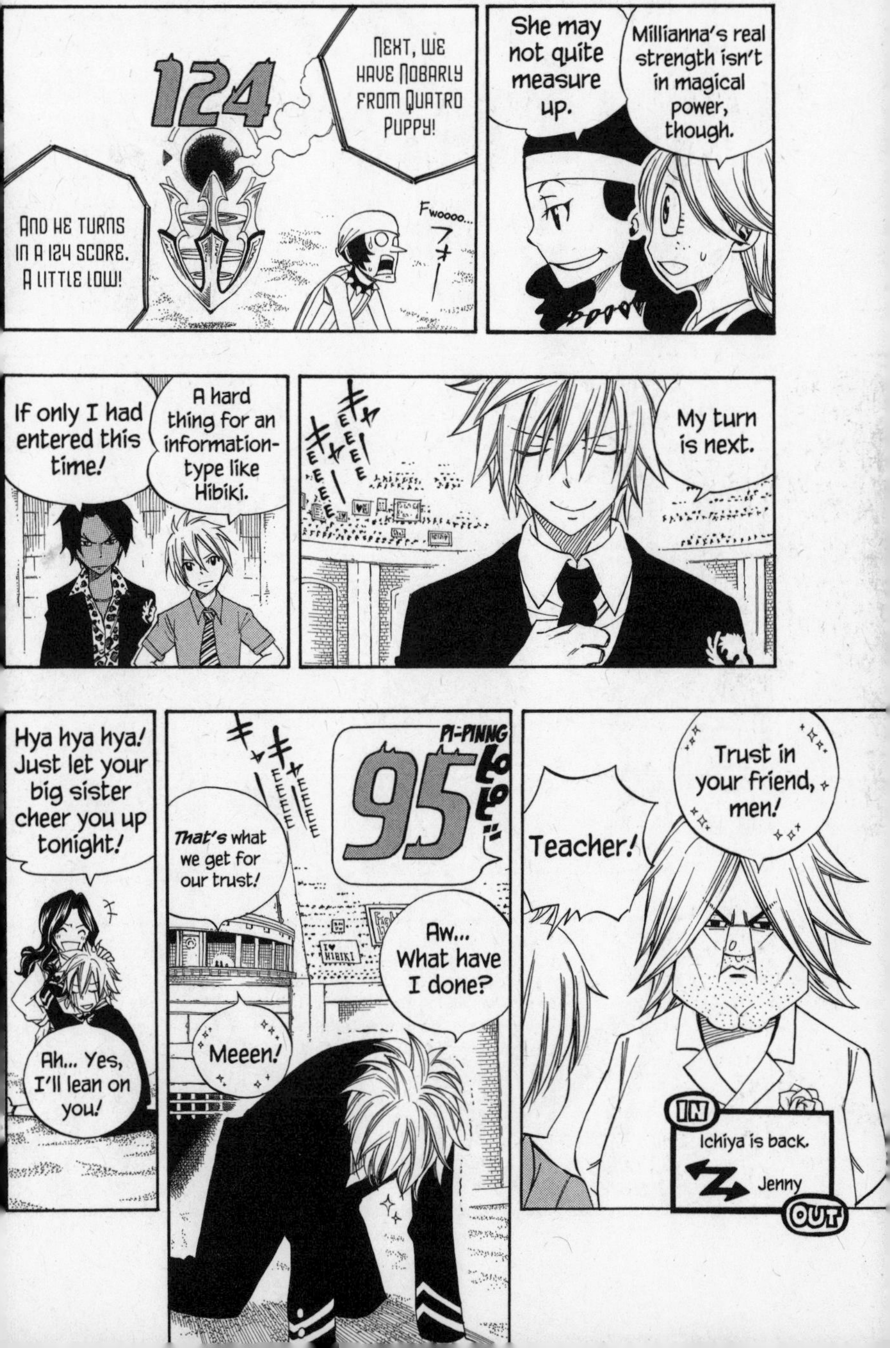
Millianna's real strength isn't in magical power, though.
She may not quite measure up.
Next, we have Nobarly from Quatro Puppy!
124
Fwoooo...
And he turns in a 124 score. A little low!
My turn is next.
EEEEE
A hard thing for an information-type like Hibiki.
If only I had entered this time!
Trust in your friend, men!
Teacher!
IN
Ichiya is back.
Jenny
OUT
PI-PING
95
EEEE
Aw... What have I done?
That's what we get for our trust!
Meeen!
Hya hya hya! Just let your big sister cheer you up tonight!
Ah... Yes, I'll lean on you!

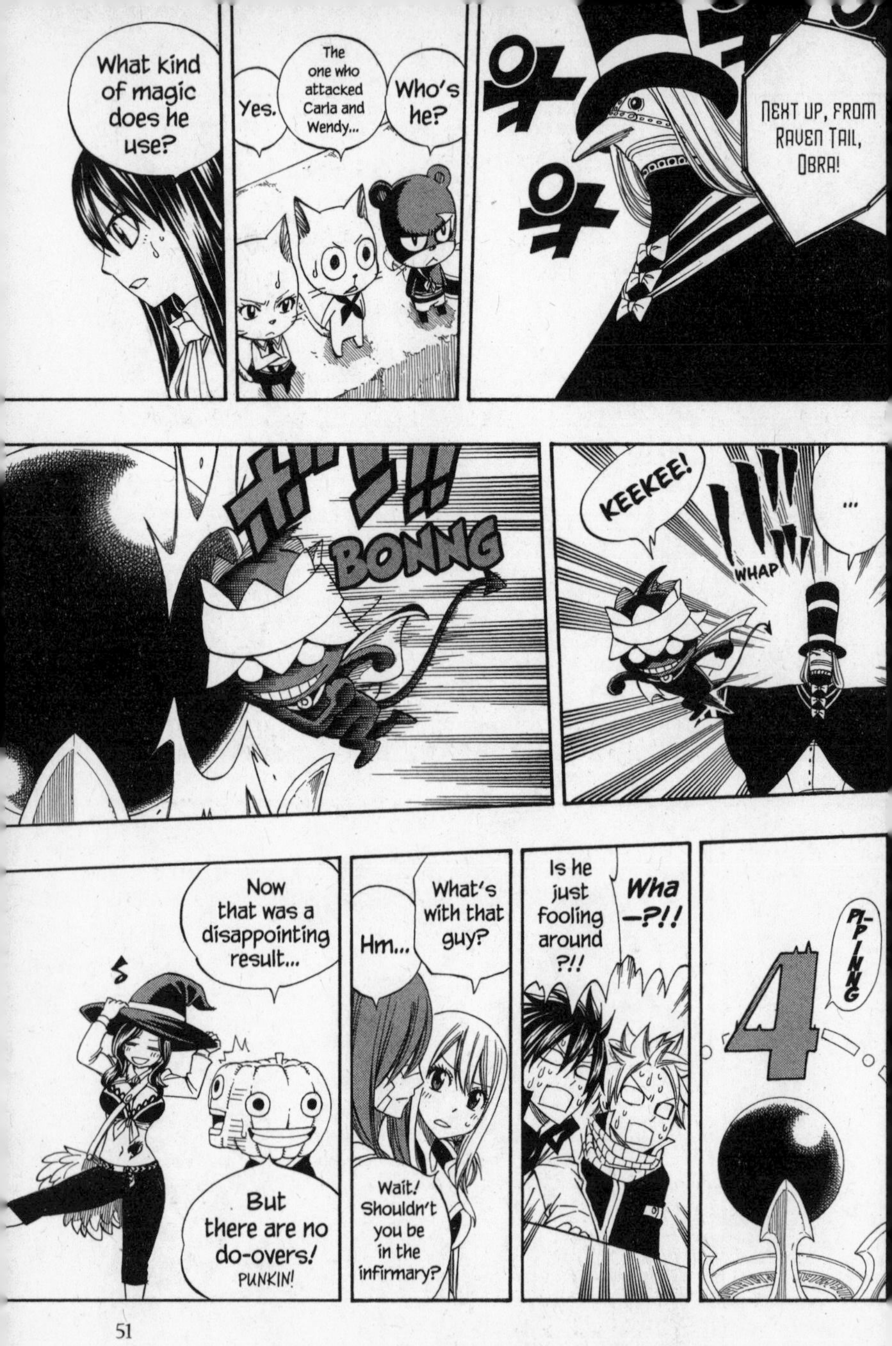

Next up, from Raven Tail, Obra!
Who's he?
The one who attacked Carla and Wendy...
Yes.
What kind of magic does he use?
...
KEEKEE!
WHAP
BONNG
PI-PINNG
4
Wha—?!!
Is he just fooling around?!!
What's with that guy?
Hm...
Wait! Shouldn't you be in the infirmary?
Now that was a disappointing result...
But there are no do-overs!
PUNKIN!

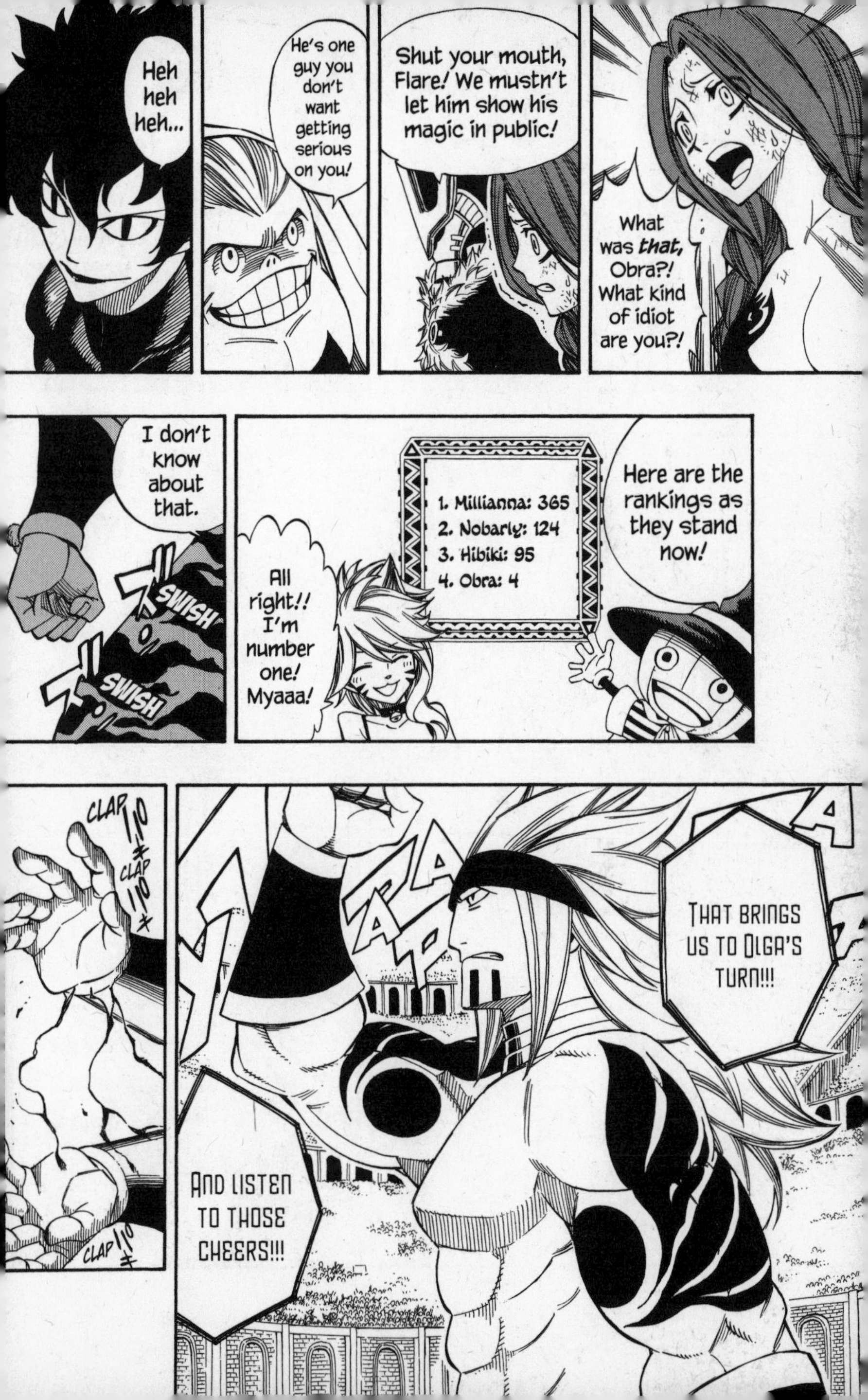
What was *that*, Obra?! What kind of idiot are you?!
Shut your mouth, Flare! We mustn't let him show his magic in public!
He's one guy you don't want getting serious on you!
Heh heh heh...
Here are the rankings as they stand now!
1. Millianna: 365
2. Nobarly: 124
3. Hibiki: 95
4. Obra: 4
All right!! I'm number one! Myaaa!
I don't know about that.
SWISH
SWISH
THAT BRINGS US TO OLGA'S TURN!!!
AND LISTEN TO THOSE CHEERS!!!
CLAP
CLAP
CLAP

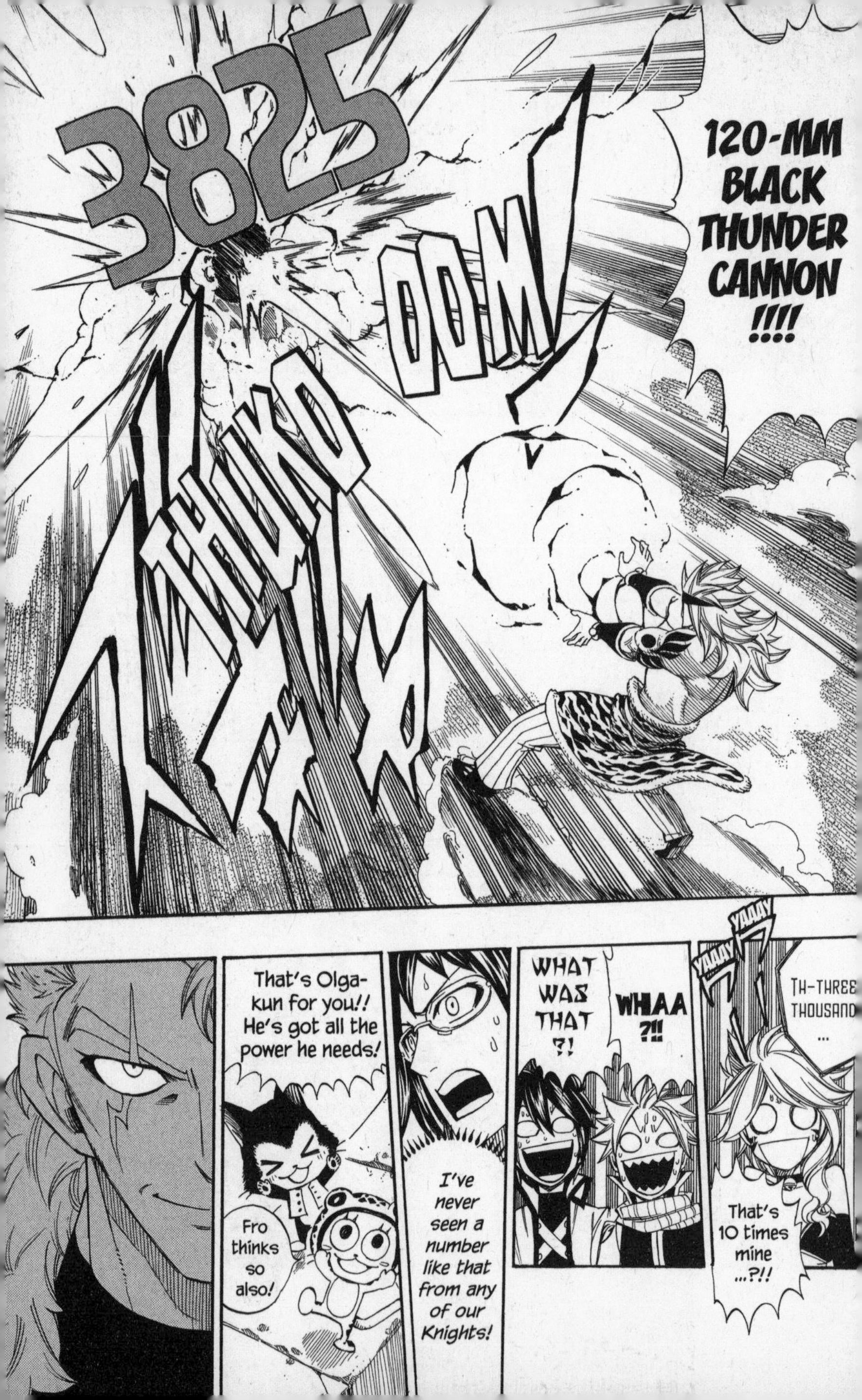
3825
120-MM BLACK THUNDER CANNON!!!!
THUKOOOM
YAAAY
YAAAY
TH-THREE THOUSAND...
That's 10 times mine...?!!
WHAA?!!
WHAT WAS THAT?!
I've never seen a number like that from any of our Knights!
That's Olga-kun for you!! He's got all the power he needs!
Fro thinks so also!

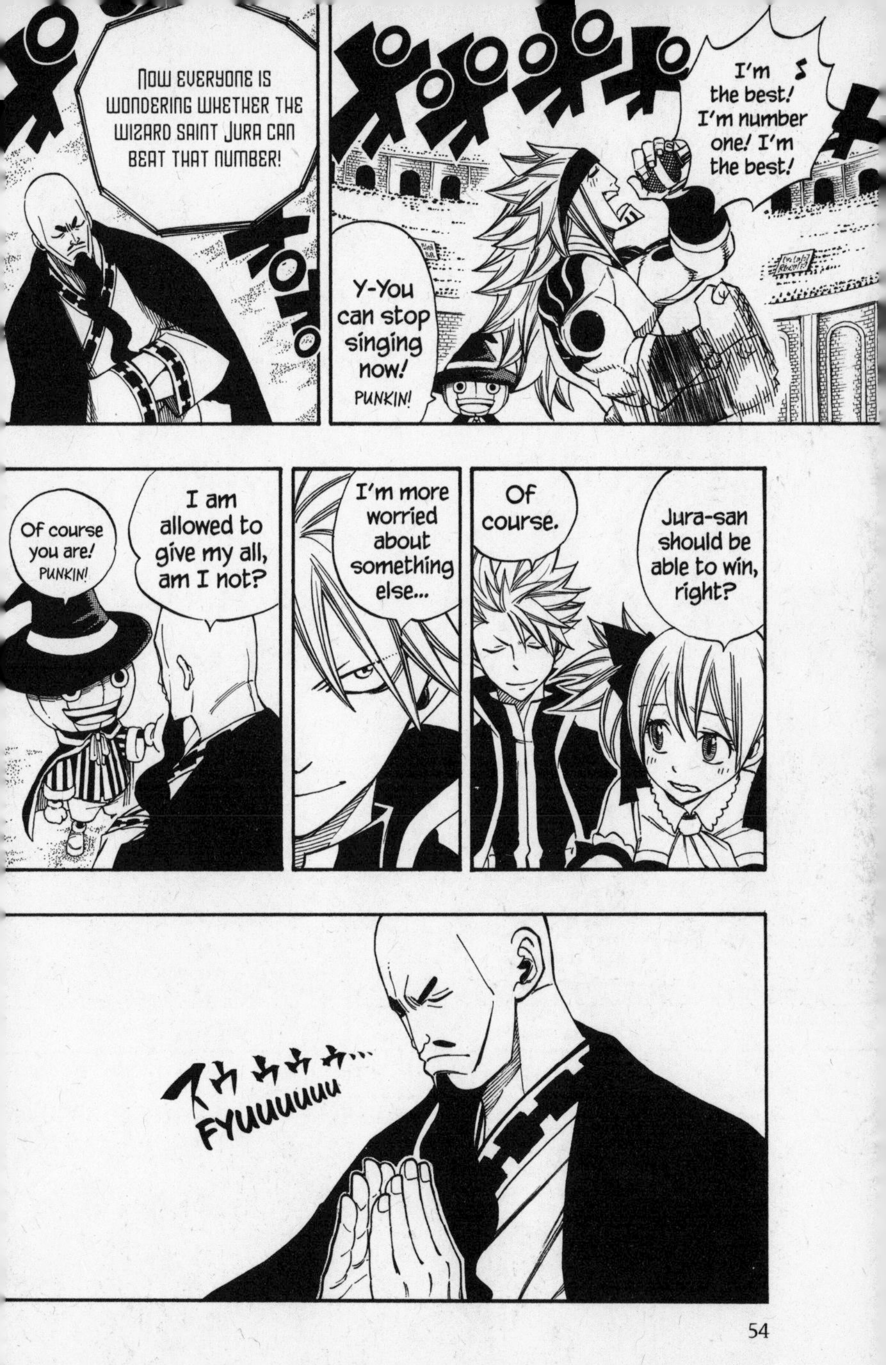
I'm the best! I'm number one! I'm the best!
Y-You can stop singing now! PUNKIN!
Now everyone is wondering whether the Wizard Saint Jura can beat that number!
Jura-san should be able to win, right?
Of course.
I'm more worried about something else...
I am allowed to give my all, am I not?
Of course you are! PUNKIN!
FYUUUUUU

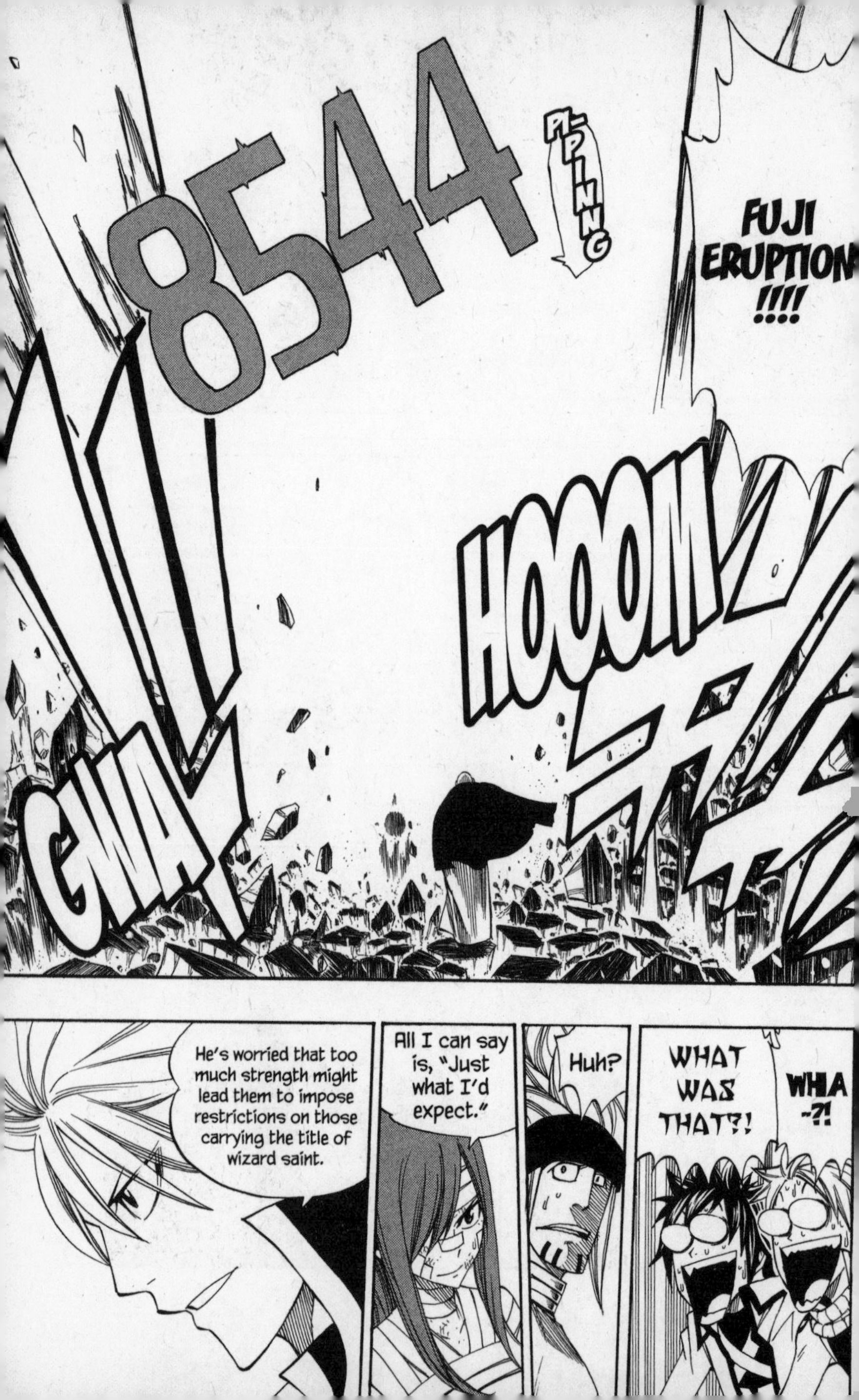
FUJI ERUPTION!!!!
PI-PINNG
8544
HOOOM
GWA
WHIA-?!
WHAT WAS THAT?!
Huh?
All I can say is, "Just what I'd expect."
He's worried that too much strength might lead them to impose restrictions on those carrying the title of wizard saint.

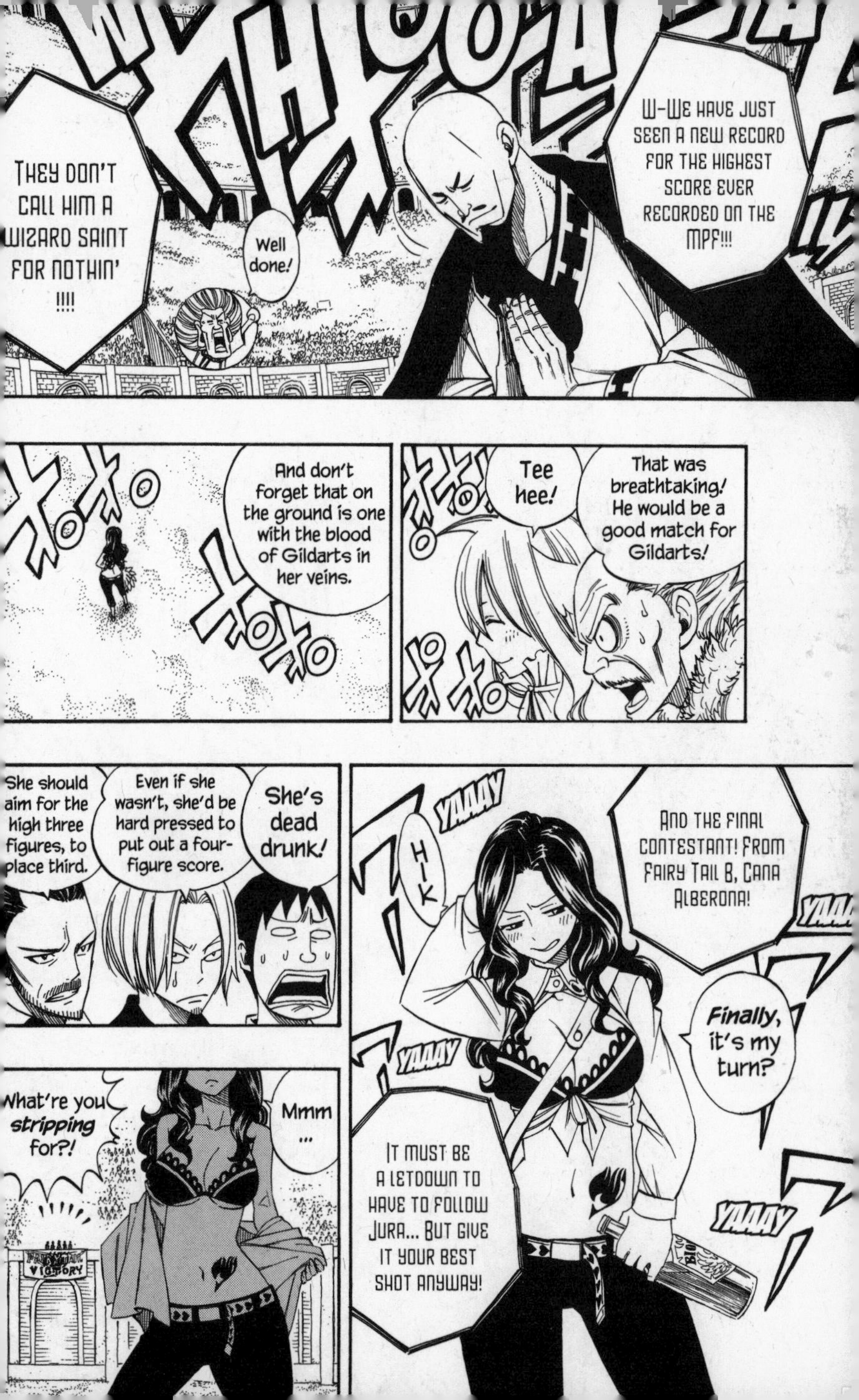
W-We have just seen a new record for the highest score ever recorded on the MPF!!!
Well done!
They don't call him a Wizard Saint for nothin' !!!!
That was breathtaking! He would be a good match for Gildarts!
Tee hee!
And don't forget that on the ground is one with the blood of Gildarts in her veins.
YAAAY
And the final contestant! From Fairy Tail B, Cana Alberona!
HIK
YAAAY
Finally, it's my turn?
YAAAY
YAAAY
It must be a letdown to have to follow Jura... But give it your best shot anyway!
She's dead drunk!
Even if she wasn't, she'd be hard pressed to put out a four-figure score.
She should aim for the high three figures, to place third.
Mmm ...
What're you stripping for?!

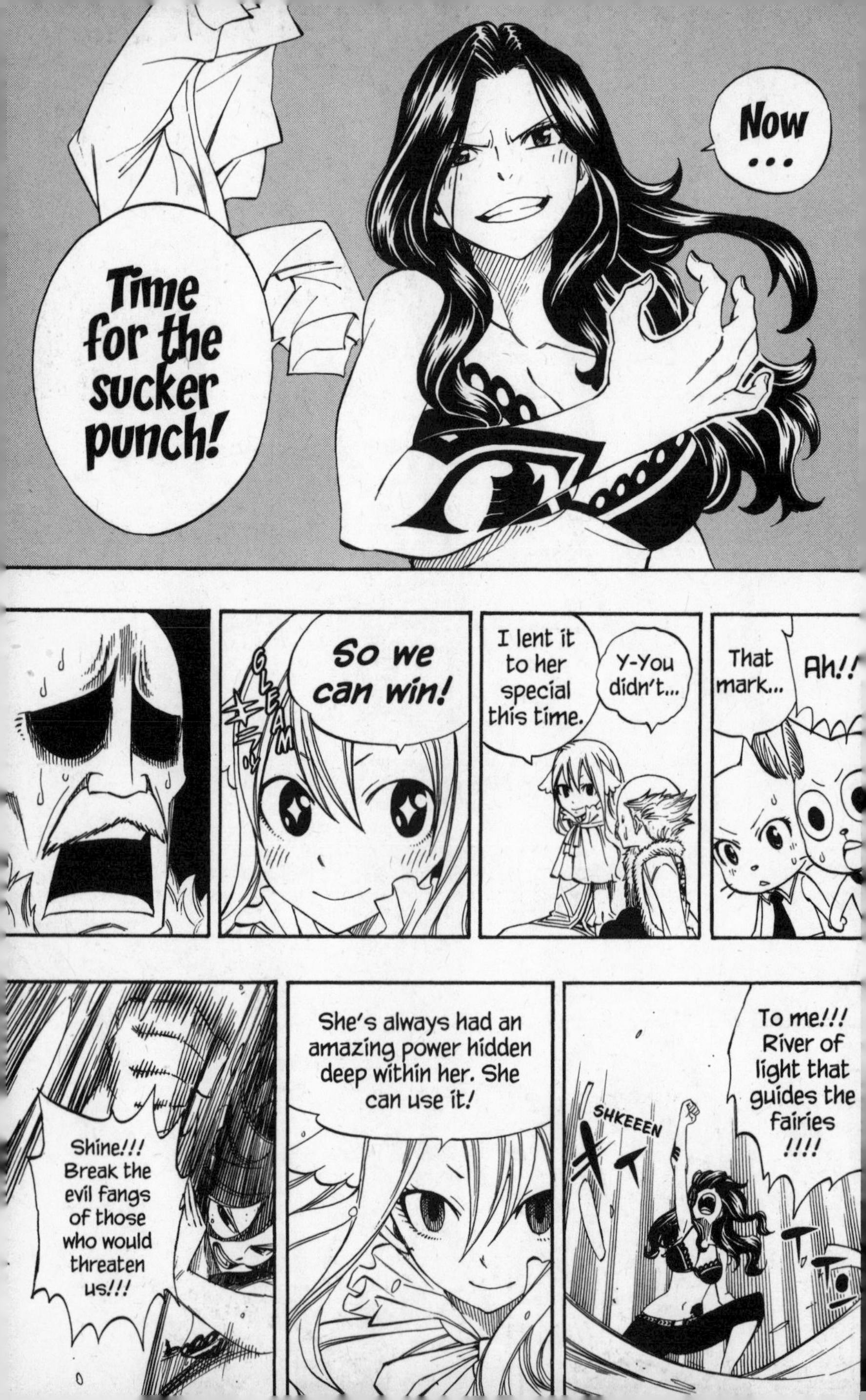
Now...
Time for the sucker punch!
Ah!!
That mark...
Y-You didn't...
I lent it to her special this time.
So we can win!
GLEAM
To me!!! River of light that guides the fairies !!!!
SHKEEEN
She's always had an amazing power hidden deep within her. She can use it!
Shine!!! Break the evil fangs of those who would threaten us!!!

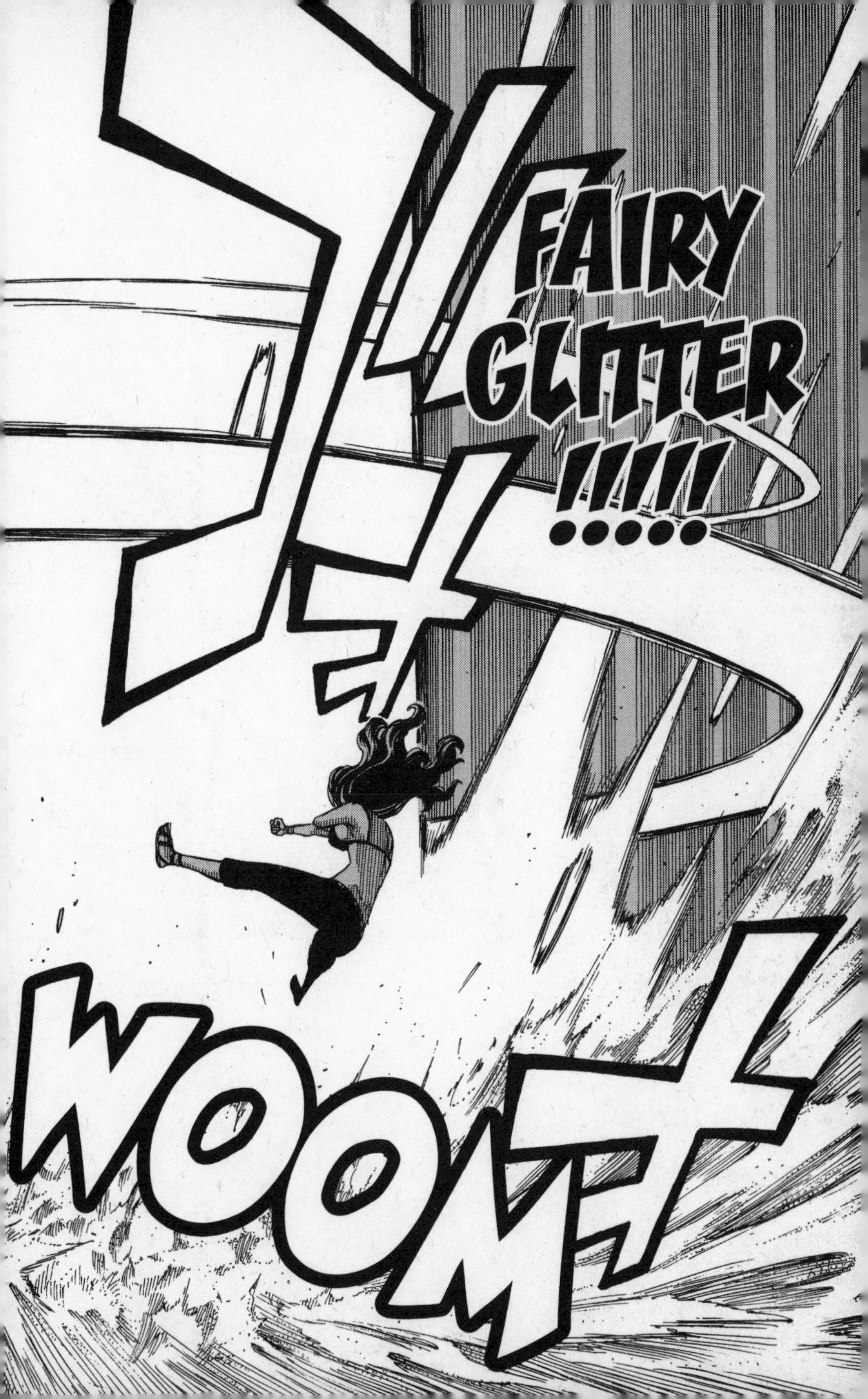
FAIRY GLITTER!!!!!
WOOM

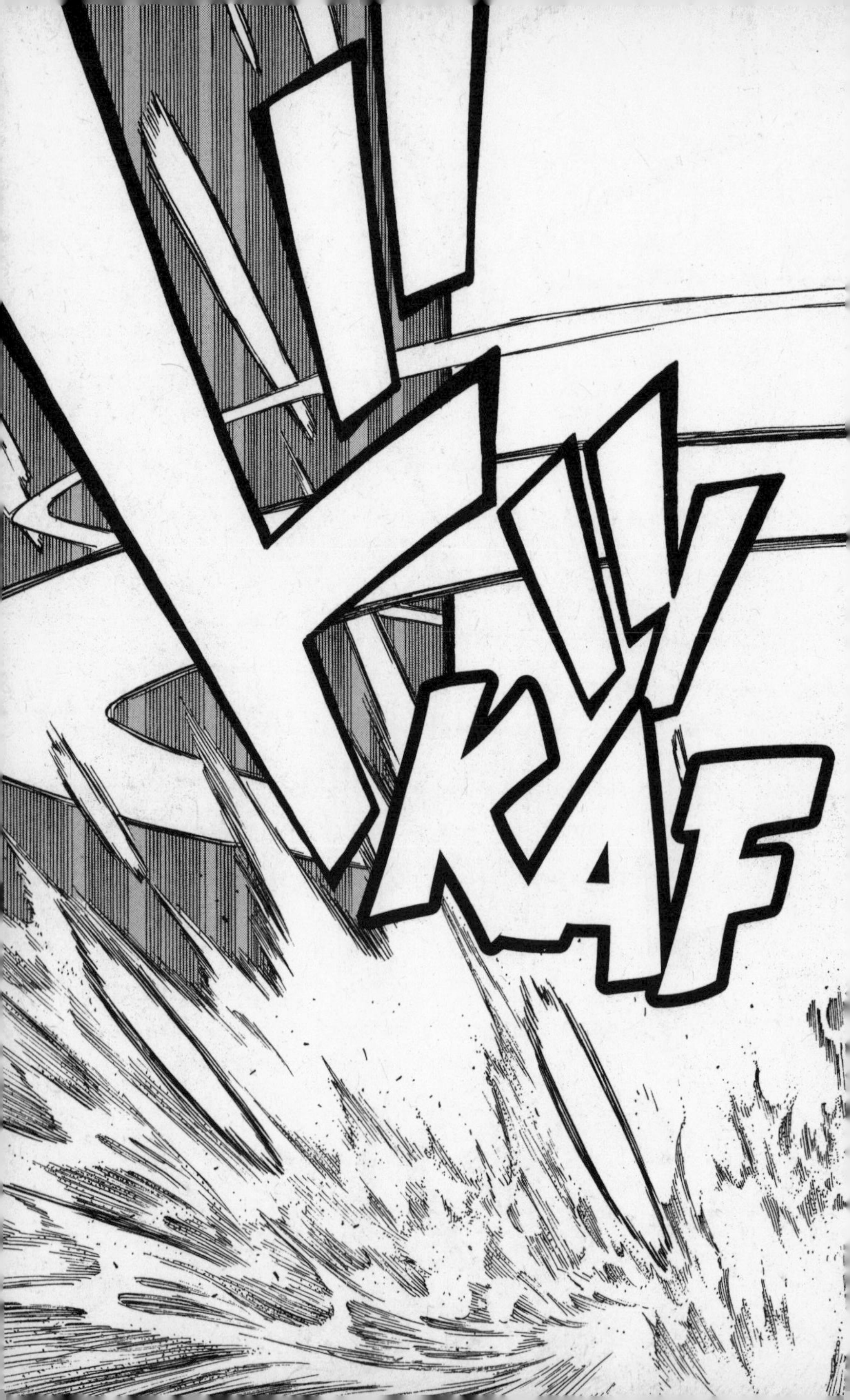
KAF

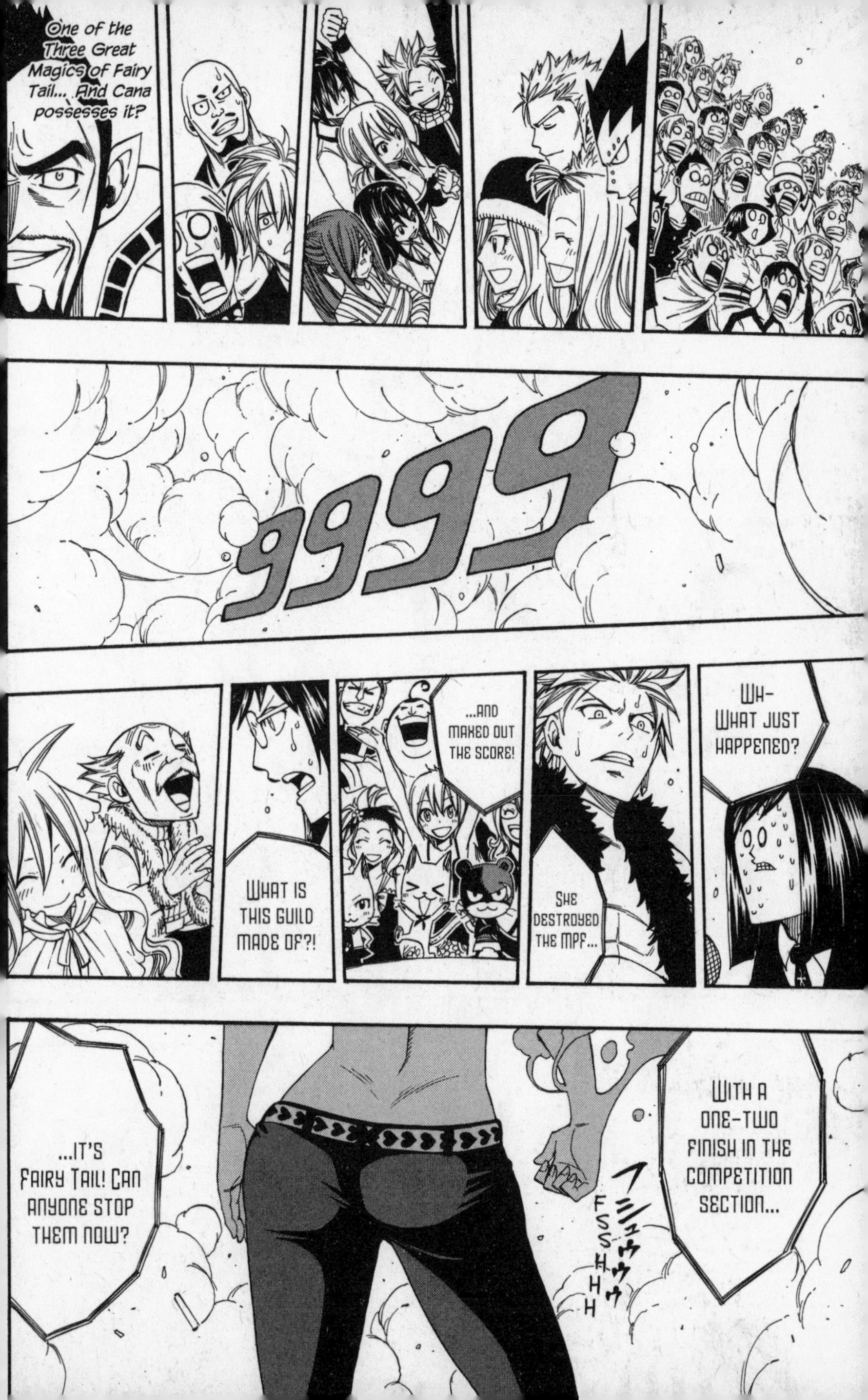
One of the Three Great Magics of Fairy Tail... And Cana possesses it?
9999
WH- WHAT JUST HAPPENED?
SHE DESTROYED THE MPF...
...AND MAXED OUT THE SCORE!
WHAT IS THIS GUILD MADE OF?!
WITH A ONE-TWO FINISH IN THE COMPETITION SECTION...
FSSHHH
...IT'S FAIRY TAIL! CAN ANYONE STOP THEM NOW?

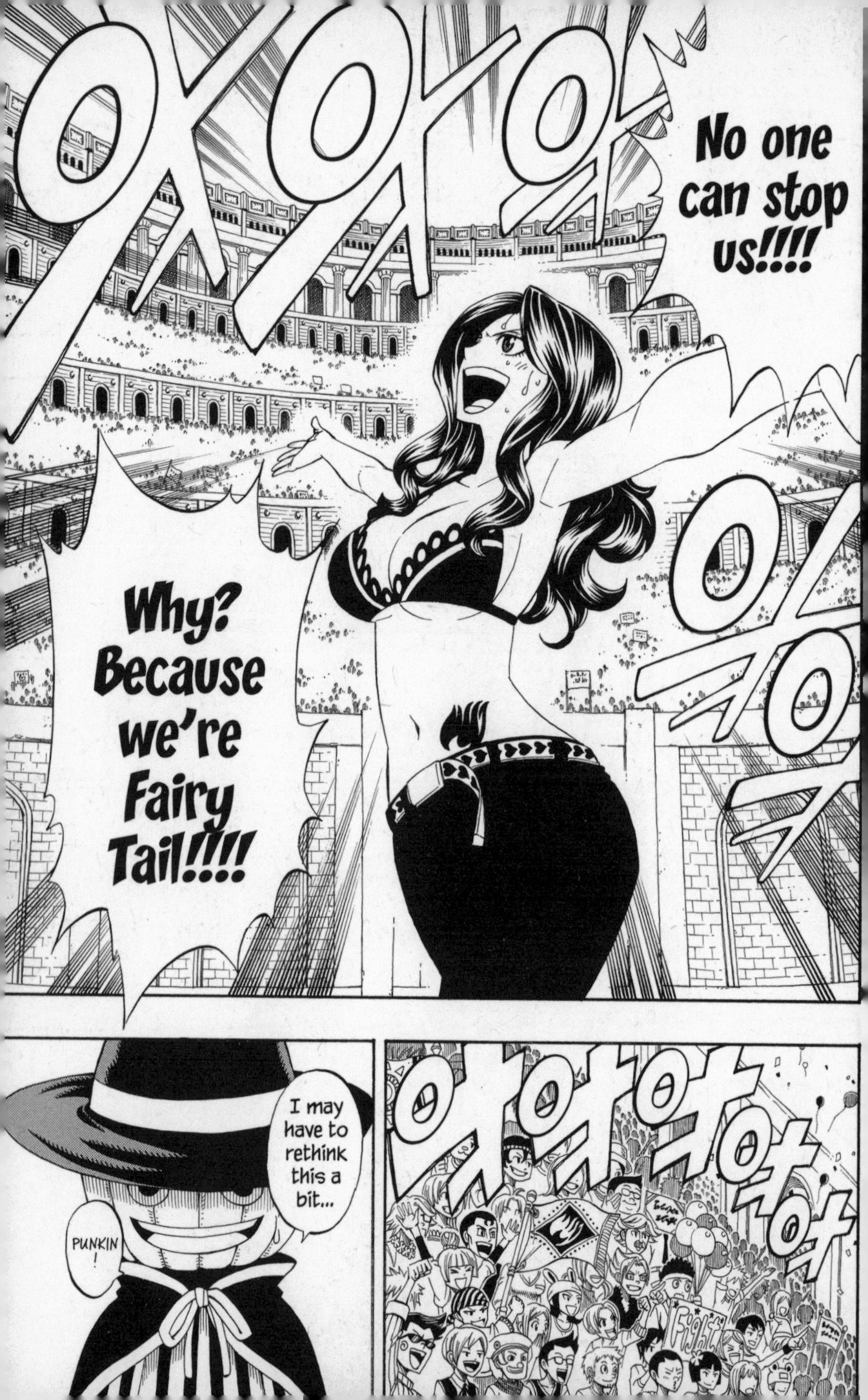
No one can stop us!!!!
Why? Because we're Fairy Tail!!!!
I may have to rethink this a bit...
PUNKIN!

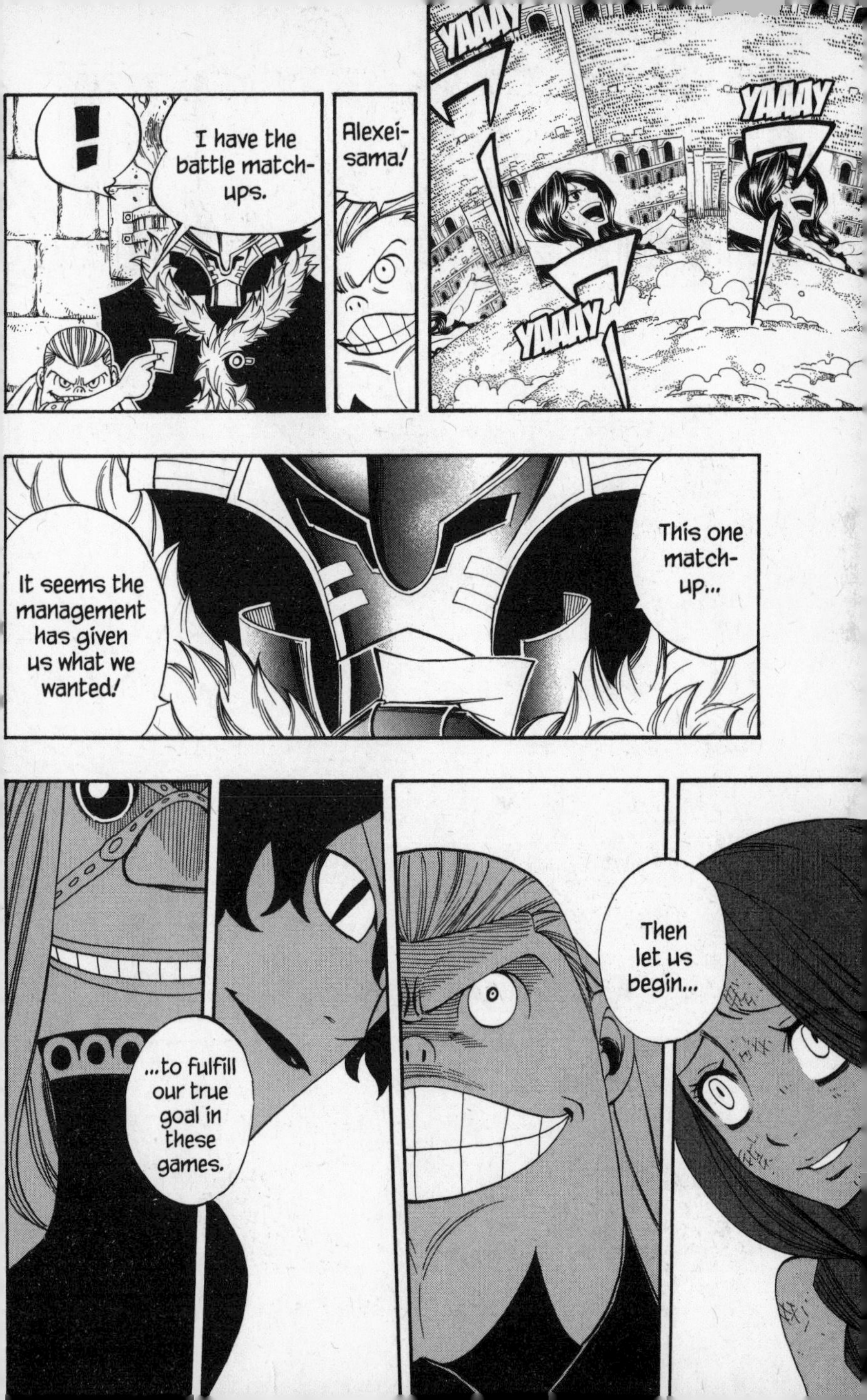
YAAAY
YAAAY
YAAAY
Alexei-sama!
I have the battle match-ups.
!
This one match-up...
It seems the management has given us what we wanted!
Then let us begin...
...to fulfill our true goal in these games.

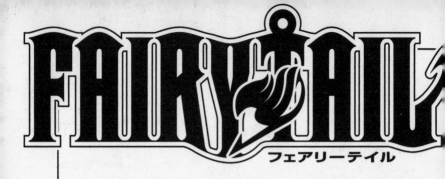

FAIRY TAIL

フェアリーテイル

Grand Magic Games Third Day Interim Results.

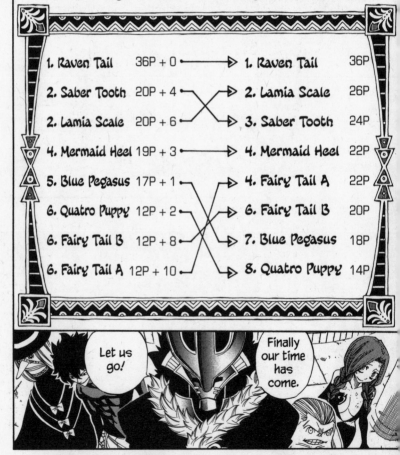

1. Raven Tail	36P + 0	1. Raven Tail	36P
2. Saber Tooth	20P + 4	2. Lamia Scale	26P
2. Lamia Scale	20P + 6	3. Saber Tooth	24P
4. Mermaid Heel	19P + 3	4. Mermaid Heel	22P
5. Blue Pegasus	17P + 1	4. Fairy Tail A	22P
6. Quatro Puppy	12P + 2	6. Fairy Tail B	20P
6. Fairy Tail B	12P + 8	7. Blue Pegasus	18P
6. Fairy Tail A	12P + 10	8. Quatro Puppy	14P

Finally our time has come.
Let us go!

Chapter 286: Laxus vs. Alexei

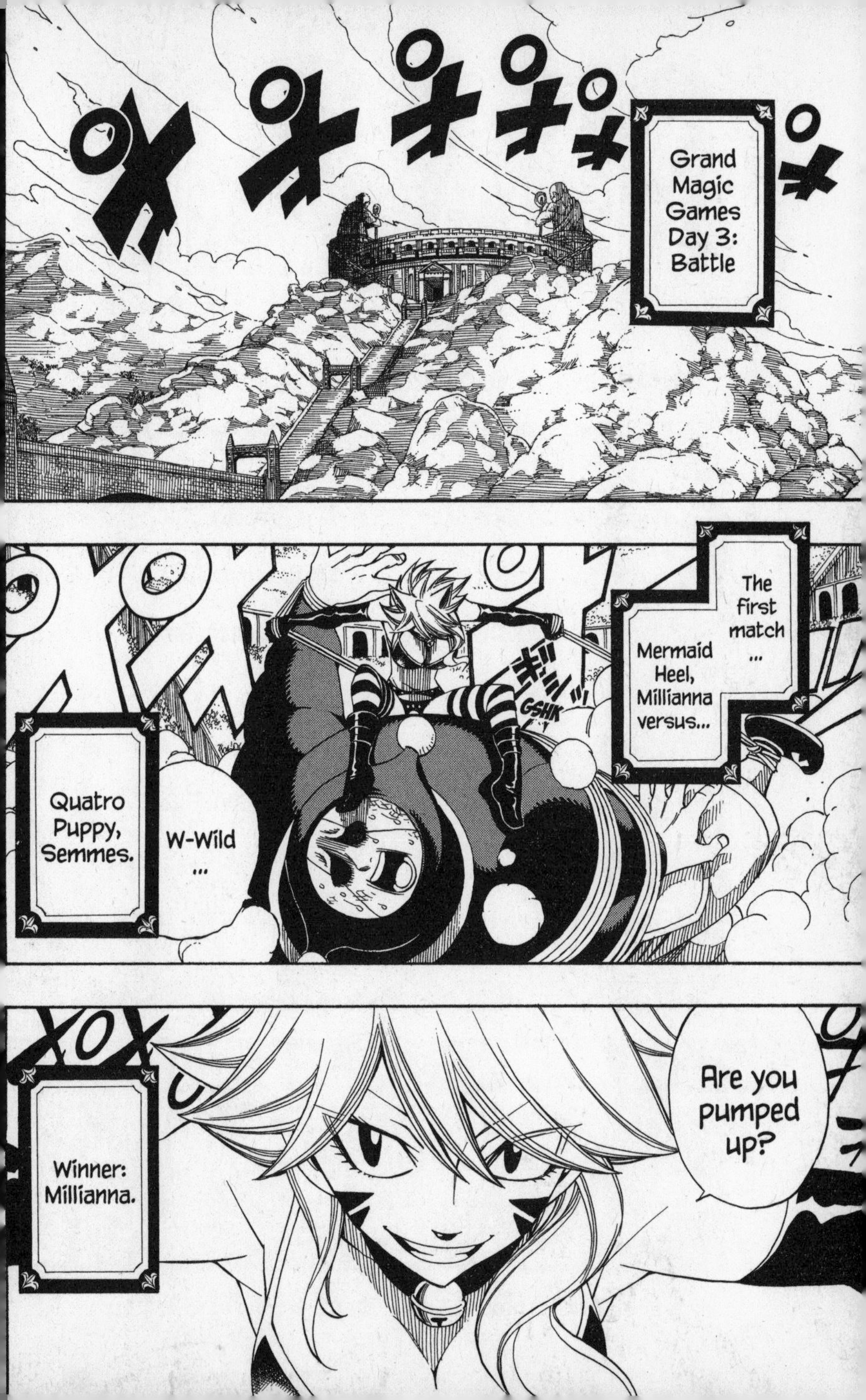
Grand Magic Games Day 3: Battle
The first match ... Mermaid Heel, Millianna versus...
GSHK
W-Wild ...
Quatro Puppy, Semmes.
Are you pumped up?
Winner: Millianna.

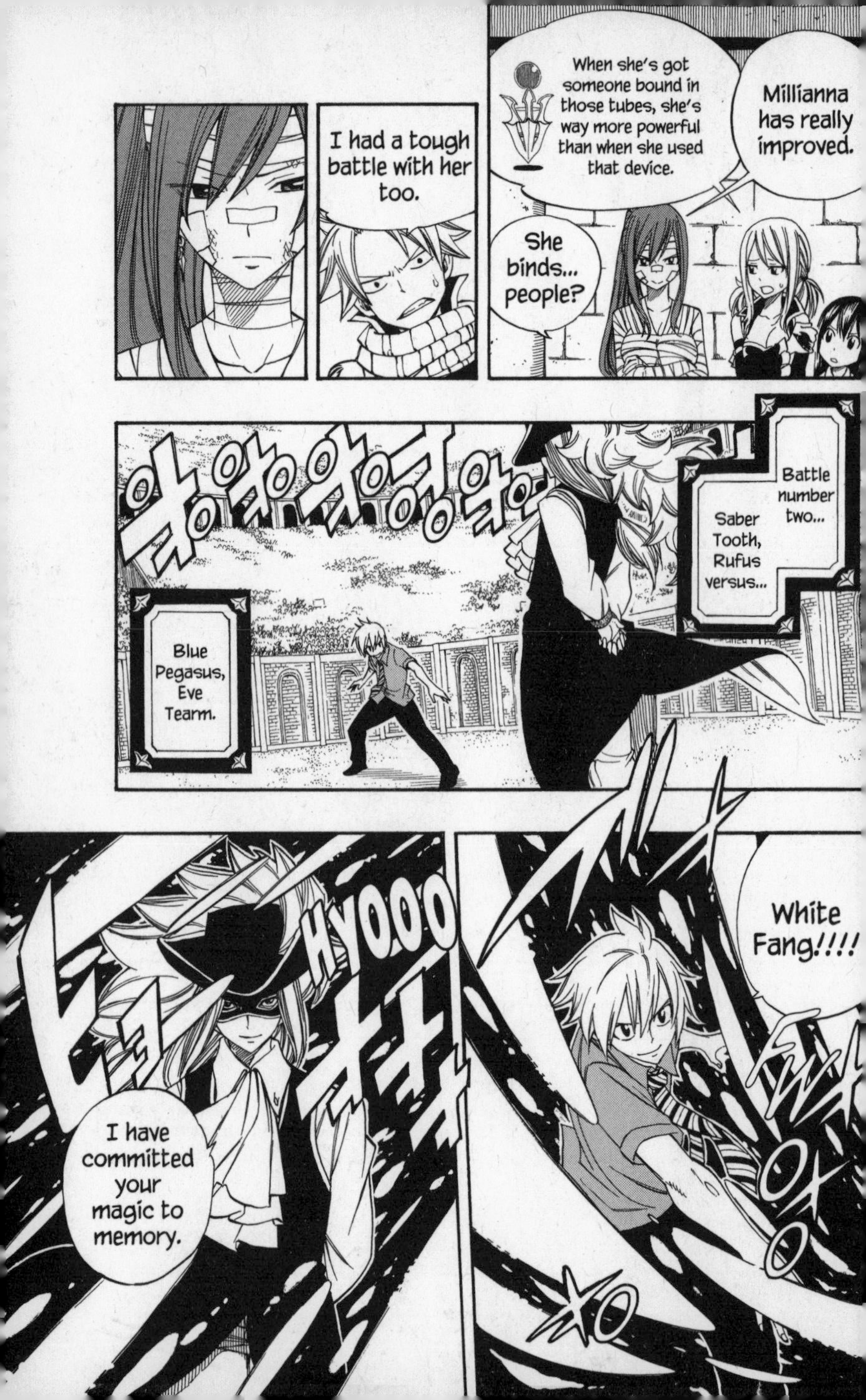
Millianna has really improved.
When she's got someone bound in those tubes, she's way more powerful than when she used that device.
She binds... people?
I had a tough battle with her too.
Battle number two...
Saber Tooth, Rufus versus...
Blue Pegasus, Eve Tearm.
White Fang!!!!
HYOOO
I have committed your magic to memory.

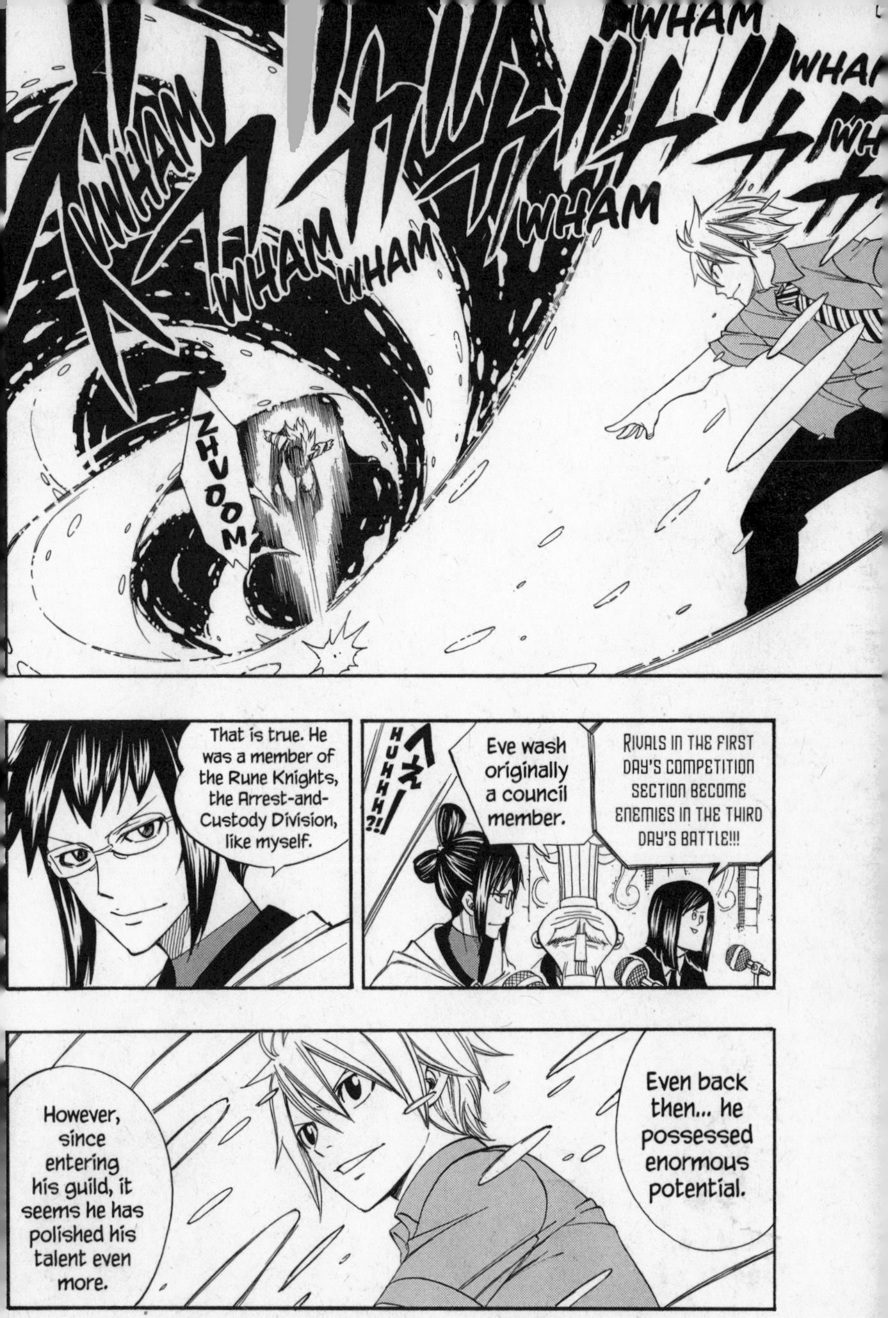
WHAM
WHAM
WHAM
WHAM
WHAM
WHAM
WHAM
WHAM
ZHVOOM
Rivals in the first day's competition section become enemies in the third day's battle!!!
Eve wash originally a council member.
HUHHH?!
That is true. He was a member of the Rune Knights, the Arrest-and-Custody Division, like myself.
Even back then... he possessed enormous potential.
However, since entering his guild, it seems he has polished his talent even more.

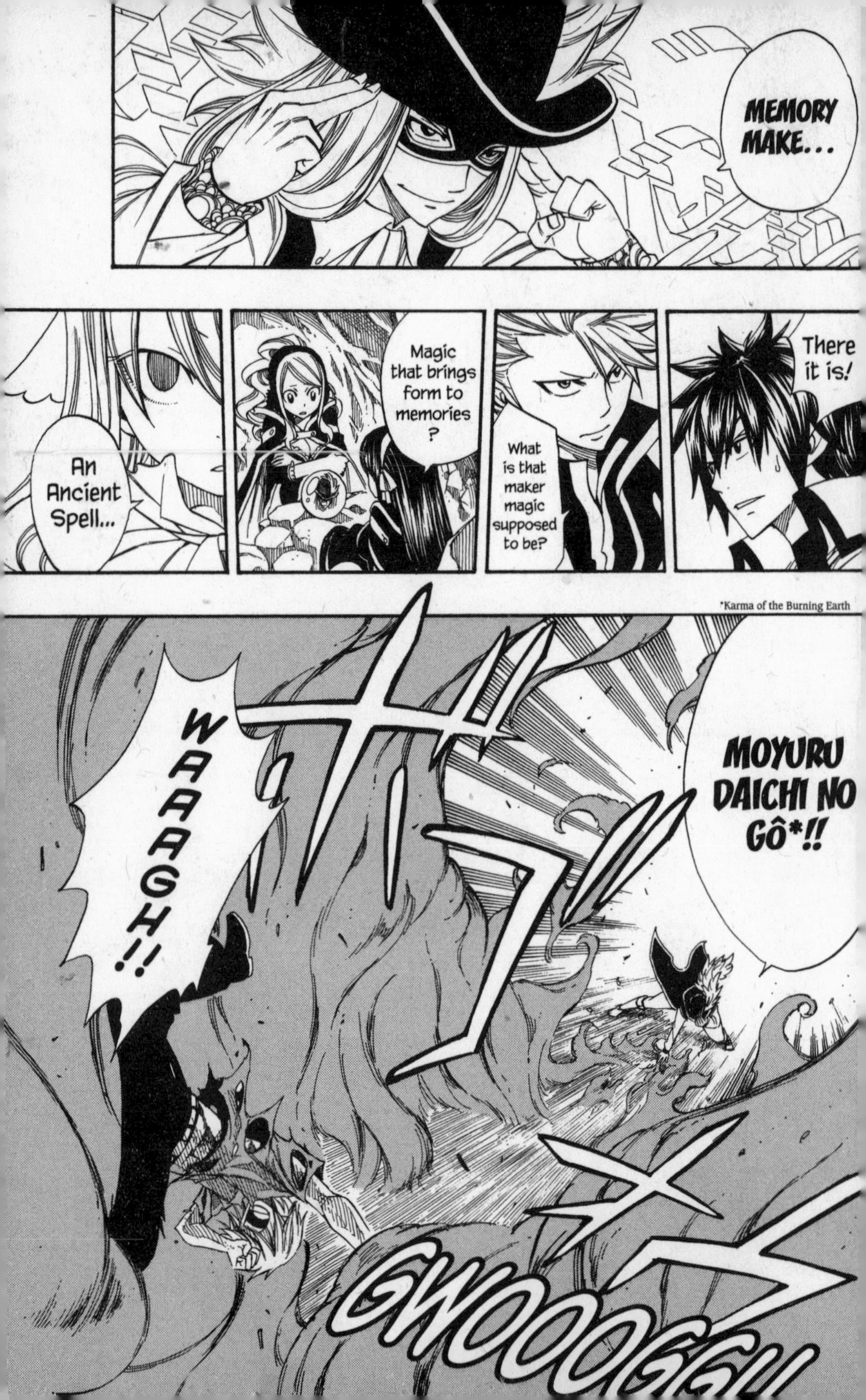
MEMORY MAKE...
There it is!
What is that maker magic supposed to be?
Magic that brings form to memories?
An Ancient Spell...
MOYURU DAICHI NO GÔ*!!
WAAAAGH!!
GWOOOGGU
*Karma of the Burning Earth

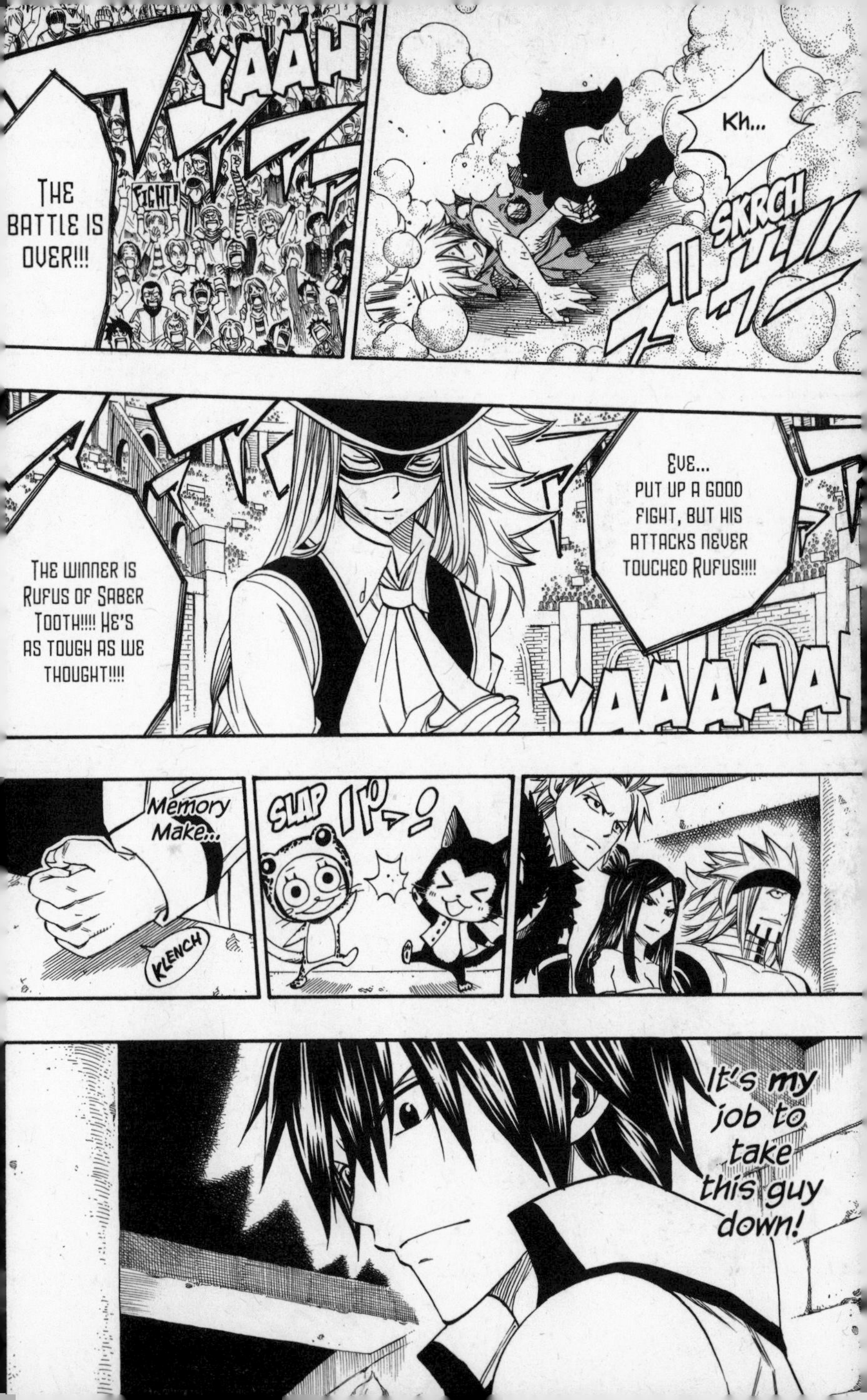

Kh...
SKRCH
YAAH
FIGHT!
THE BATTLE IS OVER!!!
Eve... put up a good fight, but his attacks never touched Rufus!!!!
The winner is Rufus of Saber Tooth!!!! He's as tough as we thought!!!!
YAAAAA
SLAP
Memory Make...
KLENCH
It's my job to take this guy down!

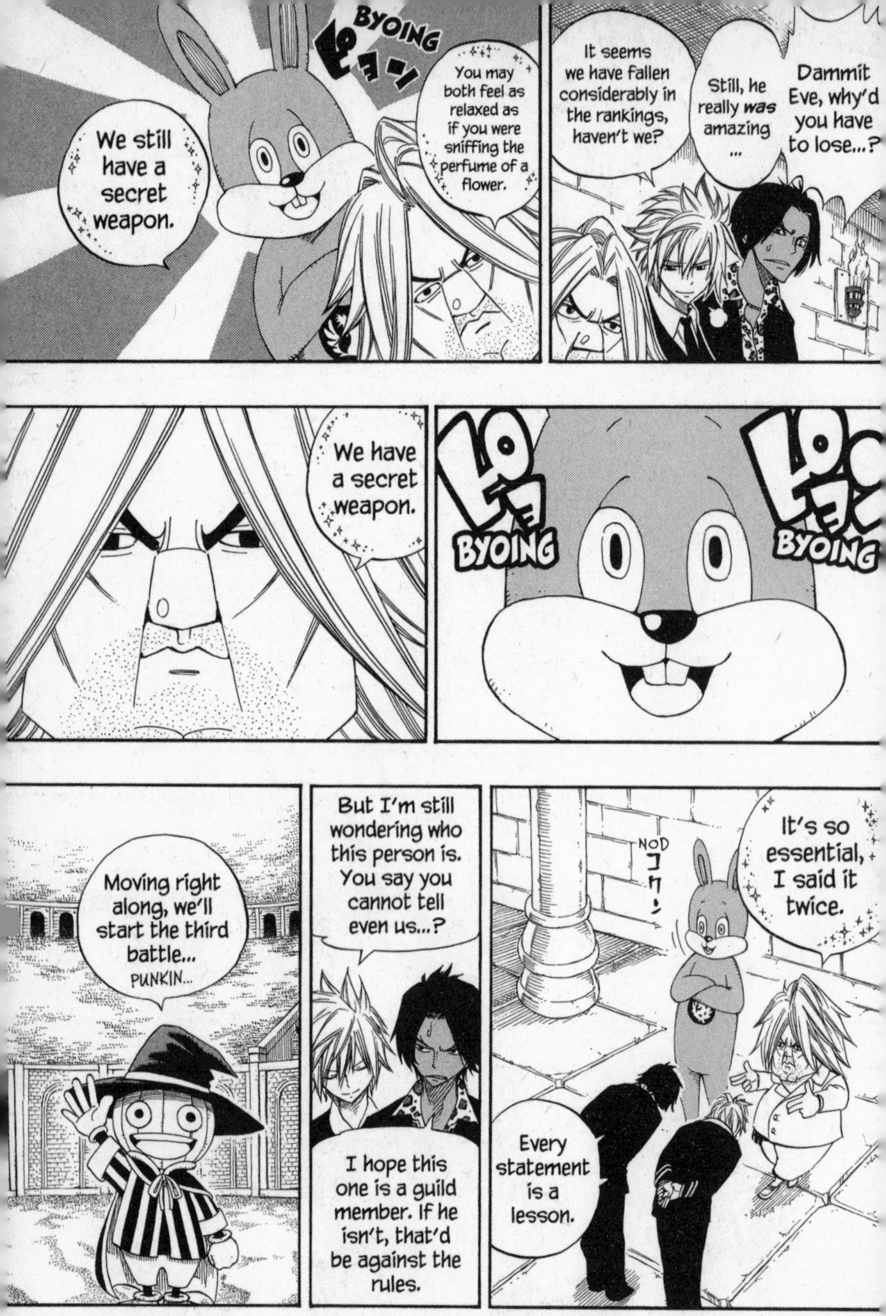
Dammit Eve, why'd you have to lose...?
Still, he really *was* amazing ...
It seems we have fallen considerably in the rankings, haven't we?
BYOING
You may both feel as relaxed as if you were sniffing the perfume of a flower.
We still have a secret weapon.
BYOING
BYOING
We have a secret weapon.
It's so essential, I said it twice.
NOD
Every statement is a lesson.
But I'm still wondering who this person is. You say you cannot tell even us...?
I hope this one is a guild member. If he isn't, that'd be against the rules.
Moving right along, we'll start the third battle...
PUNKIN...

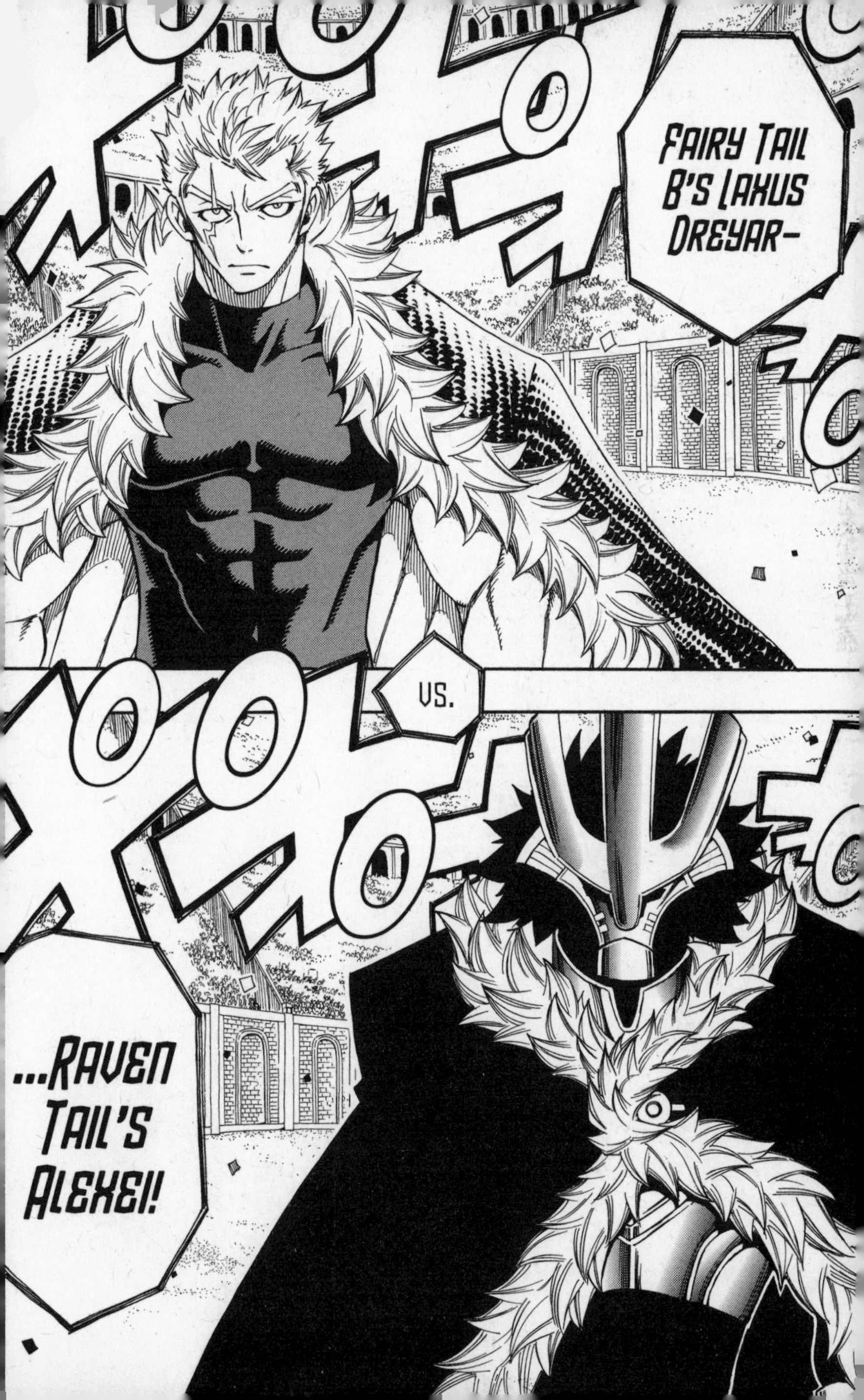
FAIRY TAIL B'S LAXUS DREYAR—
VS.
...RAVEN TAIL'S ALEXEI!

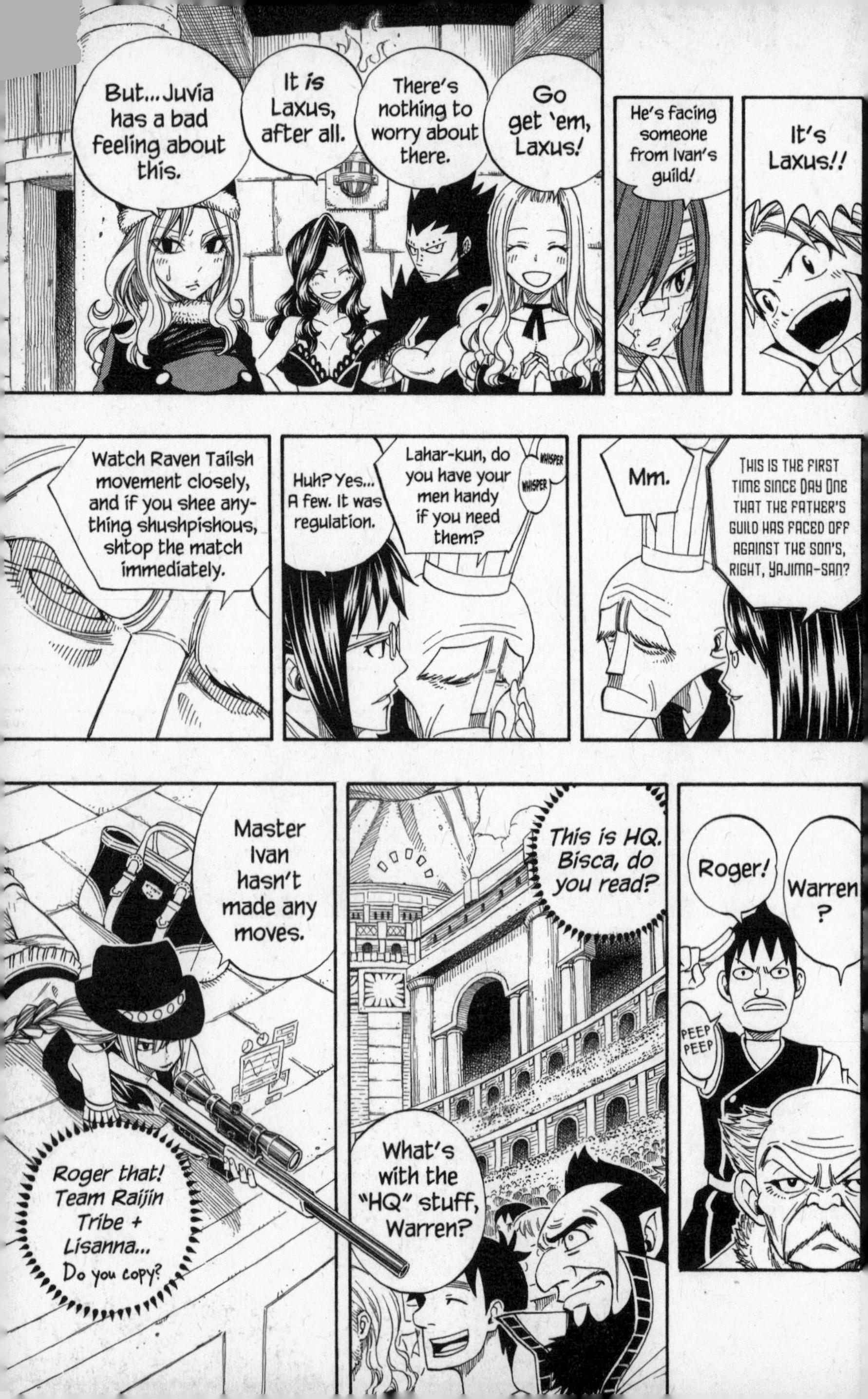
It's Laxus!!
He's facing someone from Ivan's guild!
Go get 'em, Laxus!
There's nothing to worry about there.
It *is* Laxus, after all.
But...Juvia has a bad feeling about this.
THIS IS THE FIRST TIME SINCE DAY ONE THAT THE FATHER'S GUILD HAS FACED OFF AGAINST THE SON'S, RIGHT, YAJIMA-SAN?
Mm.
WHISPER
WHISPER
Lahar-kun, do you have your men handy if you need them?
Huh? Yes... A few. It was regulation.
Watch Raven Tailsh movement closely, and if you shee any-thing shushpishous, shtop the match immediately.
Warren?
Roger!
PEEP PEEP
This is HQ. Bisca, do you read?
What's with the "HQ" stuff, Warren?
Master Ivan hasn't made any moves.
Roger that! Team Raijin Tribe + Lisanna... Do you copy?

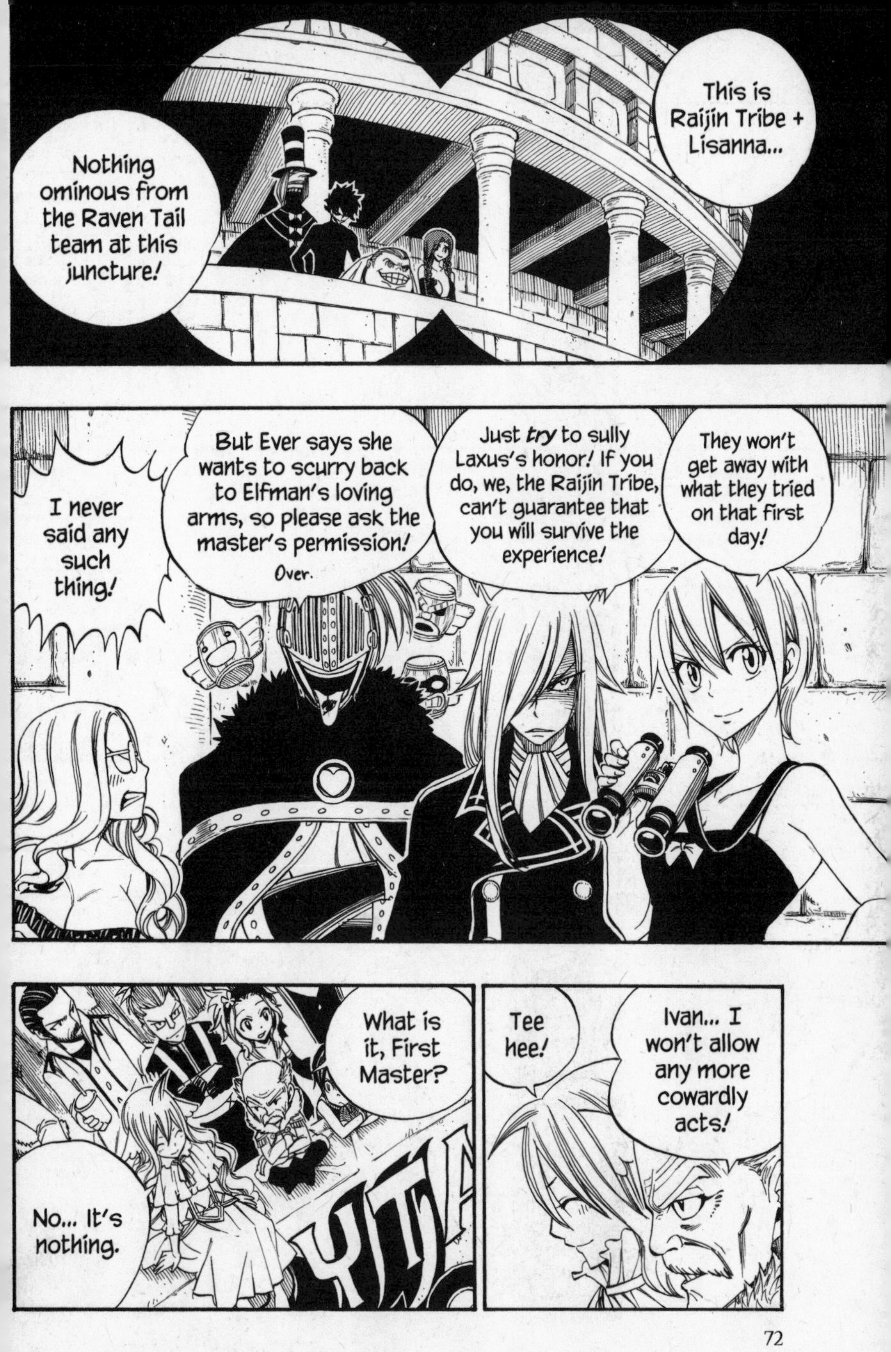

This is Raijin Tribe + Lisanna...
Nothing ominous from the Raven Tail team at this juncture!
They won't get away with what they tried on that first day!
Just *try* to sully Laxus's honor! If you do, we, the Raijin Tribe, can't guarantee that you will survive the experience!
But Ever says she wants to scurry back to Elfman's loving arms, so please ask the master's permission!
Over.
I never said any such thing!
Ivan... I won't allow any more cowardly acts!
Tee hee!
What is it, First Master?
No... It's nothing.

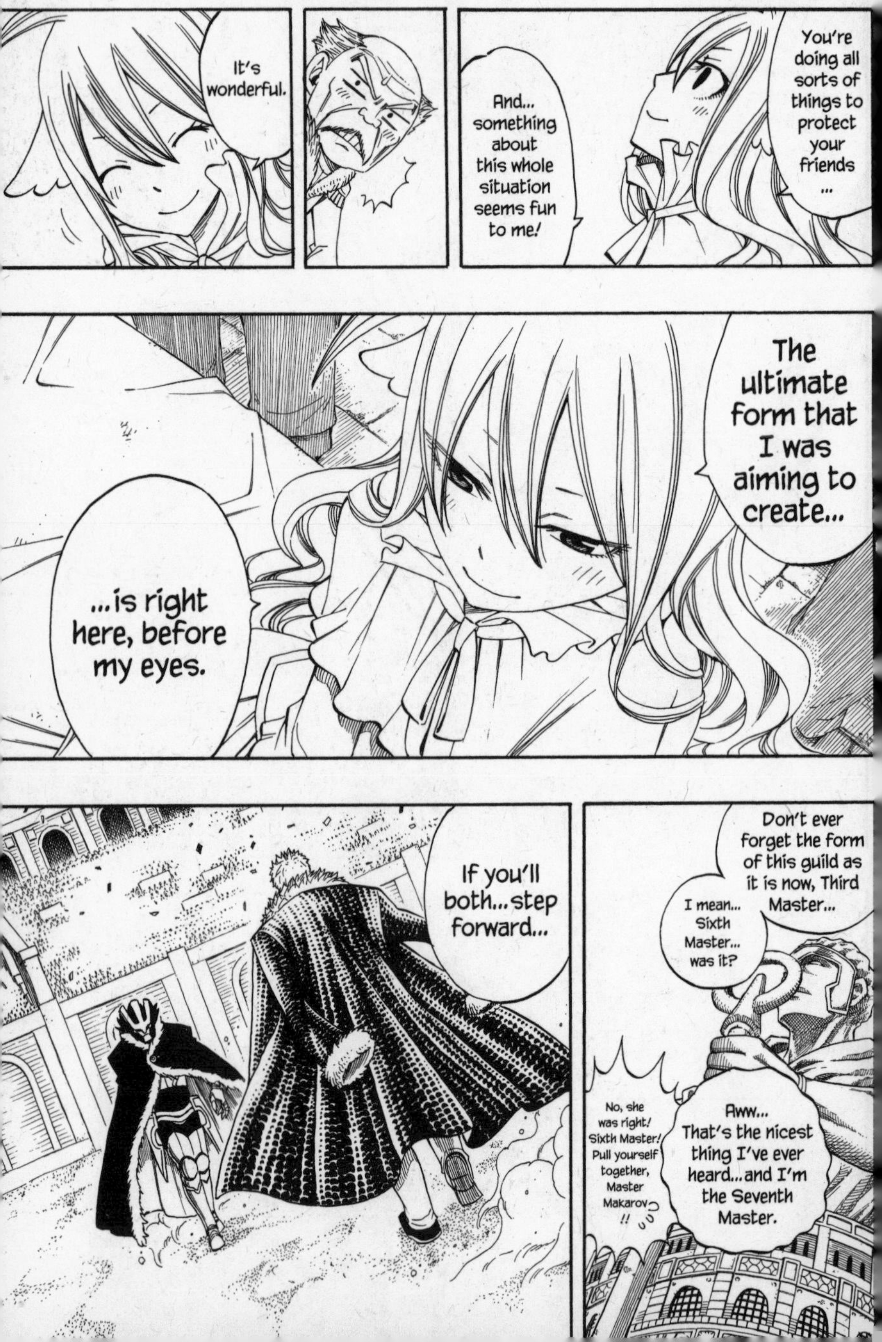
You're doing all sorts of things to protect your friends...
And... something about this whole situation seems fun to me!
It's wonderful.
The ultimate form that I was aiming to create...
...is right here, before my eyes.
Don't ever forget the form of this guild as it is now, Third Master...
I mean... Sixth Master... was it?
Aww... That's the nicest thing I've ever heard...and I'm the Seventh Master.
No, she was right! Sixth Master! Pull yourself together, Master Makarov!!
If you'll both...step forward...

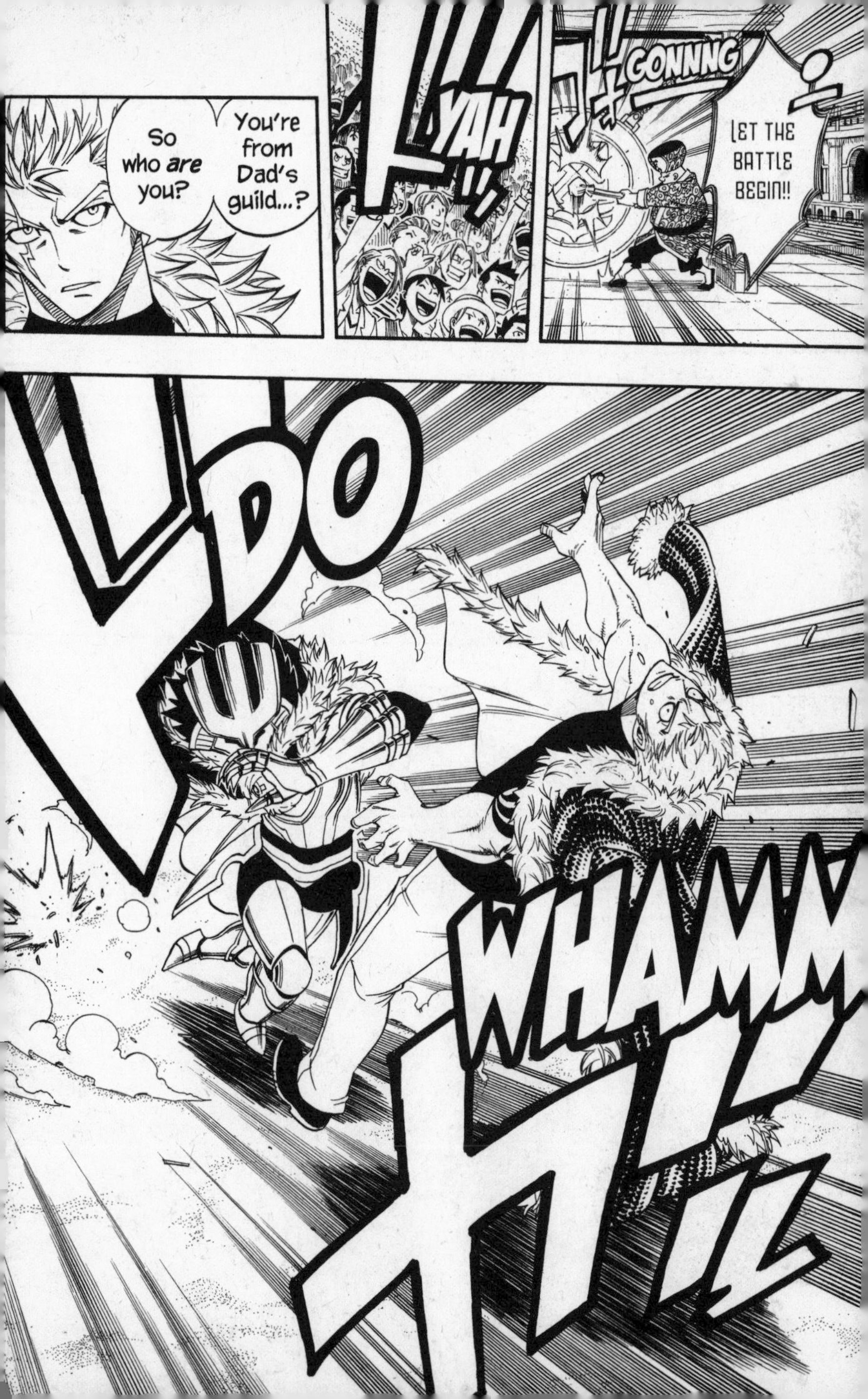
GONNNG
LET THE BATTLE BEGIN!!
YAH
You're from Dad's guild...?
So who are you?
DO
WHAMM

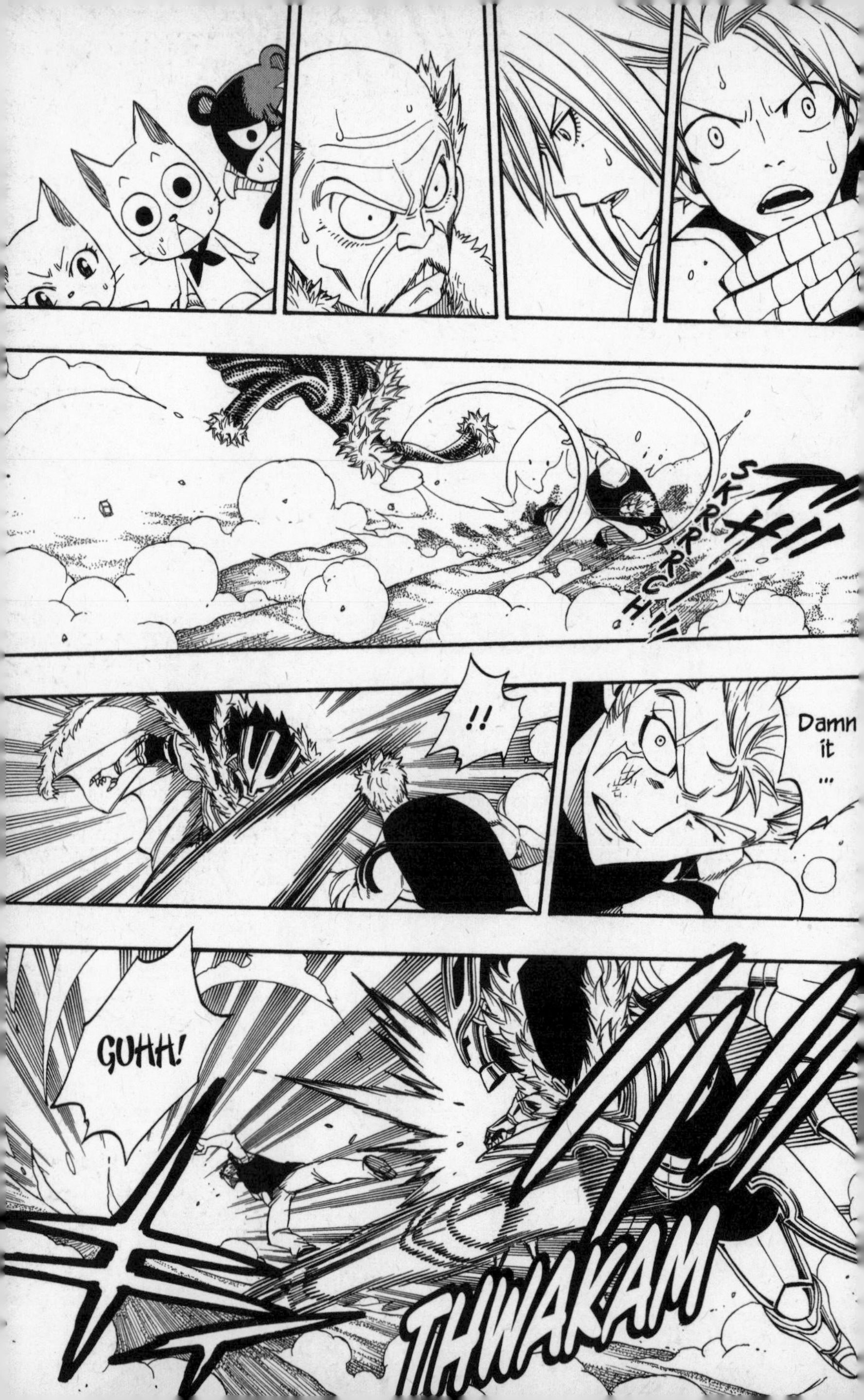
SKRRRCH!!
Damn it ...
!!
GUHH!
THWAKAM

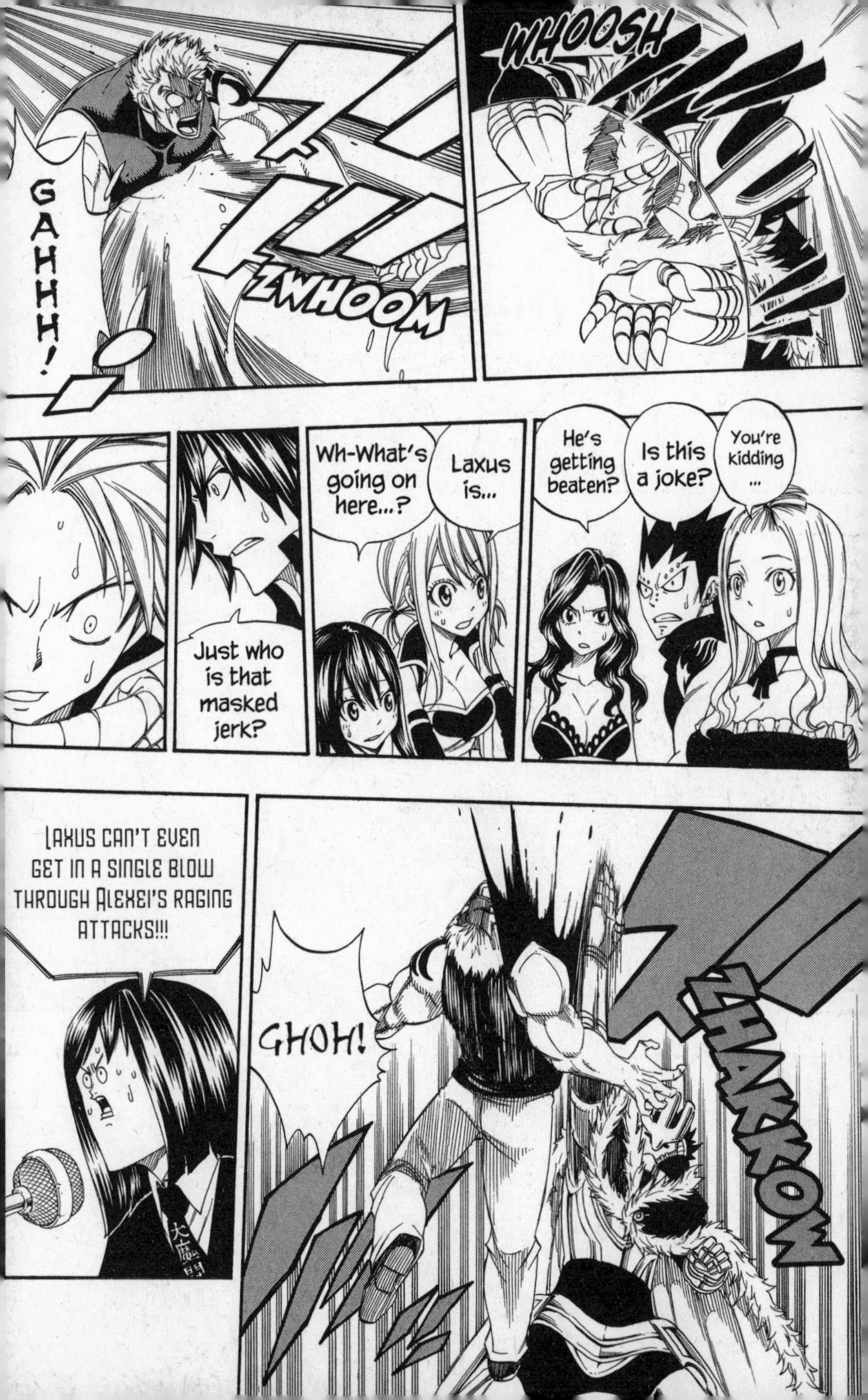
WHOOSH
ZWHOOM
GAHHH!
You're kidding ...
Is this a joke?
He's getting beaten?
Laxus is...
Wh-What's going on here...?
Just who is that masked jerk?
ZHAKKOW
GHOH!
LAXUS CAN'T EVEN GET IN A SINGLE BLOW THROUGH ALEXEI'S RAGING ATTACKS!!!

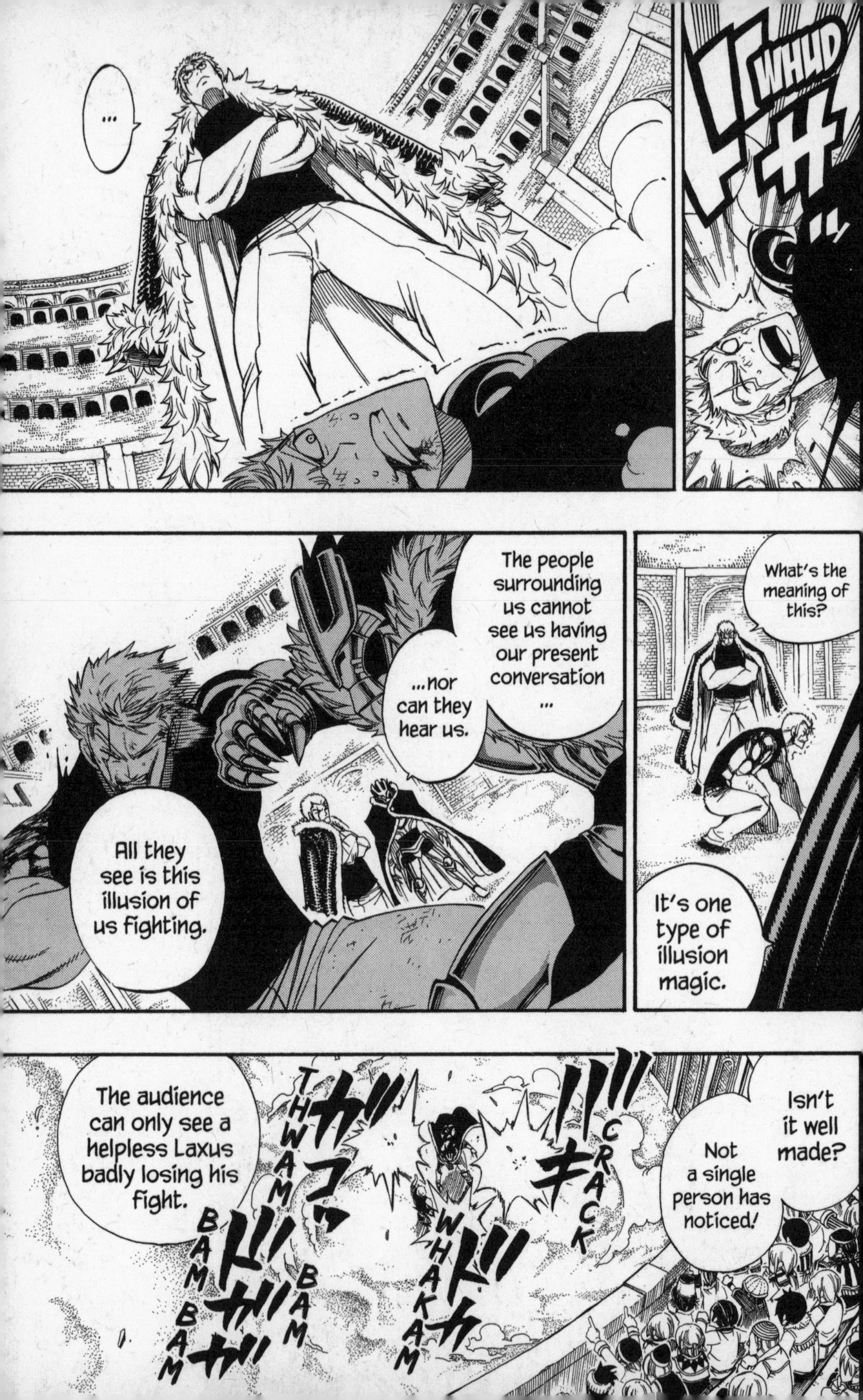
WHUD
...
What's the meaning of this?
It's one type of illusion magic.
The people surrounding us cannot see us having our present conversation...
...nor can they hear us.
All they see is this illusion of us fighting.
Isn't it well made?
Not a single person has noticed!
CRACK
WHAKAM
BAM
THWAM
BAM BAM BAM
The audience can only see a helpless Laxus badly losing his fight.

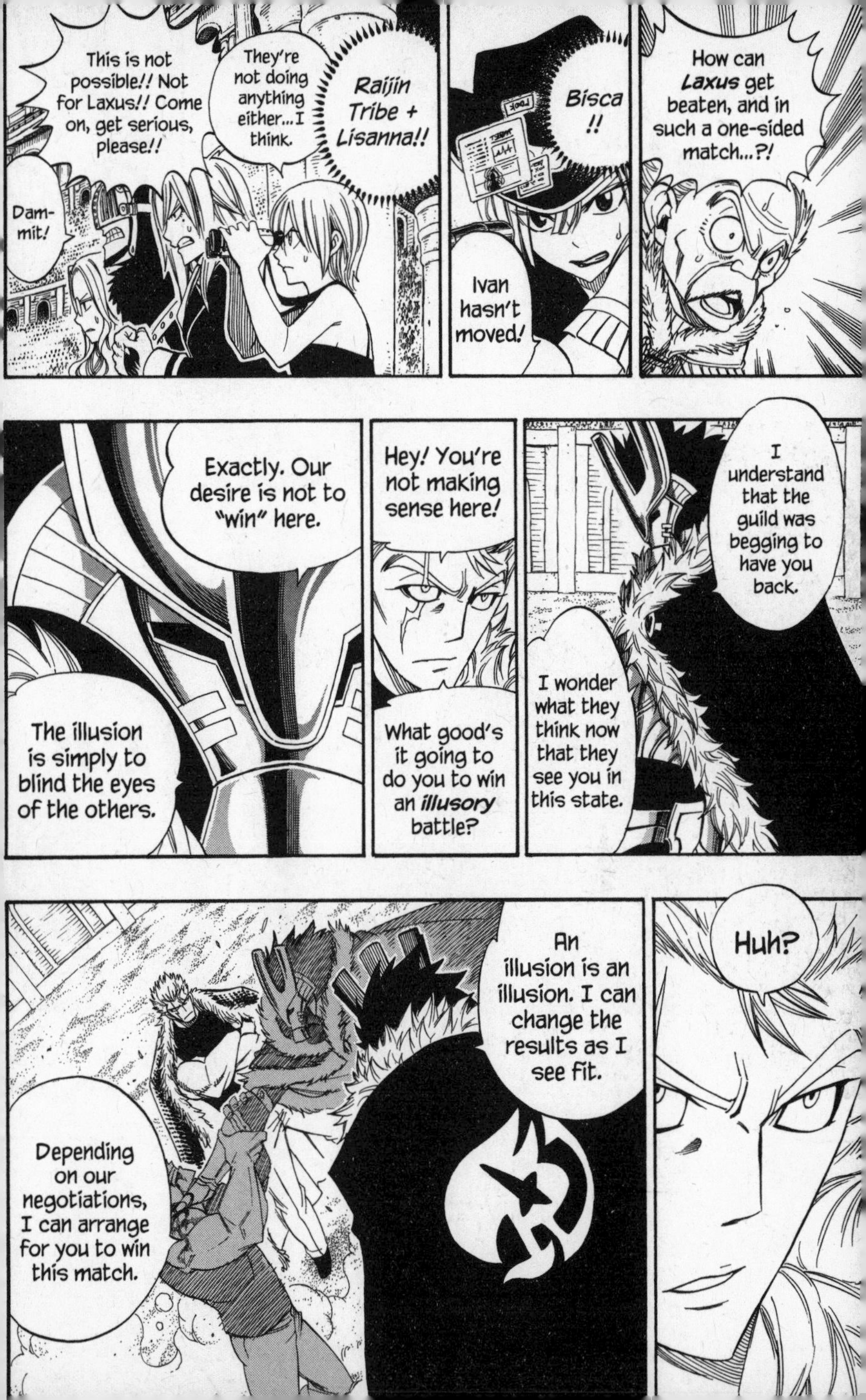
How can *Laxus* get beaten, and in such a one-sided match...?!
Bisca!!
Ivan hasn't moved!
Raijin Tribe + Lisanna!!
They're not doing anything either...I think.
This is not possible!! Not for Laxus!! Come on, get serious, please!!
Dam-mit!
I understand that the guild was begging to have you back.
I wonder what they think now that they see you in this state.
Hey! You're not making sense here!
What good's it going to do you to win an *illusory* battle?
Exactly. Our desire is not to "win" here.
The illusion is simply to blind the eyes of the others.
Huh?
An illusion is an illusion. I can change the results as I see fit.
Depending on our negotiations, I can arrange for you to win this match.

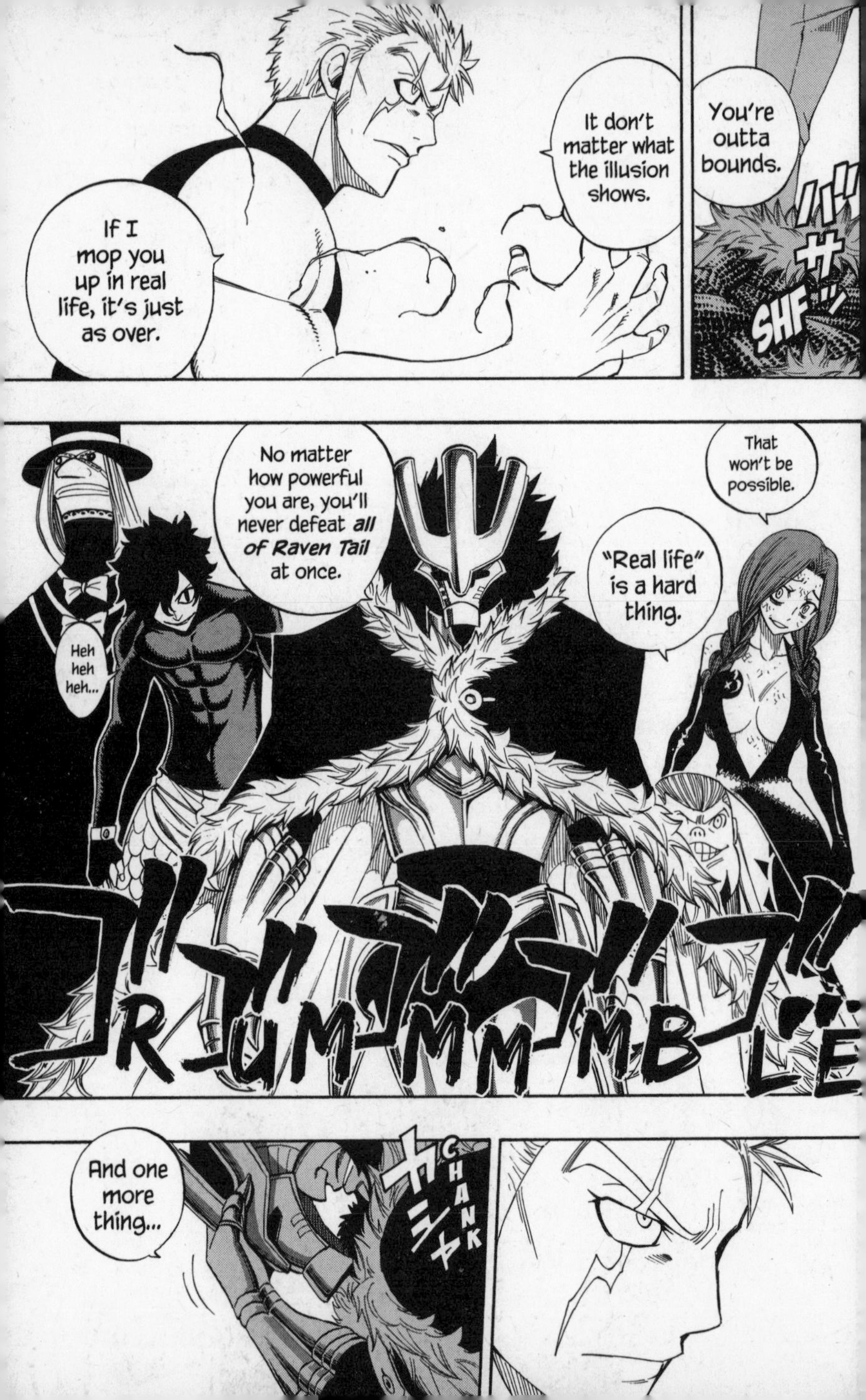
You're outta bounds.
SHF!!
It don't matter what the illusion shows.
If I mop you up in real life, it's just as over.
That won't be possible.
"Real life" is a hard thing.
No matter how powerful you are, you'll never defeat *all of Raven Tail* at once.
Heh heh heh...
RUMMMMBLE
CHANK
And one more thing...

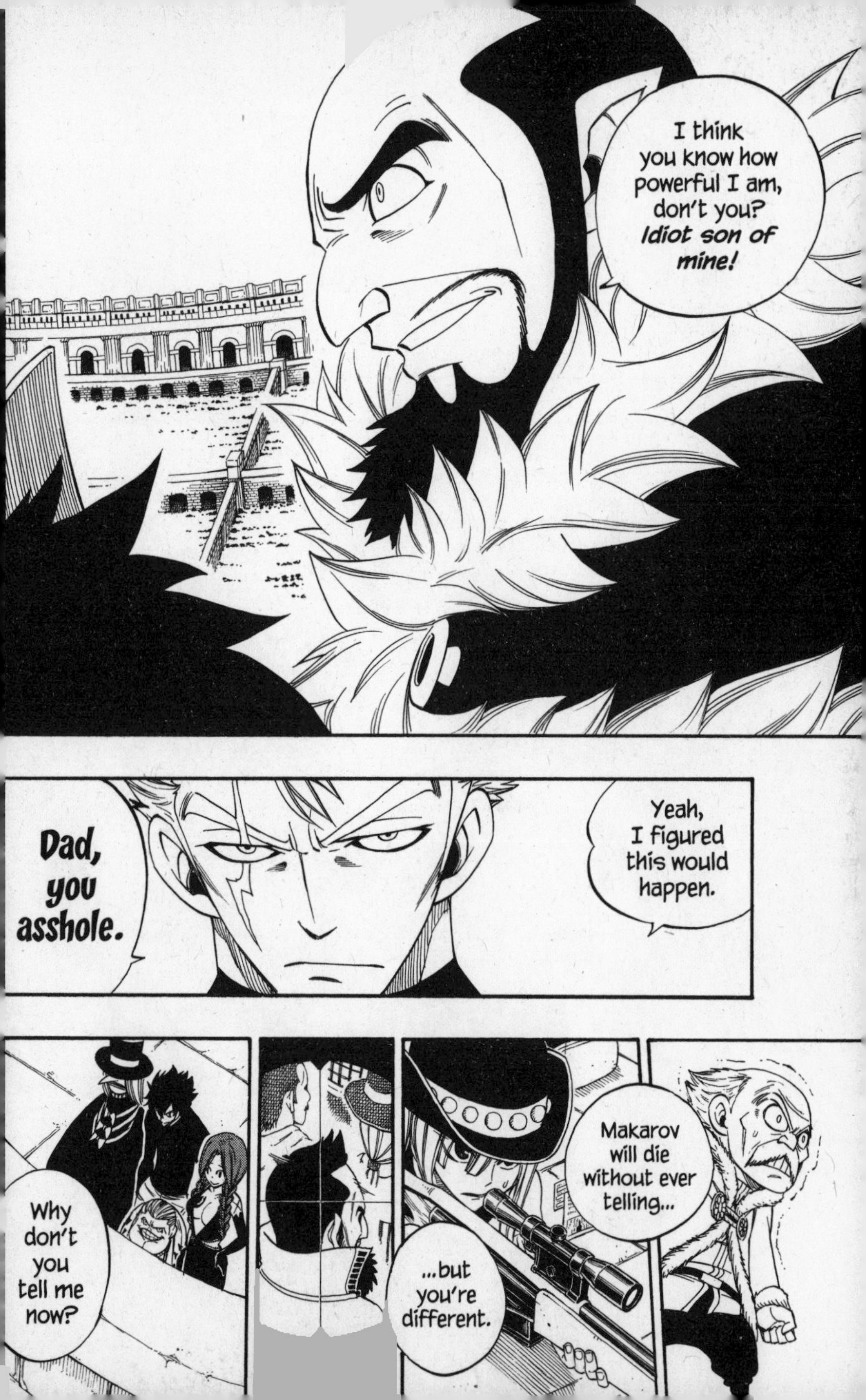
I think you know how powerful I am, don't you? *Idiot son of mine!*
Yeah, I figured this would happen.
Dad, you asshole.
Makarov will die without ever telling...
...but you're different.
Why don't you tell me now?

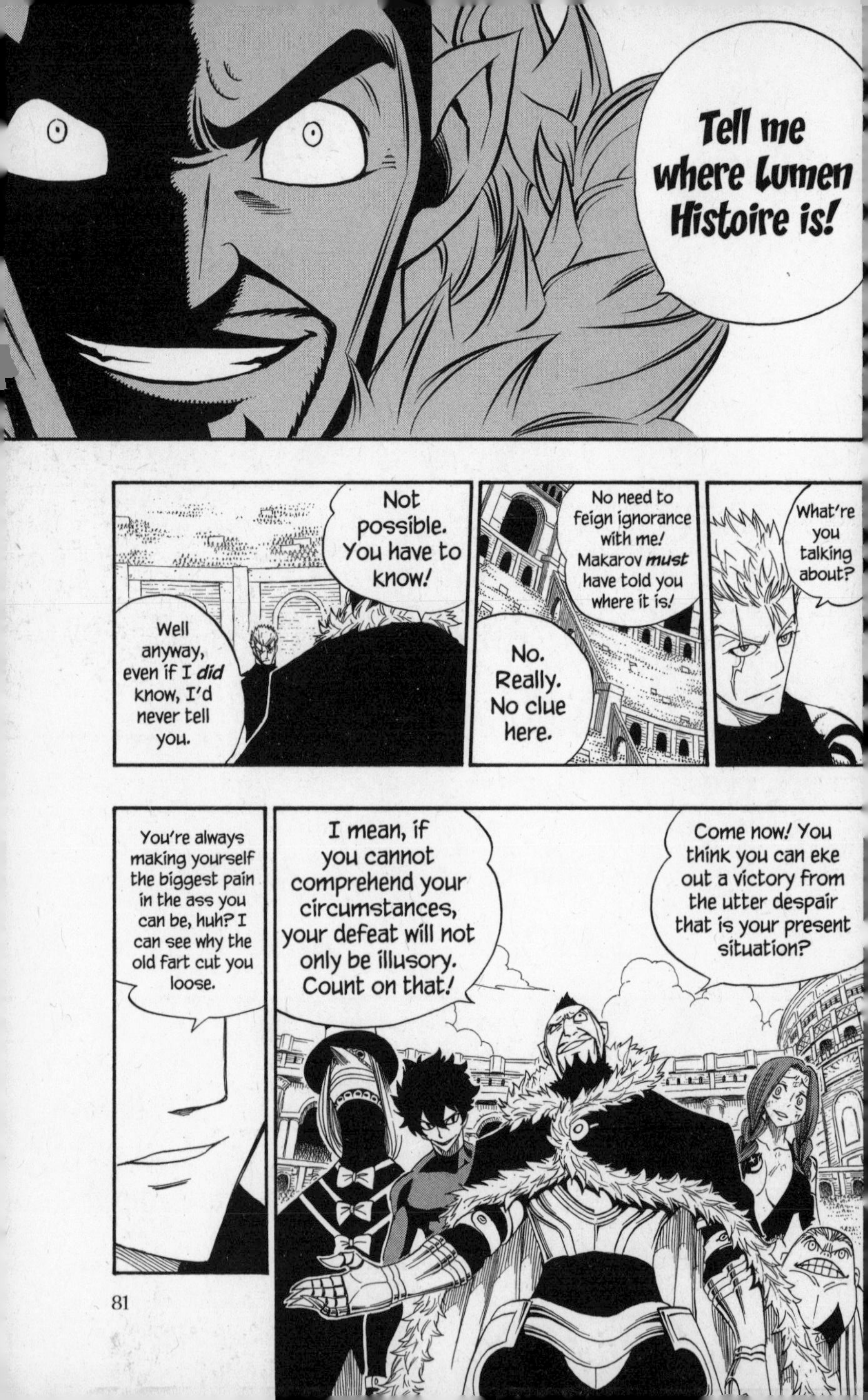
Tell me where Lumen Histoire is!
What're you talking about?
No need to feign ignorance with me! Makarov *must* have told you where it is!
No. Really. No clue here.
Not possible. You have to know!
Well anyway, even if I *did* know, I'd never tell you.
Come now! You think you can eke out a victory from the utter despair that is your present situation?
I mean, if you cannot comprehend your circumstances, your defeat will not only be illusory. Count on that!
You're always making yourself the biggest pain in the ass you can be, huh? I can see why the old fart cut you loose.

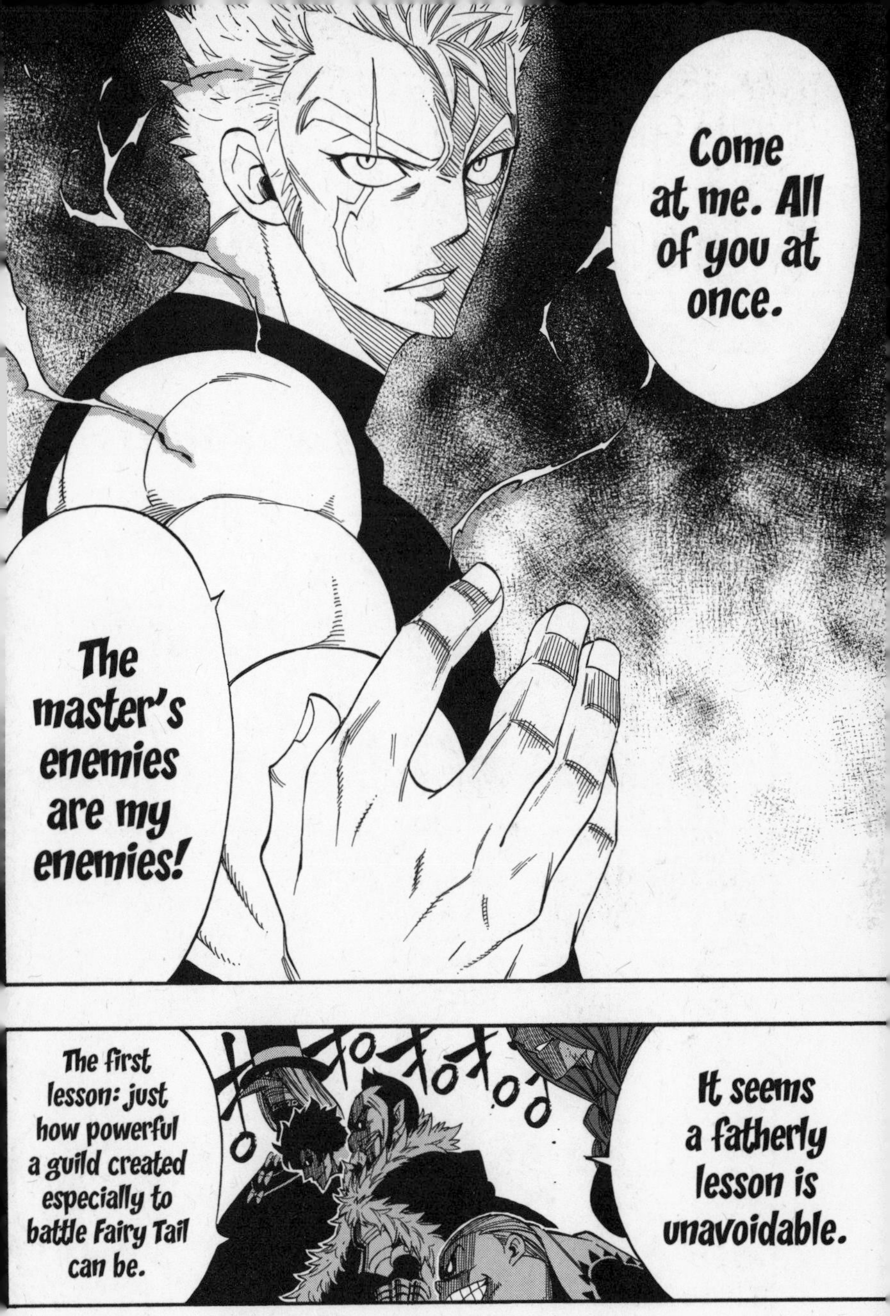
Come at me. All of you at once.
The master's enemies are my enemies!
It seems a fatherly lesson is unavoidable.
The first lesson: just how powerful a guild created especially to battle Fairy Tail can be.

FAIRY TAIL

フェアリーテイル

Chapter 287: True Family

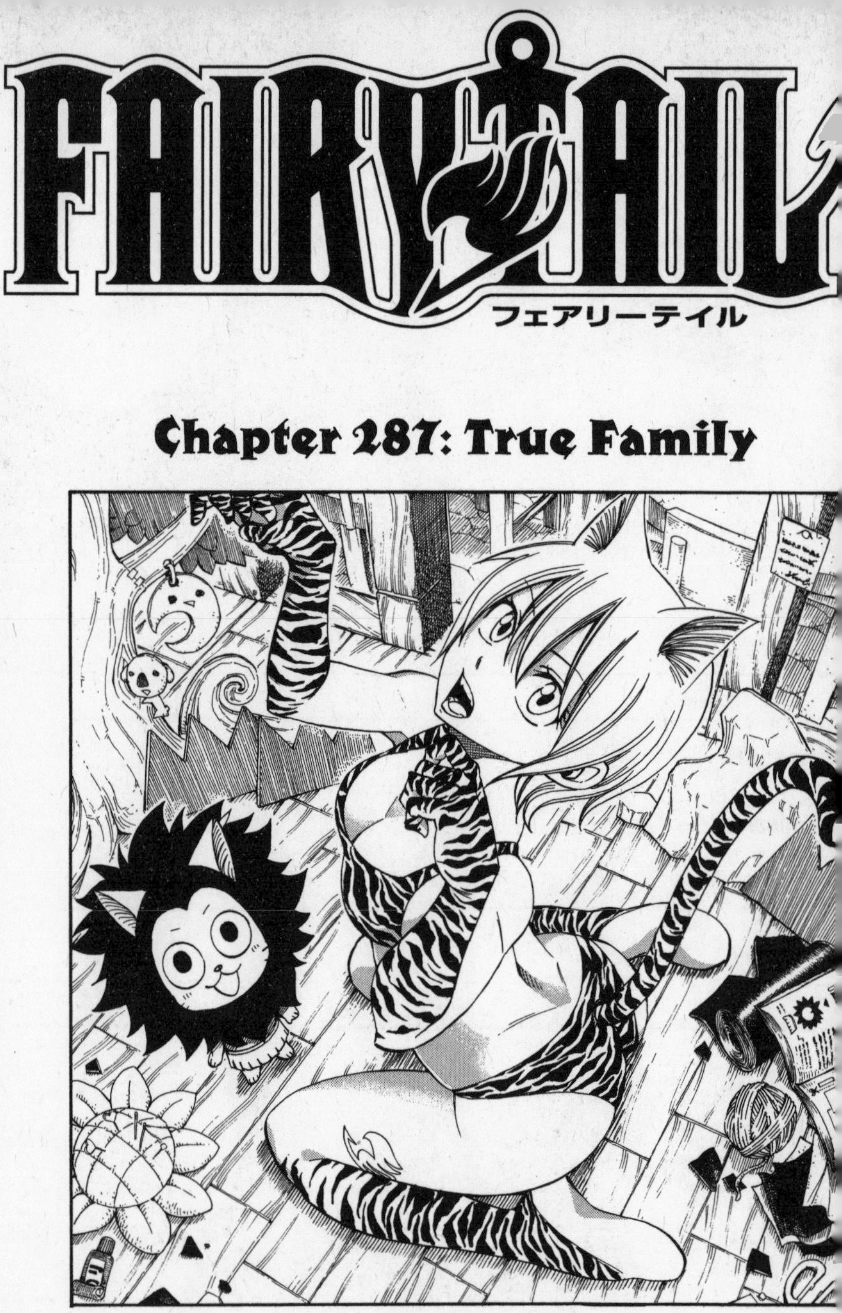

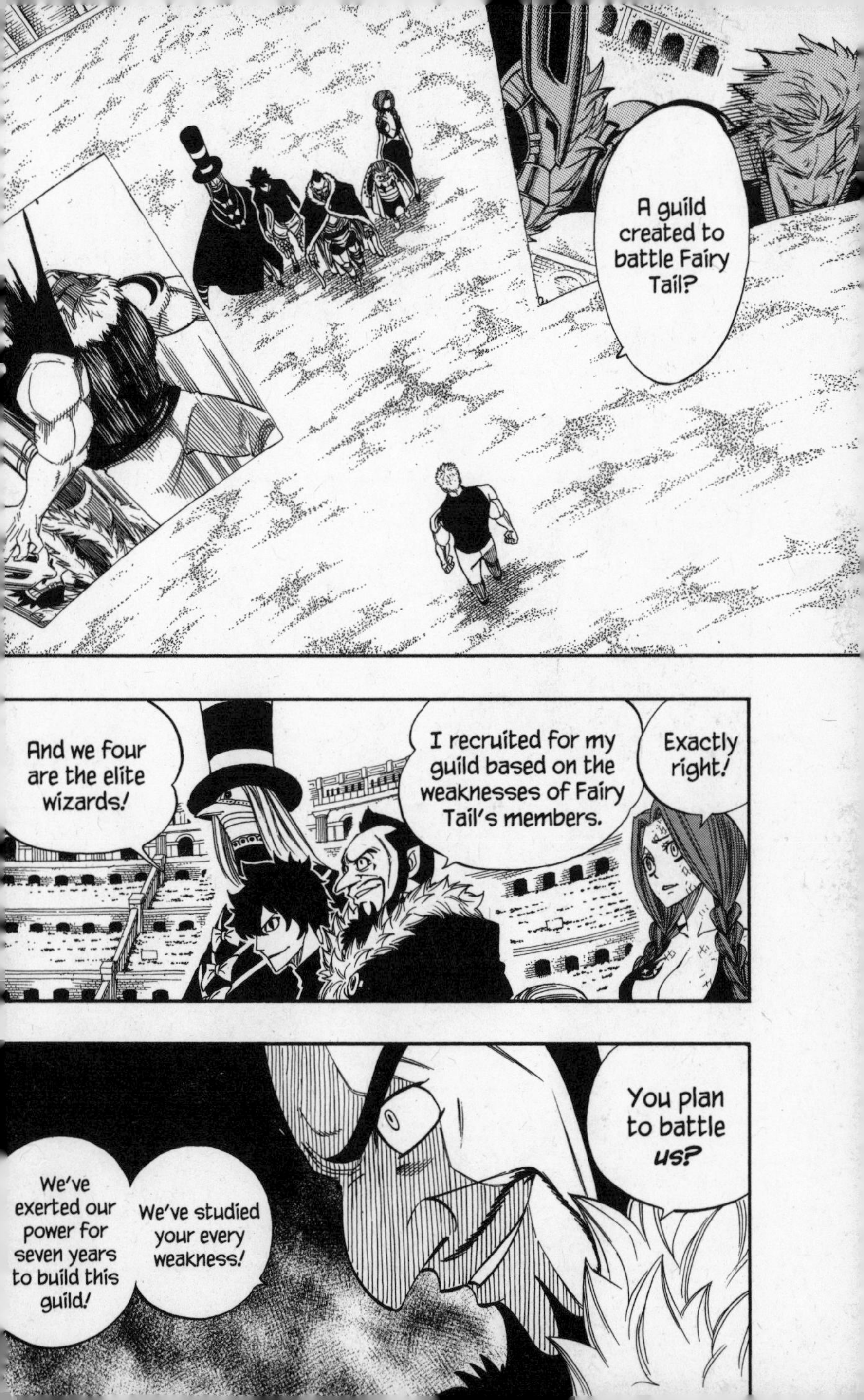
A guild created to battle Fairy Tail?
Exactly right!
I recruited for my guild based on the weaknesses of Fairy Tail's members.
And we four are the elite wizards!
You plan to battle *us*?
We've studied your every weakness!
We've exerted our power for seven years to build this guild!

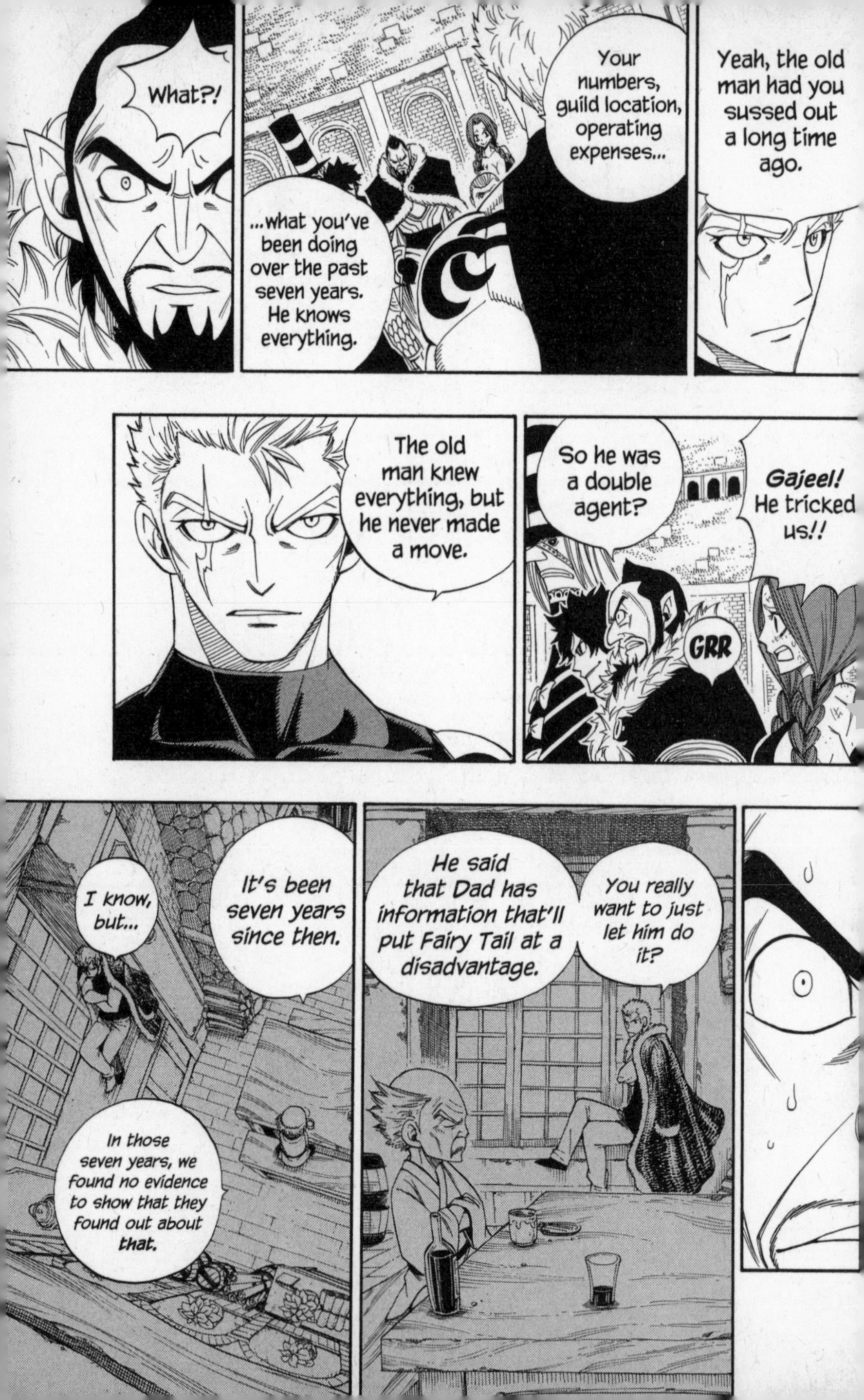
Yeah, the old man had you sussed out a long time ago.
Your numbers, guild location, operating expenses...
...what you've been doing over the past seven years. He knows everything.
What?!
Gajeel! He tricked us!!
So he was a double agent?
GRR
The old man knew everything, but he never made a move.
You really want to just let him do it?
He said that Dad has information that'll put Fairy Tail at a disadvantage.
It's been seven years since then.
I know, but...
*In those seven years, we found no evidence to show that they found out about **that**.*

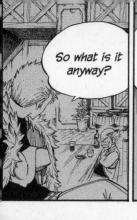

So what is it anyway?

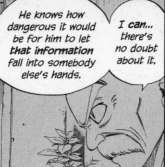

He knows how dangerous it would be for him to let *that information* fall into somebody else's hands.

I can... there's no doubt about it.

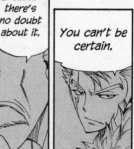

You can't be certain.

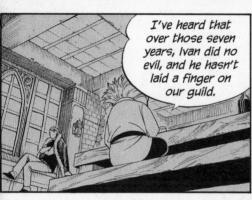

I've heard that over those seven years, Ivan did no evil, and he hasn't laid a finger on our guild.

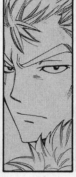

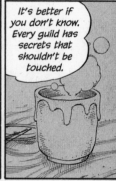

It's better if you don't know. Every guild has secrets that shouldn't be touched.

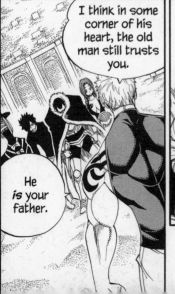

I think in some corner of his heart, the old man still trusts you.

He *is* your father.

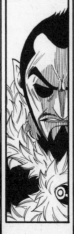

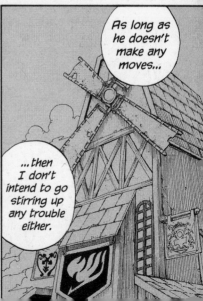

As long as he doesn't make any moves...

...then I don't intend to go stirring up any trouble either.

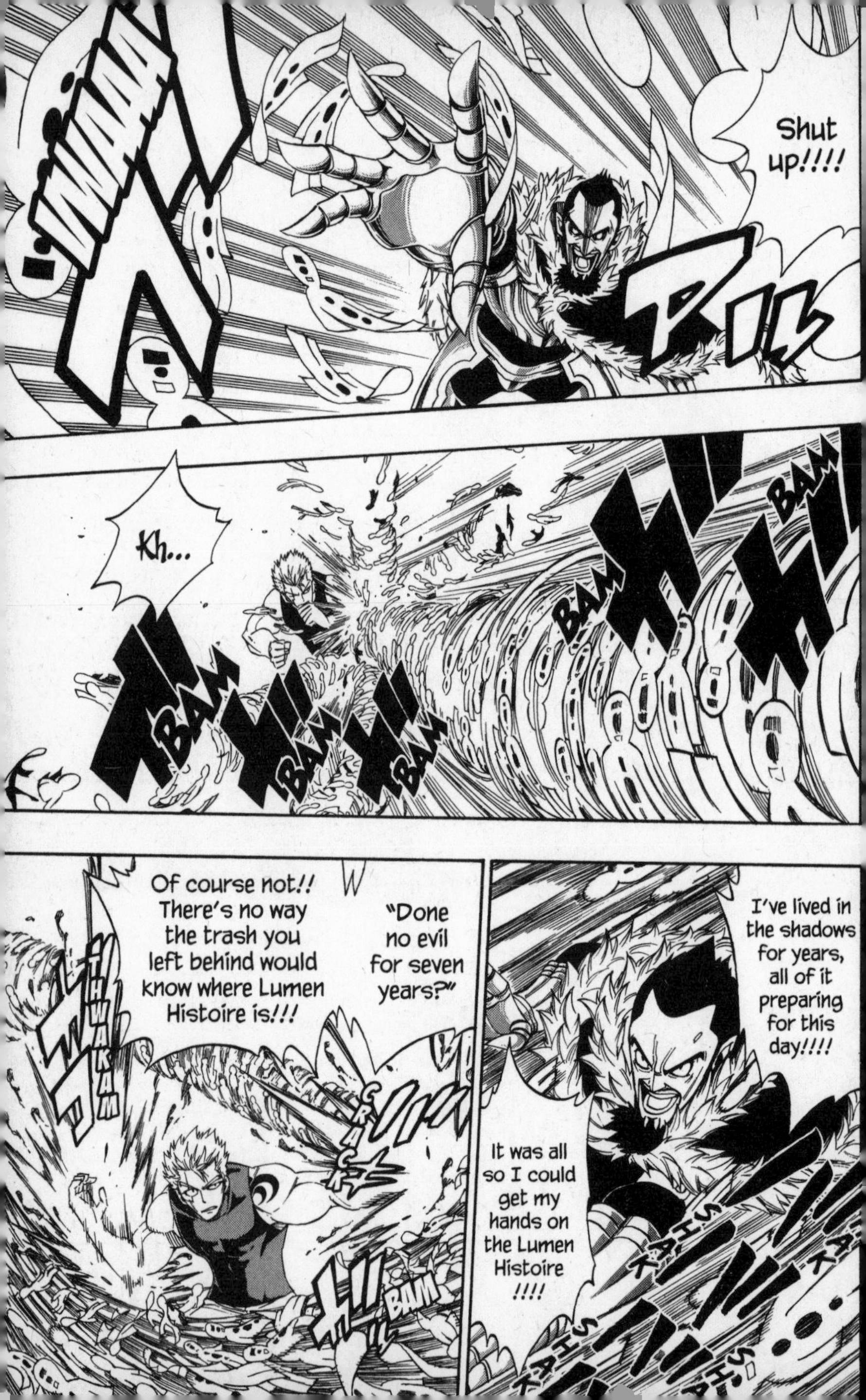

Shut up!!!!
Kh...
BAM
BAM
BAM
BAM
BAM
I've lived in the shadows for years, all of it preparing for this day!!!!
It was all so I could get my hands on the Lumen Histoire!!!!
KASHA
KASHA
"Done no evil for seven years?"
Of course not!! There's no way the trash you left behind would know where Lumen Histoire is!!!
THWAKAM
CRACK
BAM

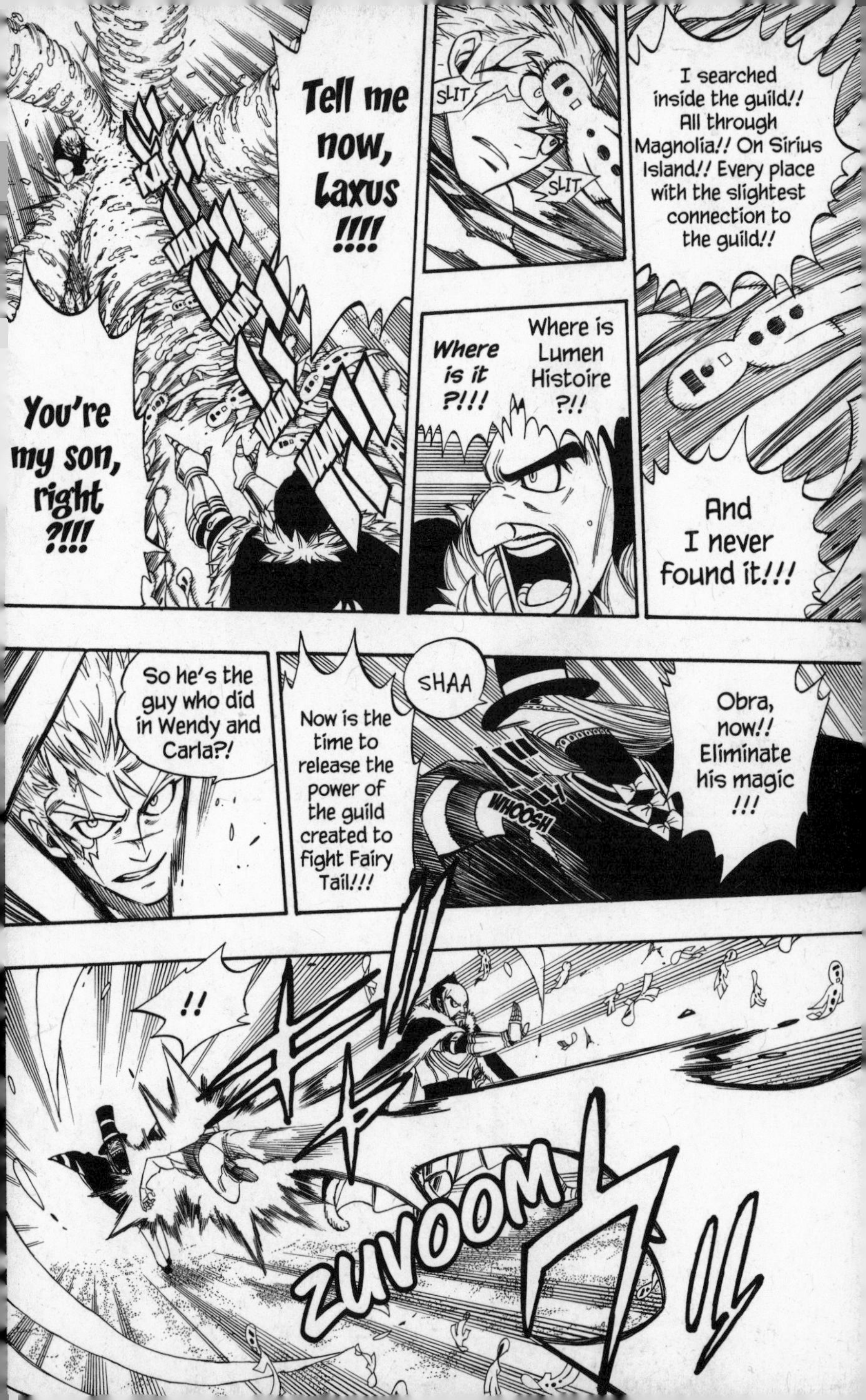
I searched inside the guild!! All through Magnolia!! On Sirius Island!! Every place with the slightest connection to the guild!!
And I never found it!!!
SLIT
SLIT
Where is Lumen Histoire?!!
Where is it?!!!
Tell me now, Laxus!!!!
You're my son, right?!!!
Obra, now!! Eliminate his magic!!!
SHAA
WHOOSH
Now is the time to release the power of the guild created to fight Fairy Tail!!!
So he's the guy who did in Wendy and Carla?!
!!
ZUVOOM

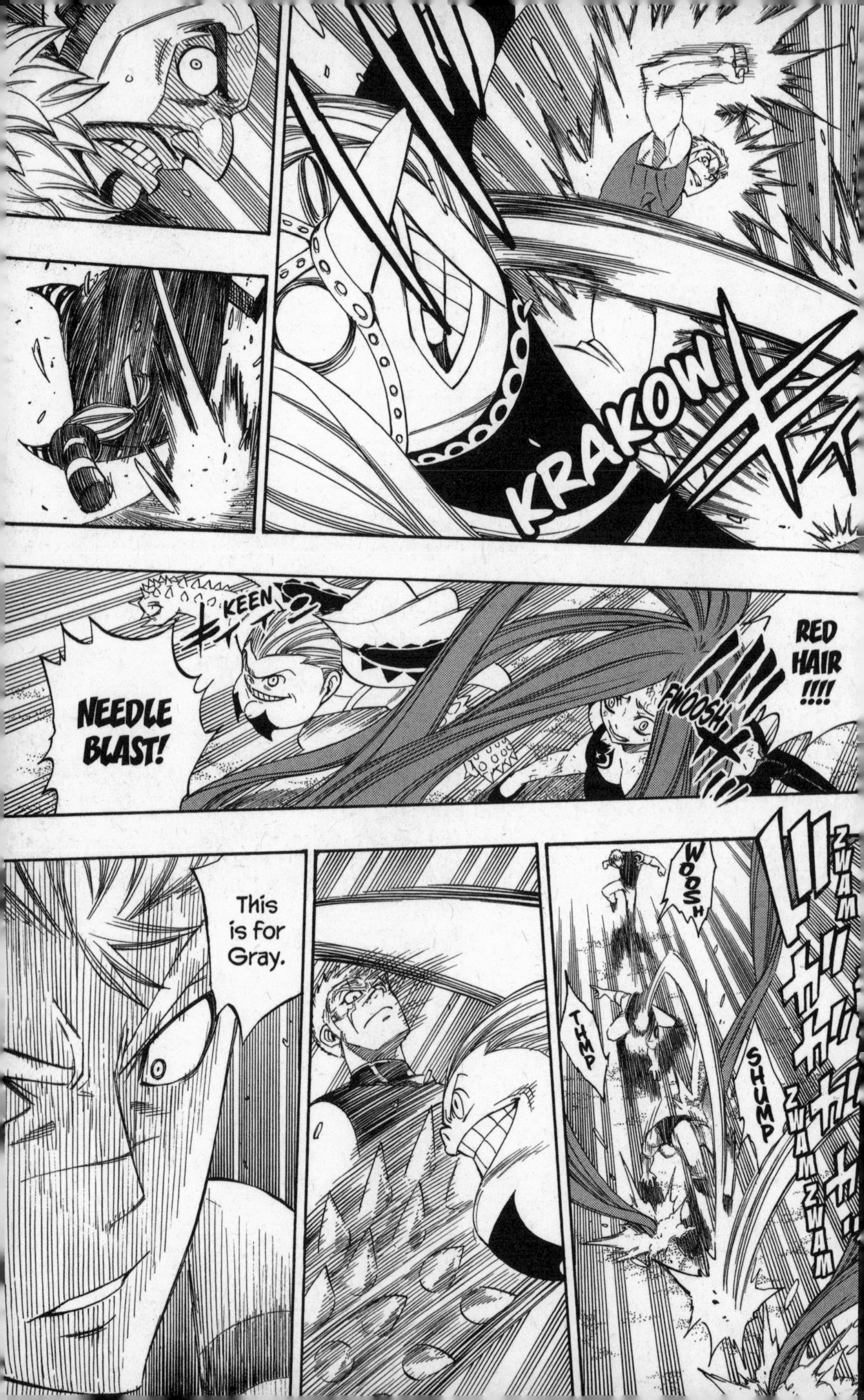
KRAKOW
RED HAIR!!!!
FWOOSH
KEEN
NEEDLE BLAST!
ZWAM
WOOSH
SHUMP
THMP
ZWAMZWAMZWAM
This is for Gray.

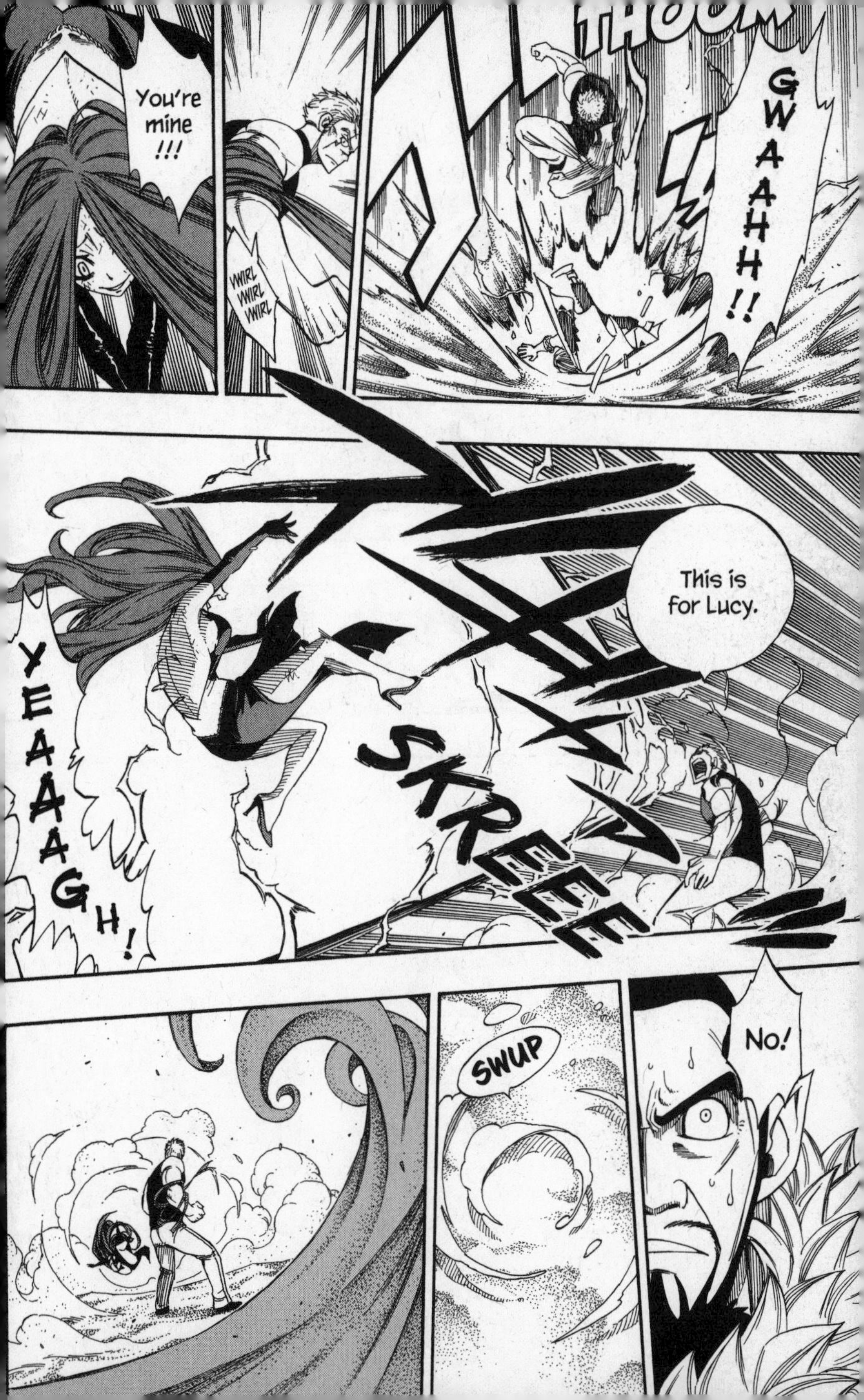
THOOM
GWAAHH!!
WHIRL
WHIRL
WHIRL
You're mine!!!
This is for Lucy.
SKREEE
YEAAAGH!
No!
SWUP

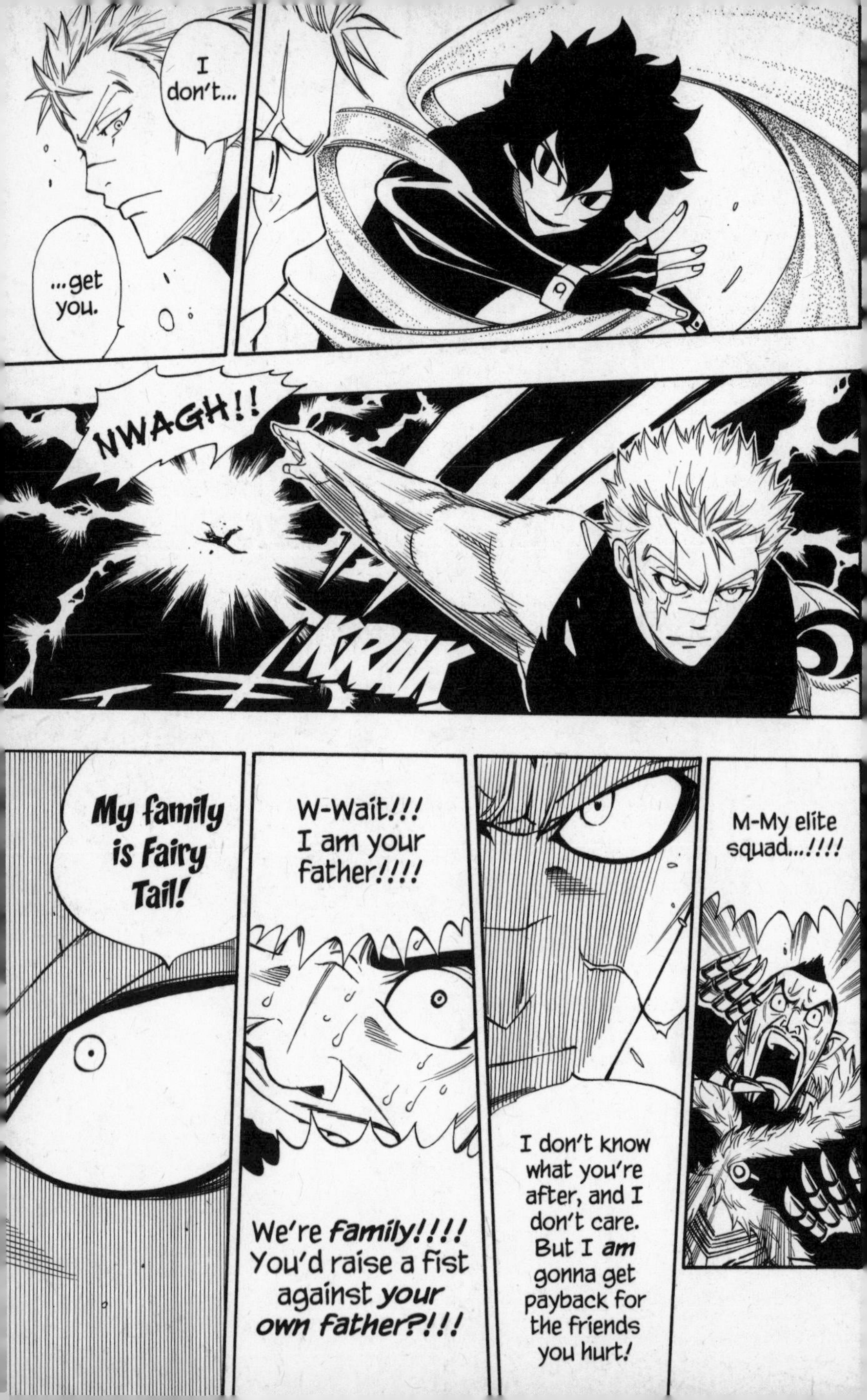
I don't...
...get you.
NWAGH!!
KRAK
M-My elite squad...!!!!
I don't know what you're after, and I don't care. But I am gonna get payback for the friends you hurt!
W-Wait!!! I am your father!!!!
We're family!!!! You'd raise a fist against your own father?!!!
My family is Fairy Tail!

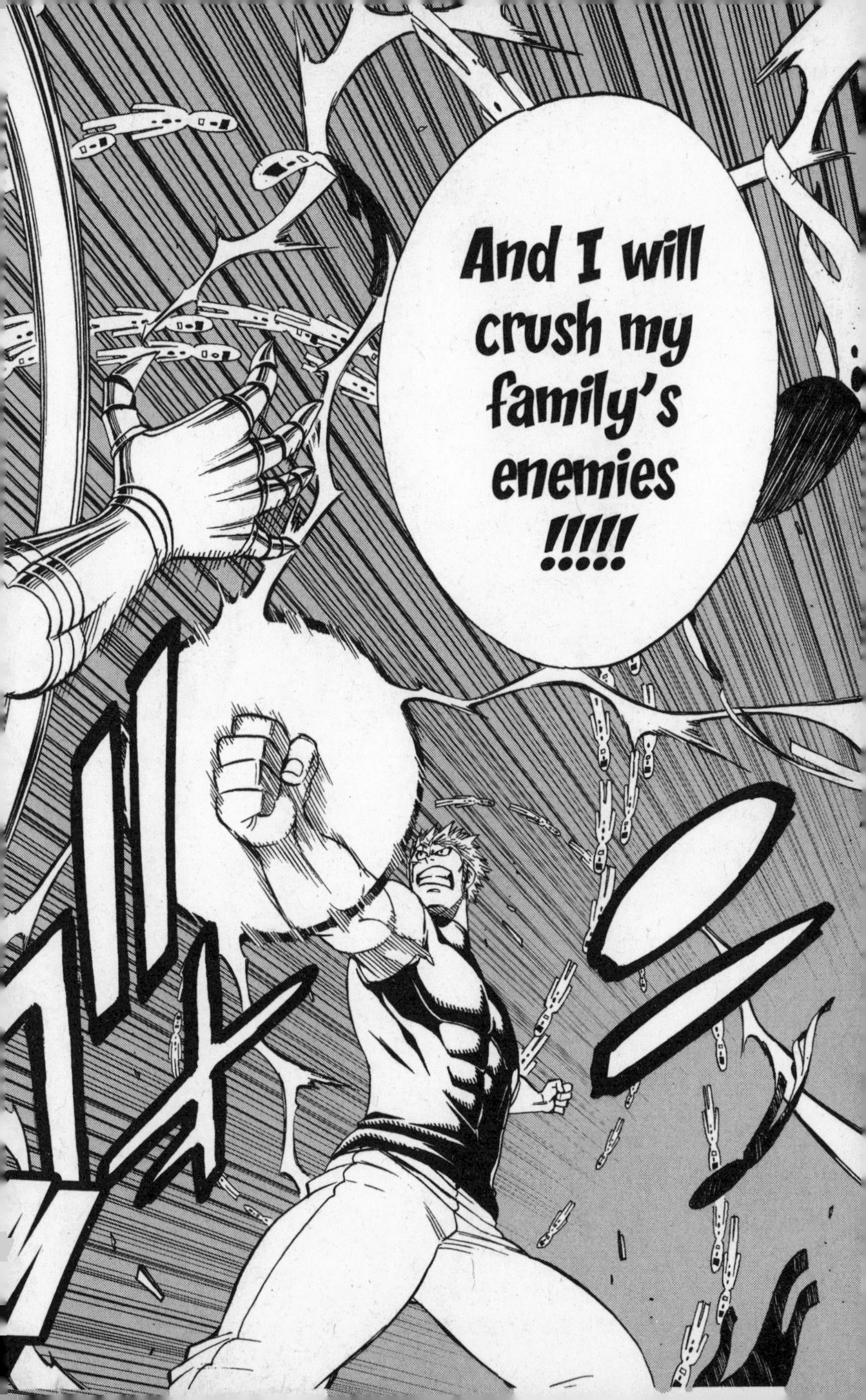
And I will crush my family's enemies !!!!!

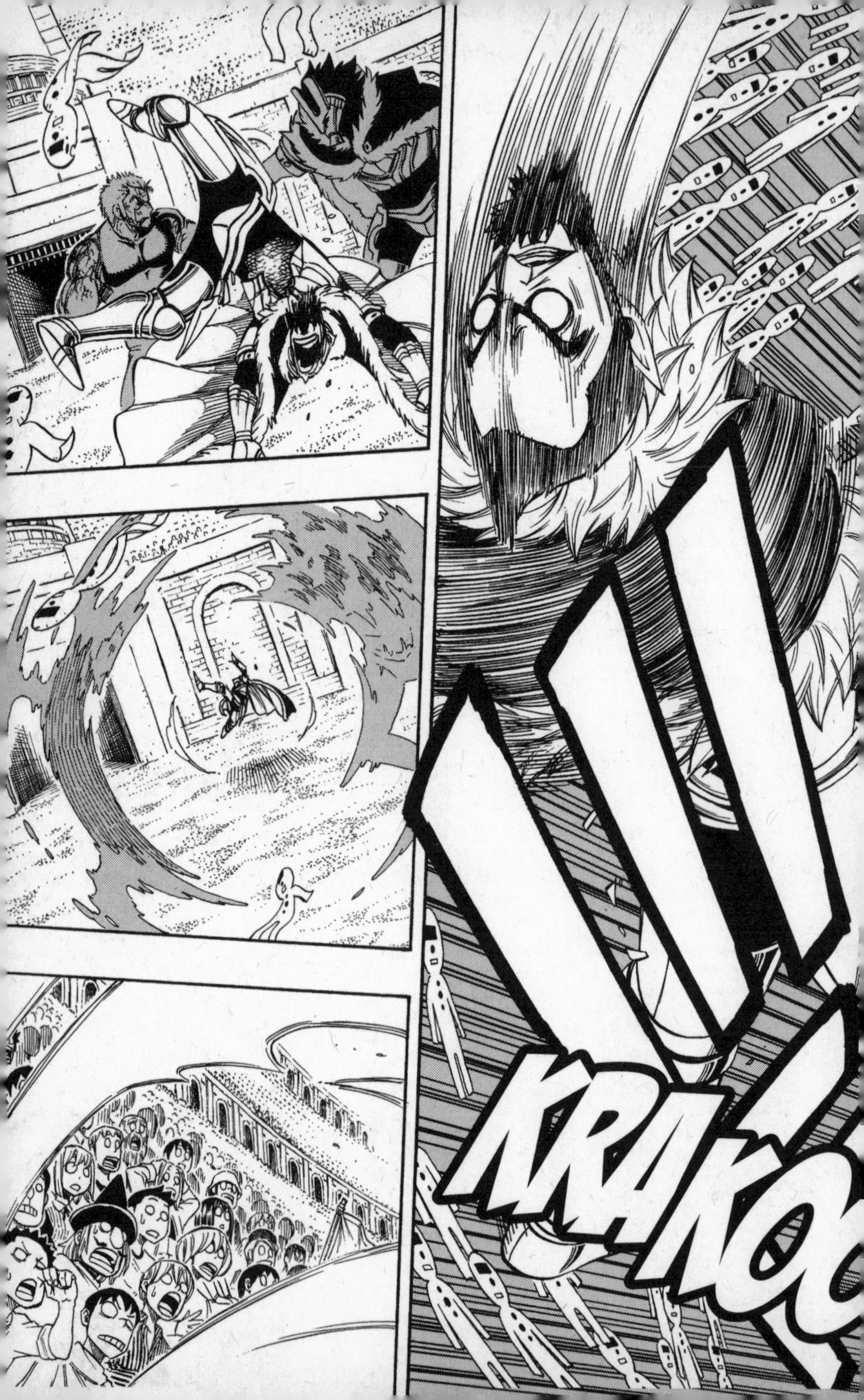
KRAKOO

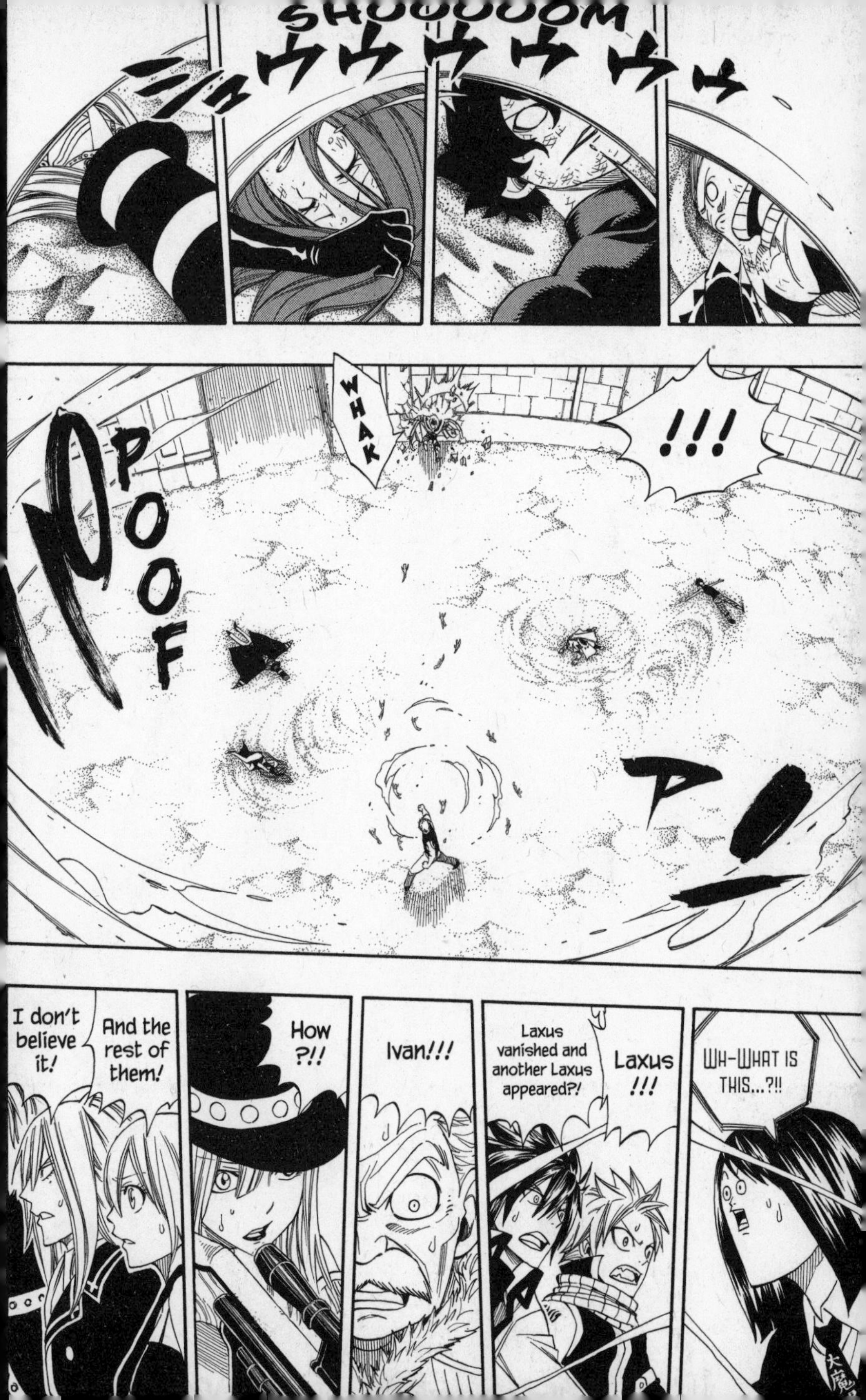

SHOOOOOOM
ジュウウウウウ
WHAK
!!!
POOF
Wh-What is this...?!!
Laxus!!!
Laxus vanished and another Laxus appeared?!
Ivan!!!
How?!!
And the rest of them!
I don't believe it!

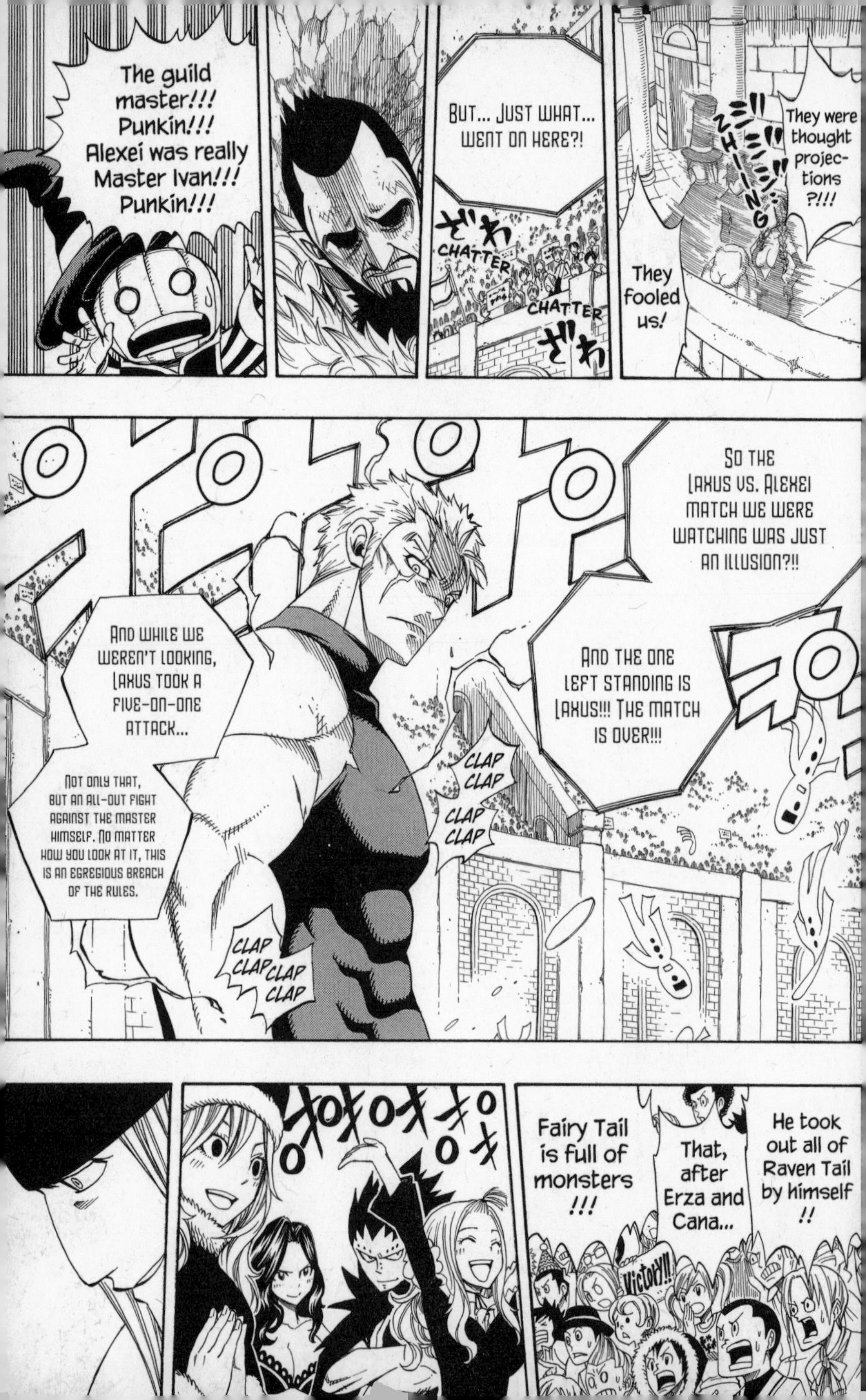
They were thought projections ?!!!
ZHIING
They fooled us!
But... just what... went on here?!
CHATTER
CHATTER
The guild master!!! Punkin!!! Alexei was really Master Ivan!!! Punkin!!!
So the Laxus vs. Alexei match we were watching was just an illusion?!!
And the one left standing is Laxus!!! The match is over!!!
CLAP CLAP
CLAP CLAP
And while we weren't looking, Laxus took a five-on-one attack...
Not only that, but an all-out fight against the master himself. No matter how you look at it, this is an egregious breach of the rules.
CLAP CLAP CLAP CLAP
He took out all of Raven Tail by himself !!
That, after Erza and Cana...
Fairy Tail is full of monsters !!!
Victory!!

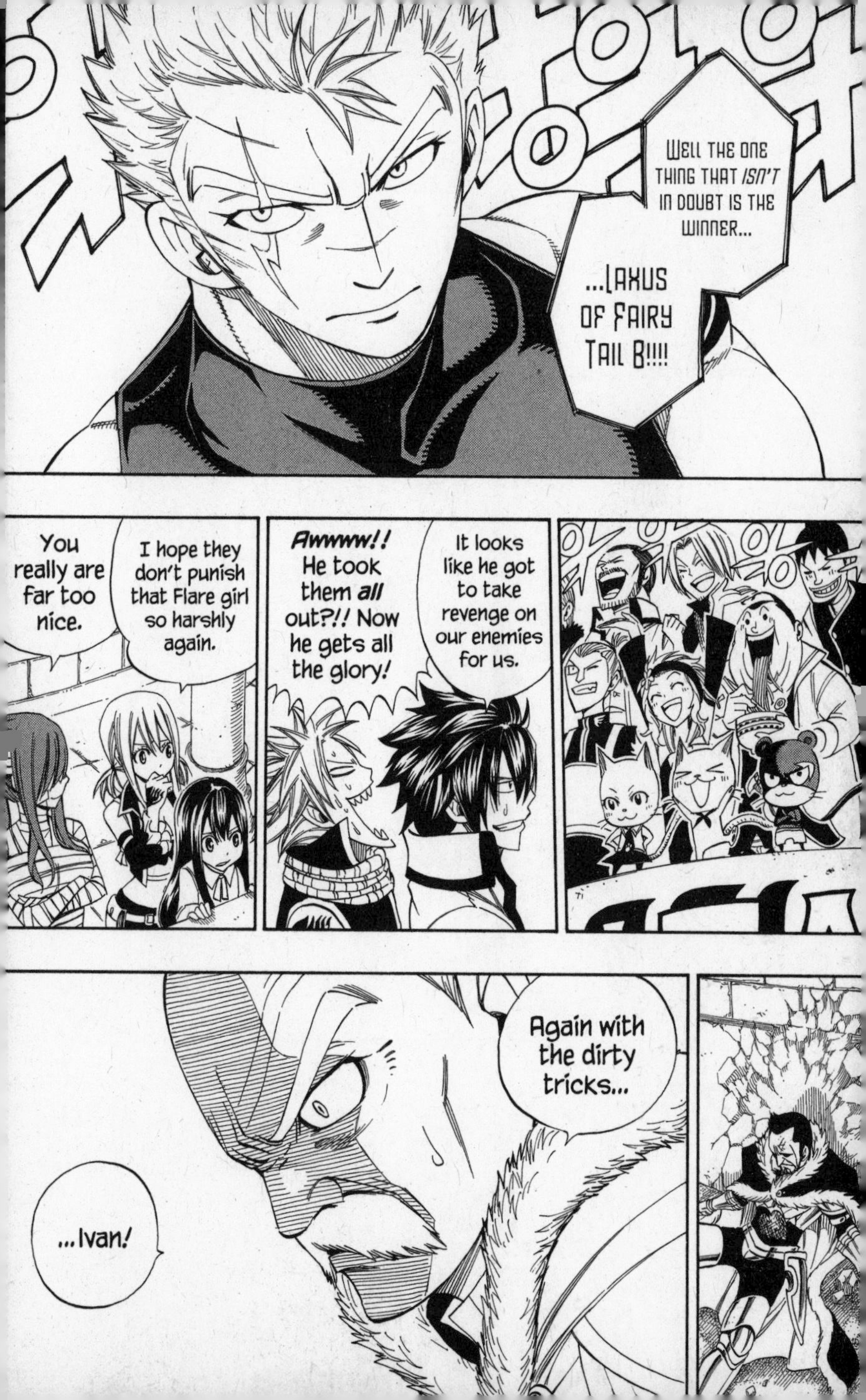
Well the one thing that *isn't* in doubt is the winner...
...Laxus of Fairy Tail B!!!!
It looks like he got to take revenge on our enemies for us.
Awwww!! He took them ***all*** out?!! Now he gets all the glory!
I hope they don't punish that Flare girl so harshly again.
You really are far too nice.
Again with the dirty tricks...
...Ivan!

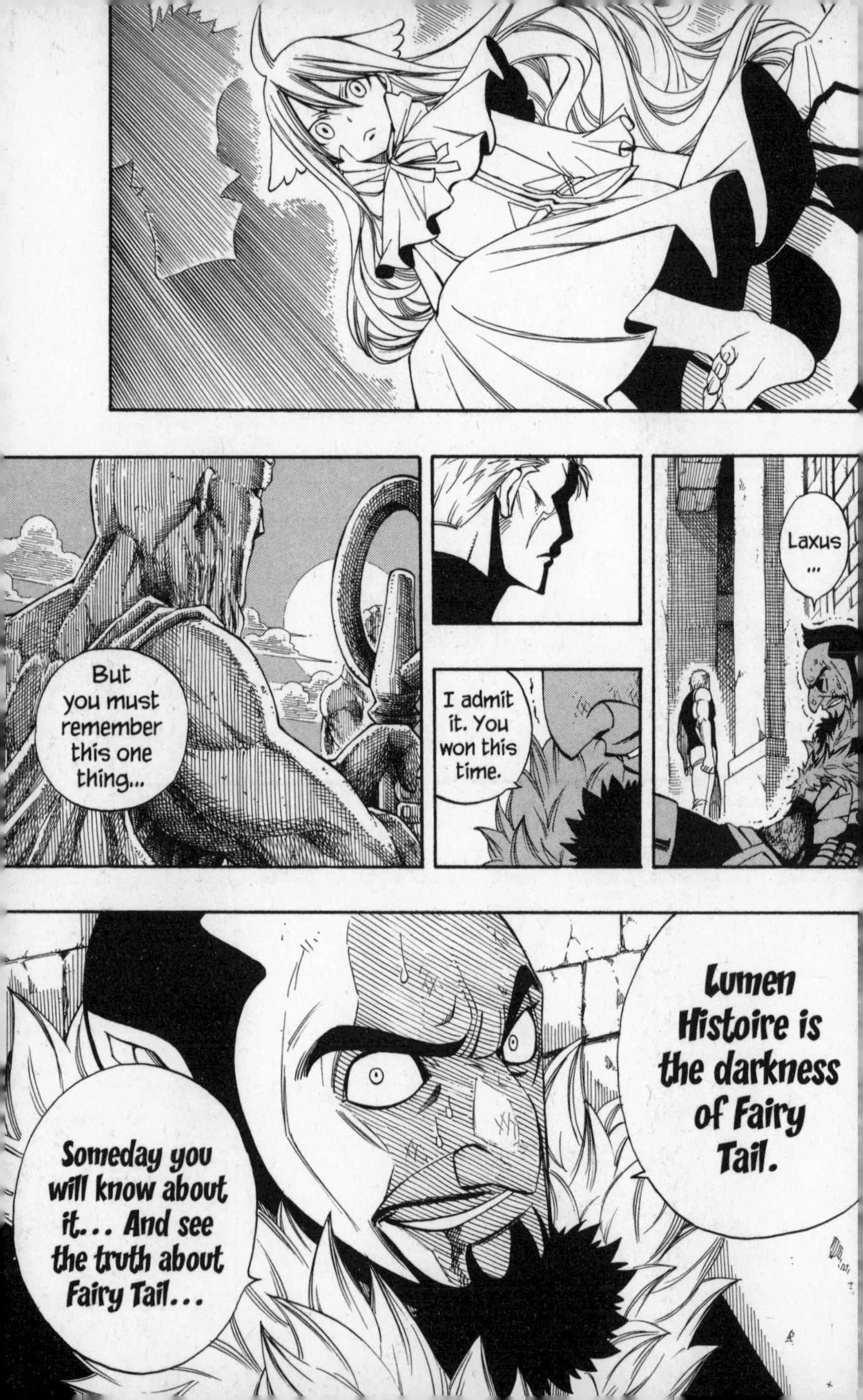
Laxus ...
I admit it. You won this time.
But you must remember this one thing...
Lumen Histoire is the darkness of Fairy Tail.
Someday you will know about it... And see the truth about Fairy Tail...

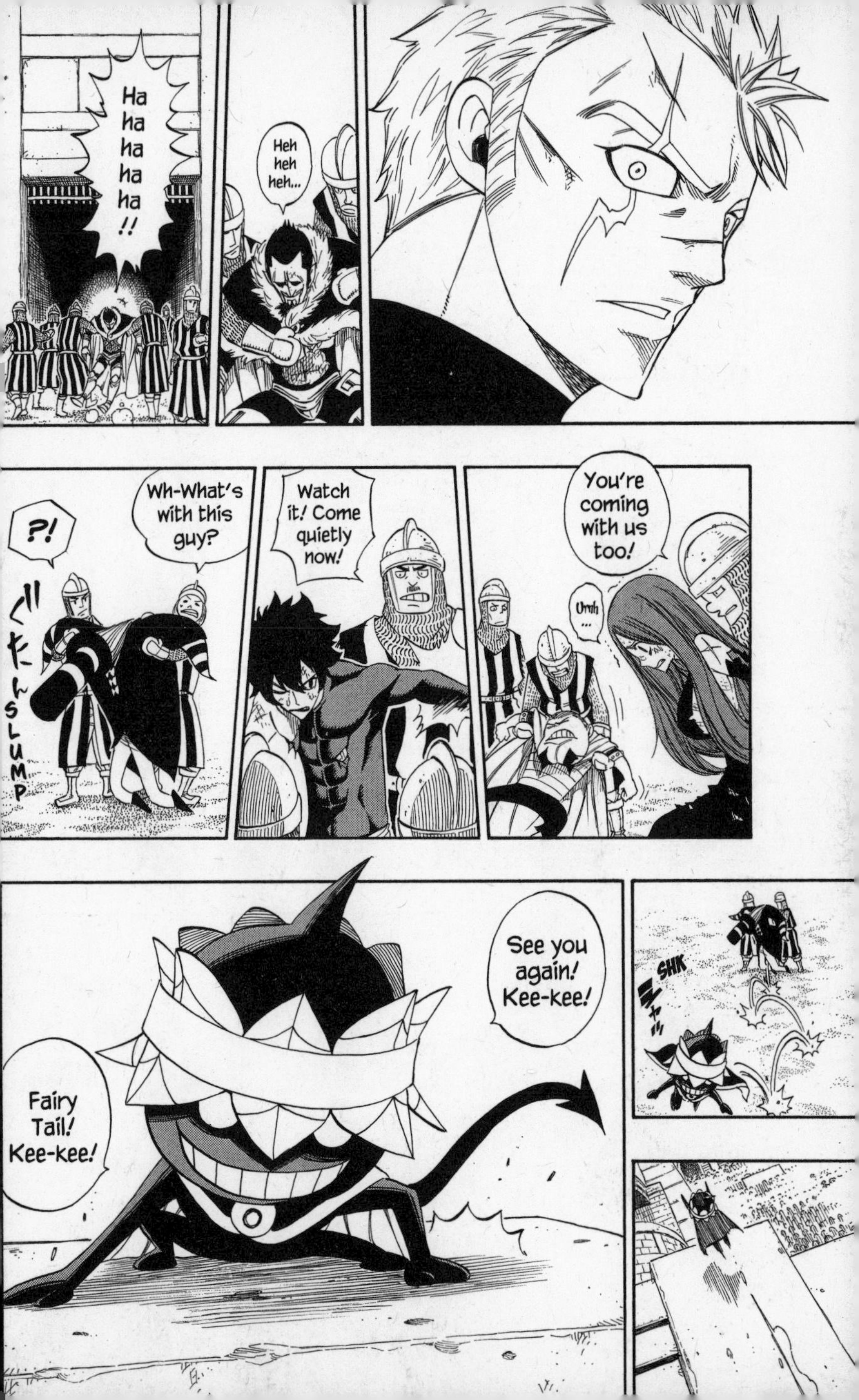
Heh heh heh...
Ha ha ha ha ha!!
You're coming with us too!
Umh...
Watch it! Come quietly now!
Wh-What's with this guy?
?!
SLUMP
SHK
See you again! Kee-kee!
Fairy Tail! Kee-kee!

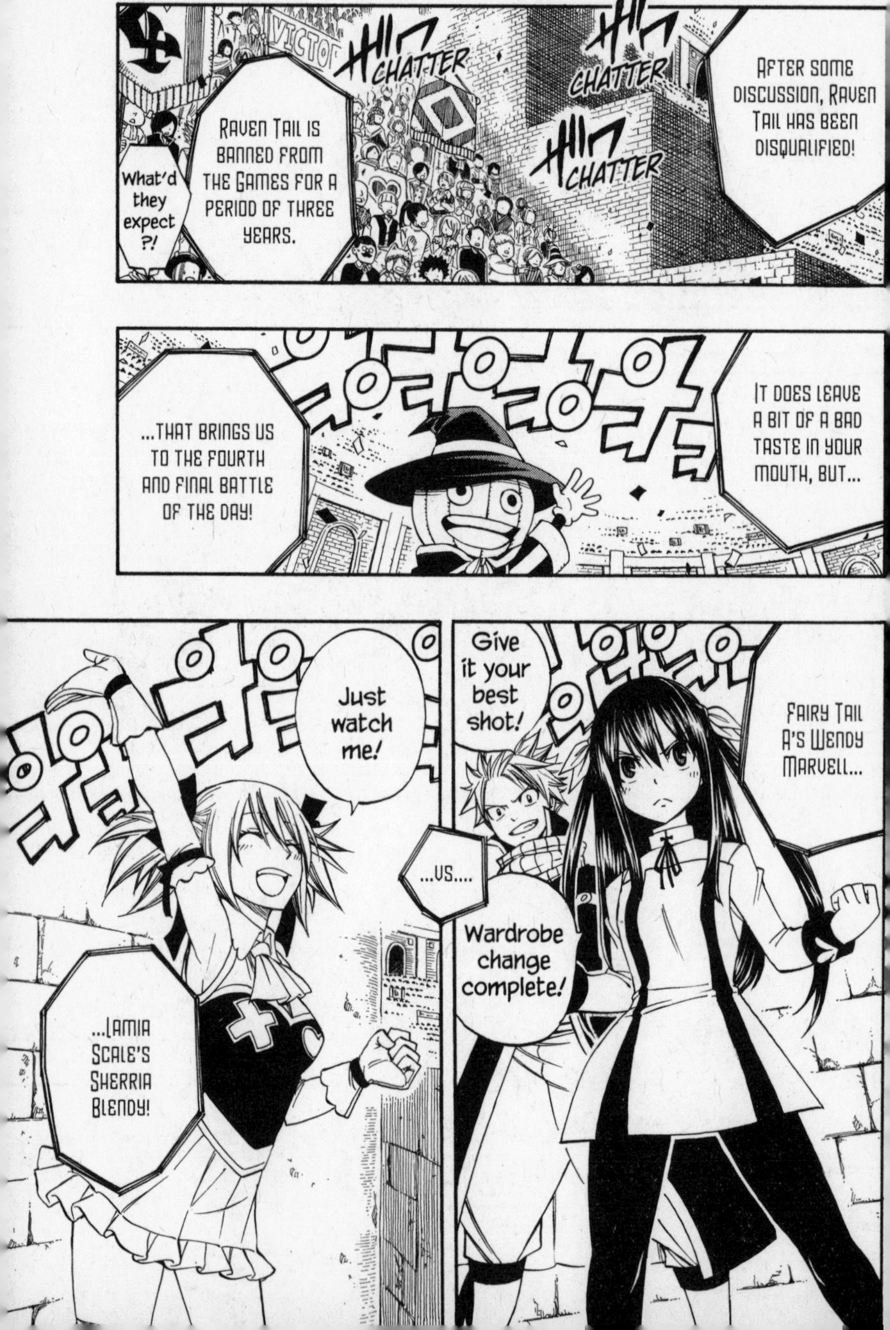

After some discussion, Raven Tail has been disqualified!
CHATTER
CHATTER
CHATTER
Raven Tail is banned from the Games for a period of three years.
What'd they expect?!
It does leave a bit of a bad taste in your mouth, but...
...that brings us to the fourth and final battle of the day!
Fairy Tail A's Wendy Marvell...
Give it your best shot!
...vs....
Wardrobe change complete!
Just watch me!
...Lamia Scale's Sherria Blendy!

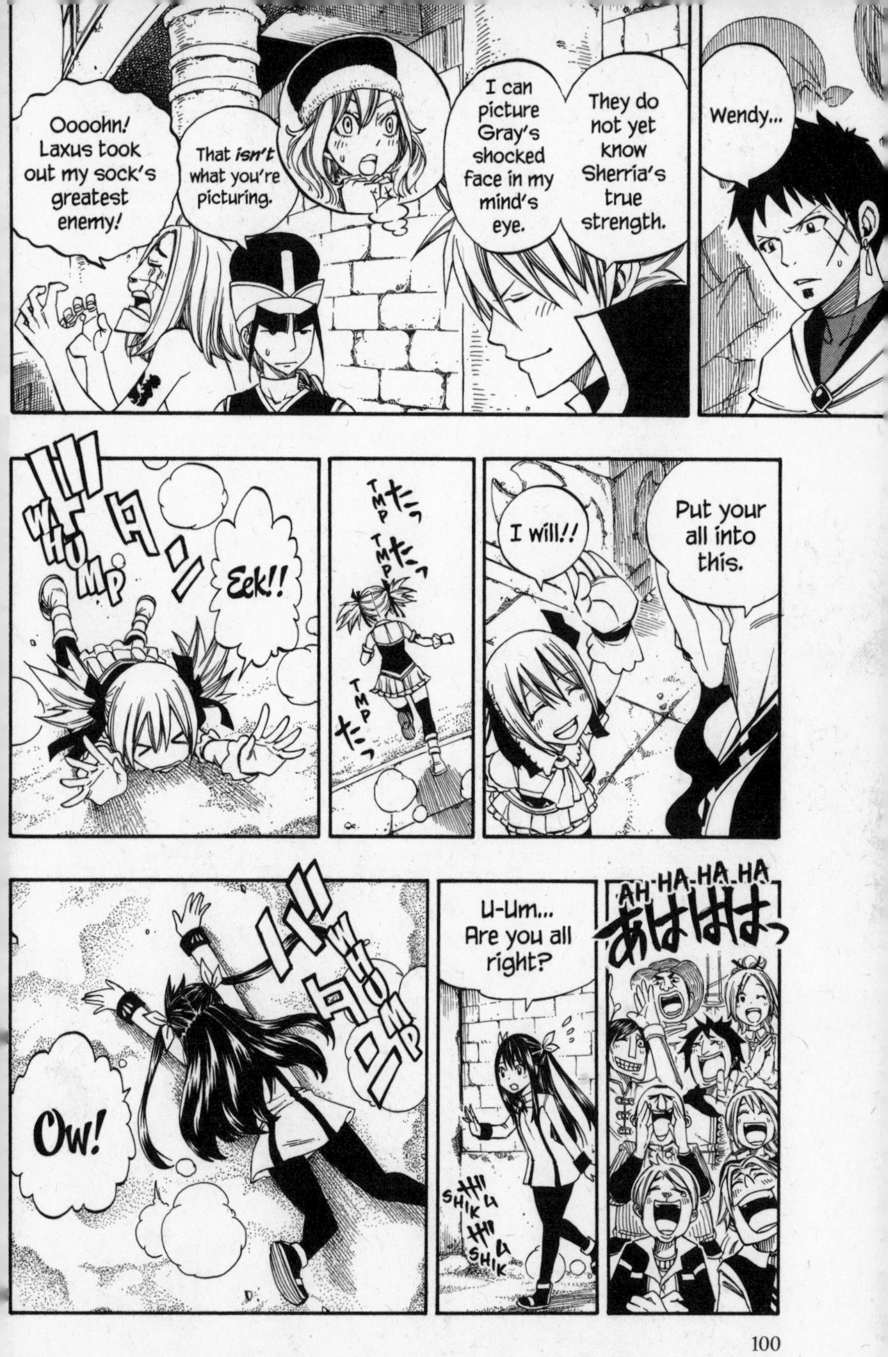

Wendy...
They do not yet know Sherria's true strength.
I can picture Gray's shocked face in my mind's eye.
That *isn't* what you're picturing.
Oooohn! Laxus took out my sock's greatest enemy!
Put your all into this.
I will!!
TMP たっ
TMP たっ
TMP たっ
WHOMP
Eek!!
AH HA HA HA
あははは っ
U-Um... Are you all right?
SHIK
SHIK
WHOMP
Ow!

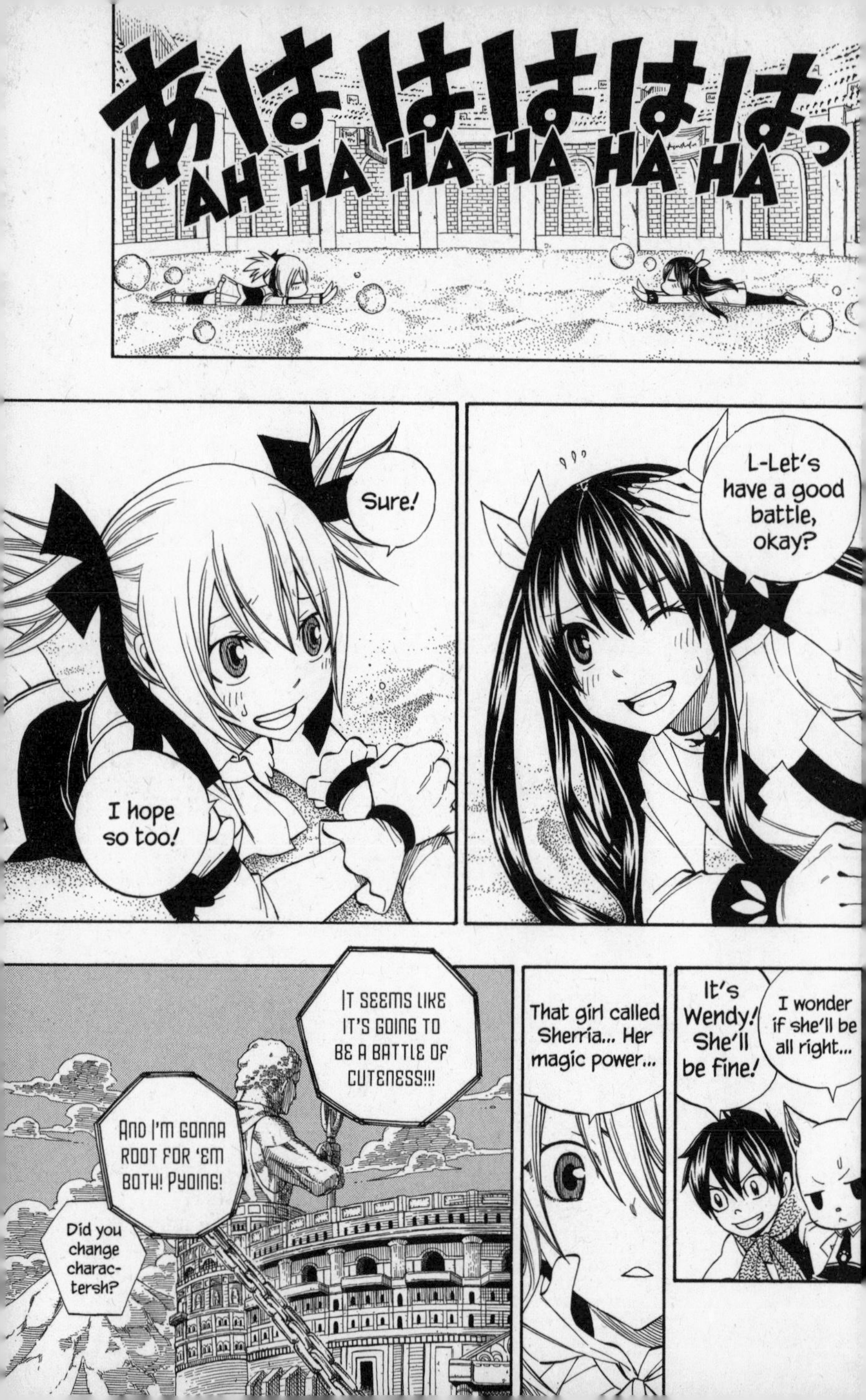
あははははは
AH HA HA HA HA HA
L-Let's have a good battle, okay?
Sure!
I hope so too!
I wonder if she'll be all right...
It's Wendy! She'll be fine!
That girl called Sherria... Her magic power...
IT SEEMS LIKE IT'S GOING TO BE A BATTLE OF CUTENESS!!!
AND I'M GONNA ROOT FOR 'EM BOTH! PYOING!
Did you change charactersh?

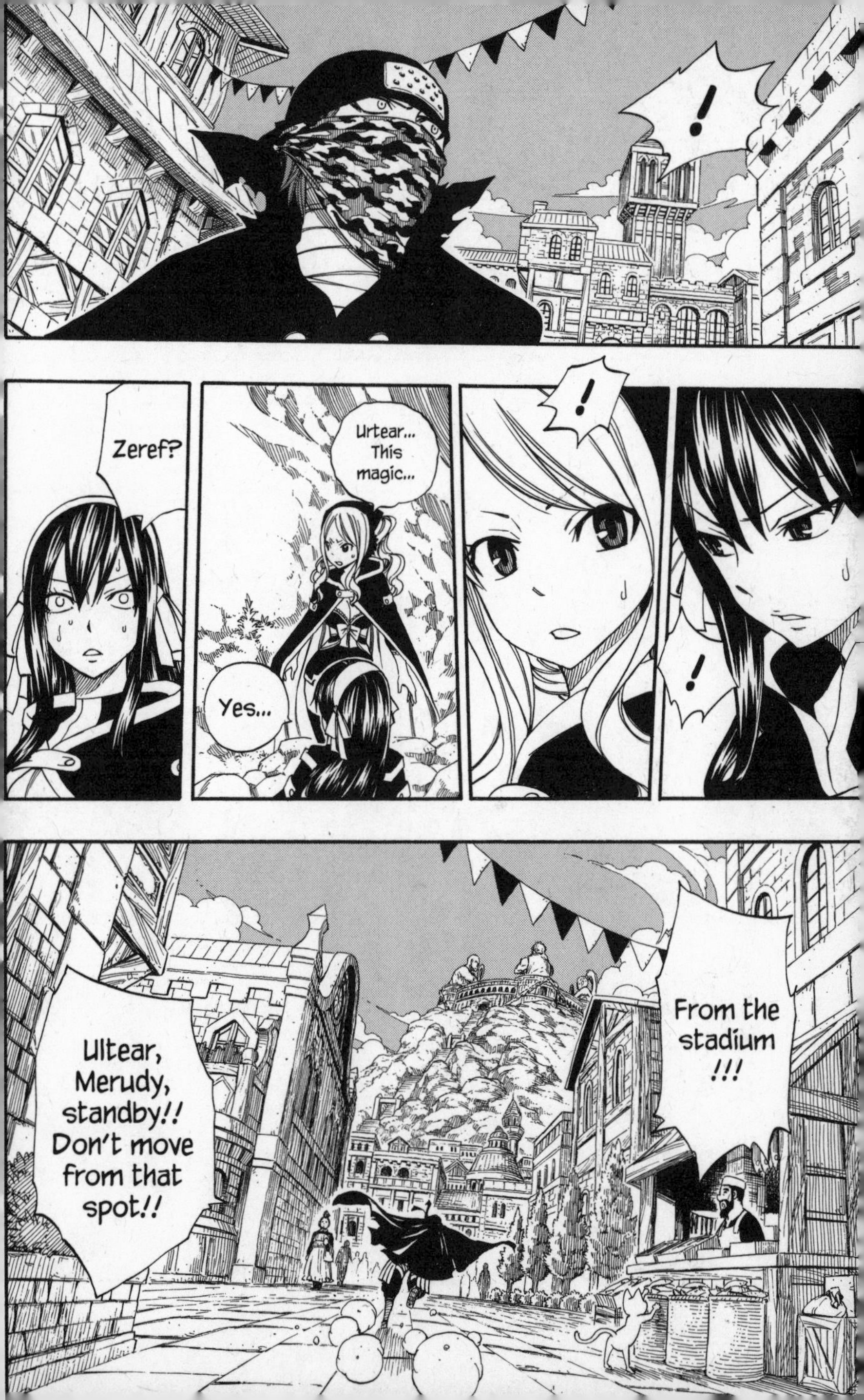
!
!
!
Urtear... This magic...
Yes...
Zeref?
From the stadium !!!
Ultear, Merudy, standby!! Don't move from that spot!!

FAIRY TAIL
フェアリーテイル

Chapter 288: Wendy vs. Sherria

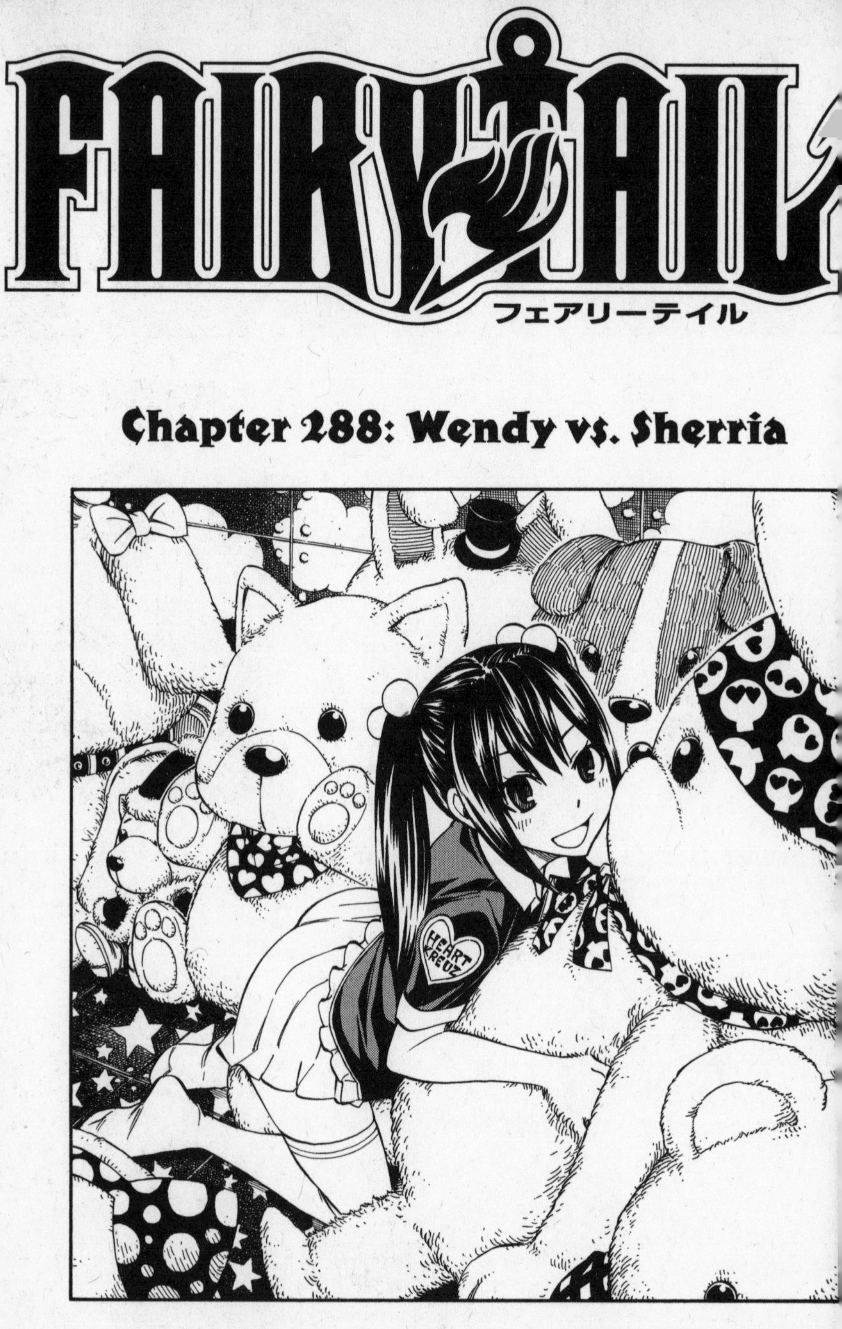
HEART KREUZ

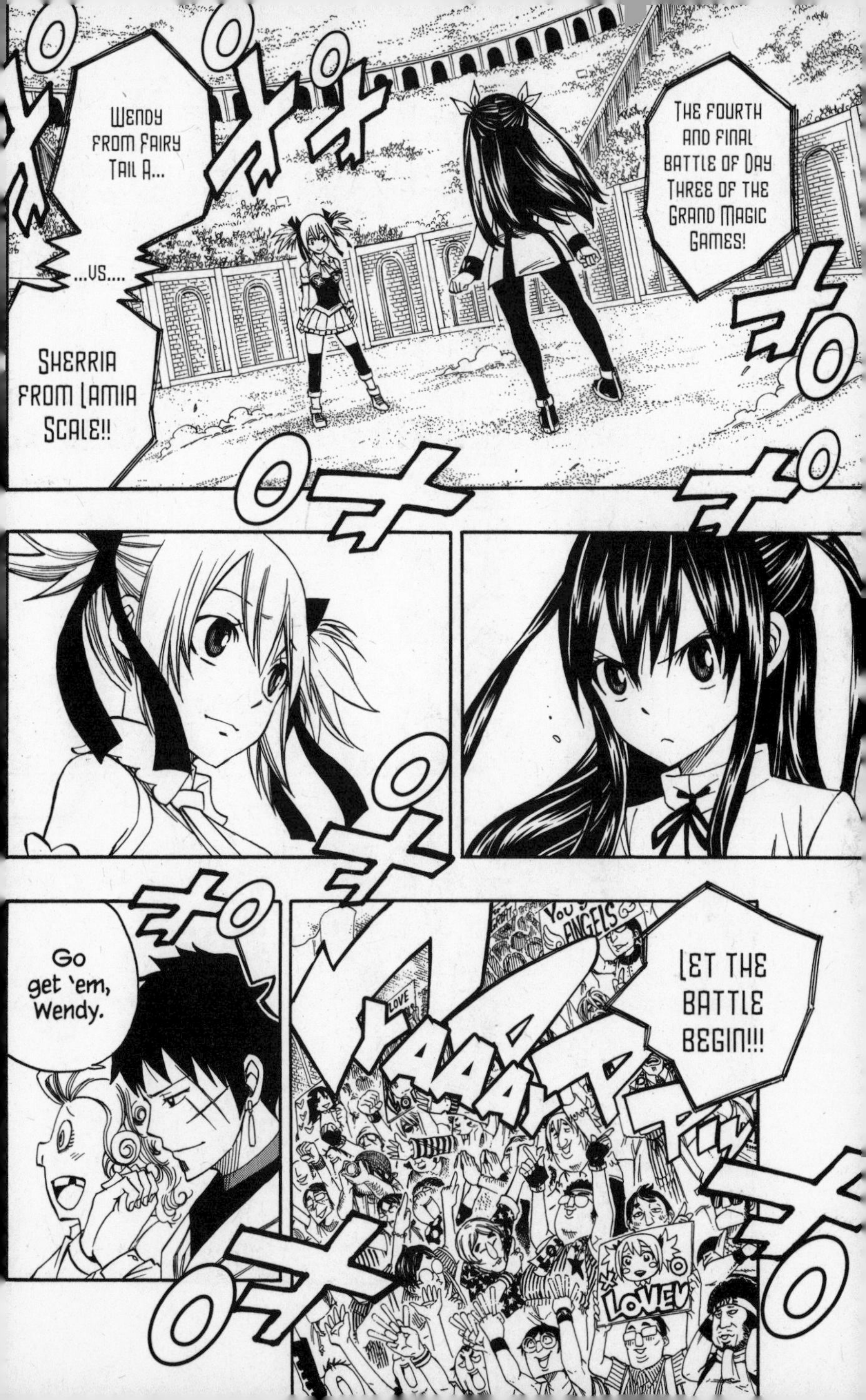
The fourth and final battle of Day Three of the Grand Magic Games!
Wendy from Fairy Tail A...
...vs....
Sherria from Lamia Scale!!
Let the battle begin!!!
LOVE
Go get 'em, Wendy.

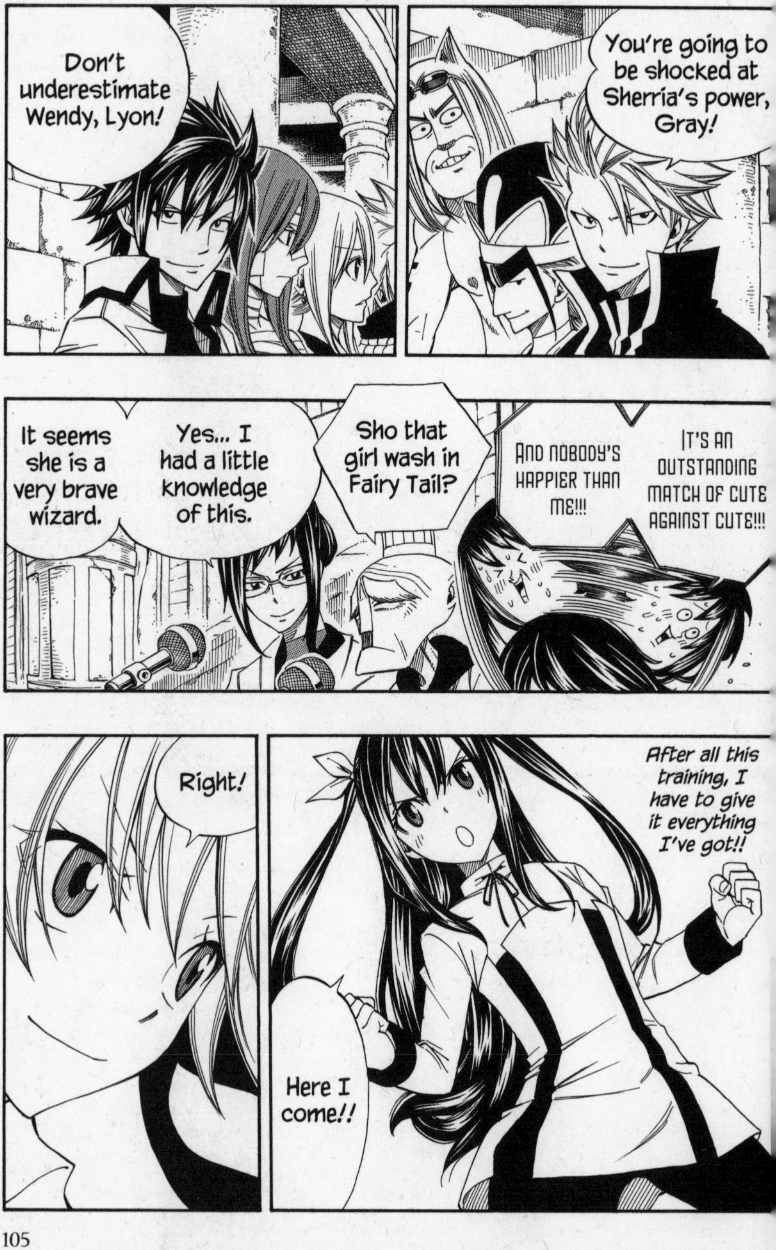
You're going to be shocked at Sherria's power, Gray!
Don't underestimate Wendy, Lyon!
IT'S AN OUTSTANDING MATCH OF CUTE AGAINST CUTE!!!
AND NOBODY'S HAPPIER THAN ME!!!
Sho that girl wash in Fairy Tail?
Yes... I had a little knowledge of this.
It seems she is a very brave wizard.
After all this training, I have to give it everything I've got!!
Here I come!!
Right!

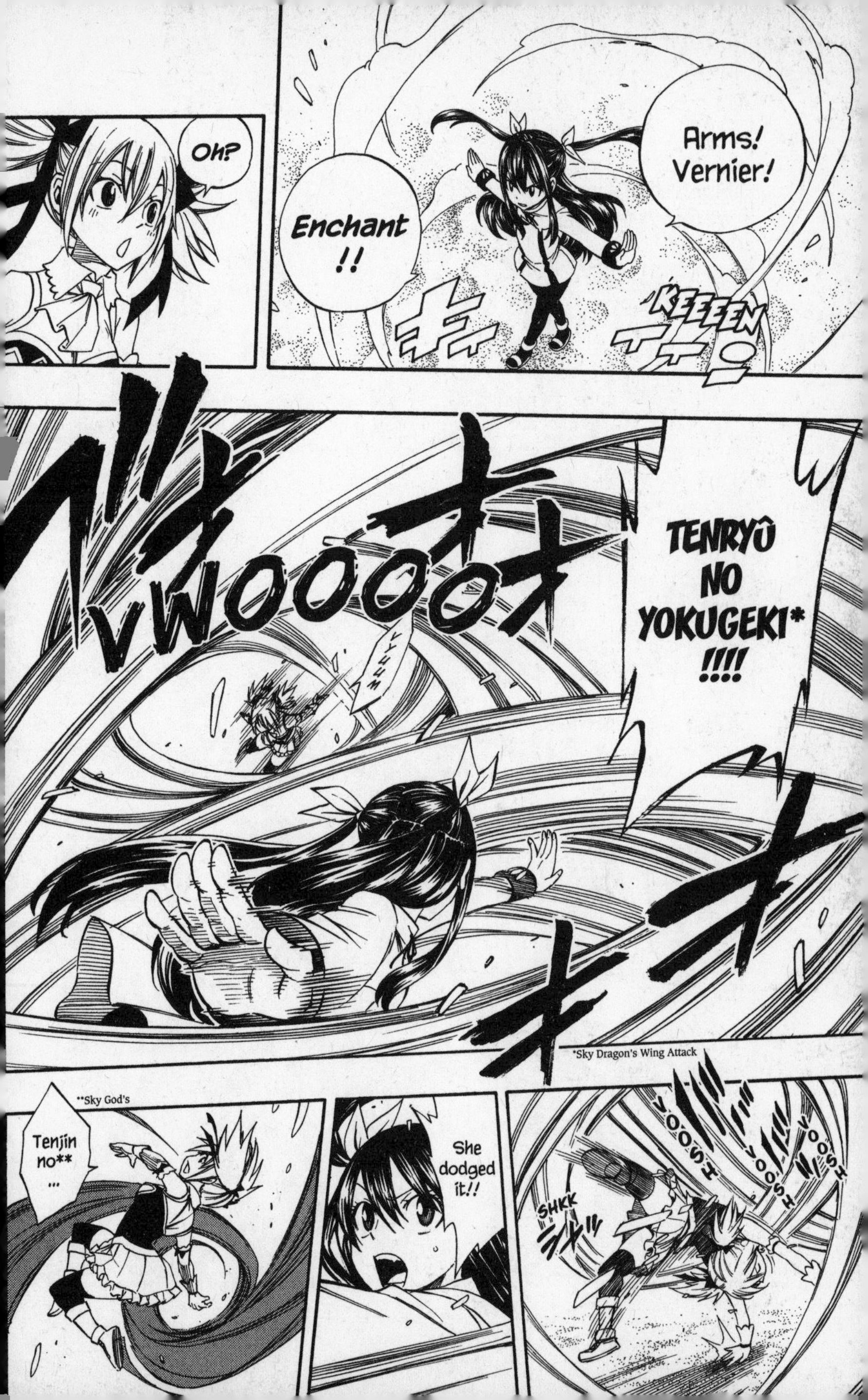

Arms! Vernier!
Enchant !!
KEEEEN
Oh?
TENRYÔ NO YOKUGEKI* !!!!
VWOOOOO
*Sky Dragon's Wing Attack
VOOSH
VOOSH
VOOSH
SHKK
She dodged it!!
Tenjin no** ...
**Sky God's

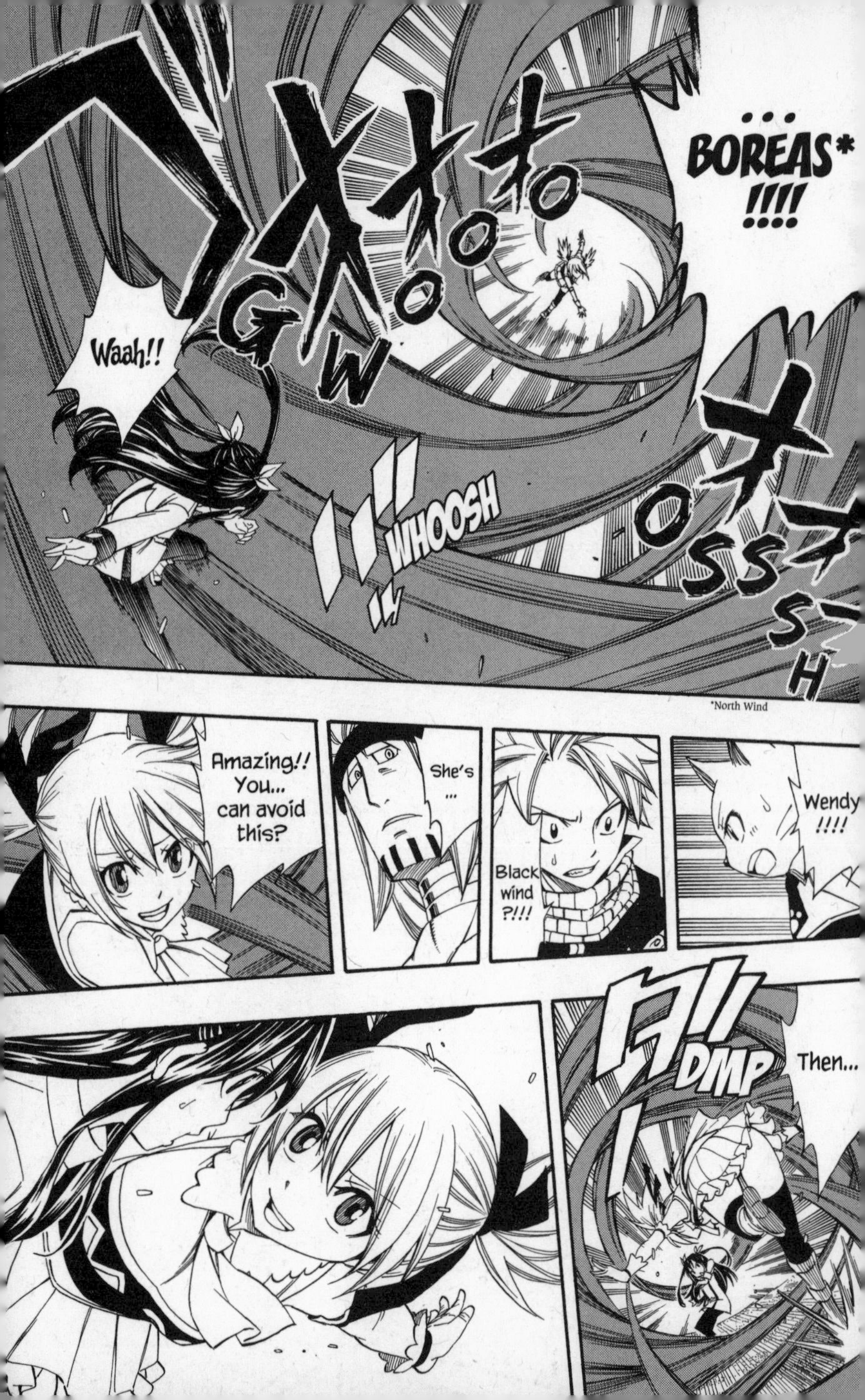
...BOREAS* !!!!
GWOOO
WHOOSH
Waah!!
Wendy !!!!
Black wind ?!!!
She's ...
Amazing!! You... can avoid this?
DMP
Then...
*North Wind

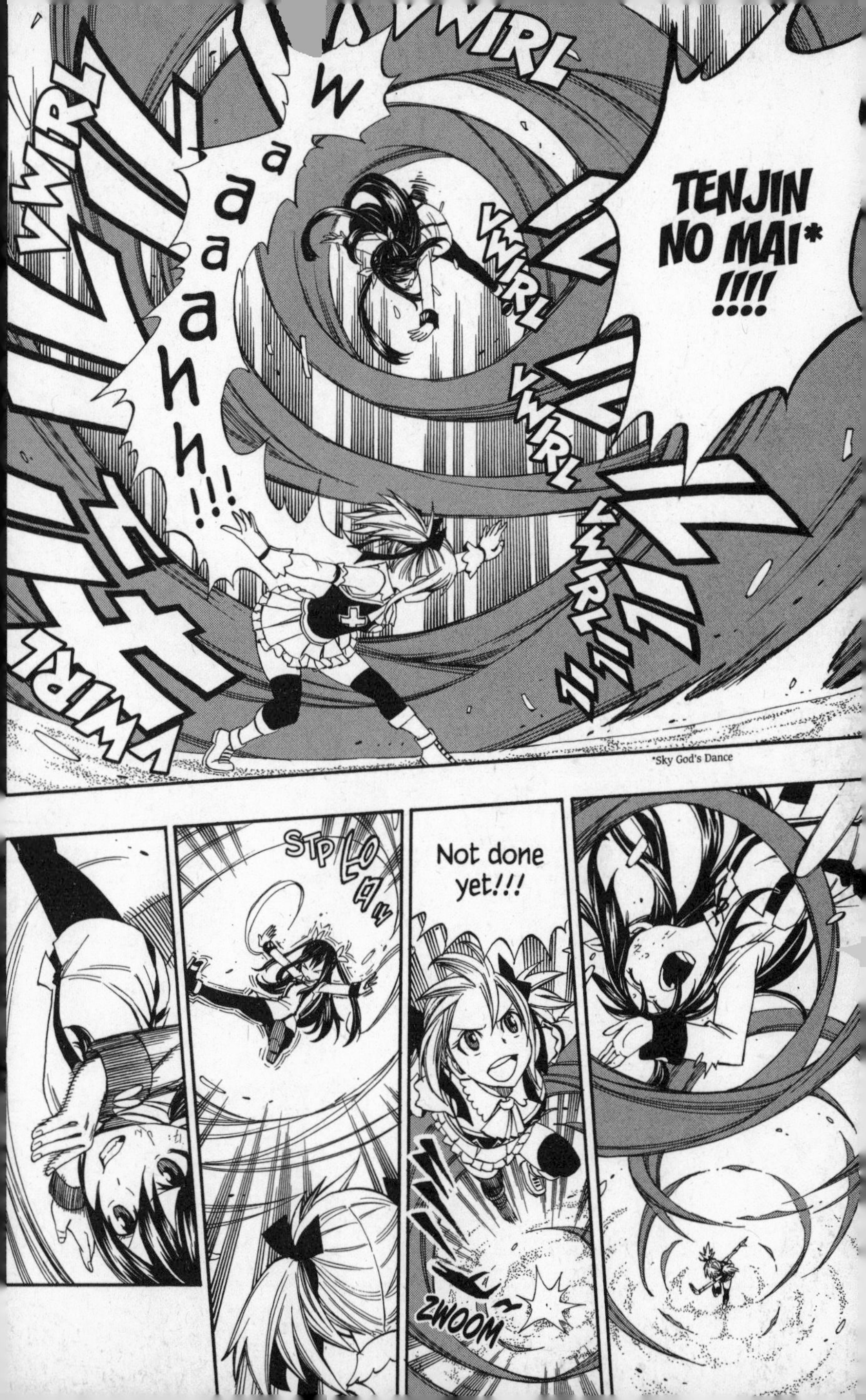
VWIRL
TENJIN NO MAI* !!!!
VWIRL
VWIRL
VWIRL!!!
Waaaahh!!!
VWIRL
VWIRL
*Sky God's Dance
Not done yet!!!
ZWOOM
STP

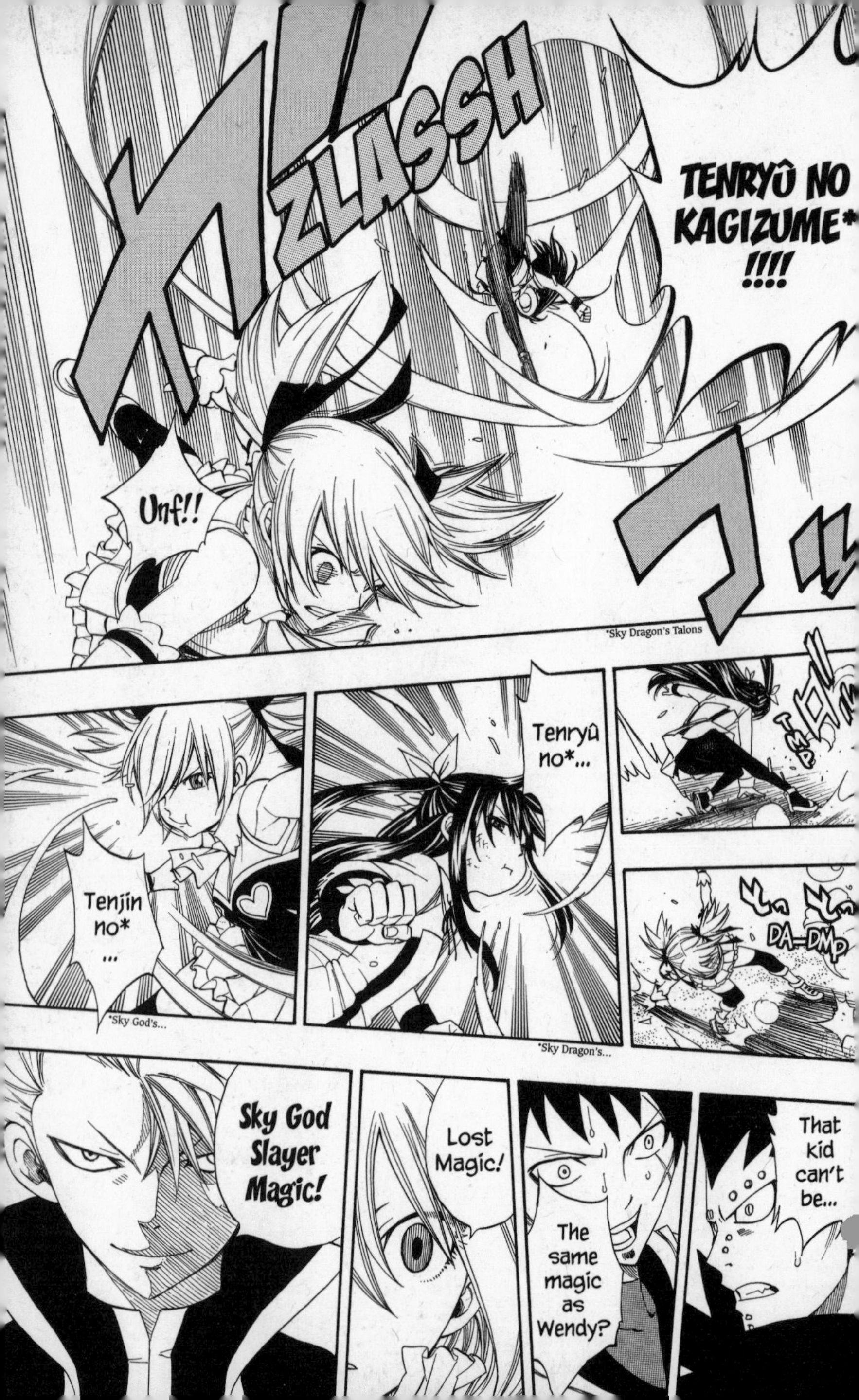
TENRYÛ NO KAGIZUME* !!!!
ZLASSH
Unf!!
*Sky Dragon's Talons
TMP
DA-DMP
Tenryû no*...
*Sky Dragon's...
Tenjin no* ...
*Sky God's...
That kid can't be...
The same magic as Wendy?
Lost Magic!
Sky God Slayer Magic!

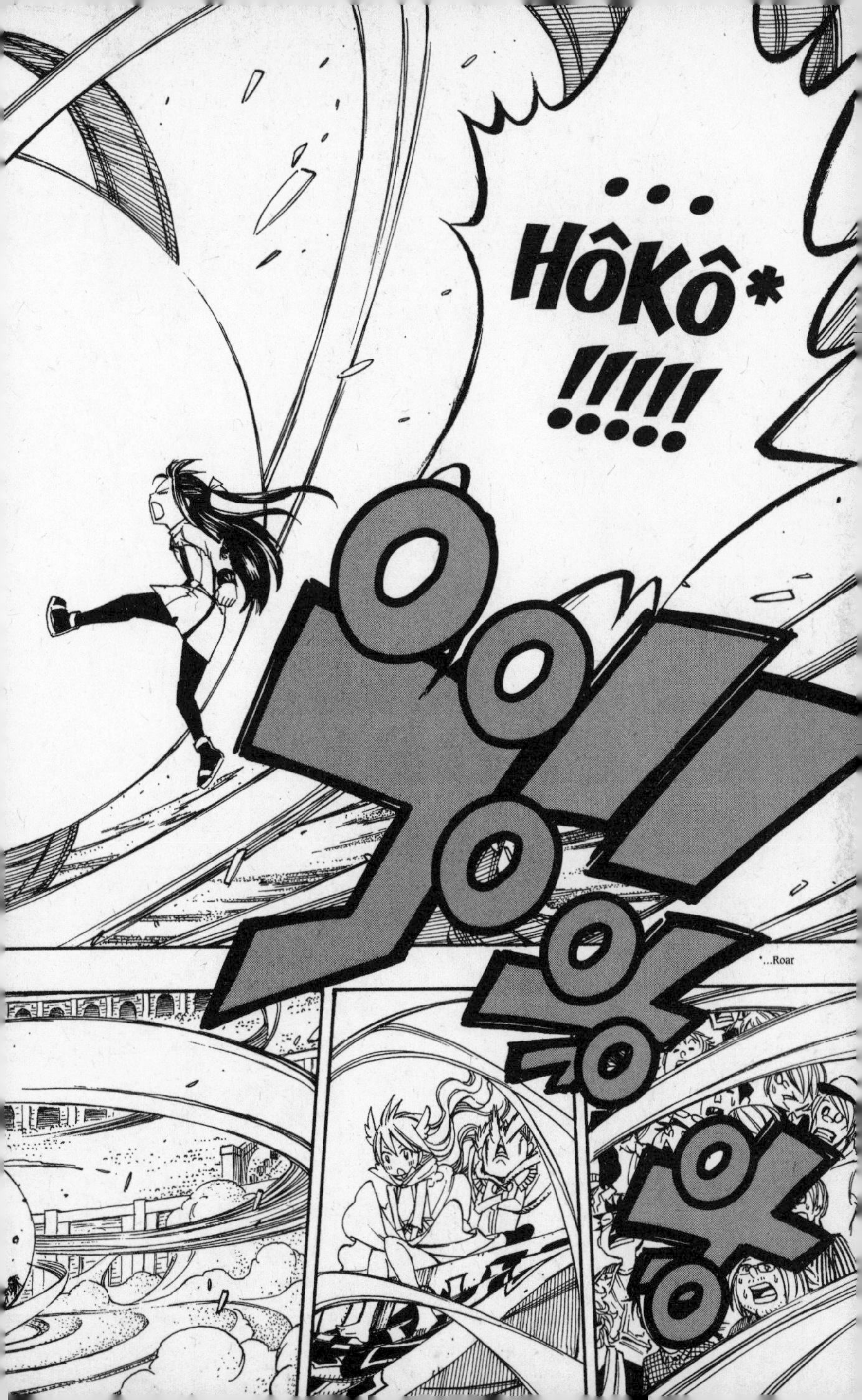
...HÔKÔ*
!!!!!
*...Roar

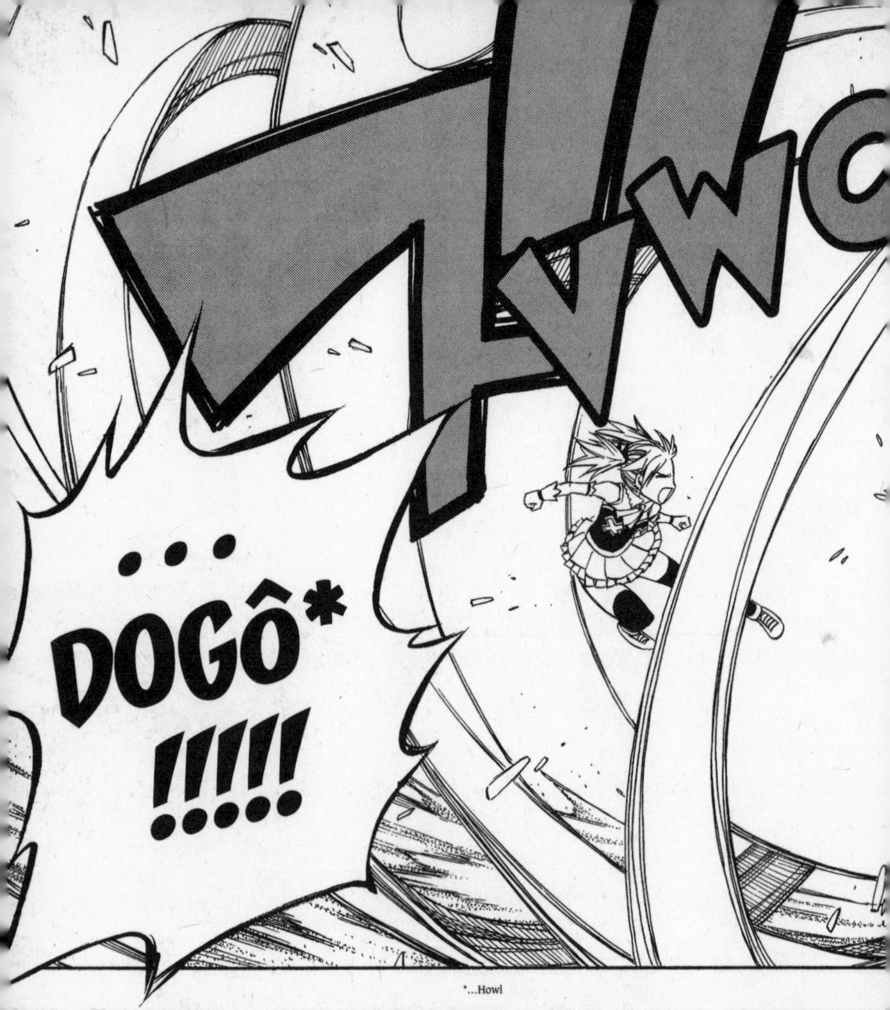
...DOGÔ*!!!!!

*...Howl

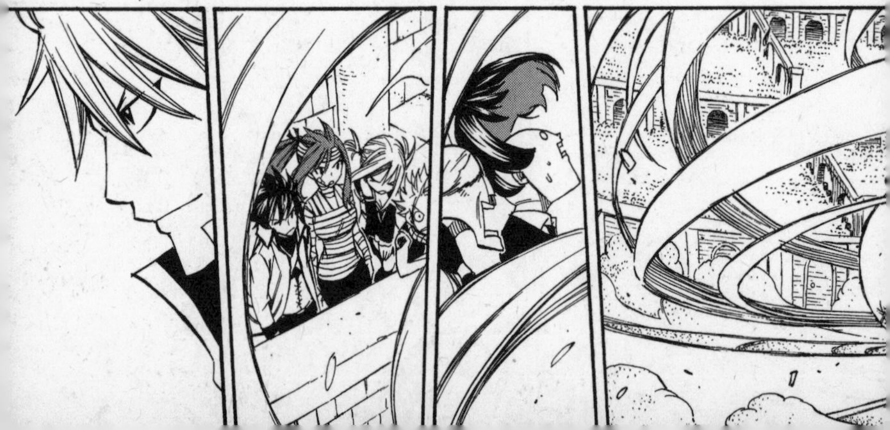

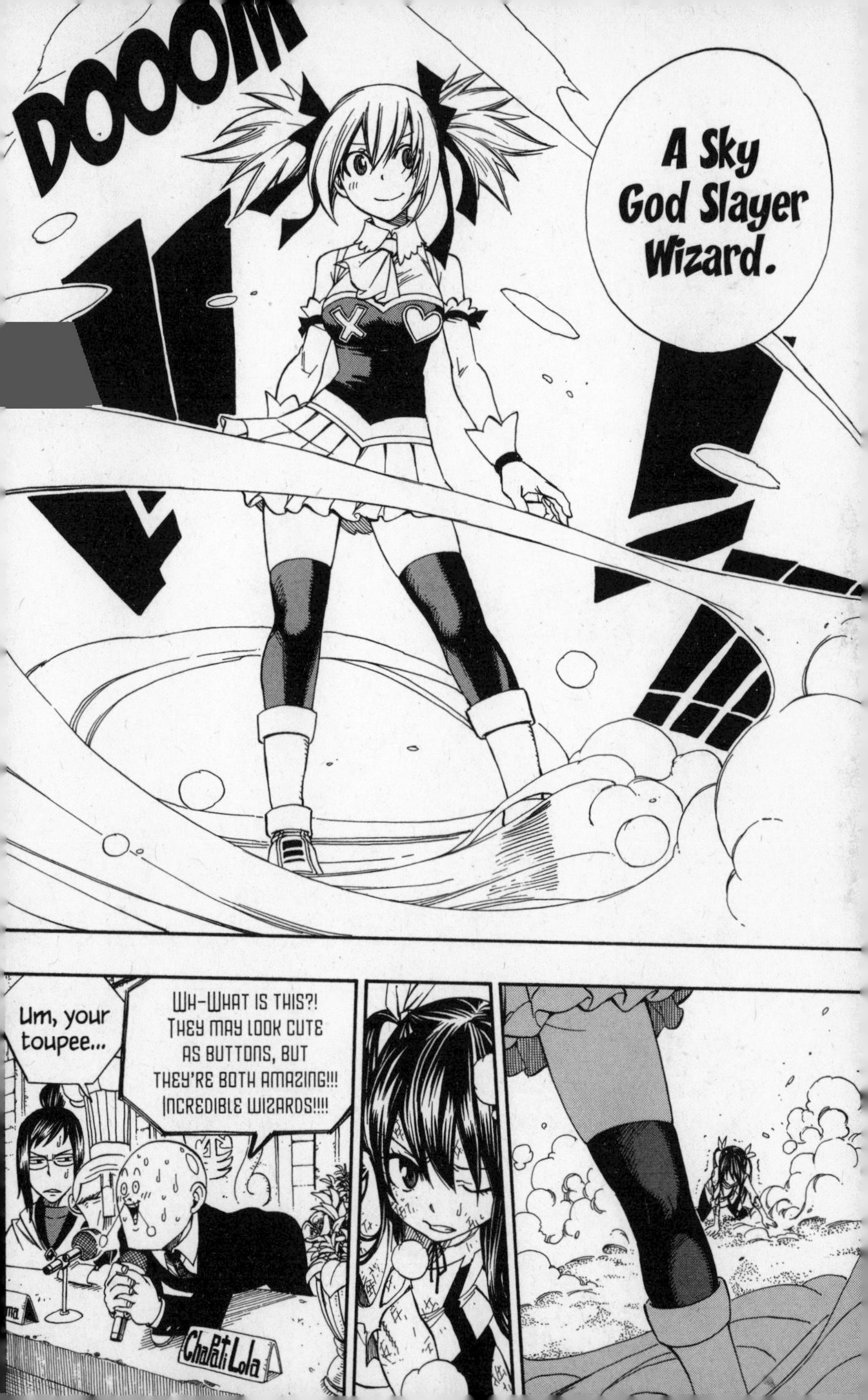
A Sky God Slayer Wizard.
DOOOM
WH-WHAT IS THIS?! THEY MAY LOOK CUTE AS BUTTONS, BUT THEY'RE BOTH AMAZING!!! INCREDIBLE WIZARDS!!!!
Um, your toupee...
ChaPaTi LoLa

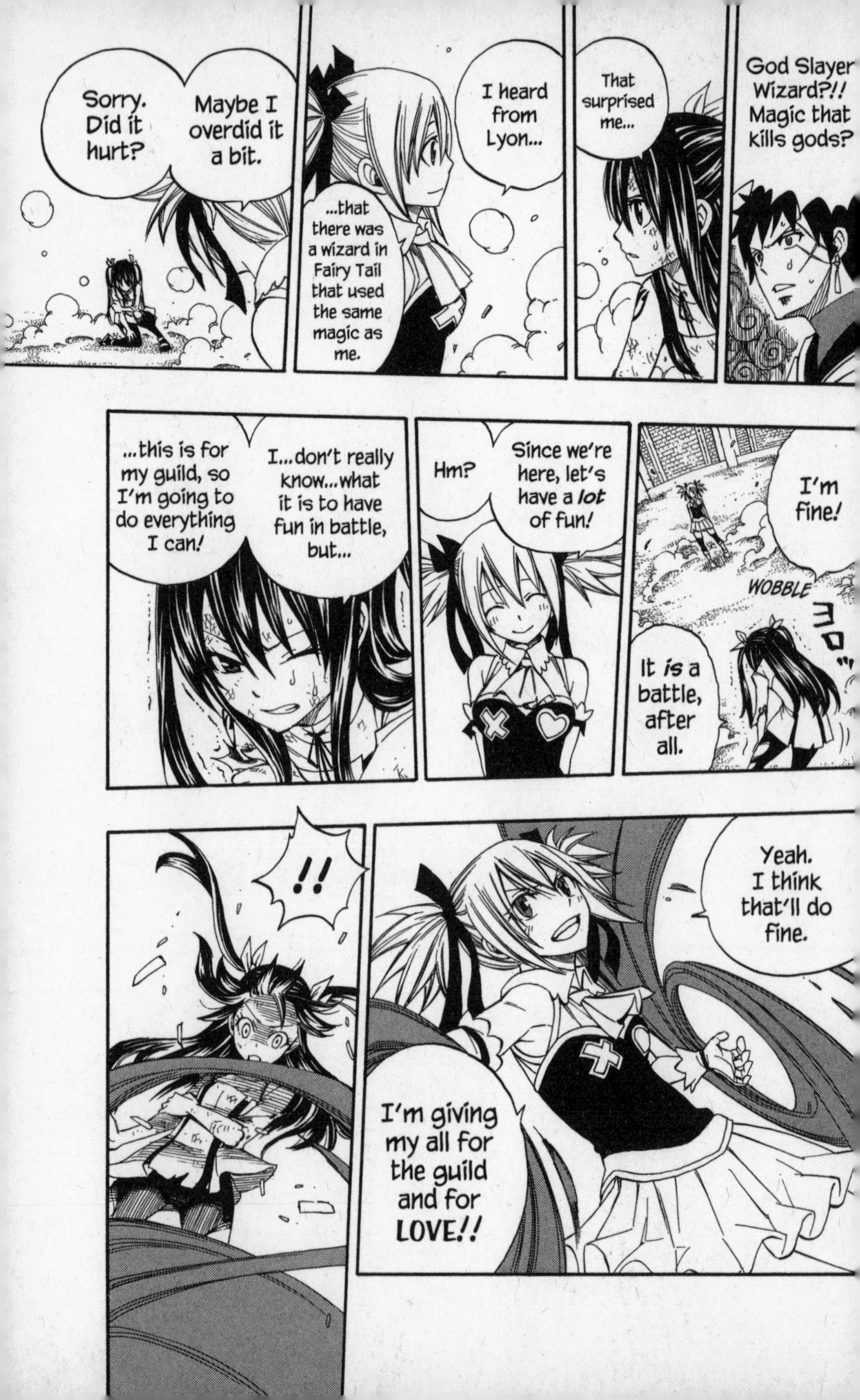
God Slayer Wizard?!! Magic that kills gods?
That surprised me...
I heard from Lyon...
...that there was a wizard in Fairy Tail that used the same magic as me.
Maybe I overdid it a bit.
Sorry. Did it hurt?
I'm fine!
WOBBLE
ヨロ…
It *is* a battle, after all.
Since we're here, let's have a *lot* of fun!
Hm?
I...don't really know...what it is to have fun in battle, but...
...this is for my guild, so I'm going to do everything I can!
Yeah. I think that'll do fine.
I'm giving my all for the guild and for **LOVE**!!
!!

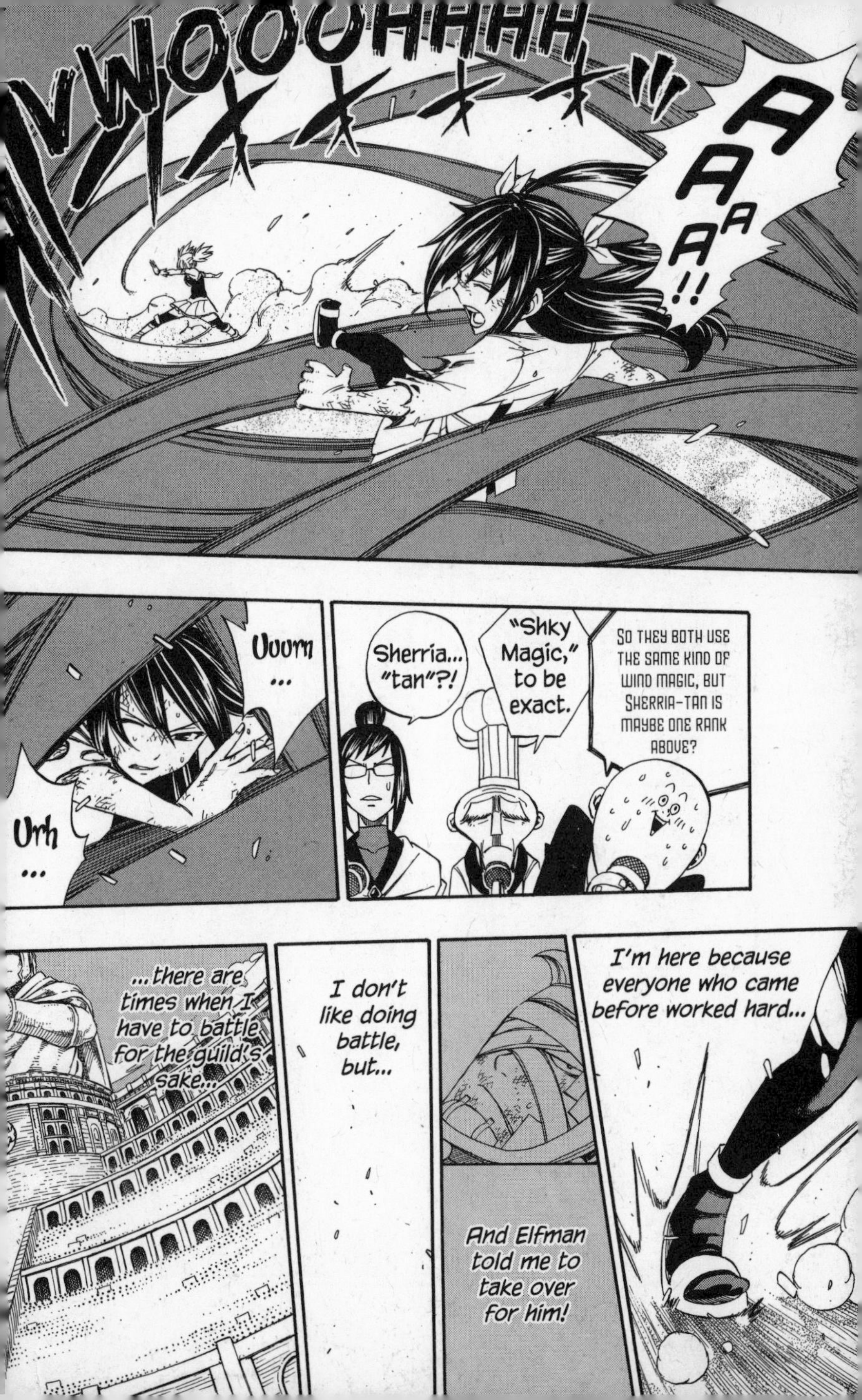
VWOOOHHHH
AAAA!!
SO THEY BOTH USE THE SAME KIND OF WIND MAGIC, BUT SHERRIA-TAN IS MAYBE ONE RANK ABOVE?
"Shky Magic," to be exact.
Sherria... "tan"?!
Uoorn...
Urh...
I'm here because everyone who came before worked hard...
And Elfman told me to take over for him!
I don't like doing battle, but...
...there are times when I have to battle for the guild's sake...

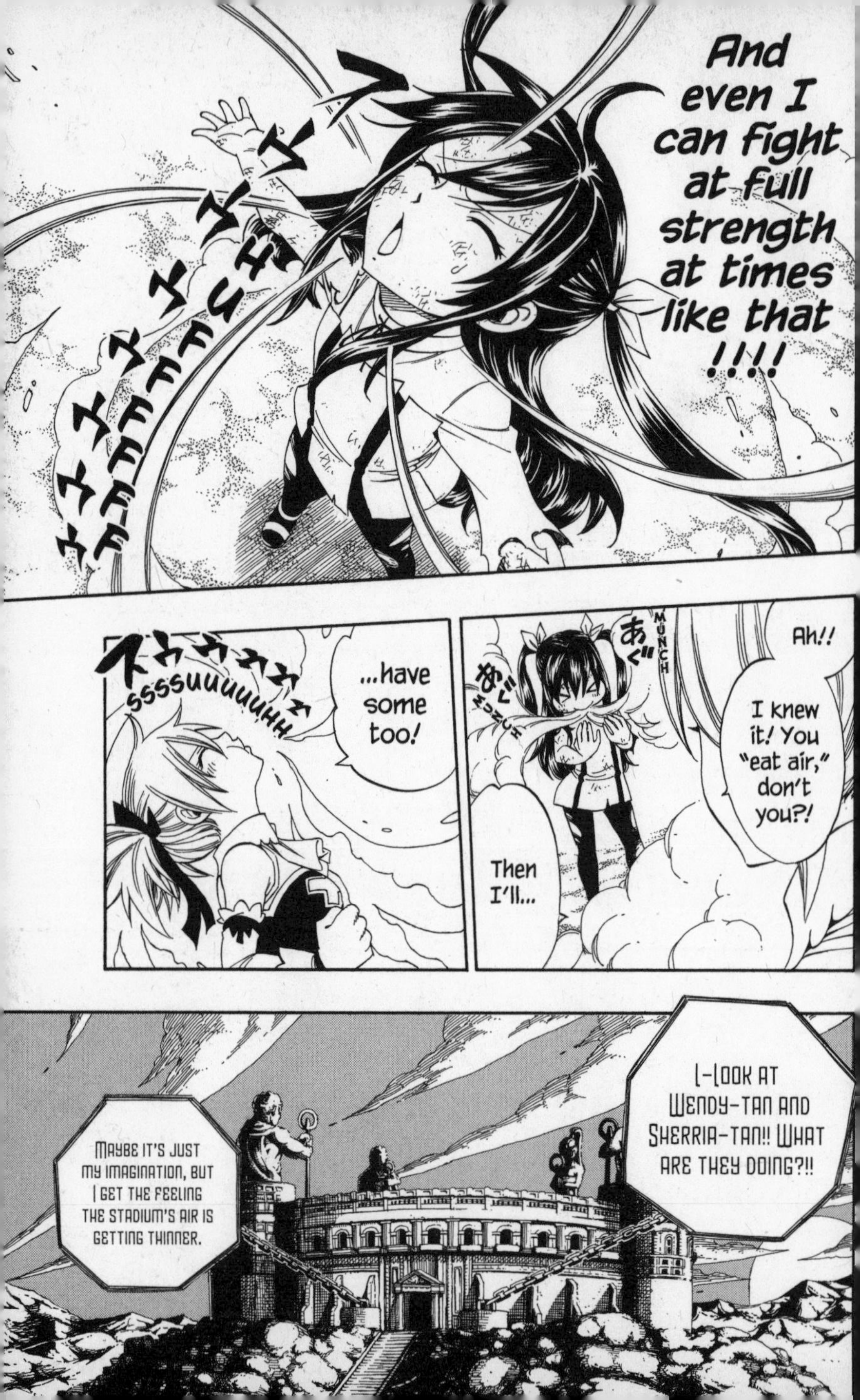

And even I can fight at full strength at times like that!!!!
HUFFFFFFFFF
Ah!!
I knew it! You "eat air," don't you?!
あぐ
MUNCH
あぐ
MUNCH
Then I'll...
...have some too!
SSSSUUUUUUHH
L-LOOK AT WENDY-TAN AND SHERRIA-TAN!! WHAT ARE THEY DOING?!!
MAYBE IT'S JUST MY IMAGINATION, BUT I GET THE FEELING THE STADIUM'S AIR IS GETTING THINNER.

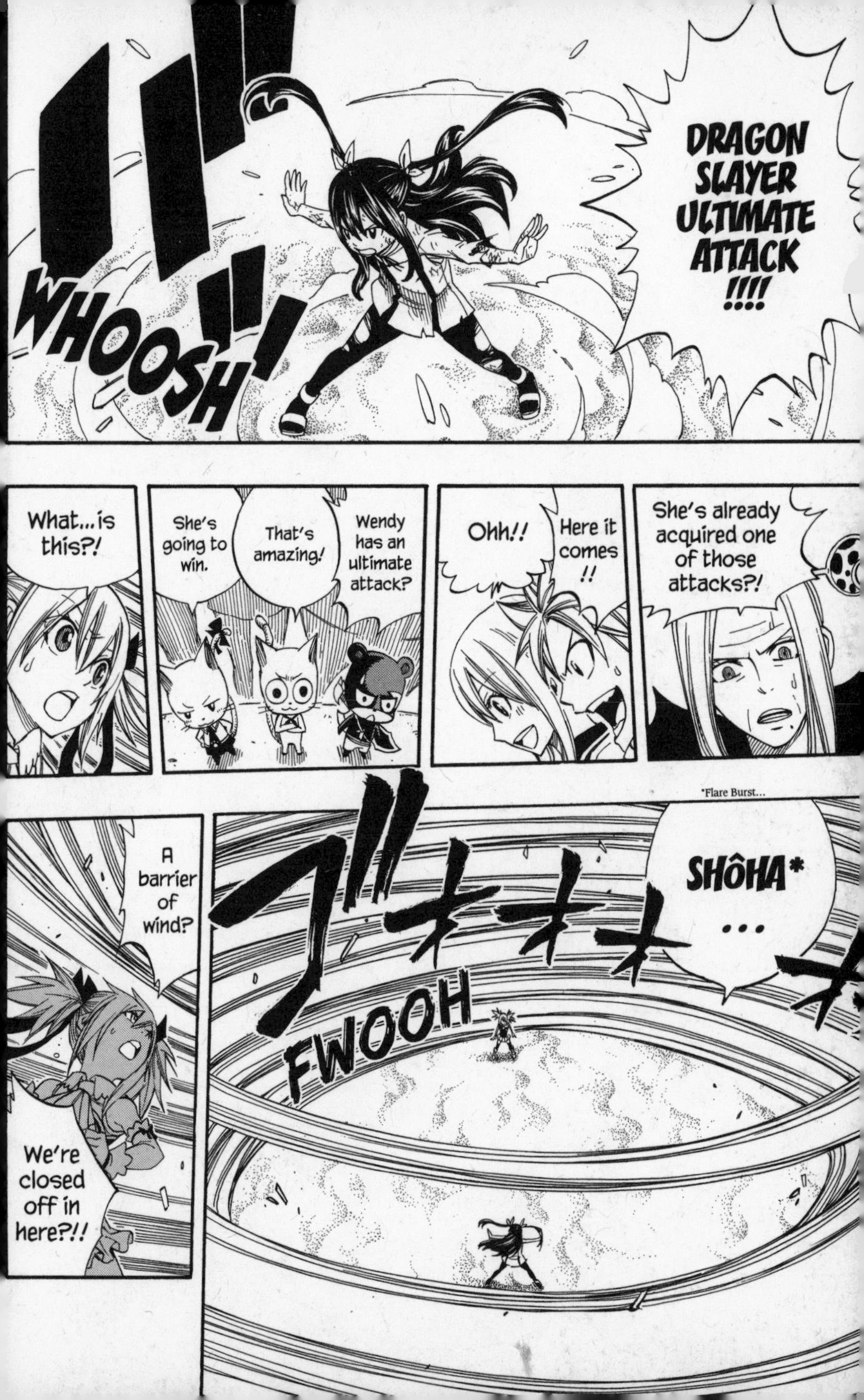
DRAGON SLAYER ULTIMATE ATTACK!!!!
WHOOSH!!
She's already acquired one of those attacks?!
Here it comes!!
Ohh!!
Wendy has an ultimate attack?
That's amazing!
She's going to win.
What...is this?!
SHÔHA*...
FWOOH
A barrier of wind?
We're closed off in here?!!
*Flare Burst...

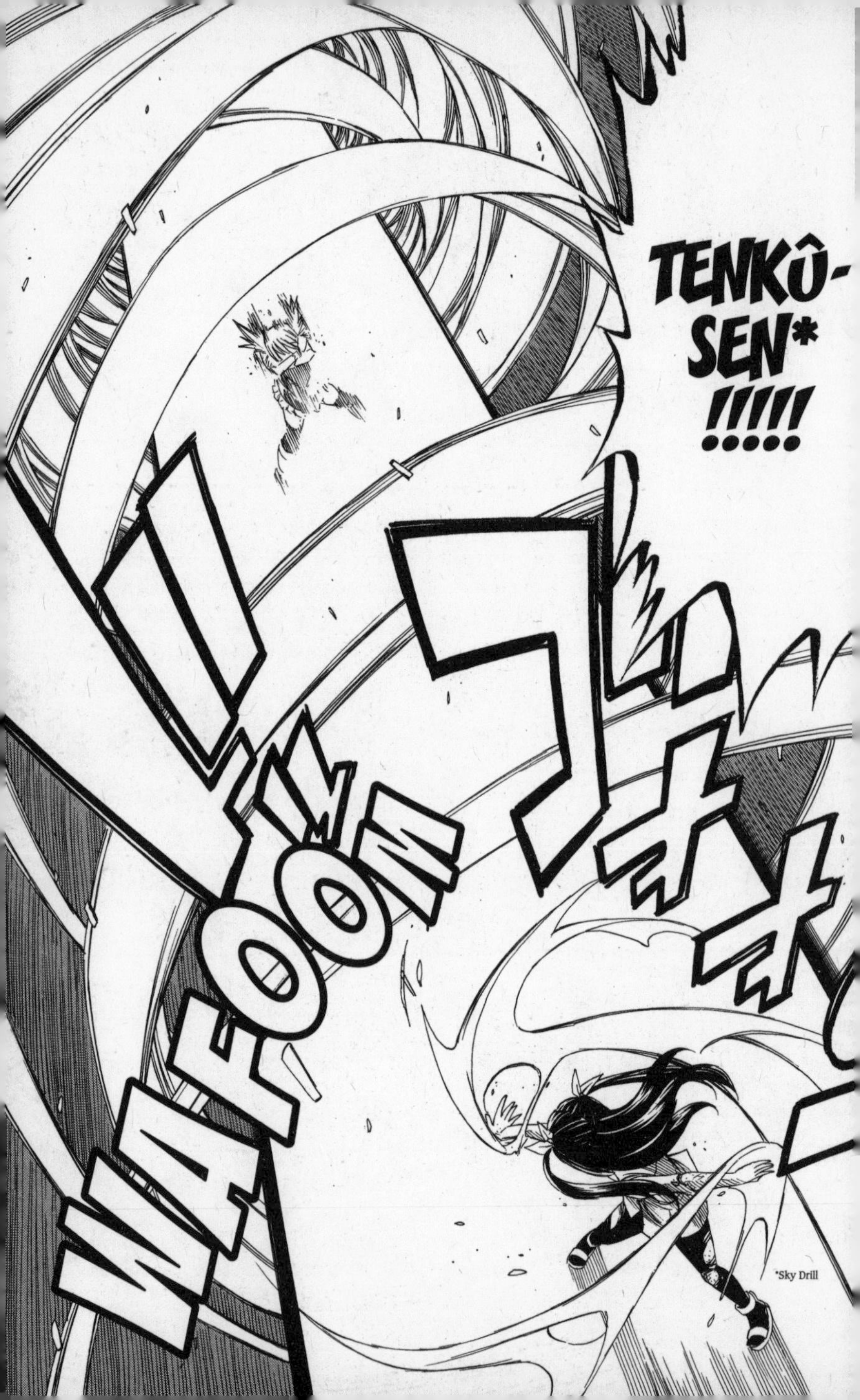
TENKÛ-SEN*!!!!!
WHOOOM

*Sky Drill

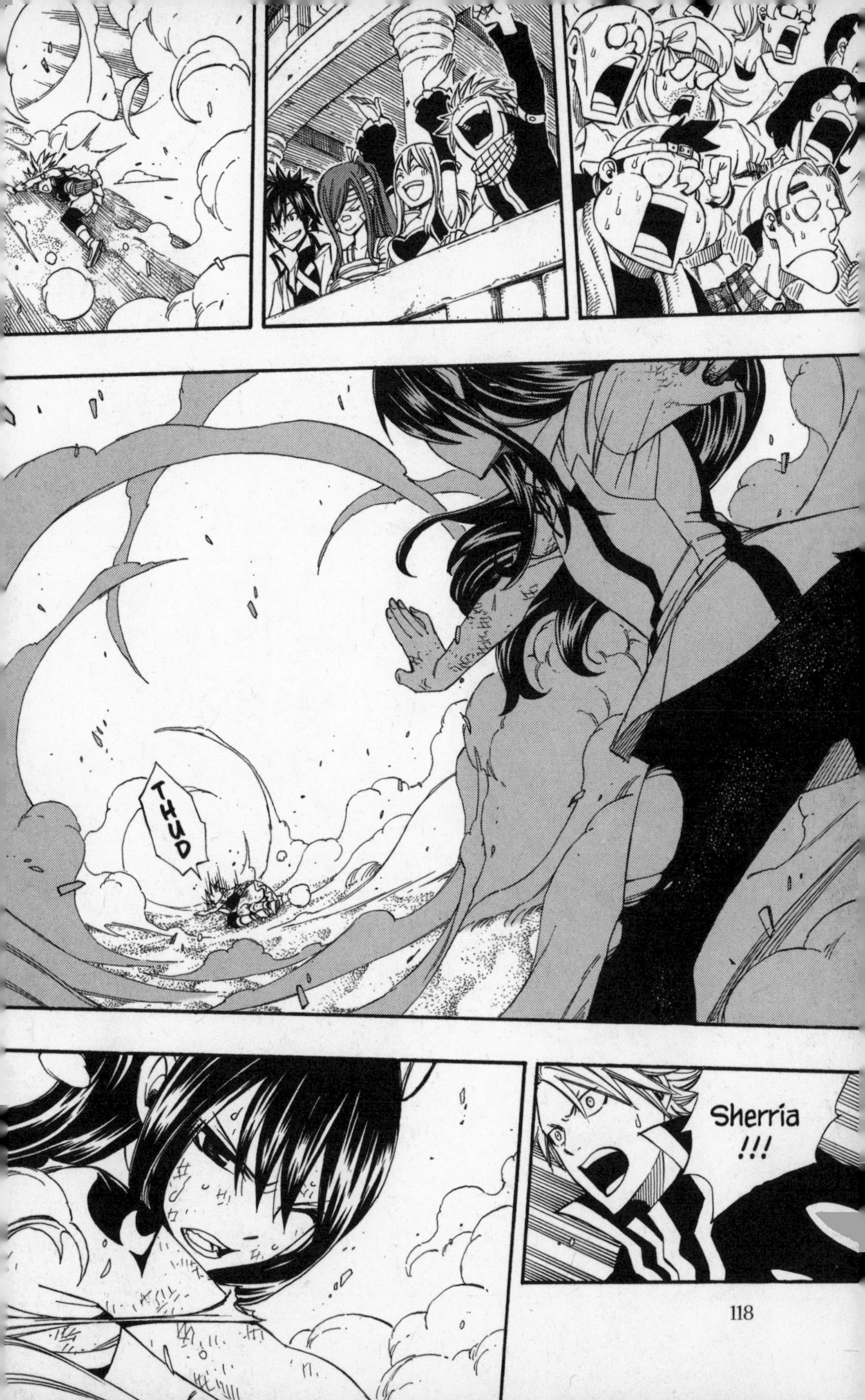
THUD
Sherria !!!

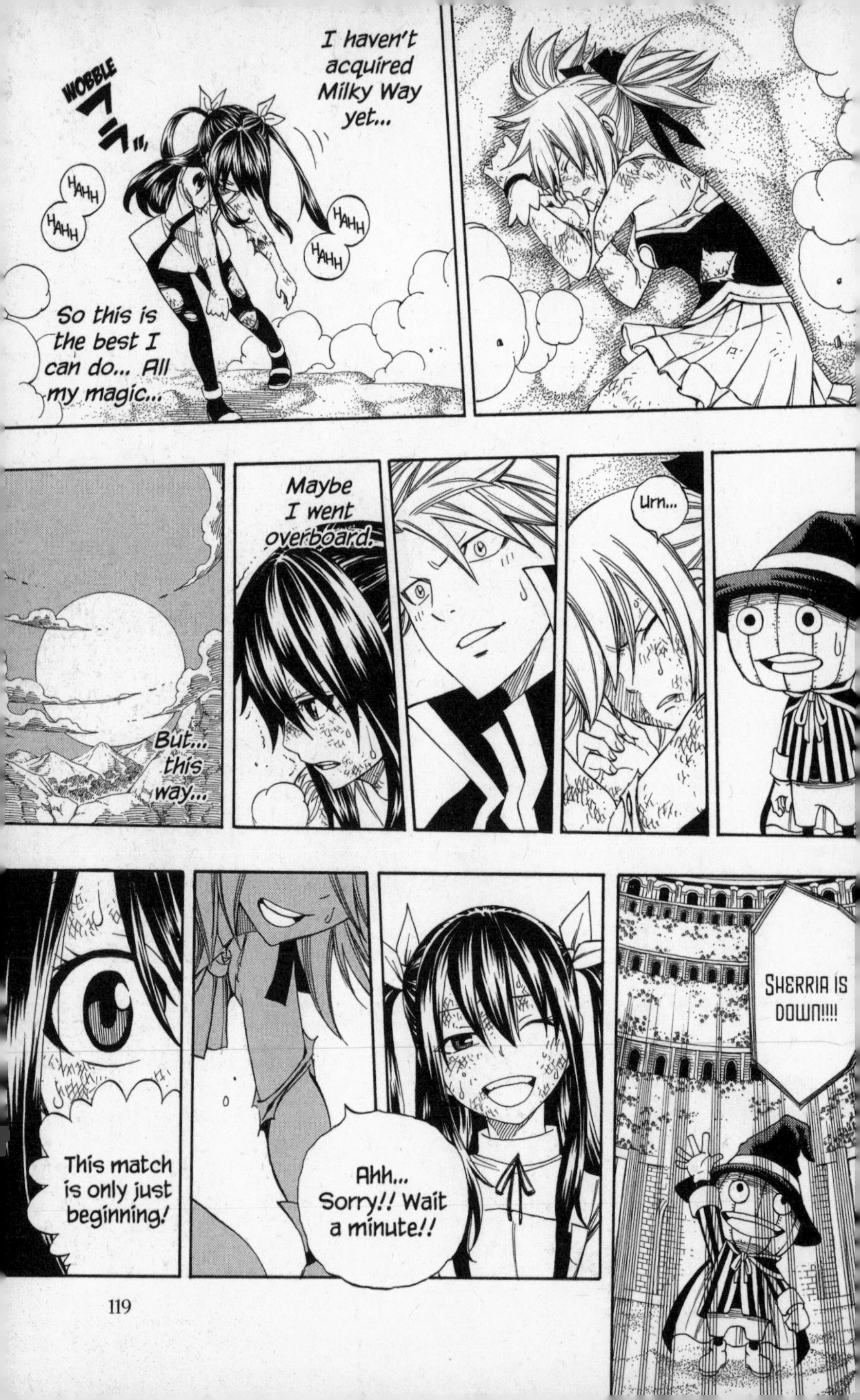
I haven't acquired Milky Way yet...
WOBBLE
HAHH
HAHH
HAHH
HAHH
So this is the best I can do... All my magic...
Urn...
Maybe I went overboard.
But... this way...
SHERRIA IS DOWN!!!!
Ahh... Sorry!! Wait a minute!!
This match is only just beginning!

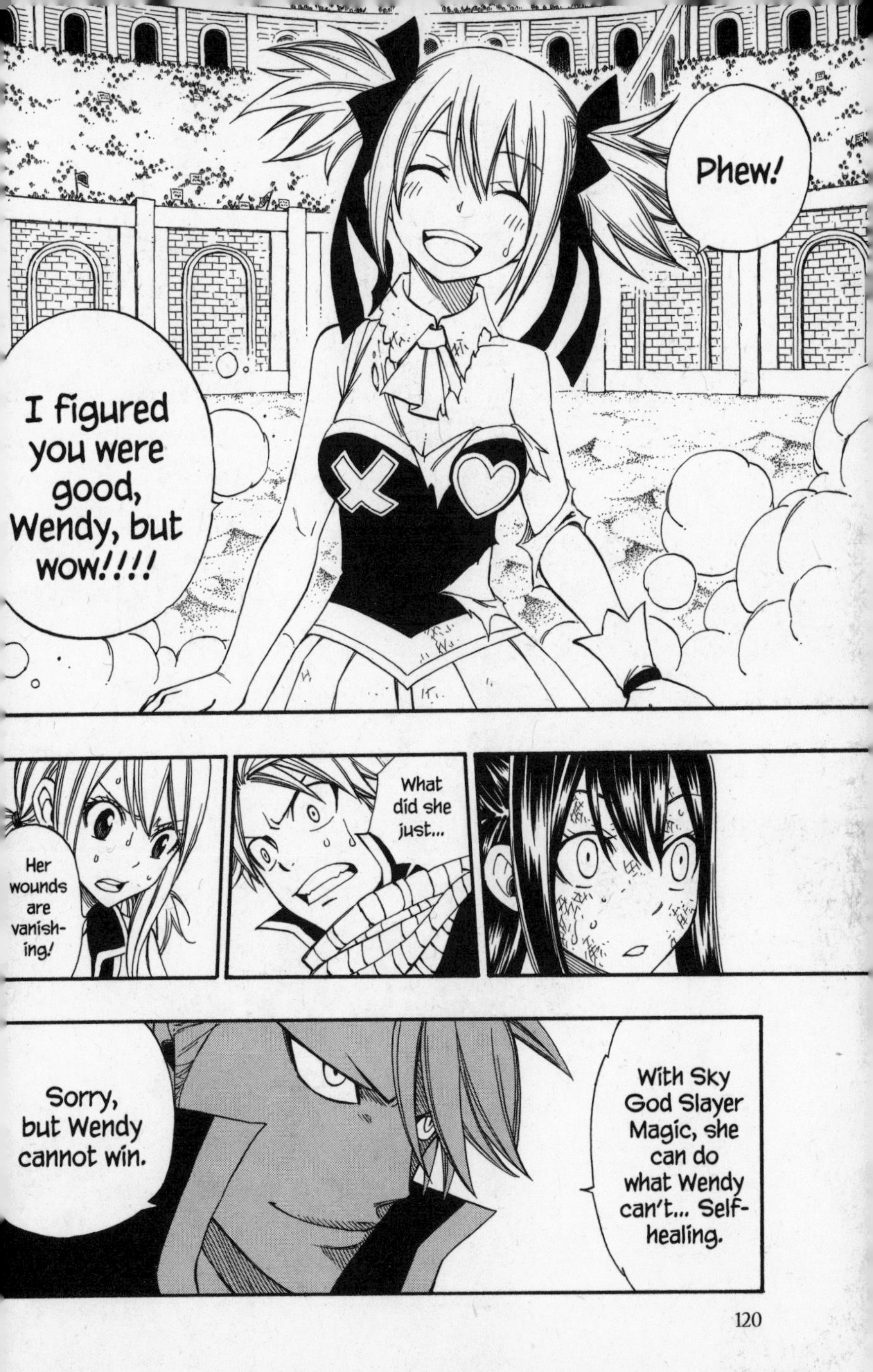
Phew!
I figured you were good, Wendy, but wow!!!!
What did she just...
Her wounds are vanish-ing!
With Sky God Slayer Magic, she can do what Wendy can't... Self-healing.
Sorry, but Wendy cannot win.

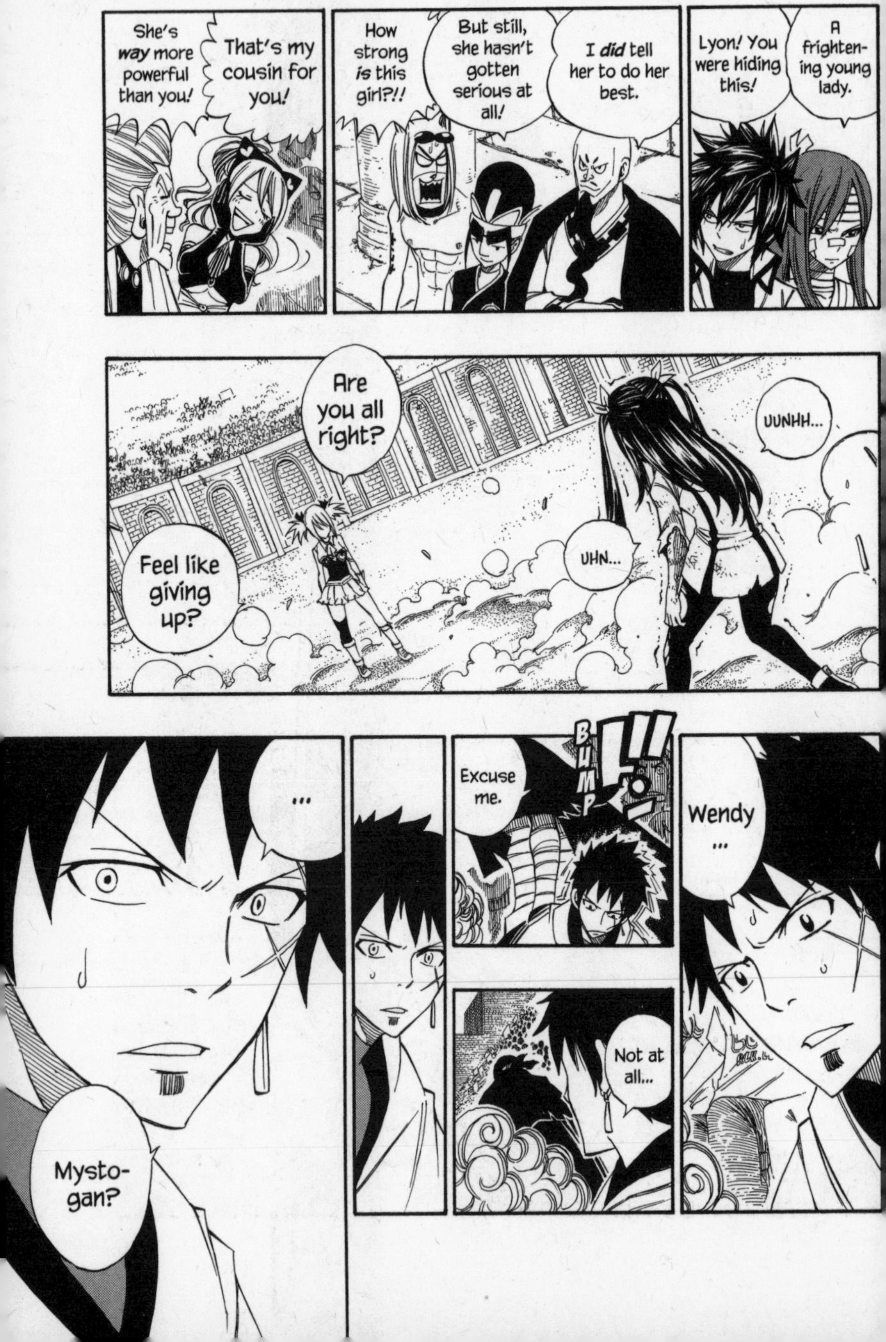
A frighten-ing young lady.
Lyon! You were hiding this!
I *did* tell her to do her best.
But still, she hasn't gotten serious at all!
How strong *is* this girl?!!
That's my cousin for you!
She's *way* more powerful than you!
UUNHH...
Are you all right?
UHN...
Feel like giving up?
Wendy ...
BUMP
Excuse me.
Not at all...
...
Mysto-gan?

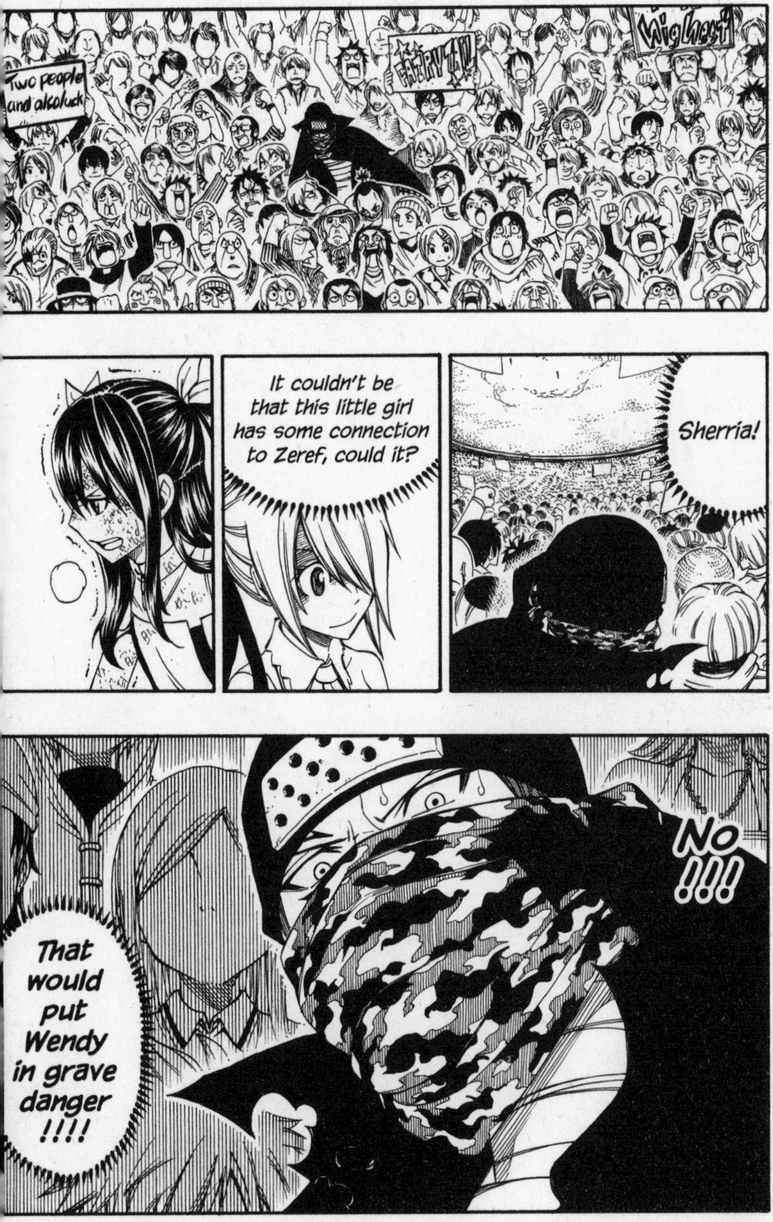
Wighest
FAIRY TAIL!!
Two people and alsoluck
Sherria!
It couldn't be that this little girl has some connection to Zeref, could it?
No!!!
That would put Wendy in grave danger!!!!

FAIRY TAIL
フェアリーテイル

Chapter 289: Tiny Fists

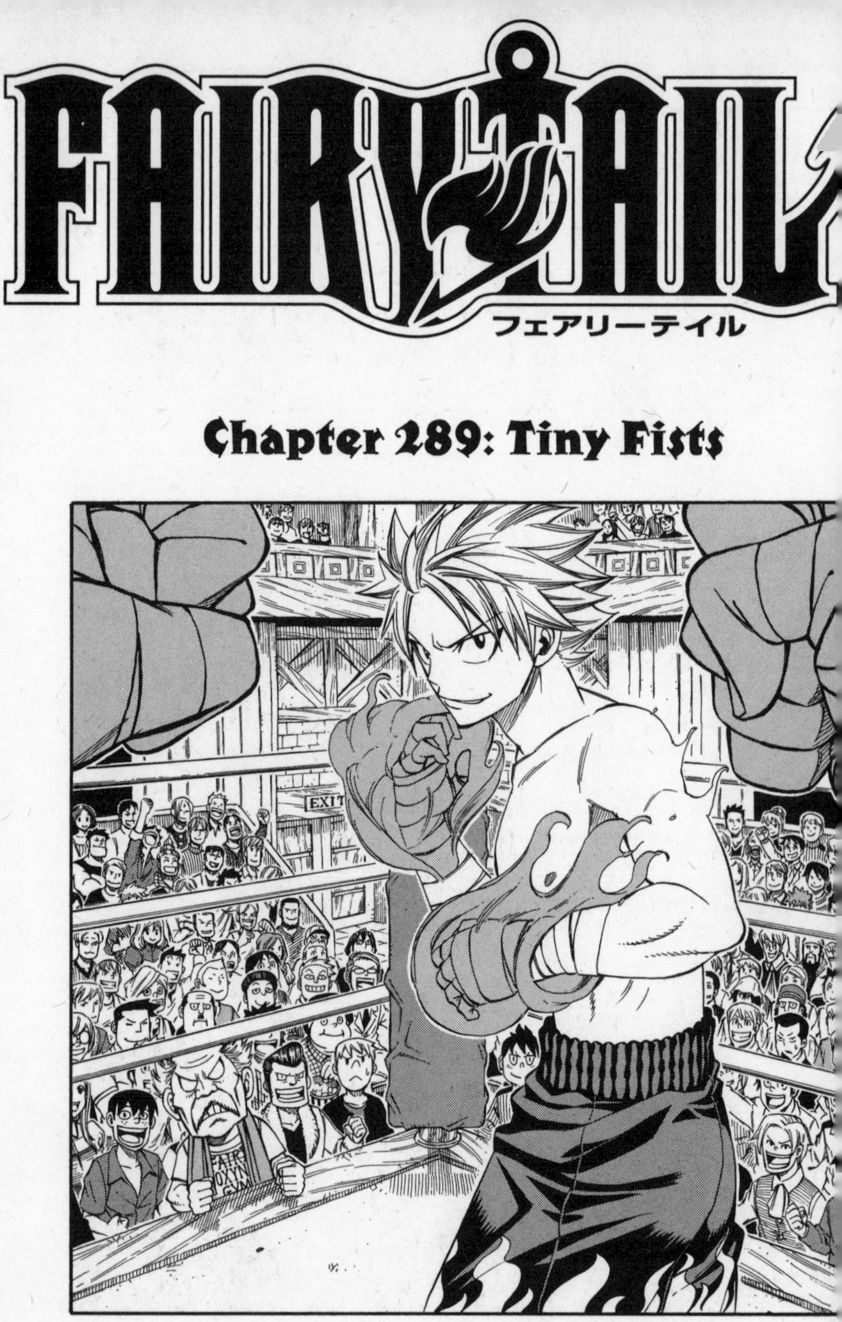
EXIT

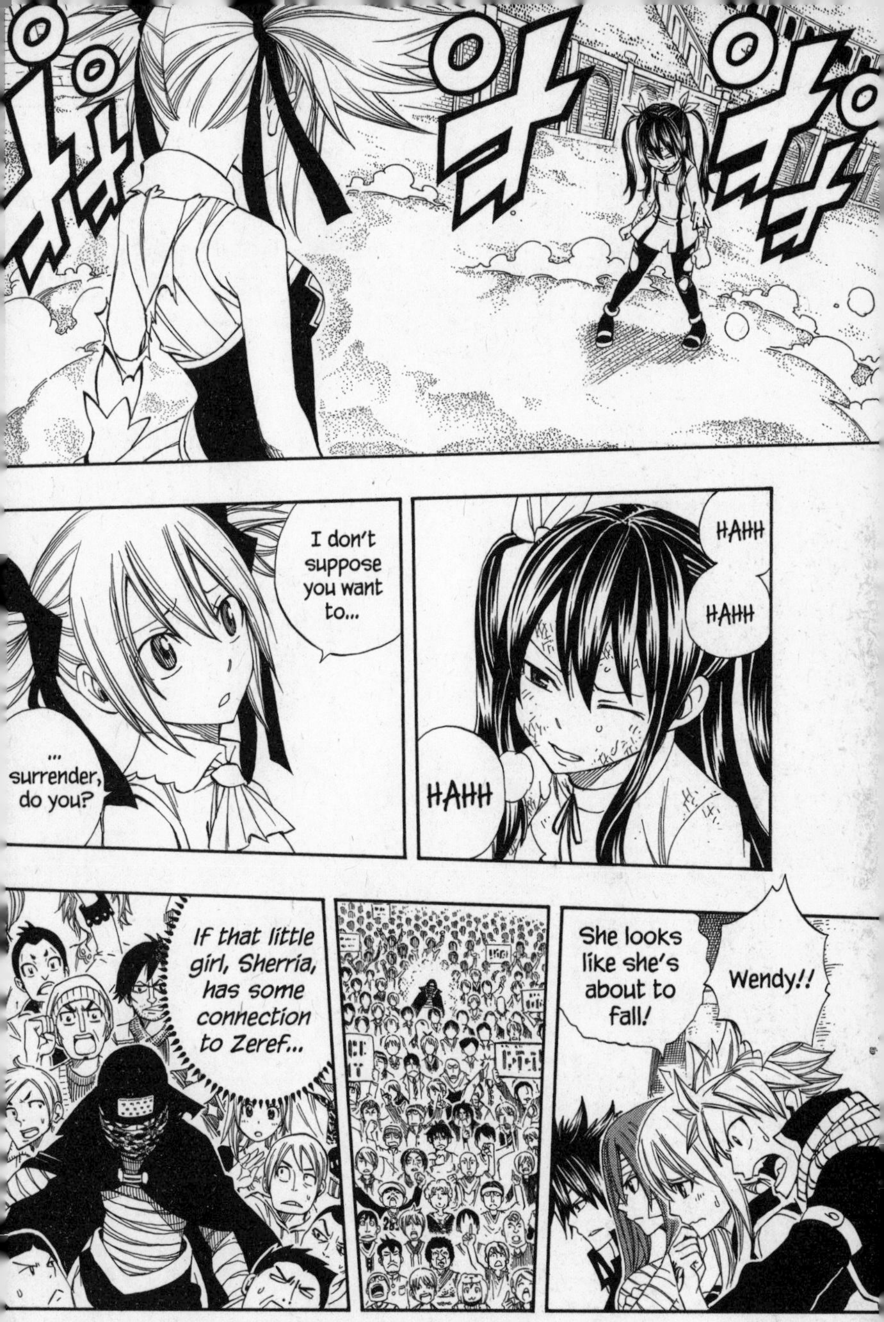
HAHH
HAHH
HAHH
I don't suppose you want to...
... surrender, do you?
Wendy!!
She looks like she's about to fall!
If that little girl, Sherria, has some connection to Zeref...

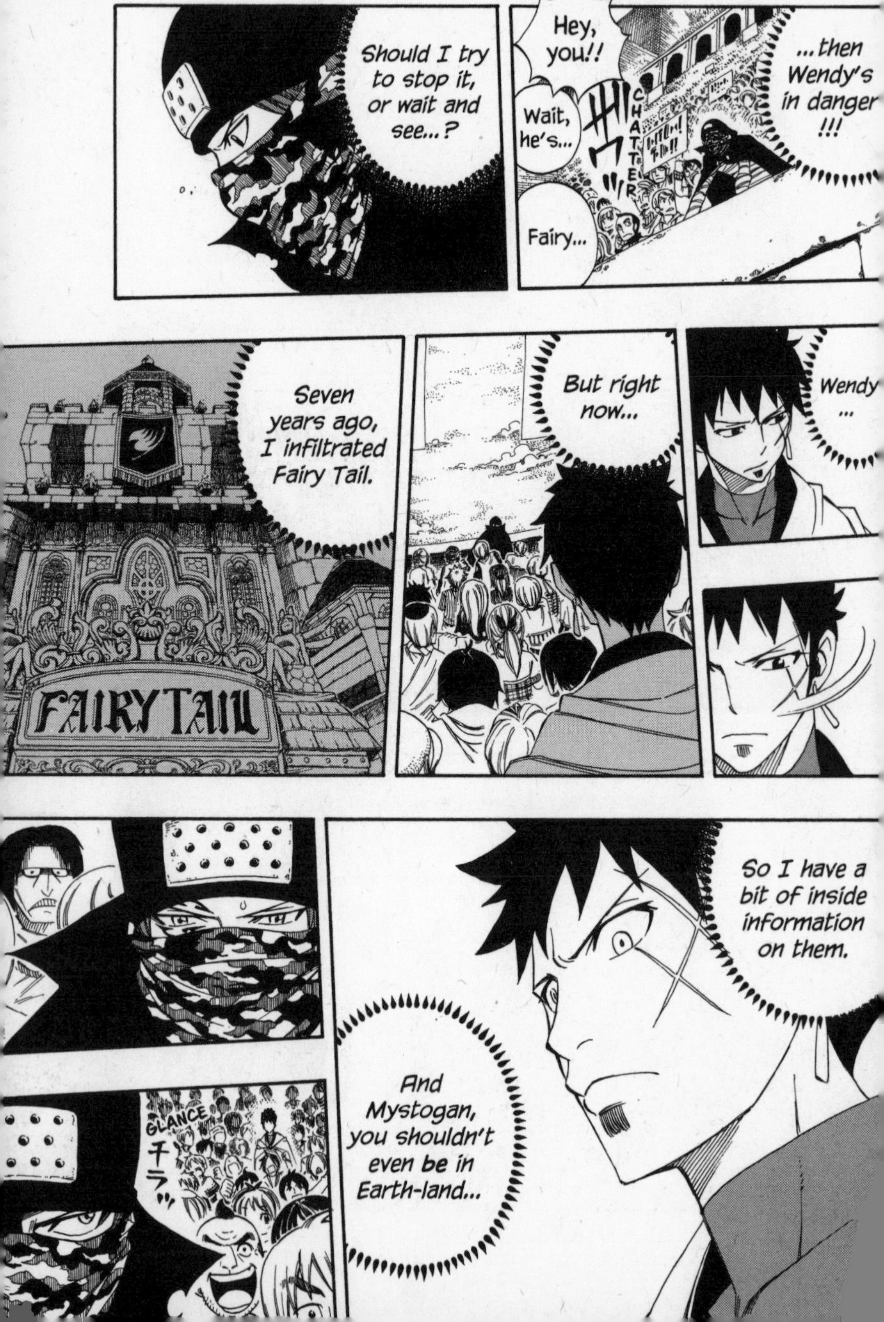
...then Wendy's in danger !!!
Hey, you!!
CHATTER
Wait, he's...
Fairy...
Should I try to stop it, or wait and see...?
Wendy ...
But right now...
Seven years ago, I infiltrated Fairy Tail.
FAIRY TAIL
So I have a bit of inside information on them.
And Mystogan, you shouldn't even be in Earth-land...
GLANCE

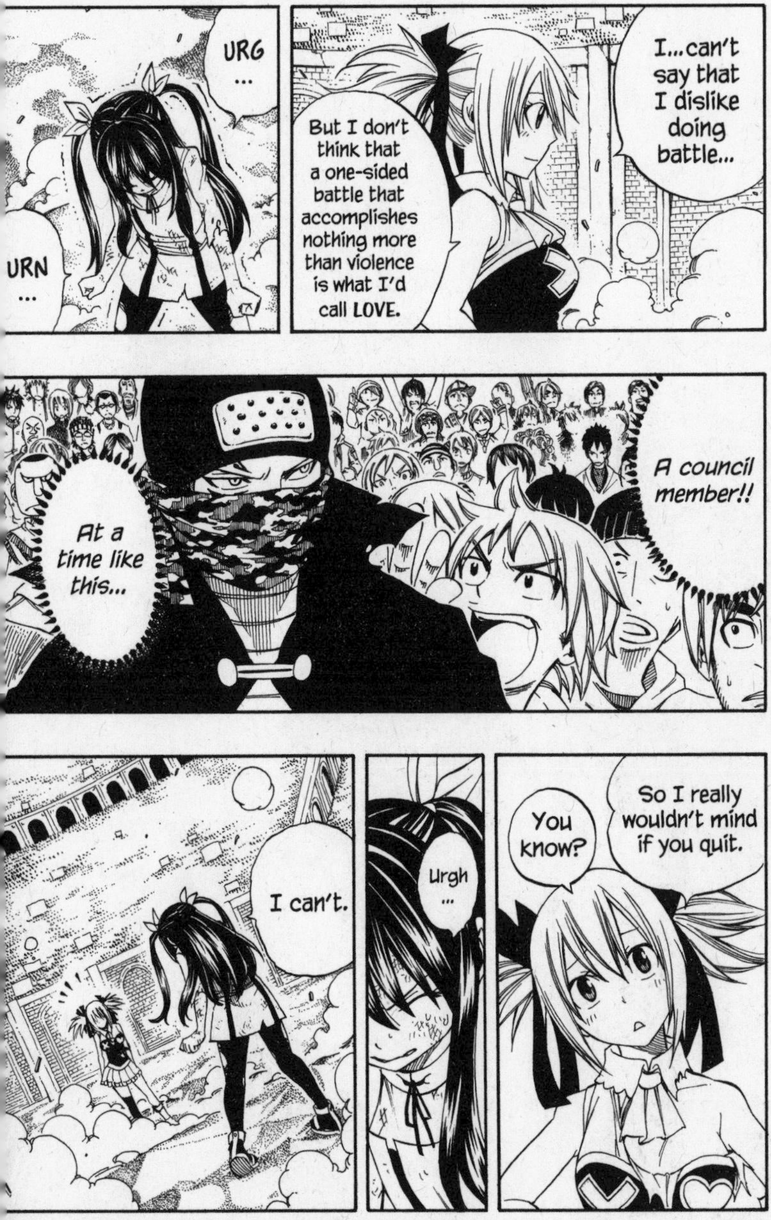
I...can't say that I dislike doing battle...
But I don't think that a one-sided battle that accomplishes nothing more than violence is what I'd call LOVE.
URG ...
URN ...
A council member!!
At a time like this...
So I really wouldn't mind if you quit.
You know?
Urgh ...
I can't.

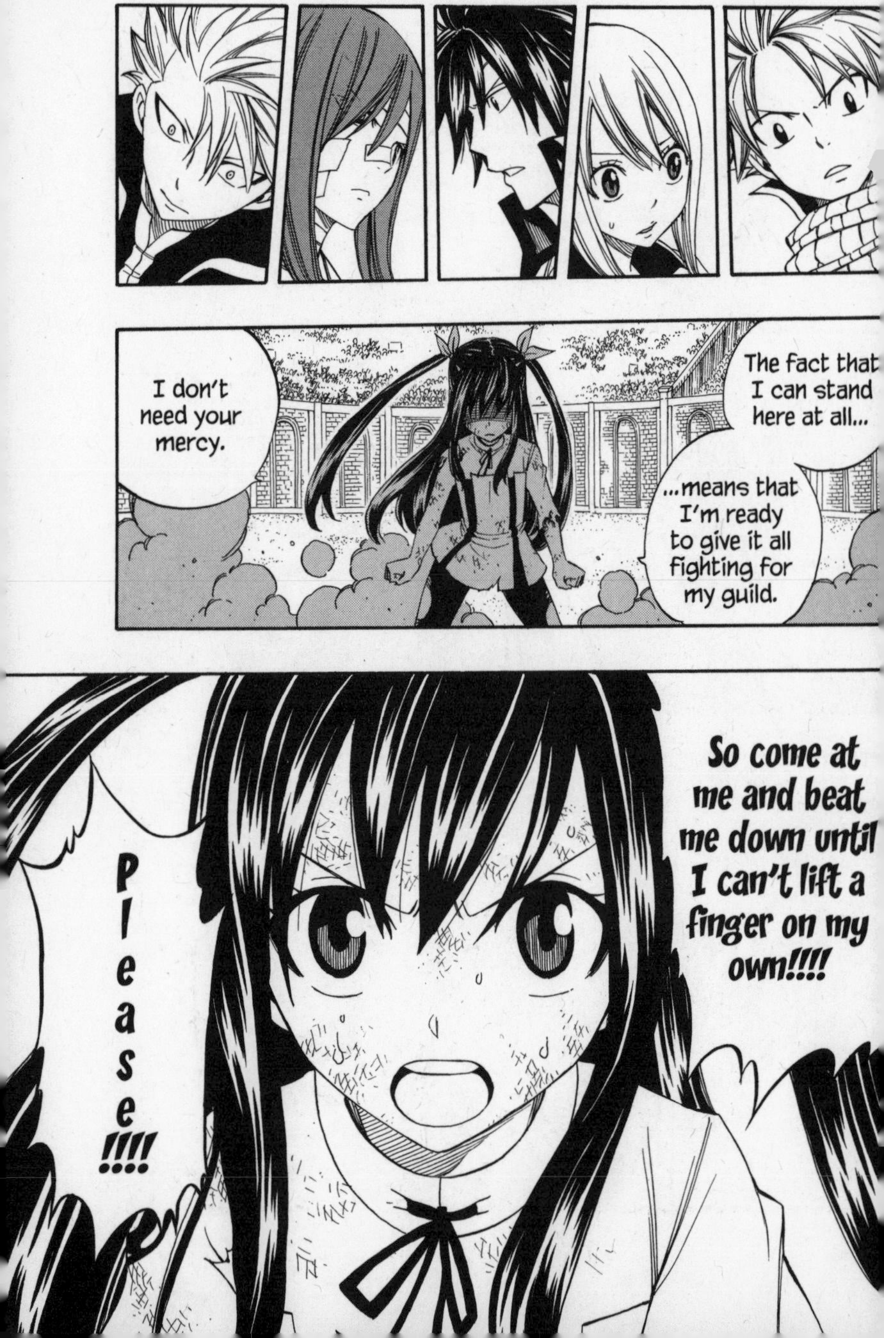
The fact that I can stand here at all...
...means that I'm ready to give it all fighting for my guild.
I don't need your mercy.
So come at me and beat me down until I can't lift a finger on my own!!!!
Please!!!!

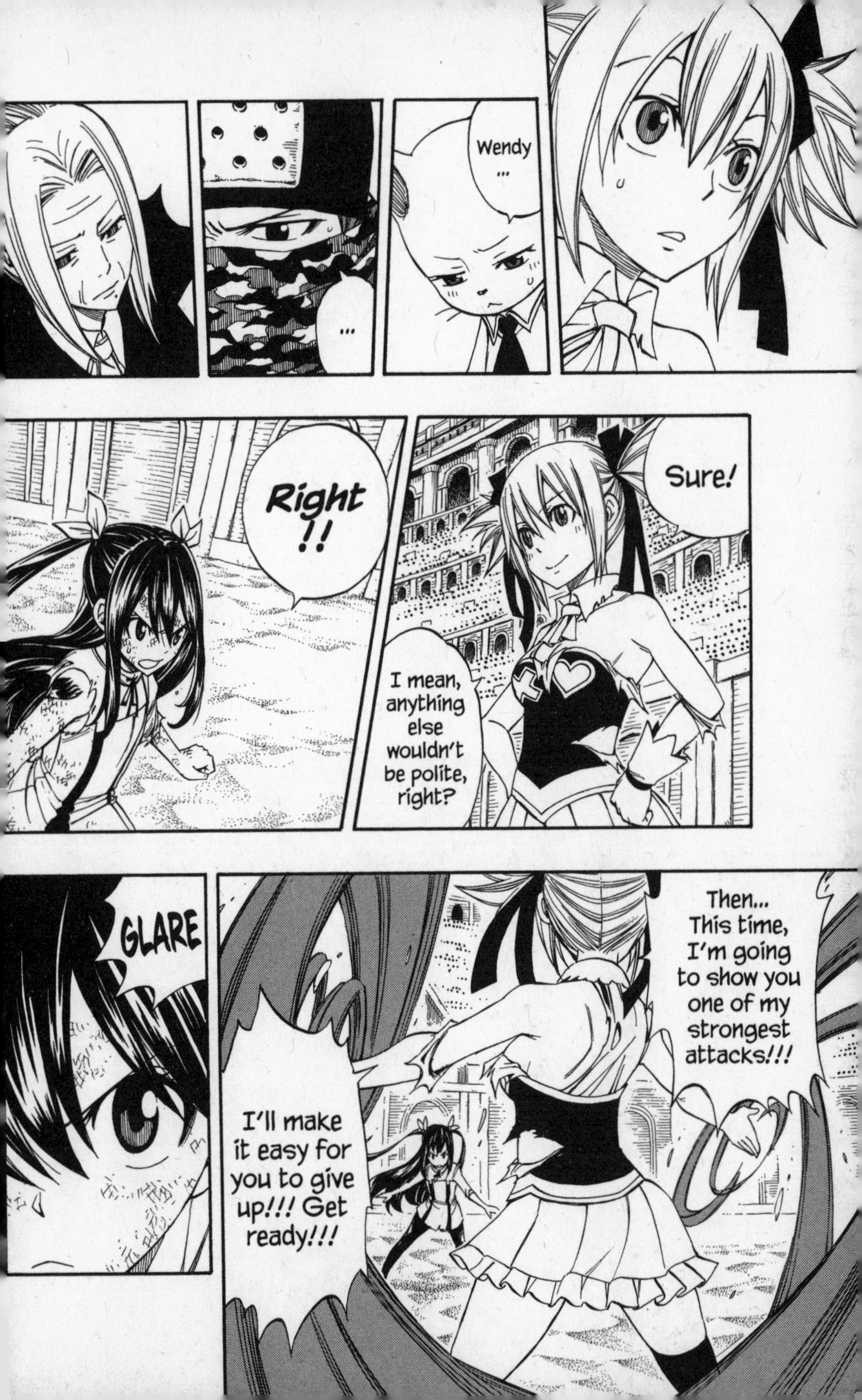
Wendy ...
...
Sure!
I mean, anything else wouldn't be polite, right?
Right !!
Then... This time, I'm going to show you one of my strongest attacks!!!
I'll make it easy for you to give up!!! Get ready!!!
GLARE

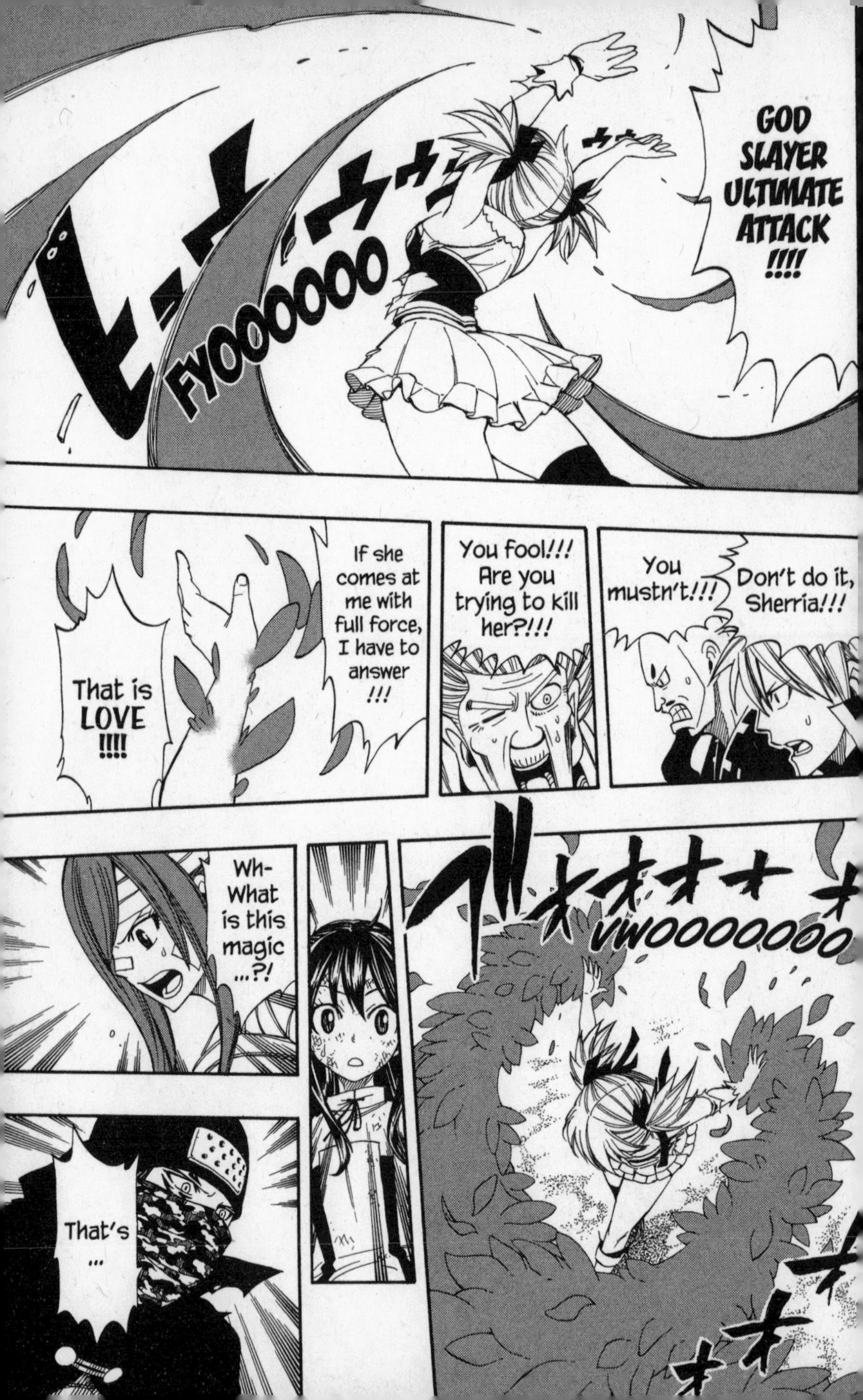
GOD SLAYER ULTIMATE ATTACK!!!!
FYOOOOOO
Don't do it, Sherria!!!
You mustn't!!!
You fool!!! Are you trying to kill her?!!!
If she comes at me with full force, I have to answer!!!
That is LOVE!!!!
VWOOOOOOOO
Wh- What is this magic...?!
That's...

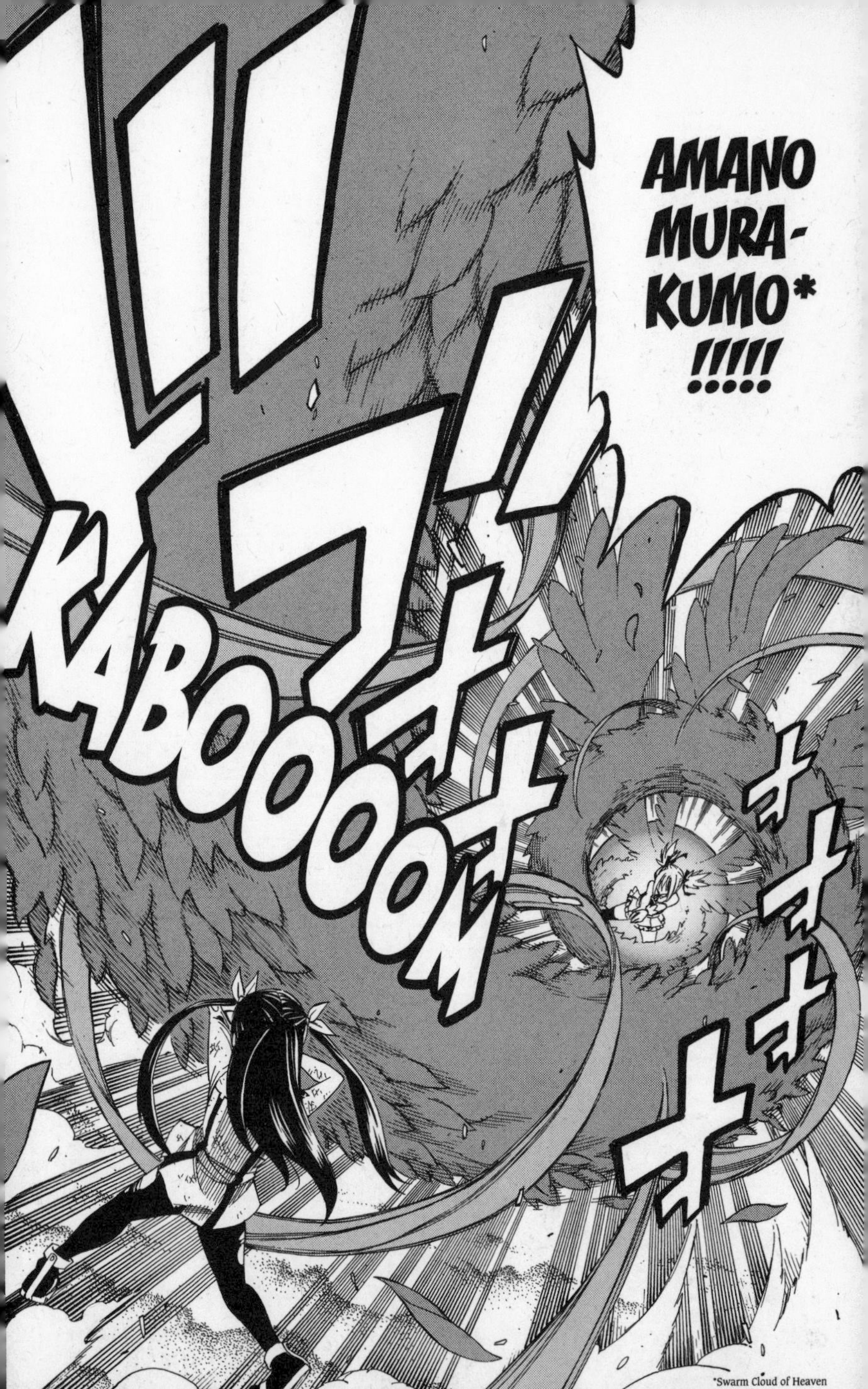
AMANO MURA-KUMO* !!!!!
KABOOOOOM

*Swarm Cloud of Heaven

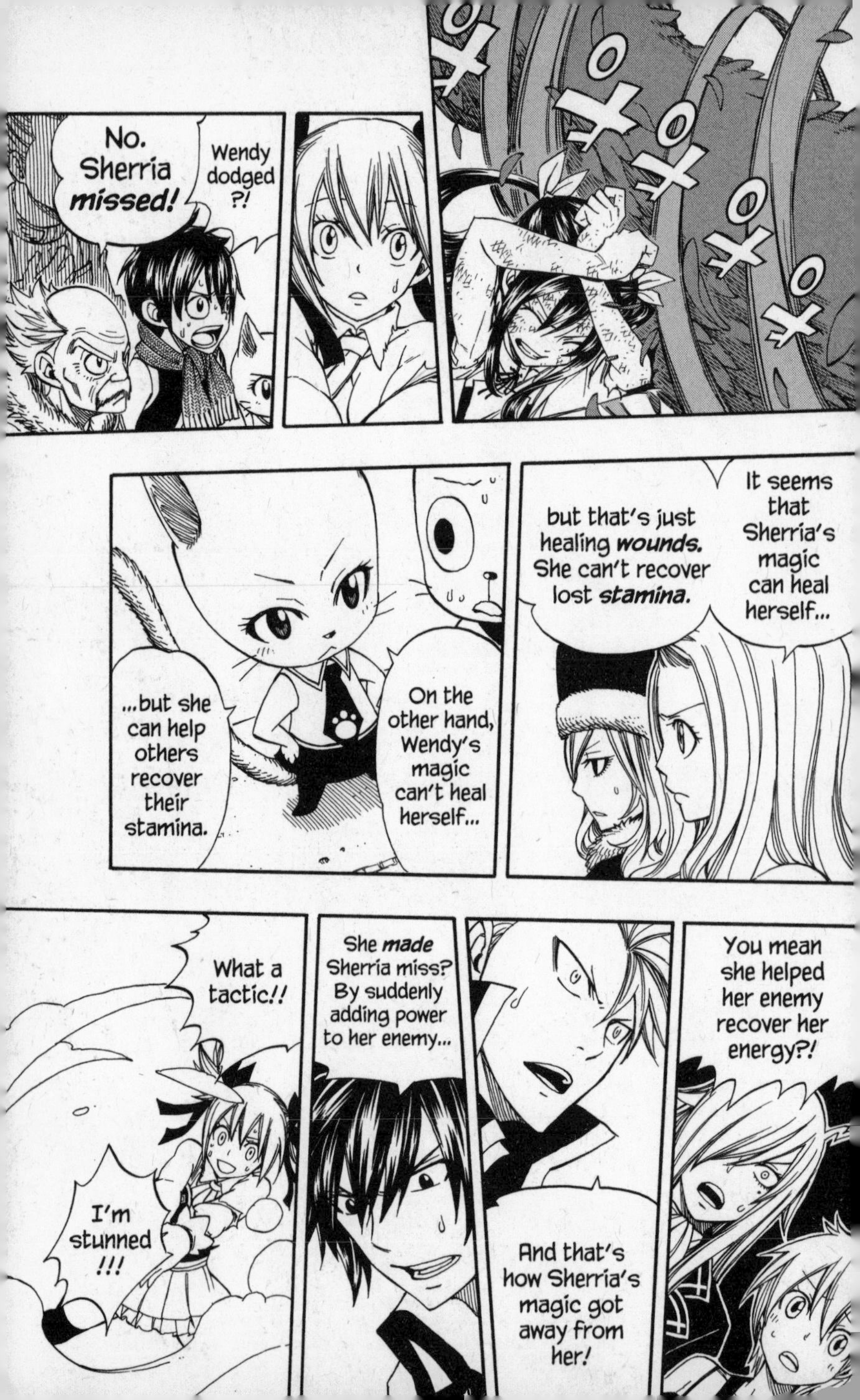
Wendy dodged?!
No. Sherria missed!
It seems that Sherria's magic can heal herself...
but that's just healing wounds. She can't recover lost stamina.
On the other hand, Wendy's magic can't heal herself...
...but she can help others recover their stamina.
You mean she helped her enemy recover her energy?!
She made Sherria miss? By suddenly adding power to her enemy...
And that's how Sherria's magic got away from her!
What a tactic!!
I'm stunned!!!

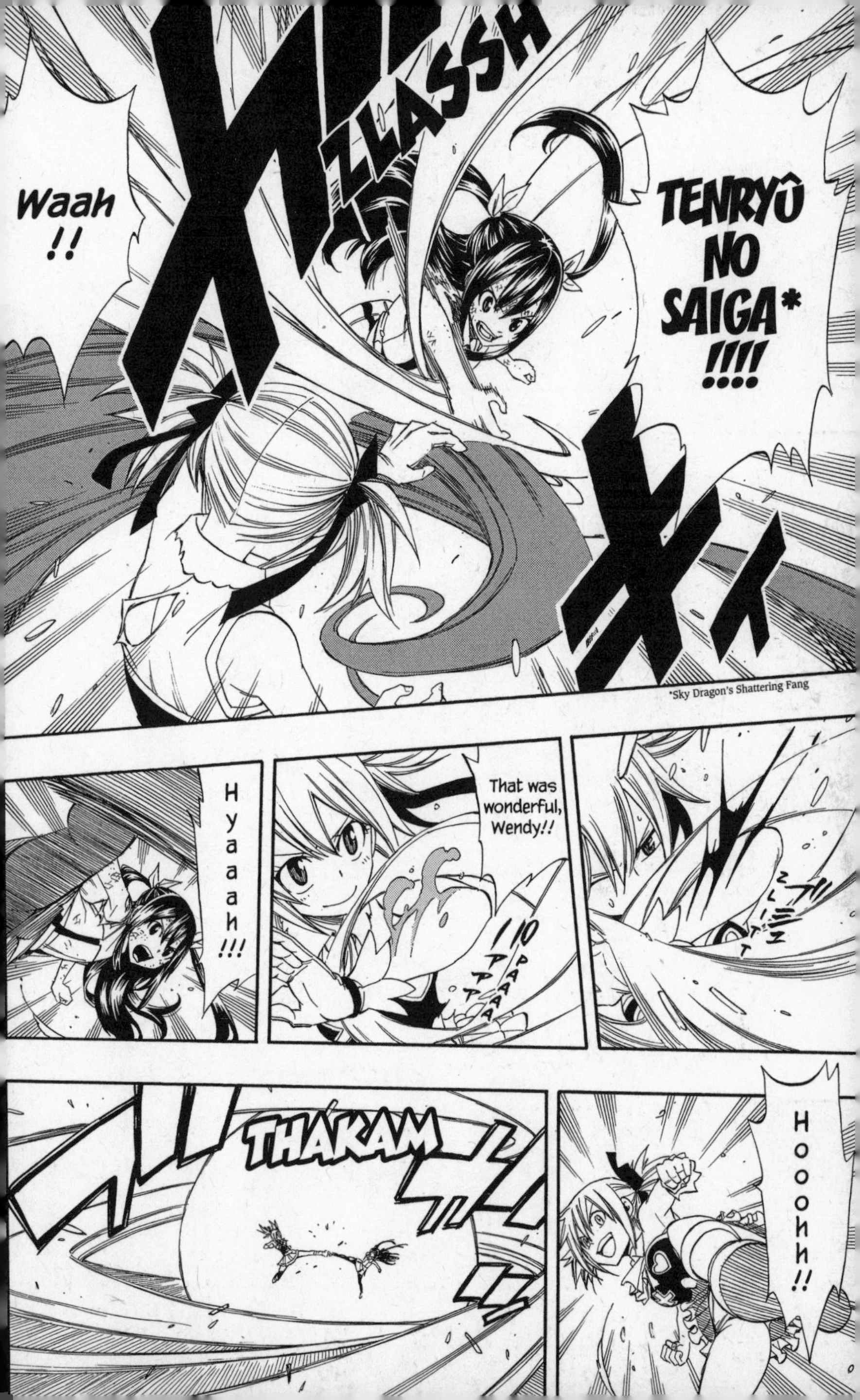
TENRYÛ NO SAIGA* !!!!
ZLASSH
Waah !!
That was wonderful, Wendy!!
Hyaaah!!!
Hooohh!!
THAKAM
*Sky Dragon's Shattering Fang

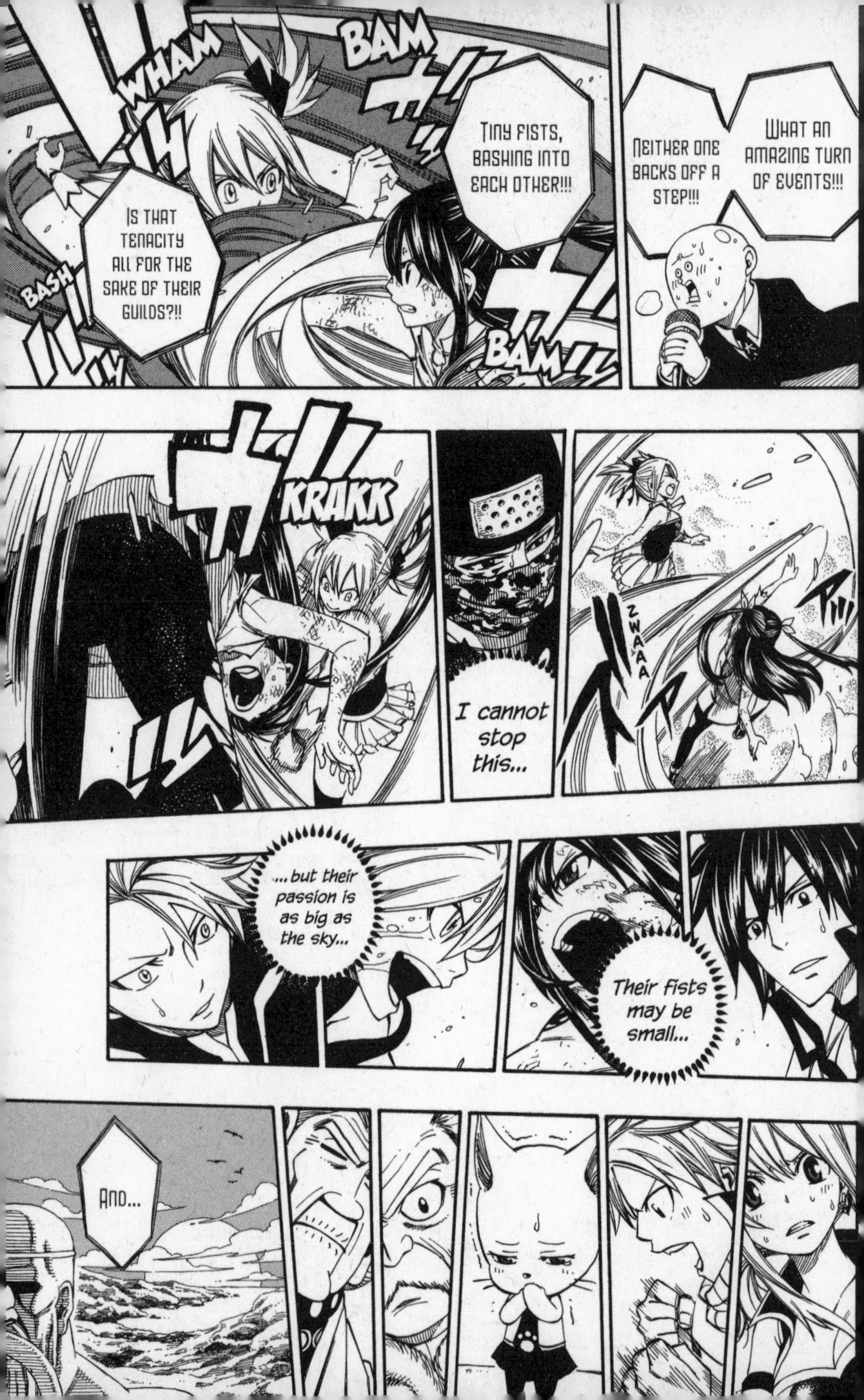

WHAT AN AMAZING TURN OF EVENTS!!!
NEITHER ONE BACKS OFF A STEP!!!
BAM
TINY FISTS, BASHING INTO EACH OTHER!!!
WHAM
IS THAT TENACITY ALL FOR THE SAKE OF THEIR GUILDS?!!
BASH
BAM!!
ZWAAA
I cannot stop this...
KRAKK
Their fists may be small...
...but their passion is as big as the sky...
AND...

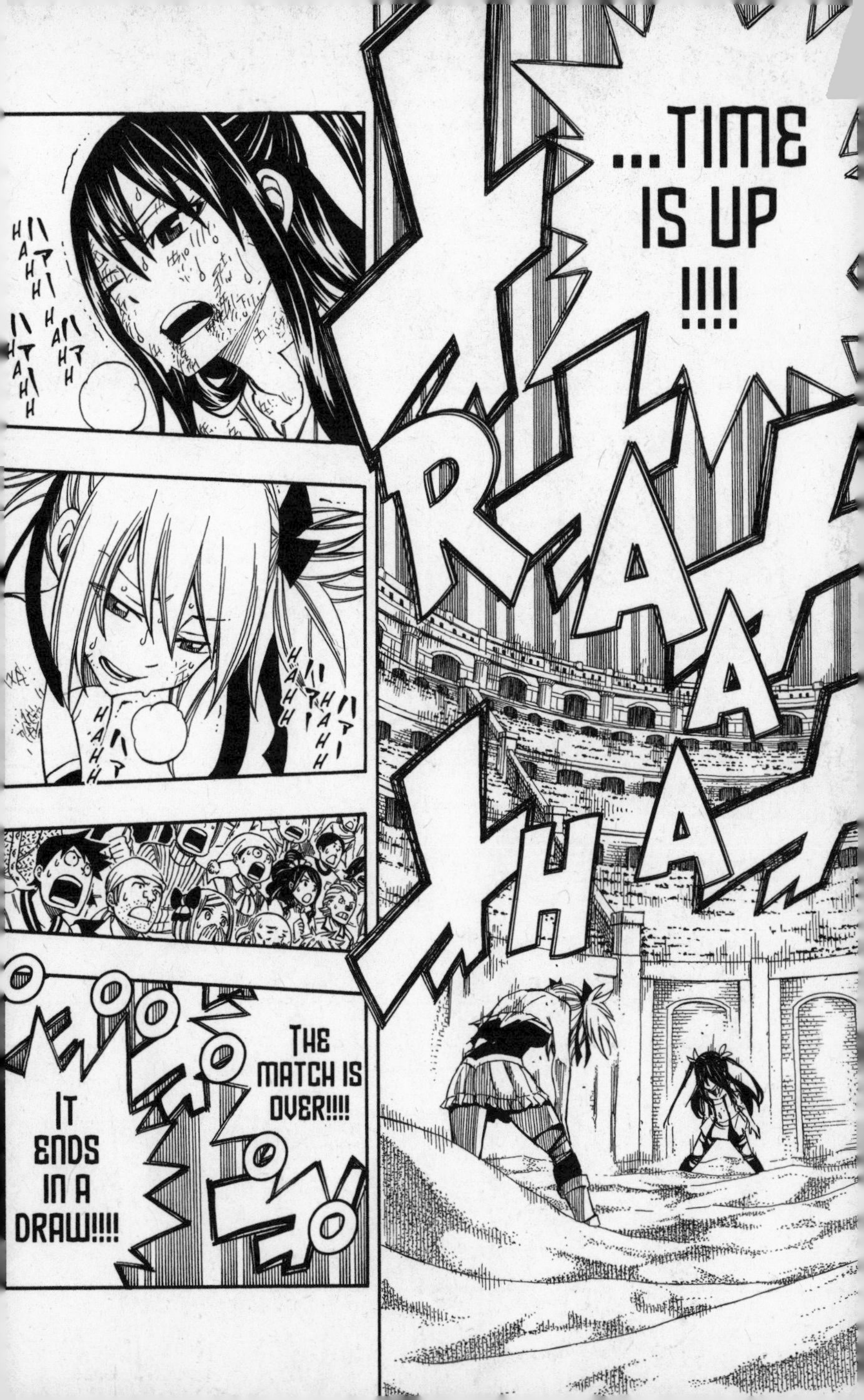
...TIME IS UP!!!!
THE MATCH IS OVER!!!!
IT ENDS IN A DRAW!!!!

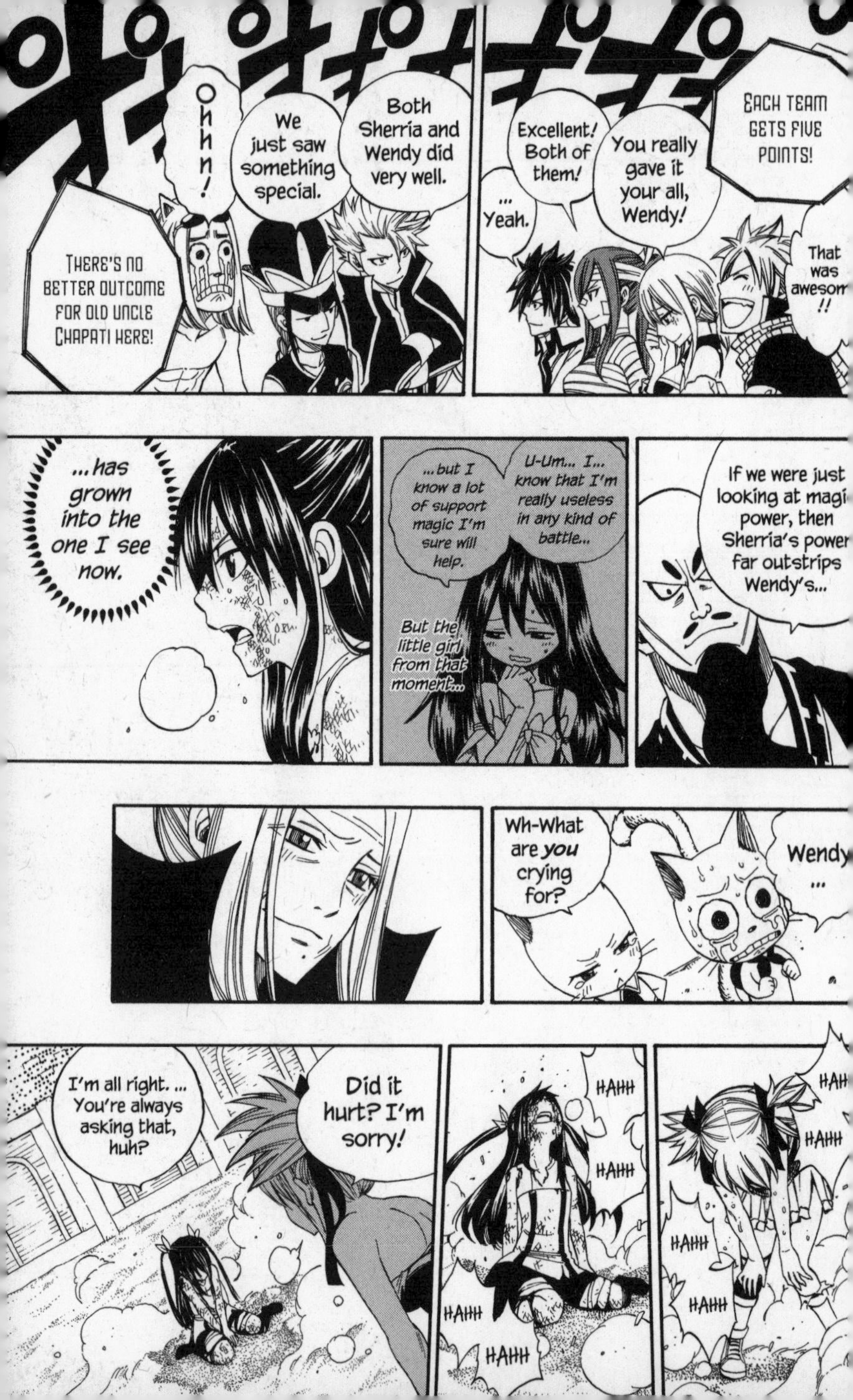
EACH TEAM GETS FIVE POINTS!
That was awesom !!
You really gave it your all, Wendy!
Excellent! Both of them!
... Yeah.
Both Sherria and Wendy did very well.
We just saw something special.
Ohhn!
THERE'S NO BETTER OUTCOME FOR OLD UNCLE CHAPATI HERE!
If we were just looking at magi power, then Sherria's power far outstrips Wendy's...
U-Um... I... know that I'm really useless in any kind of battle...
...but I know a lot of support magic I'm sure will help.
But the little girl from that moment...
...has grown into the one I see now.
Wendy ...
Wh-What are *you* crying for?
HAH
HAHH
HAHH
HAHH
HAHH
HAHH
HAHH
HAHH
Did it hurt? I'm sorry!
I'm all right. ... You're always asking that, huh?

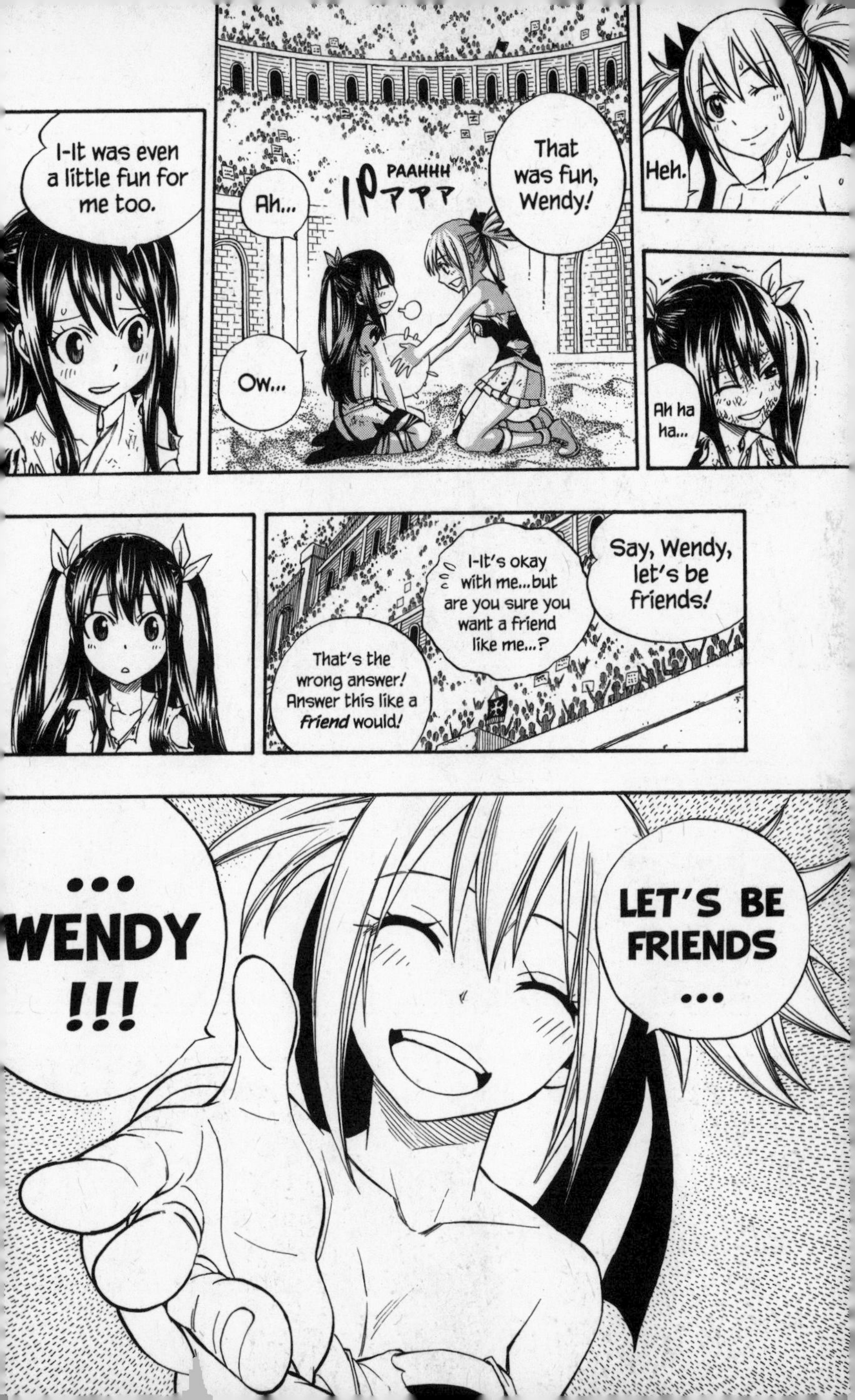

Heh.
Ah ha ha...
That was fun, Wendy!
PAAHHH
Ah...
Ow...
I-It was even a little fun for me too.
Say, Wendy, let's be friends!
I-It's okay with me...but are you sure you want a friend like me...?
That's the wrong answer! Answer this like a *friend* would!
LET'S BE FRIENDS...
...WENDY!!!

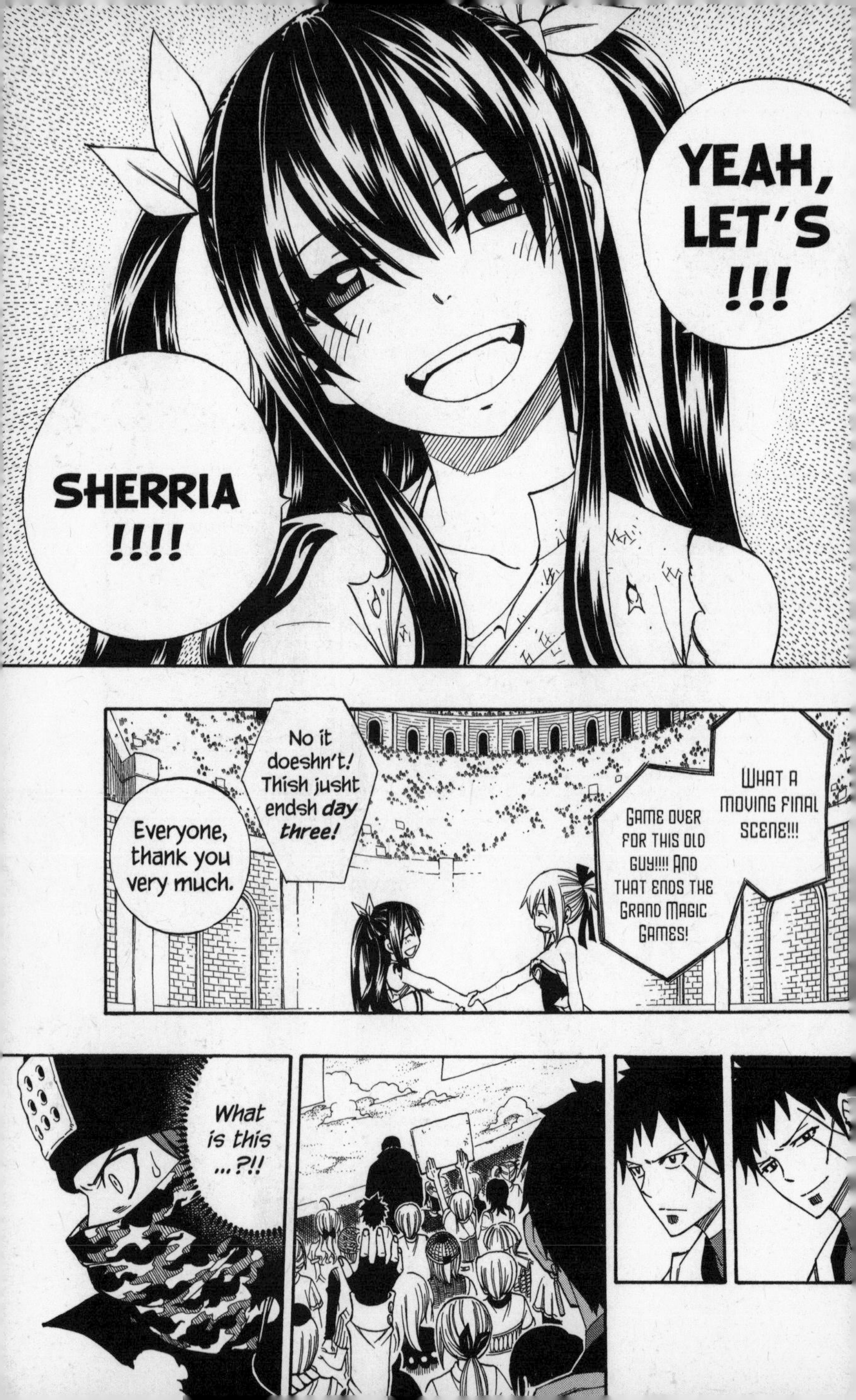
YEAH, LET'S !!!
SHERRIA !!!!
WHAT A MOVING FINAL SCENE!!!
GAME OVER FOR THIS OLD GUY!!!! AND THAT ENDS THE GRAND MAGIC GAMES!
No it doeshn't! Thish jusht endsh *day three!*
Everyone, thank you very much.
What is this ...?!!

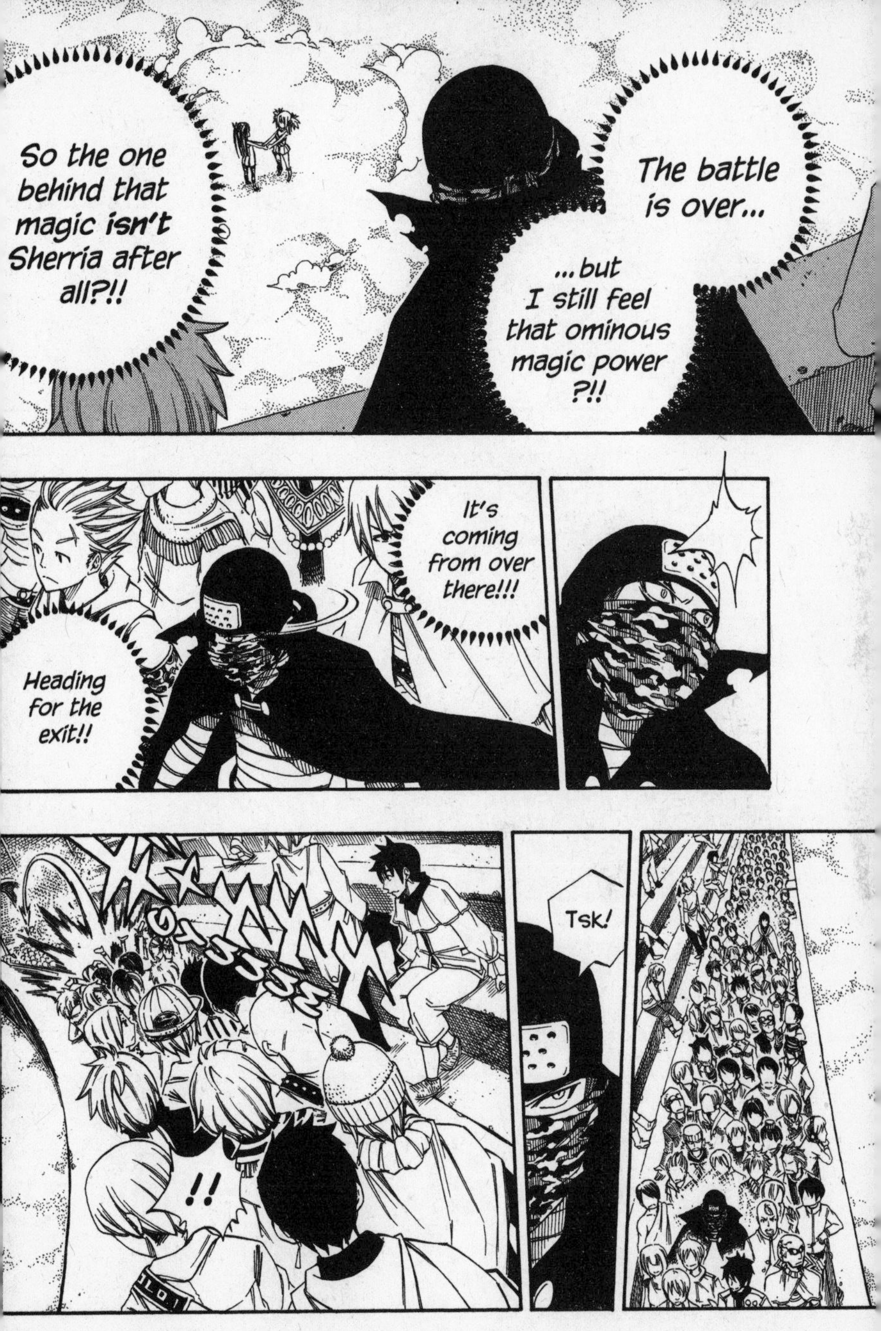
The battle is over...
...but I still feel that ominous magic power ?!!
So the one behind that magic isn't Sherria after all?!!
It's coming from over there!!!
Heading for the exit!!
Tsk!
!!

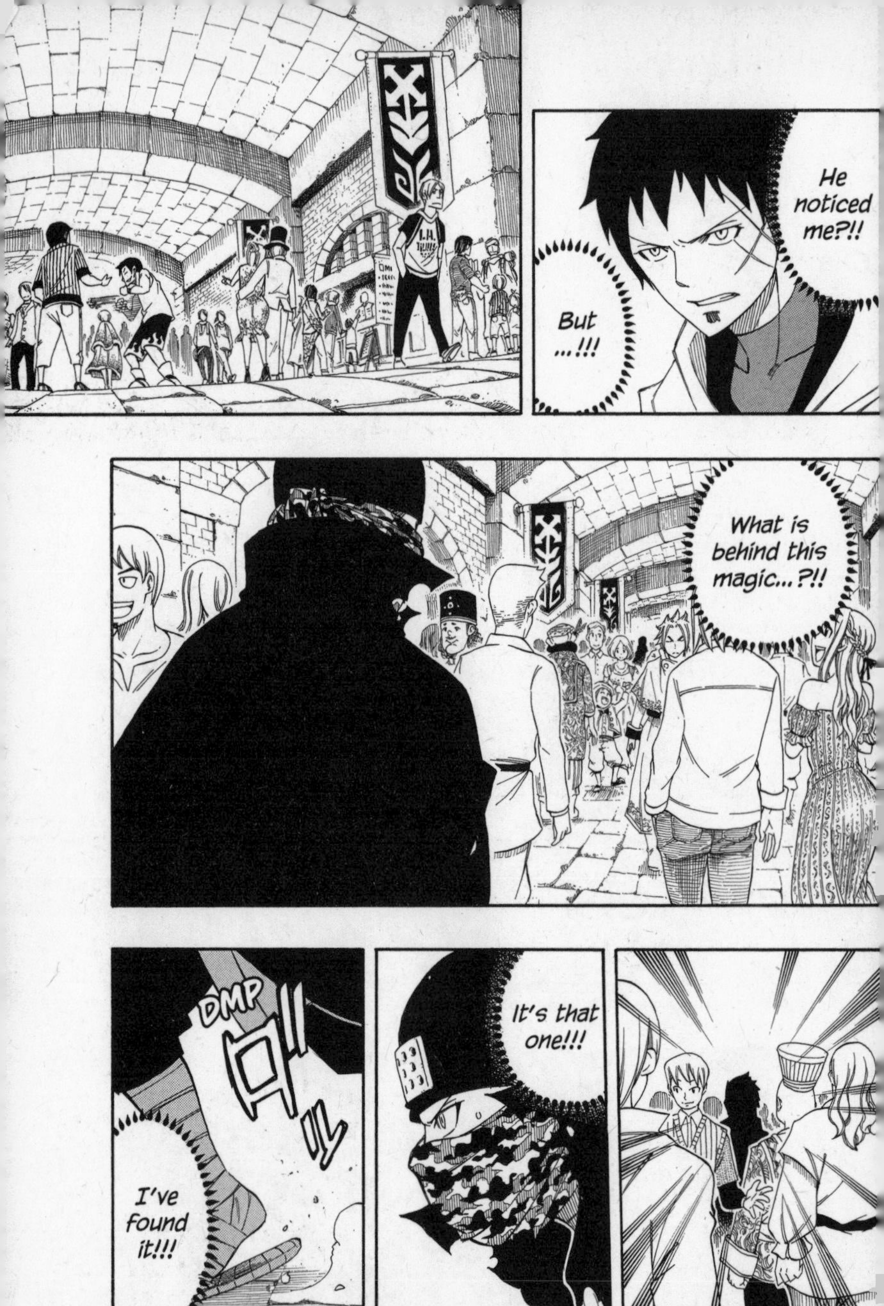
He noticed me?!!
But ...!!!
What is behind this magic...?!!
It's that one!!!
DMP
I've found it!!!

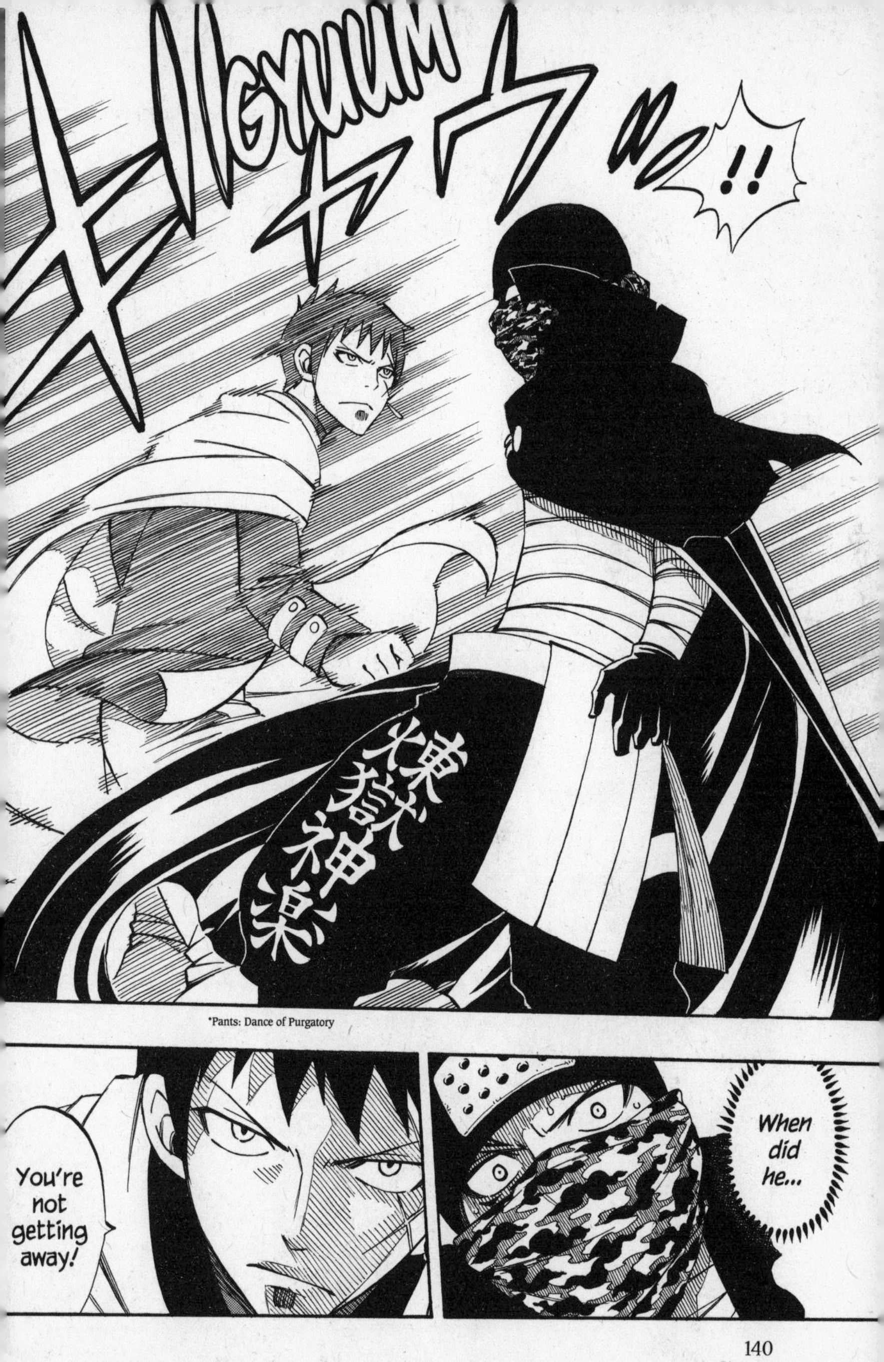
GYUUUM
!!
煉獄神楽
When did he...
You're not getting away!
*Pants: Dance of Purgatory

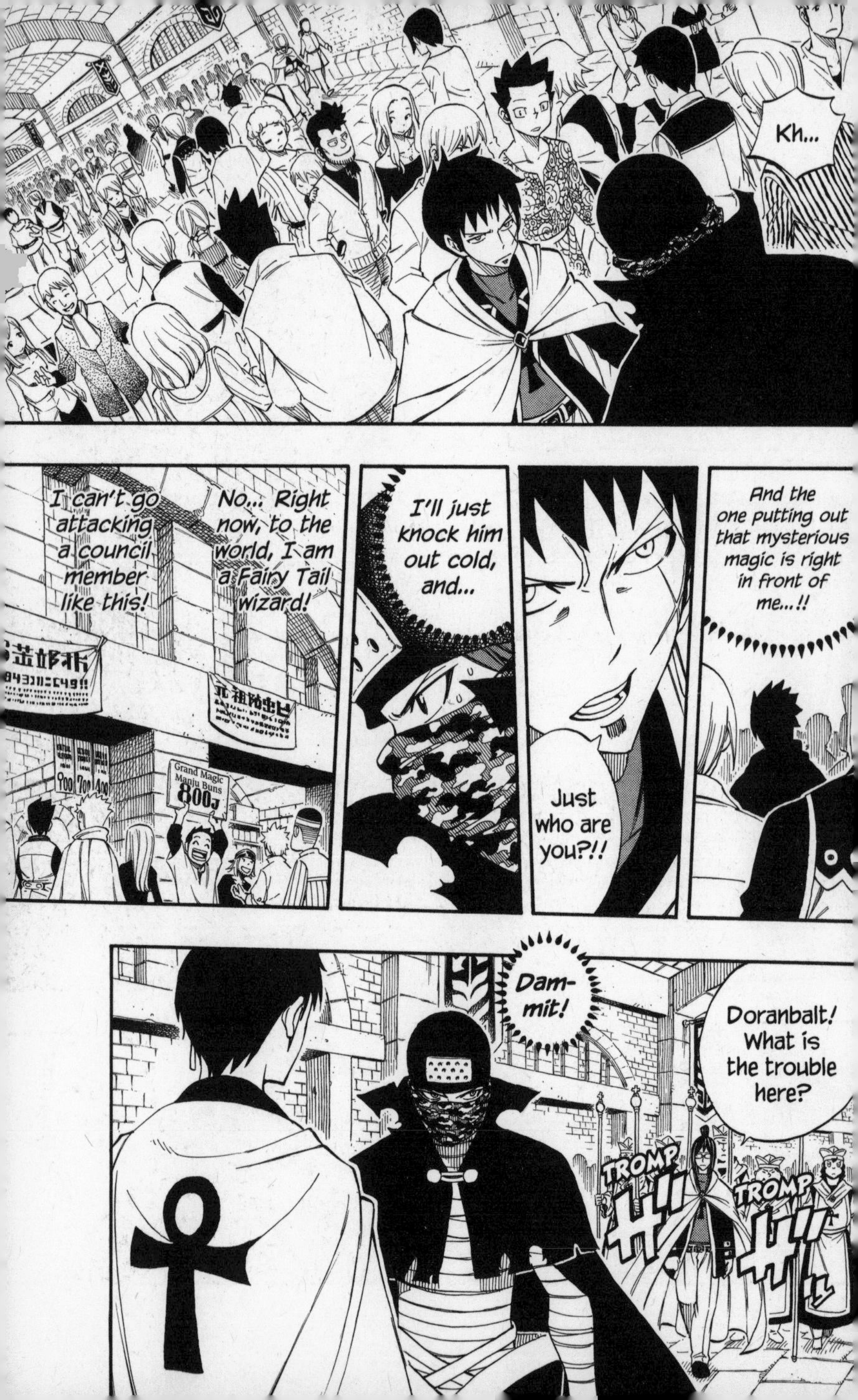
Kh...
And the one putting out that mysterious magic is right in front of me...!!
Just who are you?!!
I'll just knock him out cold, and...
No... Right now, to the world, I am a Fairy Tail wizard!
I can't go attacking a council member like this!
Grand Magic Manju Buns 800J
Doranbalt! What is the trouble here?
Dam-mit!
TROMP
TROMP

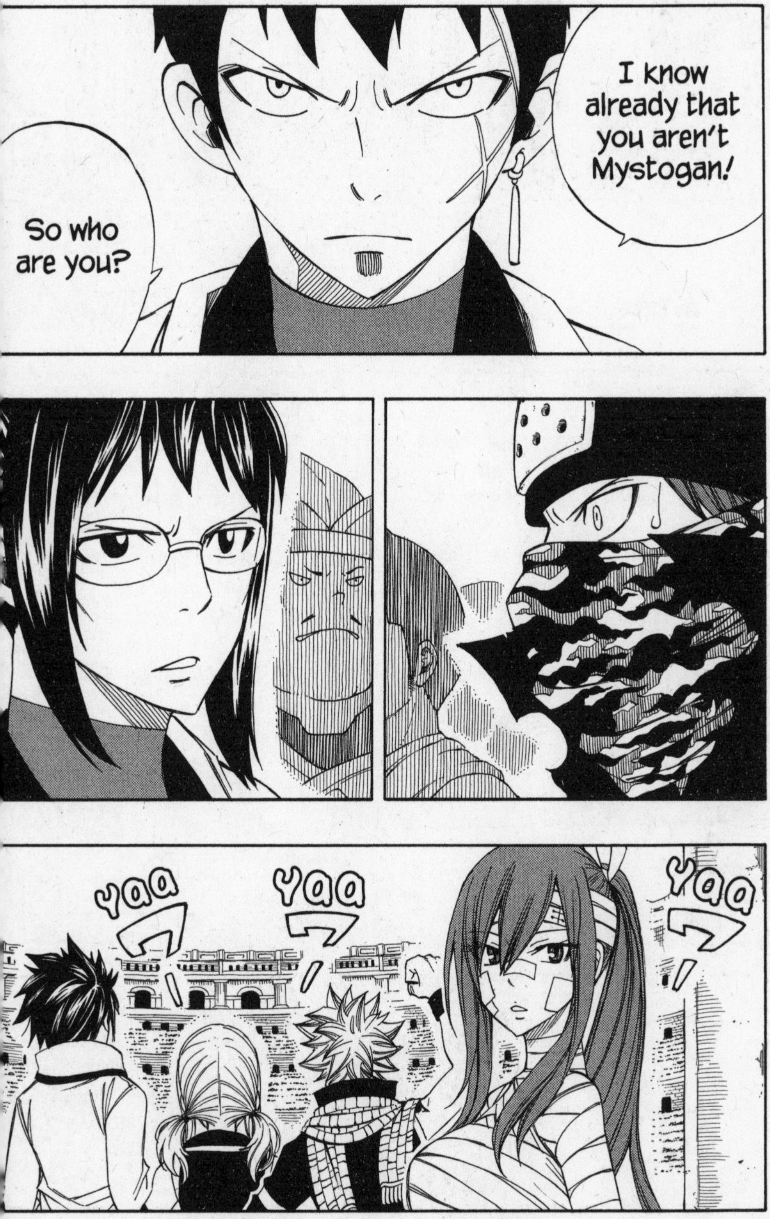
I know already that you aren't Mystogan!
So who are you?
Yaa
Yaa
Yaa

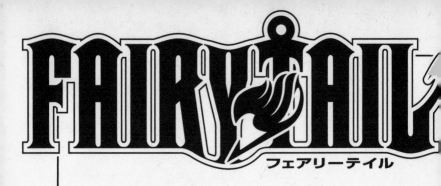

FAIRY TAIL

フェアリーテイル

Grand Magic Games Results of the 3rd Day

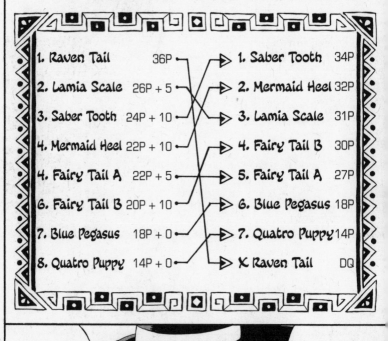

1. Raven Tail	36P	1. Saber Tooth	34P
2. Lamia Scale	26P + 5	2. Mermaid Heel	32P
3. Saber Tooth	24P + 10	3. Lamia Scale	31P
4. Mermaid Heel	22P + 10	4. Fairy Tail B	30P
4. Fairy Tail A	22P + 5	5. Fairy Tail A	27P
6. Fairy Tail B	20P + 10	6. Blue Pegasus	18P
7. Blue Pegasus	18P + 0	7. Quatro Puppy	14P
8. Quatro Puppy	14P + 0	X Raven Tail	DQ

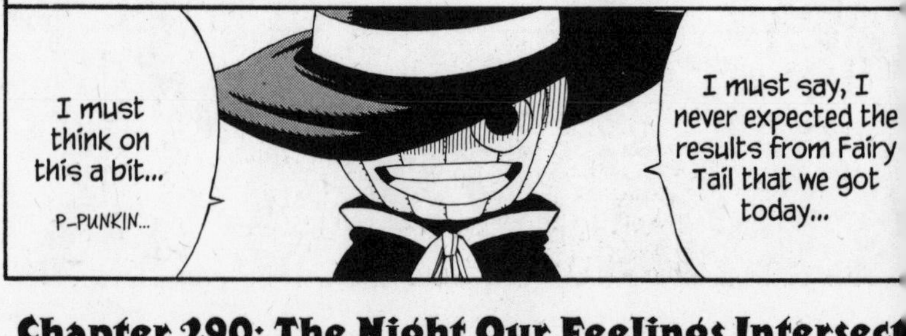

I must say, I never expected the results from Fairy Tail that we got today...
I must think on this a bit...
P-PUNKIN...

Chapter 290: The Night Our Feelings Intersect

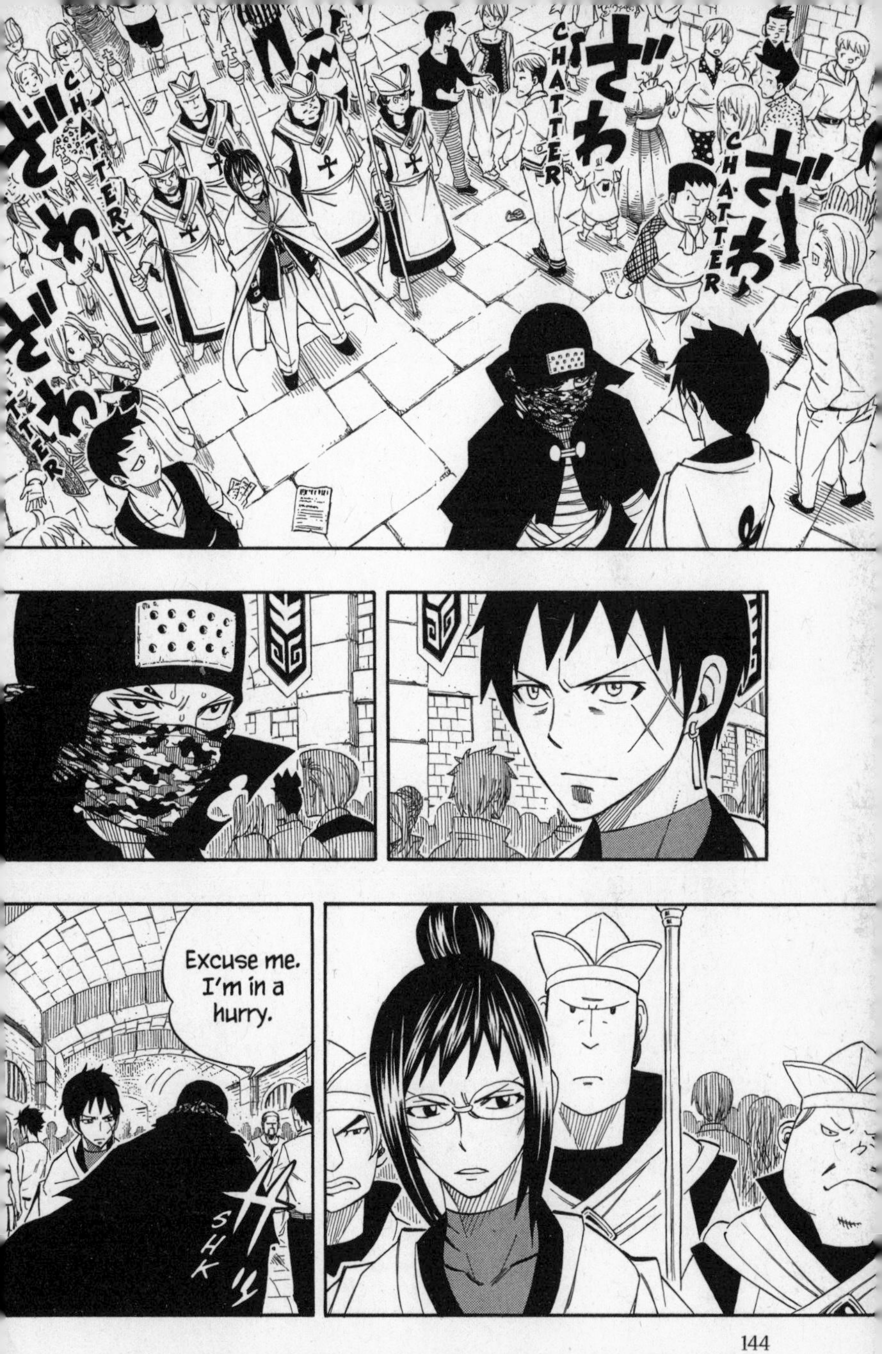
ざわ
CHATTER
ざわ
CHATTER
ざわ
CHATTER
ざわ
TTER
Excuse me. I'm in a hurry.
SHK

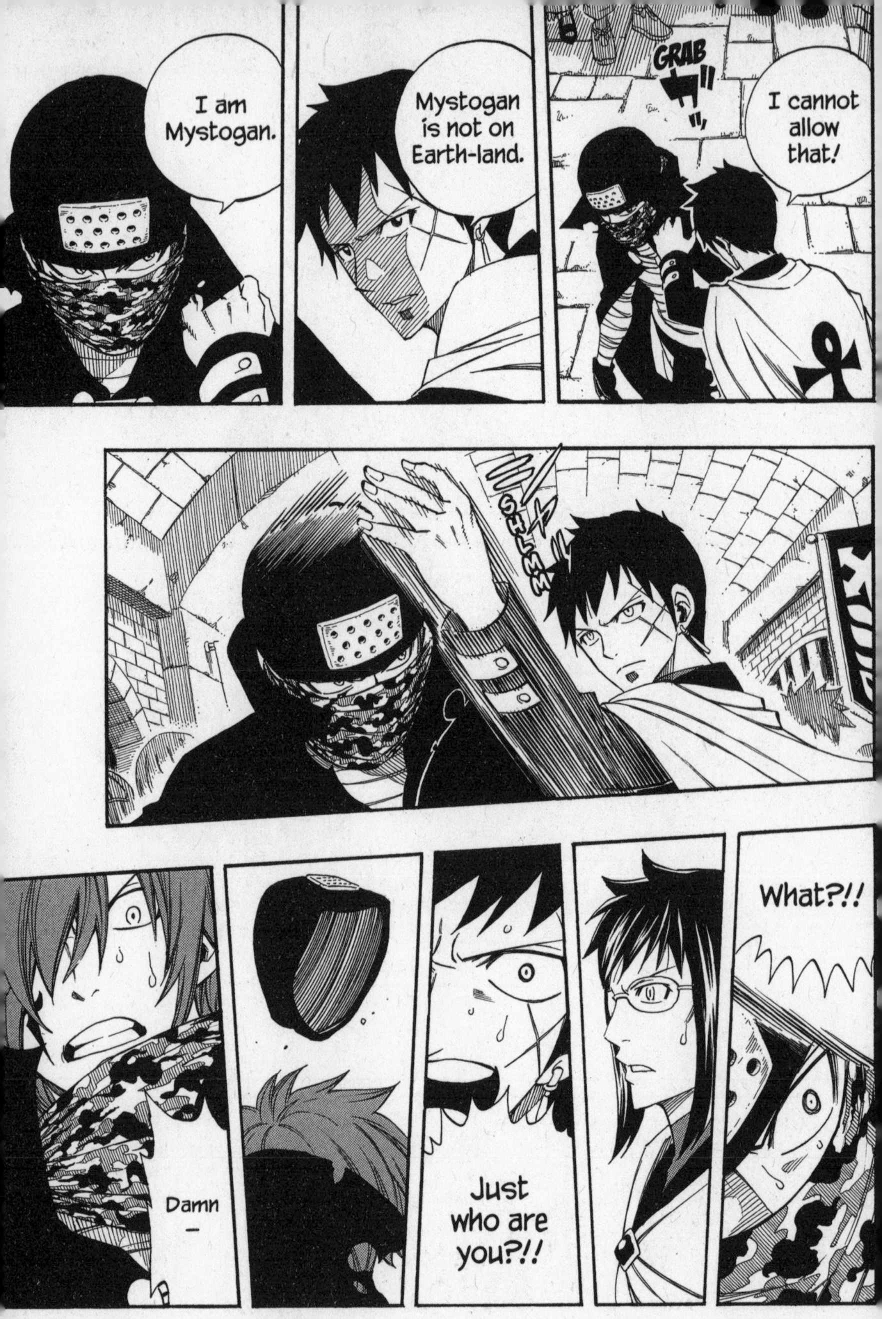
GRAB
I cannot allow that!
Mystogan is not on Earth-land.
I am Mystogan.
SHLMMM
What?!!
Just who are you?!!
Damn –

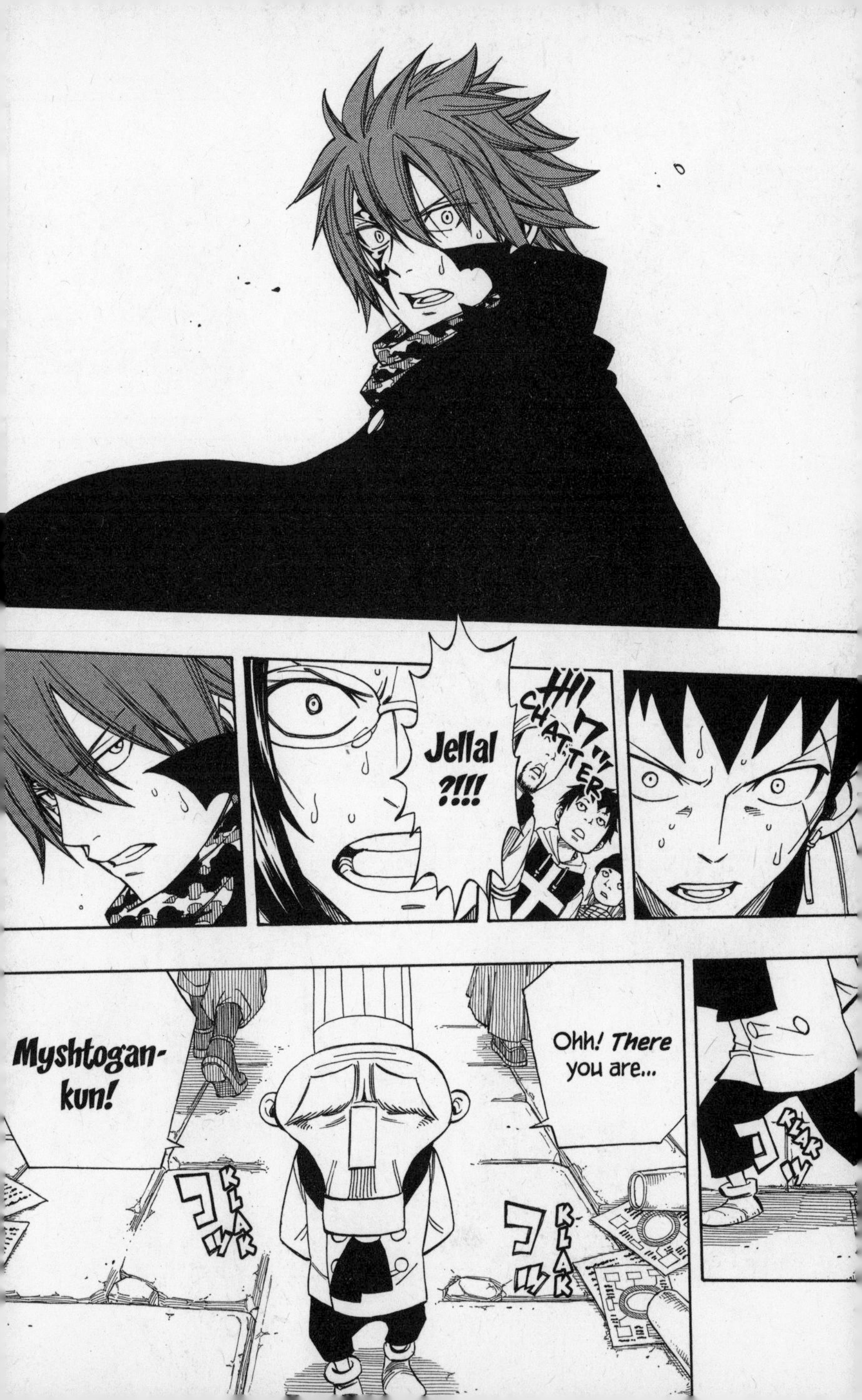
CHATTER
Jellal ?!!!
KLAK
Ohh! There you are...
KLAK
KLAK
Myshtogan-kun!

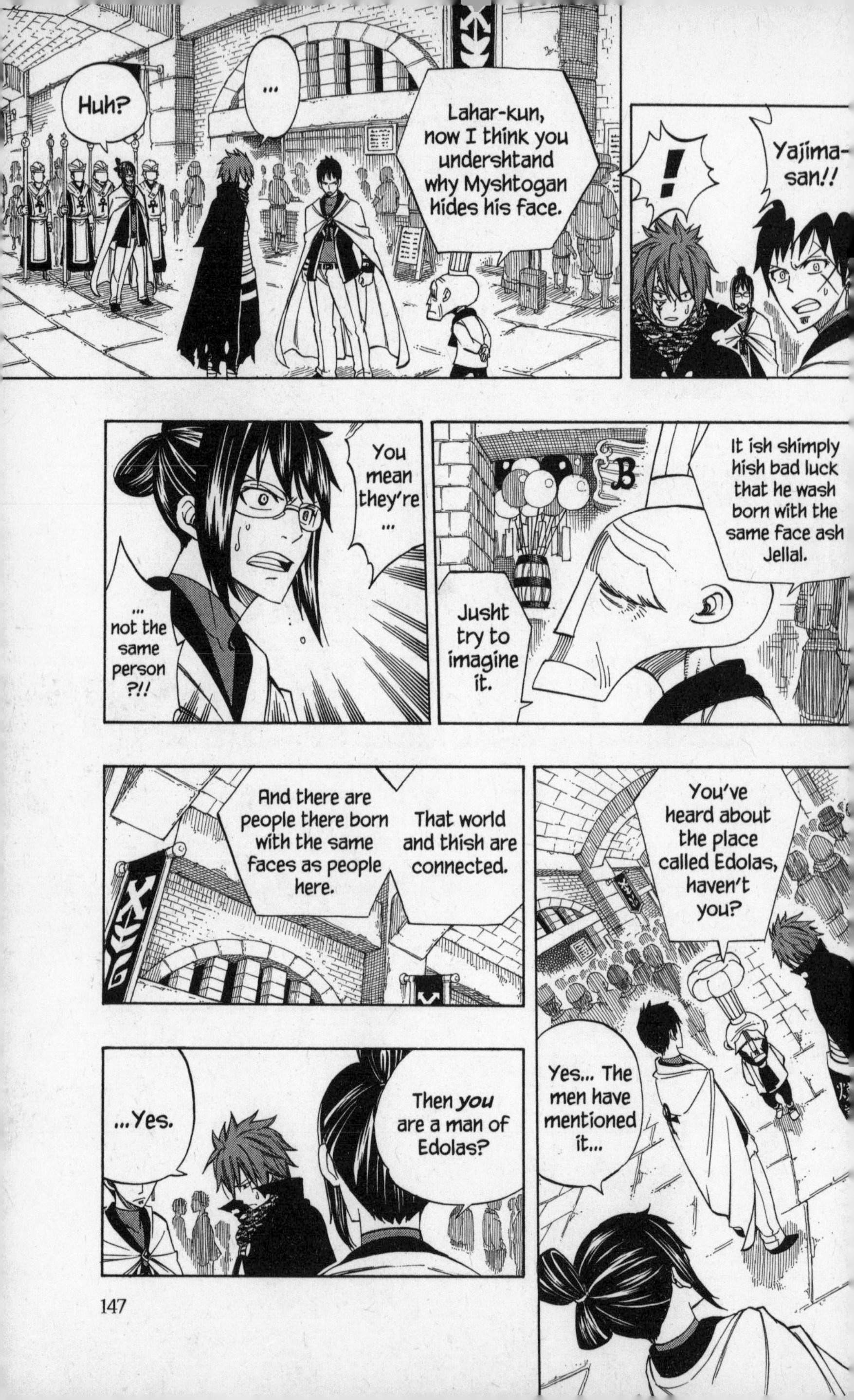
!
Yajima-san!!
Lahar-kun, now I think you undershtand why Myshtogan hides his face.
...
Huh?
It ish shimply hish bad luck that he wash born with the same face ash Jellal.
Jusht try to imagine it.
You mean they're ...
... not the same person?!!
You've heard about the place called Edolas, haven't you?
Yes... The men have mentioned it...
That world and thish are connected.
And there are people there born with the same faces as people here.
Then *you* are a man of Edolas?
...Yes.

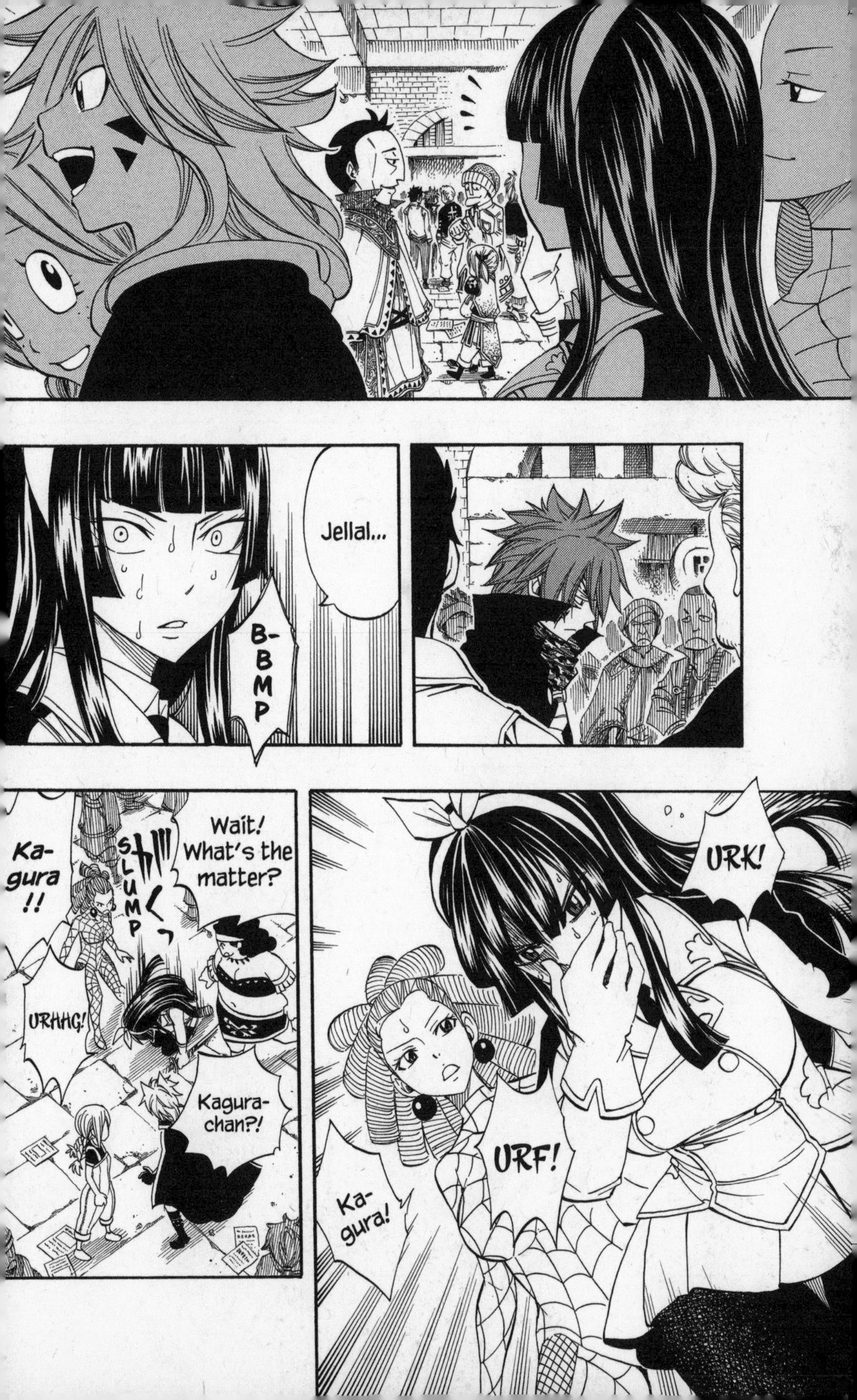
Jellal...
B-BMP
URK!
URF!
Ka-gura!
Wait! What's the matter?
SLUMP
Ka-gura!!
URHHG!
Kagura-chan?!

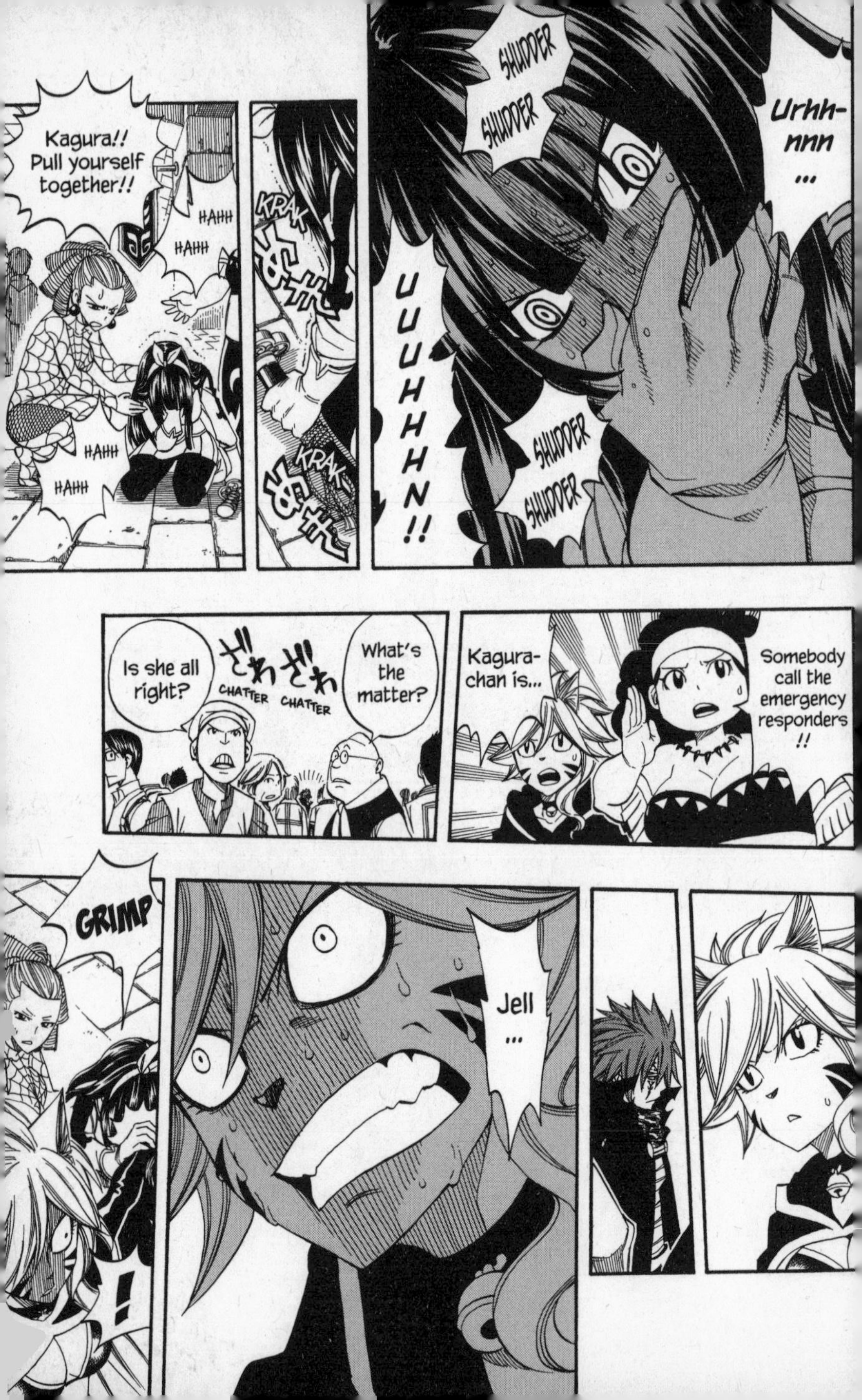
Urhh-nnn ...
SHUDDER SHUDDER
UUUUHHHHN!!
SHUDDER SHUDDER
KRAK
KRAK
Kagura!! Pull yourself together!!
HAHH HAHH
HAHH HAHH
Somebody call the emergency responders!!
Kagura-chan is...
What's the matter?
ざわざわ CHATTER CHATTER
Is she all right?
Jell ...
GRIMP
!

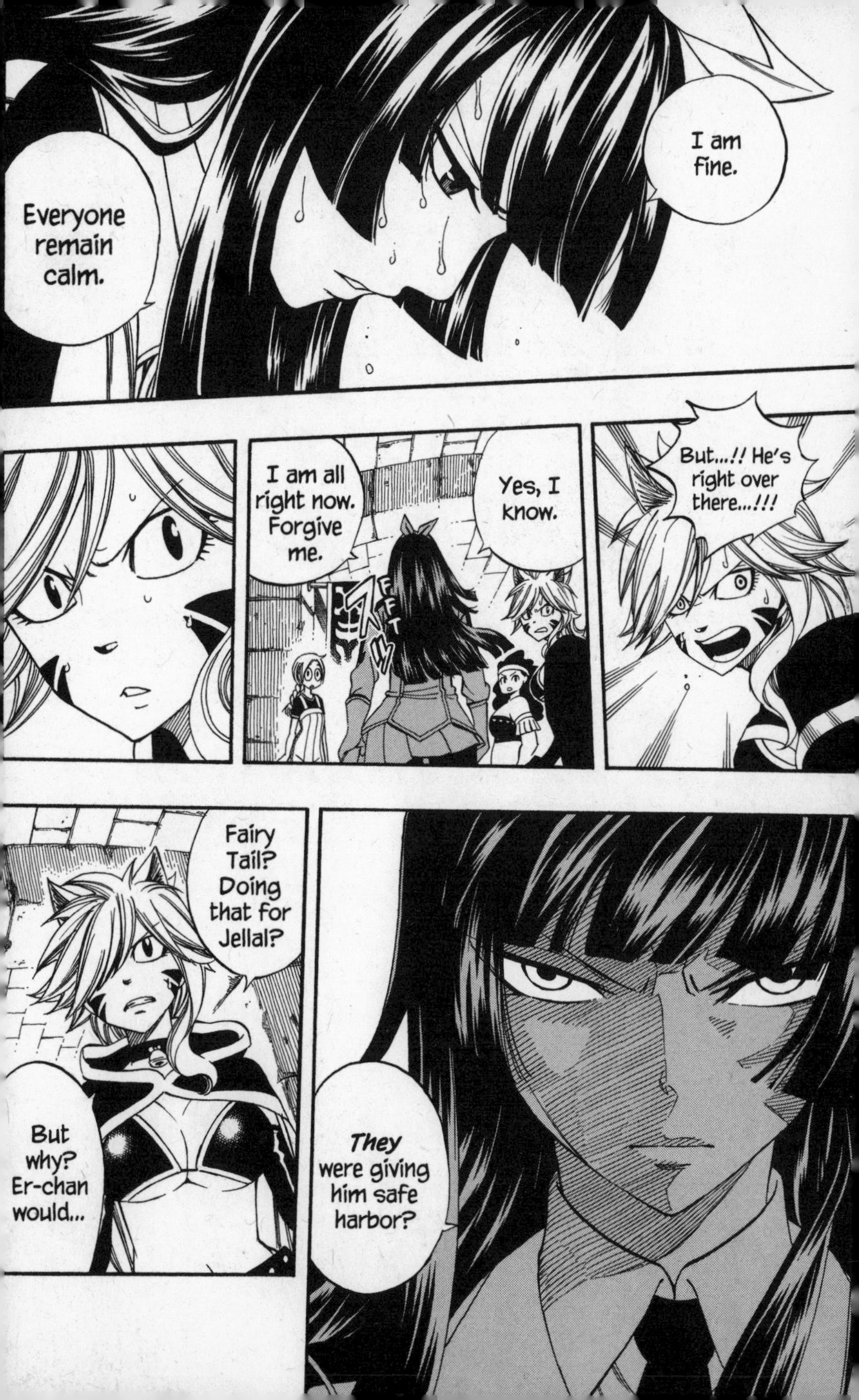
I am fine.
Everyone remain calm.
But...!! He's right over there...!!!
Yes, I know.
I am all right now. Forgive me.
FFFT
They were giving him safe harbor?
Fairy Tail? Doing that for Jellal?
But why? Er-chan would...

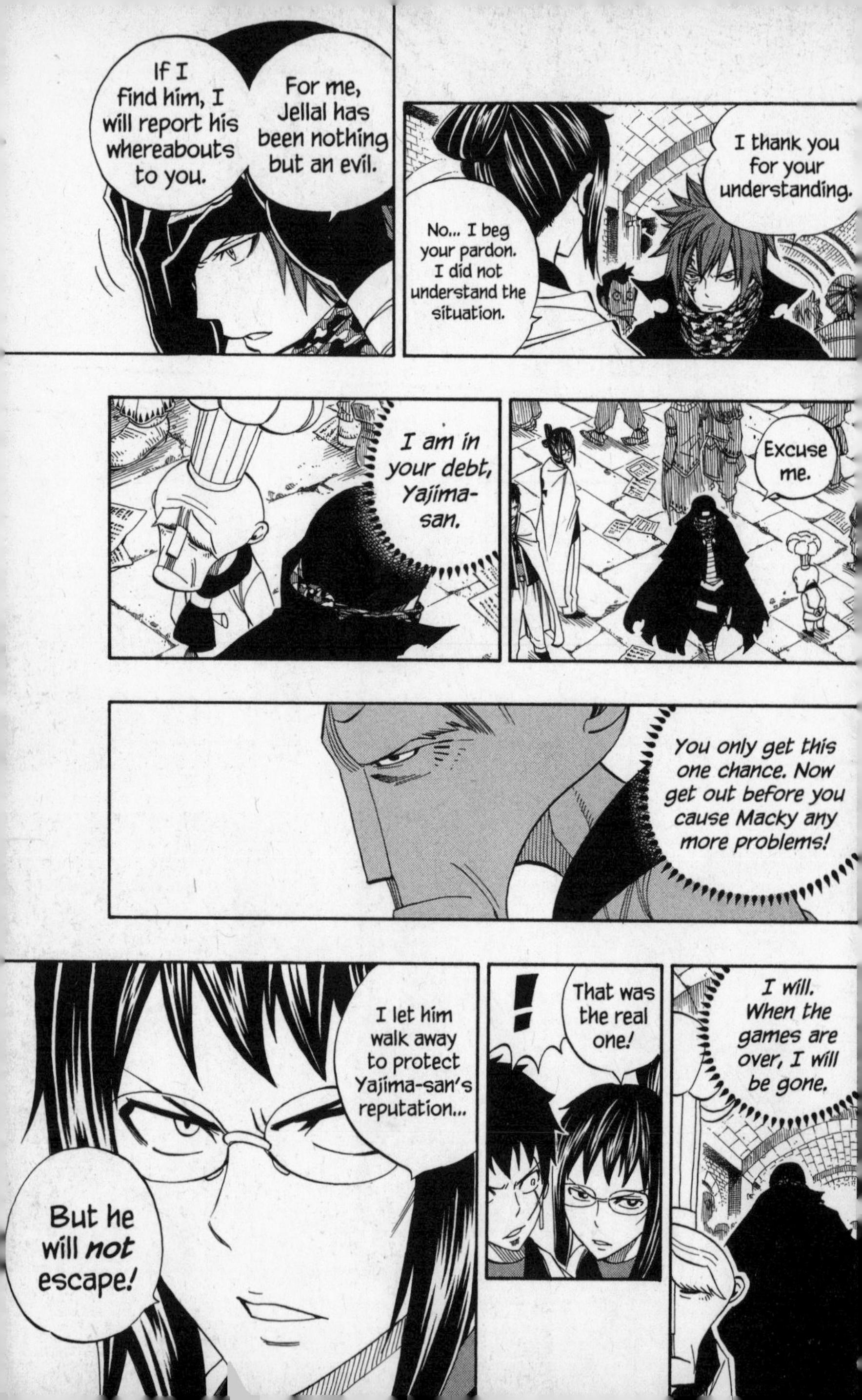
I thank you for your understanding.
No... I beg your pardon. I did not understand the situation.
For me, Jellal has been nothing but an evil.
If I find him, I will report his whereabouts to you.
Excuse me.
I am in your debt, Yajima-san.
You only get this one chance. Now get out before you cause Macky any more problems!
I will. When the games are over, I will be gone.
!
That was the real one!
I let him walk away to protect Yajima-san's reputation...
But he will **not** escape!

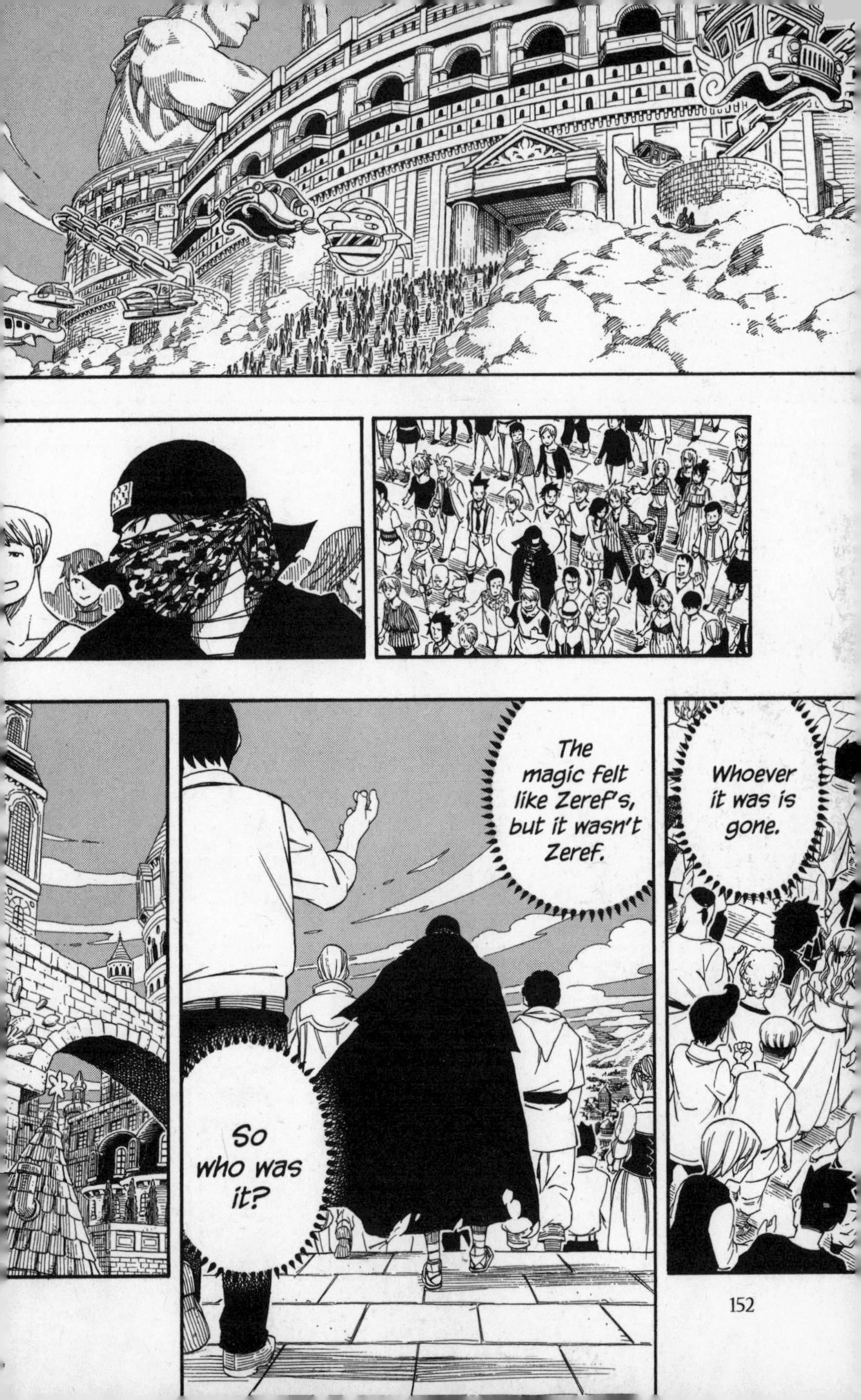
Whoever it was is gone.
The magic felt like Zeref's, but it wasn't Zeref.
So who was it?

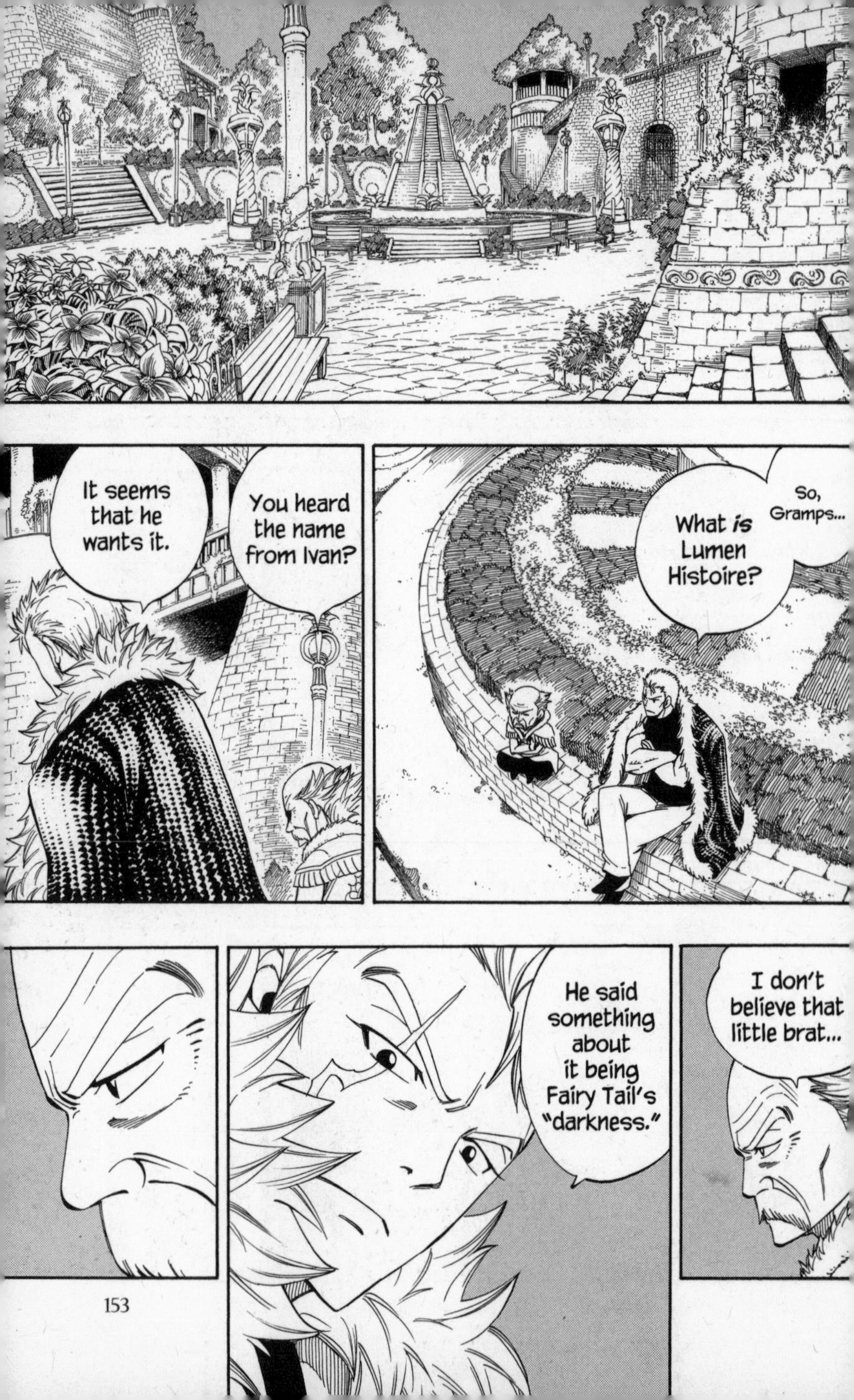
So, Gramps...
What *is* Lumen Histoire?
You heard the name from Ivan?
It seems that he wants it.
I don't believe that little brat...
He said something about it being Fairy Tail's "darkness."

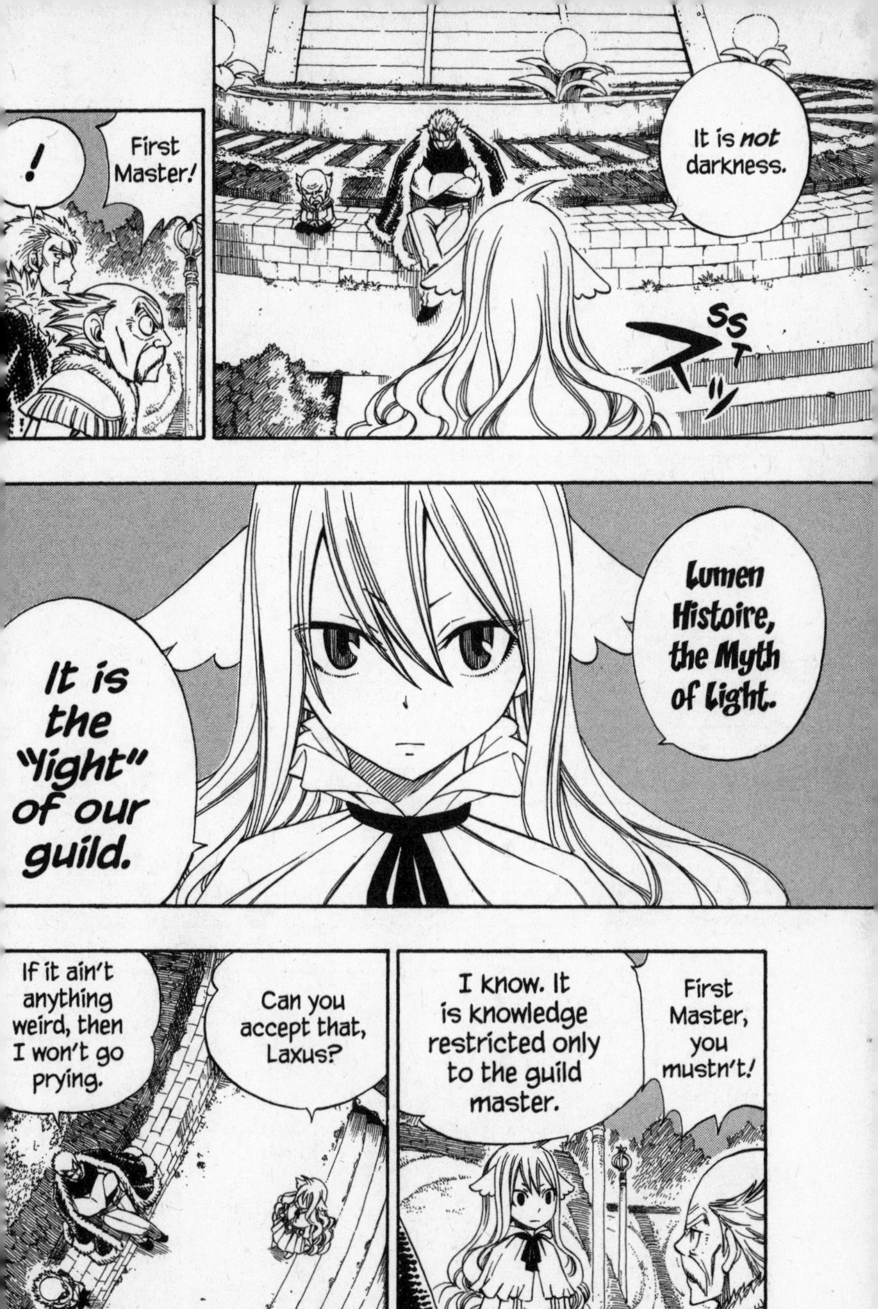
It is *not* darkness.
SST
First Master!
!
Lumen Histoire, the Myth of Light.
It is the "light" of our guild.
First Master, you mustn't!
I know. It is knowledge restricted only to the guild master.
Can you accept that, Laxus?
If it ain't anything weird, then I won't go prying.

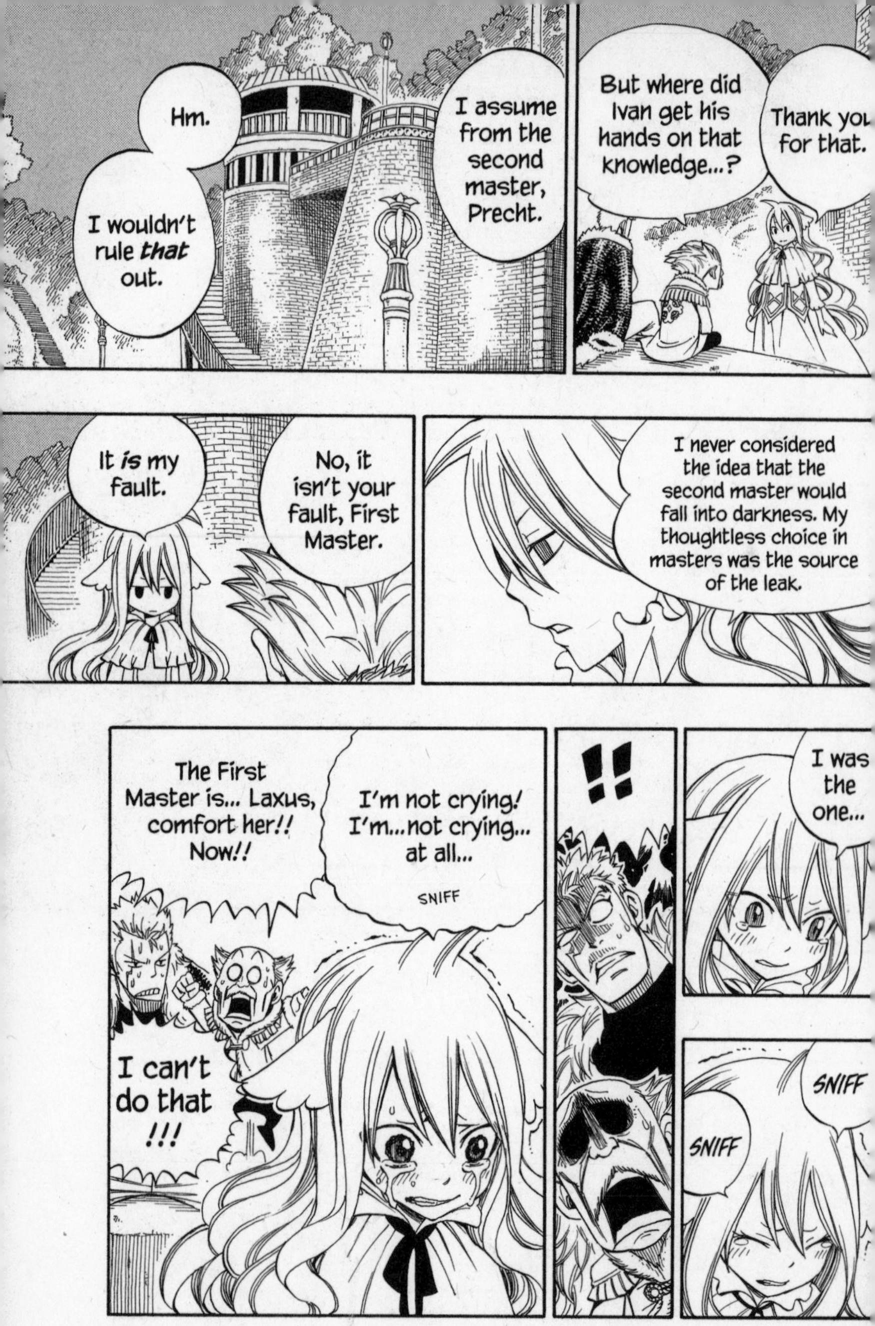
Thank you for that.
But where did Ivan get his hands on that knowledge...?
I assume from the second master, Precht.
Hm.
I wouldn't rule *that* out.
I never considered the idea that the second master would fall into darkness. My thoughtless choice in masters was the source of the leak.
No, it isn't your fault, First Master.
It *is* my fault.
I was the one...
SNIFF
SNIFF
!!
I'm not crying! I'm...not crying... at all...
SNIFF
The First Master is... Laxus, comfort her!! Now!!
I can't do that!!!

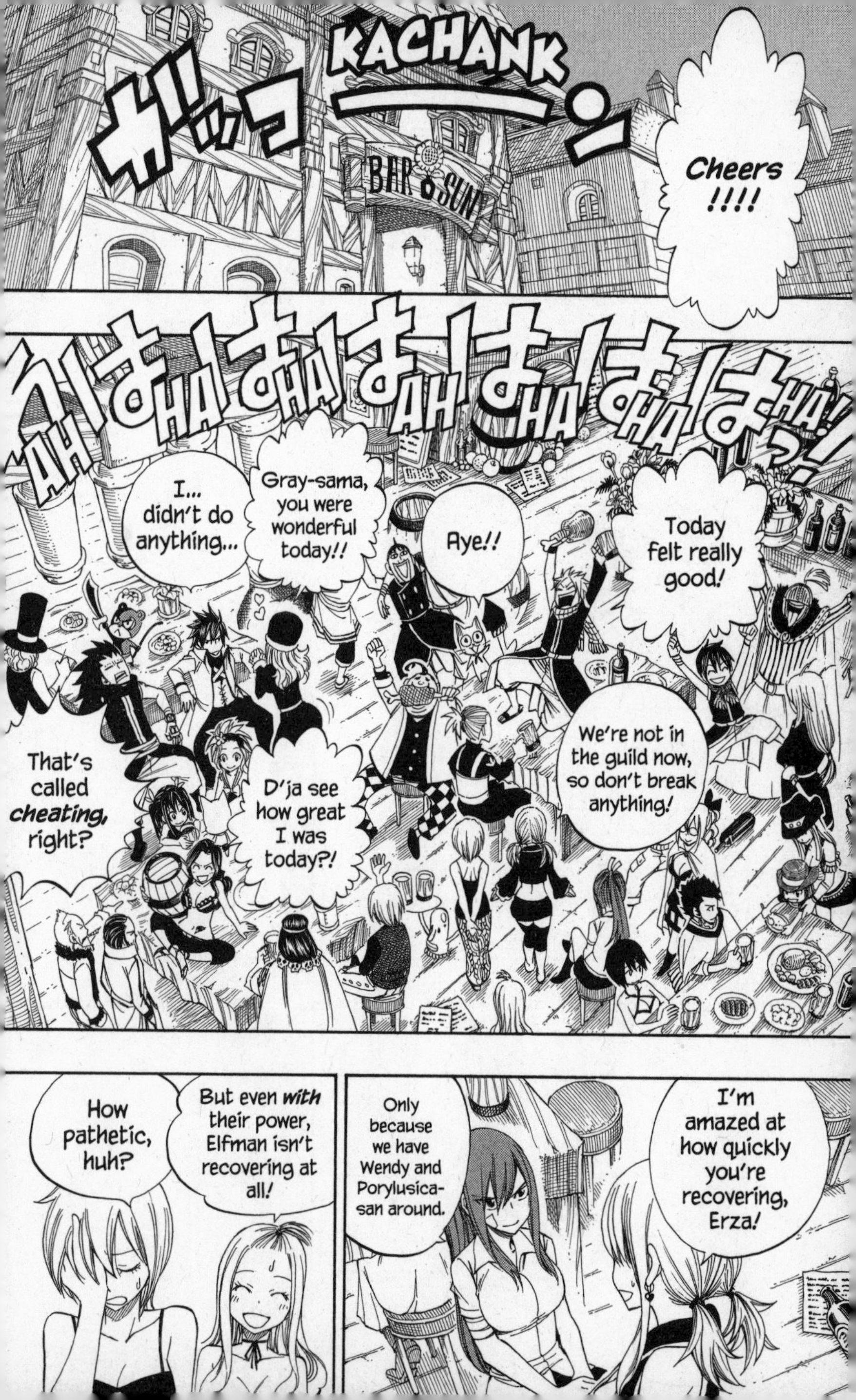
KACHANK
Cheers !!!!
AH HA AH HA AH HA!
Today felt really good!
Aye!!
Gray-sama, you were wonderful today!!
I... didn't do anything...
We're not in the guild now, so don't break anything!
D'ja see how great I was today?!
That's called *cheating*, right?
I'm amazed at how quickly you're recovering, Erza!
Only because we have Wendy and Porylusica-san around.
But even *with* their power, Elfman isn't recovering at all!
How pathetic, huh?

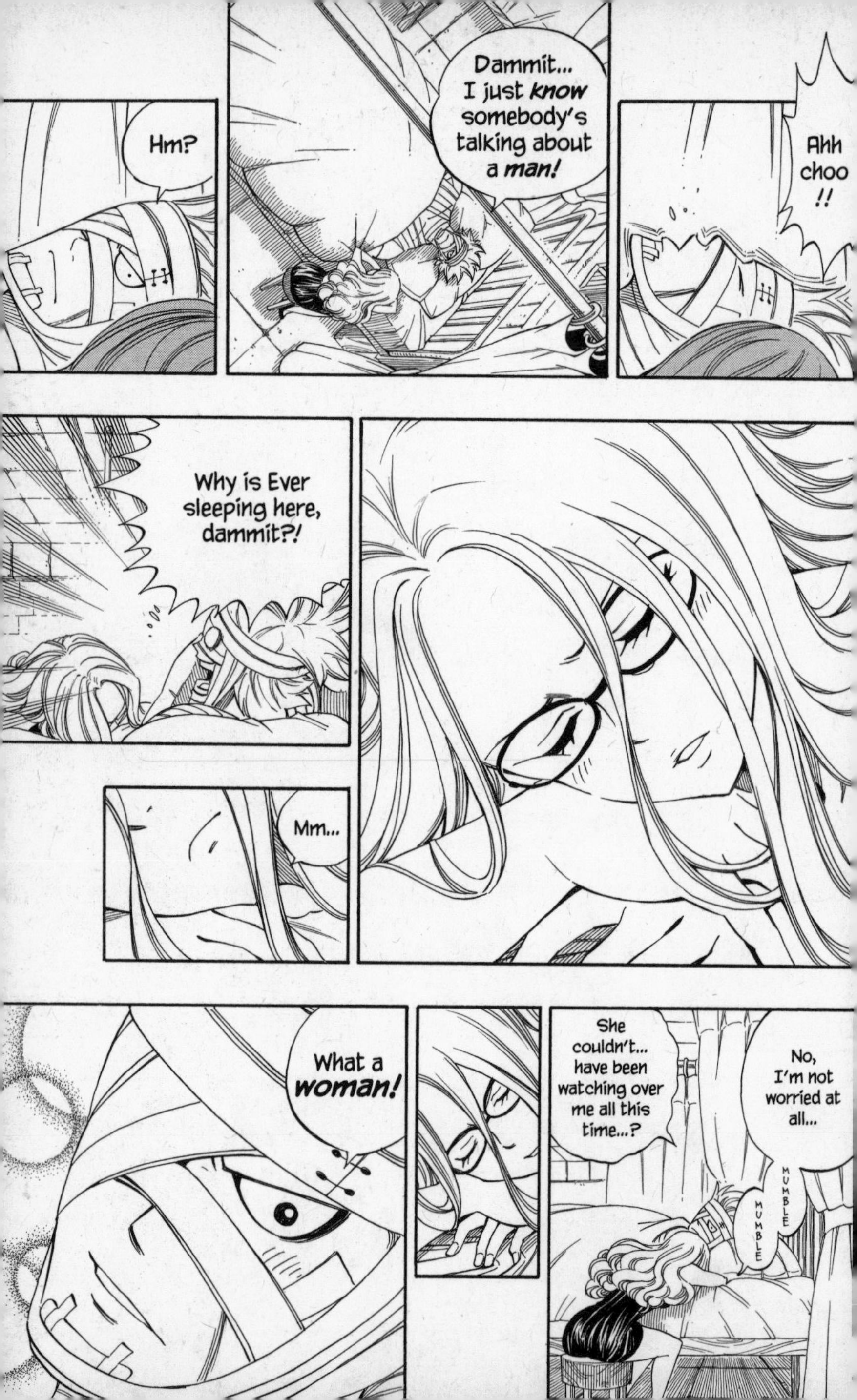
Ahh choo!!
Dammit... I just know somebody's talking about a man!
Hm?
Why is Ever sleeping here, dammit?!
Mm...
No, I'm not worried at all...
She couldn't... have been watching over me all this time...?
MUMBLE
MUMBLE
What a woman!

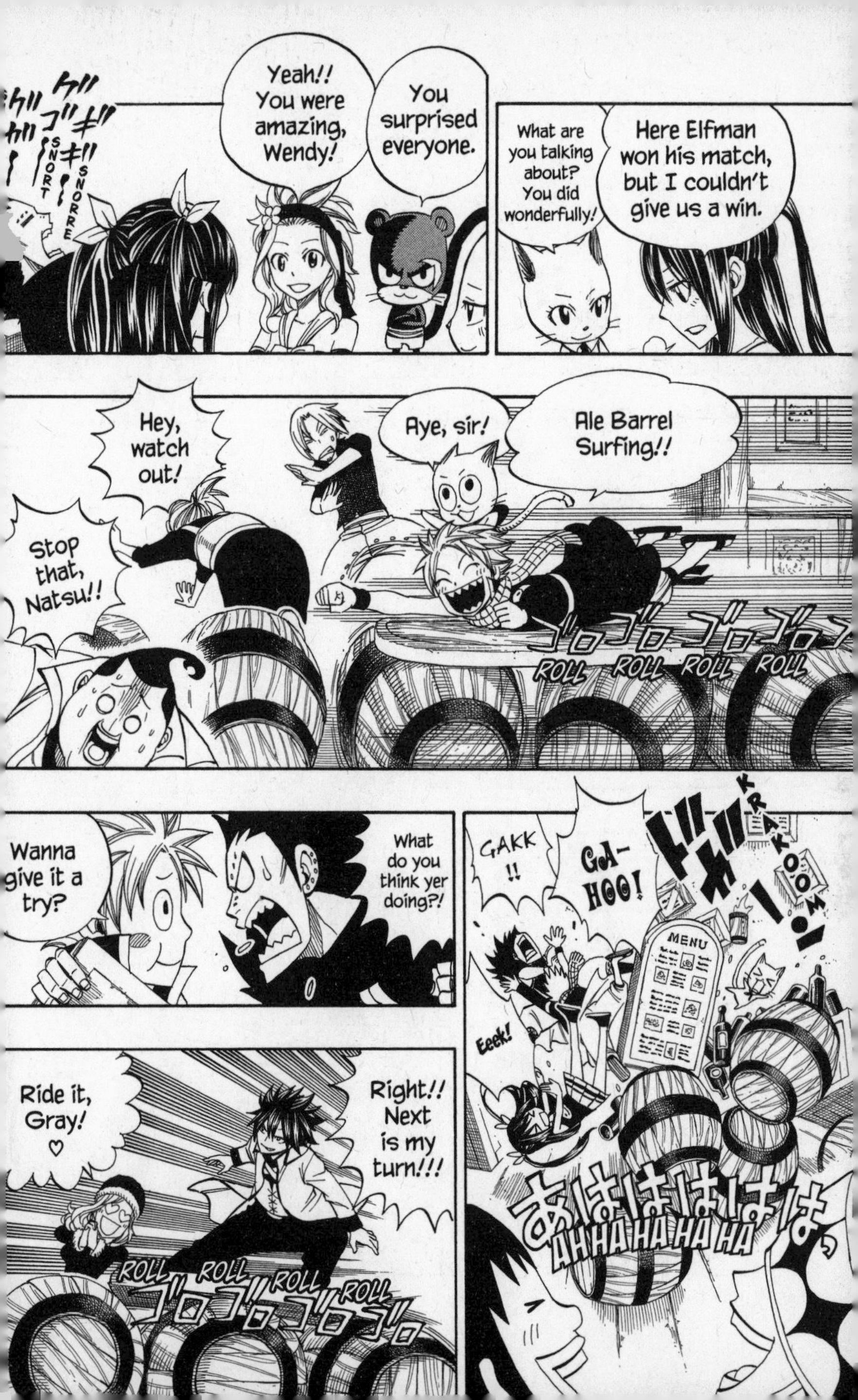
Here Elfman won his match, but I couldn't give us a win.
What are you talking about? You did wonderfully!
You surprised everyone.
Yeah!! You were amazing, Wendy!
SNORRE
SNORT
Ale Barrel Surfing!!
Aye, sir!
ROLL ROLL ROLL ROLL
Hey, watch out!
Stop that, Natsu!!
What do you think yer doing?!
Wanna give it a try?
Right!! Next is my turn!!!
Ride it, Gray! ♡
ROLL ROLL ROLL ROLL
KRAKOOOM!
GA-HOO!
GAKK!!
MENU
Eeek!
AHHAHAHAHA

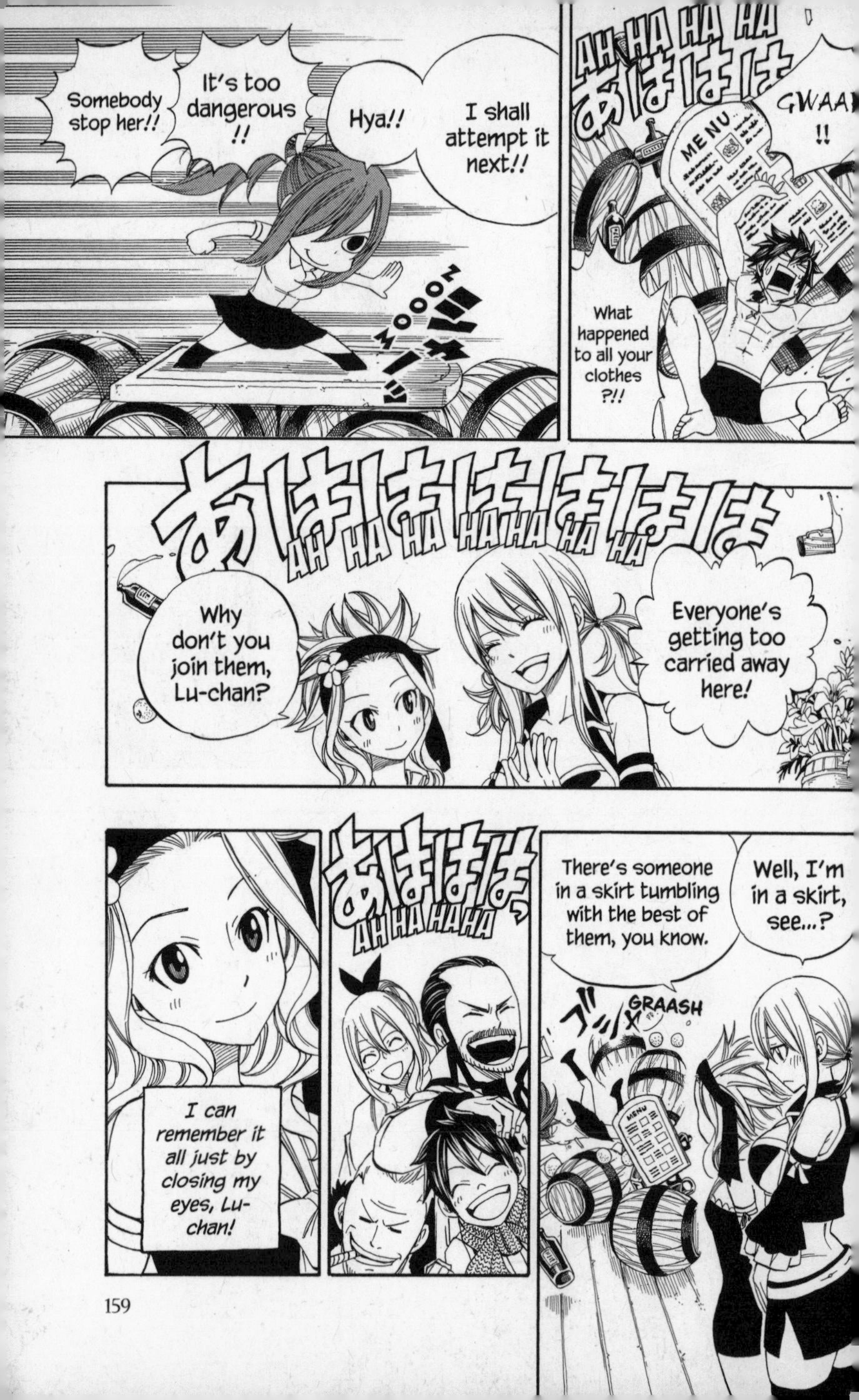
AH HA HA HA
GWAA!!
What happened to all your clothes?!!
I shall attempt it next!!
Hya!!
It's too dangerous!!
Somebody stop her!!
AH HA HA HA HA HA HA HA
Everyone's getting too carried away here!
Why don't you join them, Lu-chan?
Well, I'm in a skirt, see...?
There's someone in a skirt tumbling with the best of them, you know.
GRAASH
AH HA HA HA HA
I can remember it all just by closing my eyes, Lu-chan!

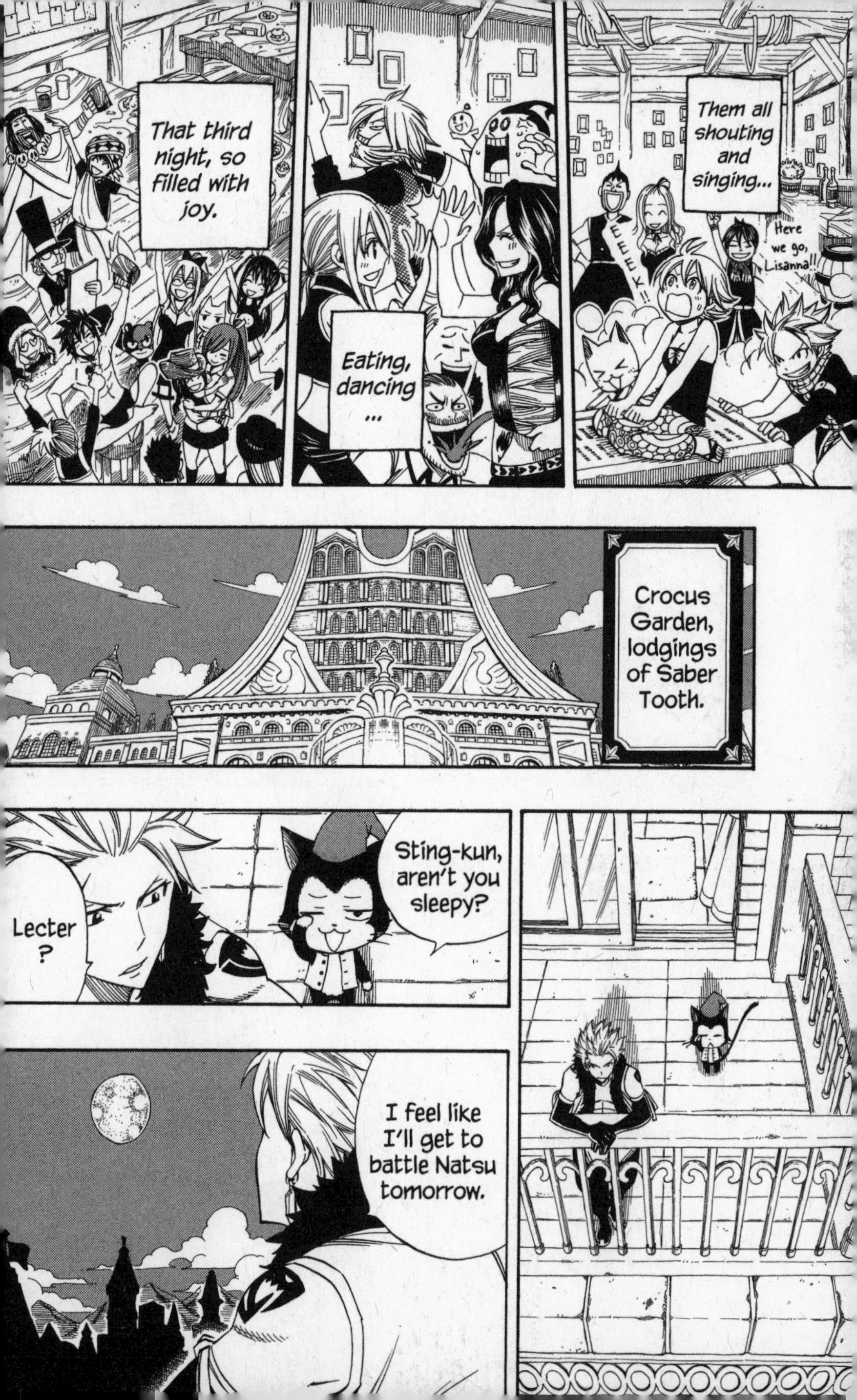
Them all shouting and singing...
Here we go, Lisanna!!
EEEEK!!
Eating, dancing ...
That third night, so filled with joy.
Crocus Garden, lodgings of Saber Tooth.
Sting-kun, aren't you sleepy?
Lecter ?
I feel like I'll get to battle Natsu tomorrow.

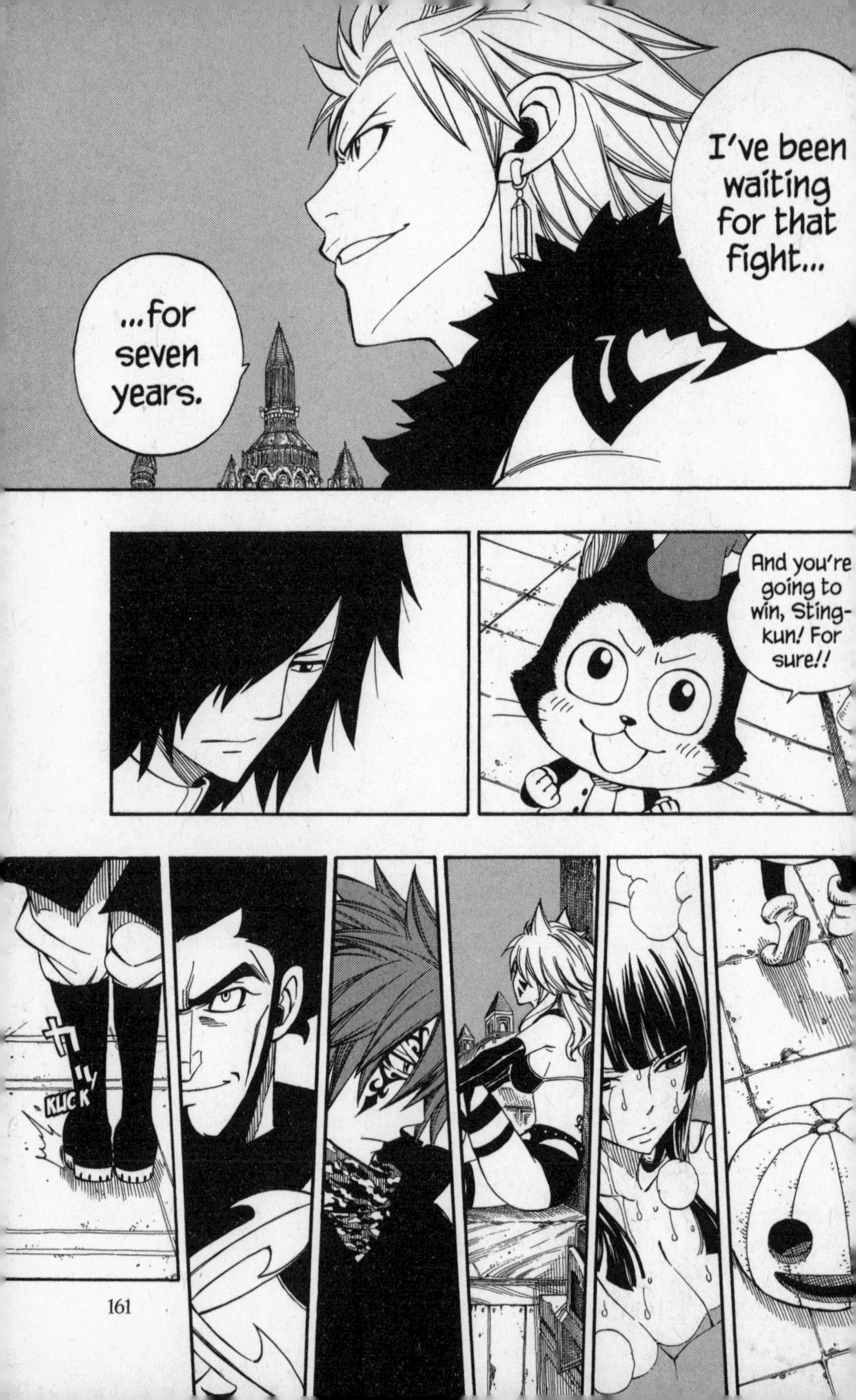
I've been waiting for that fight...
...for seven years.
And you're going to win, Sting-kun! For sure!!
KUCK

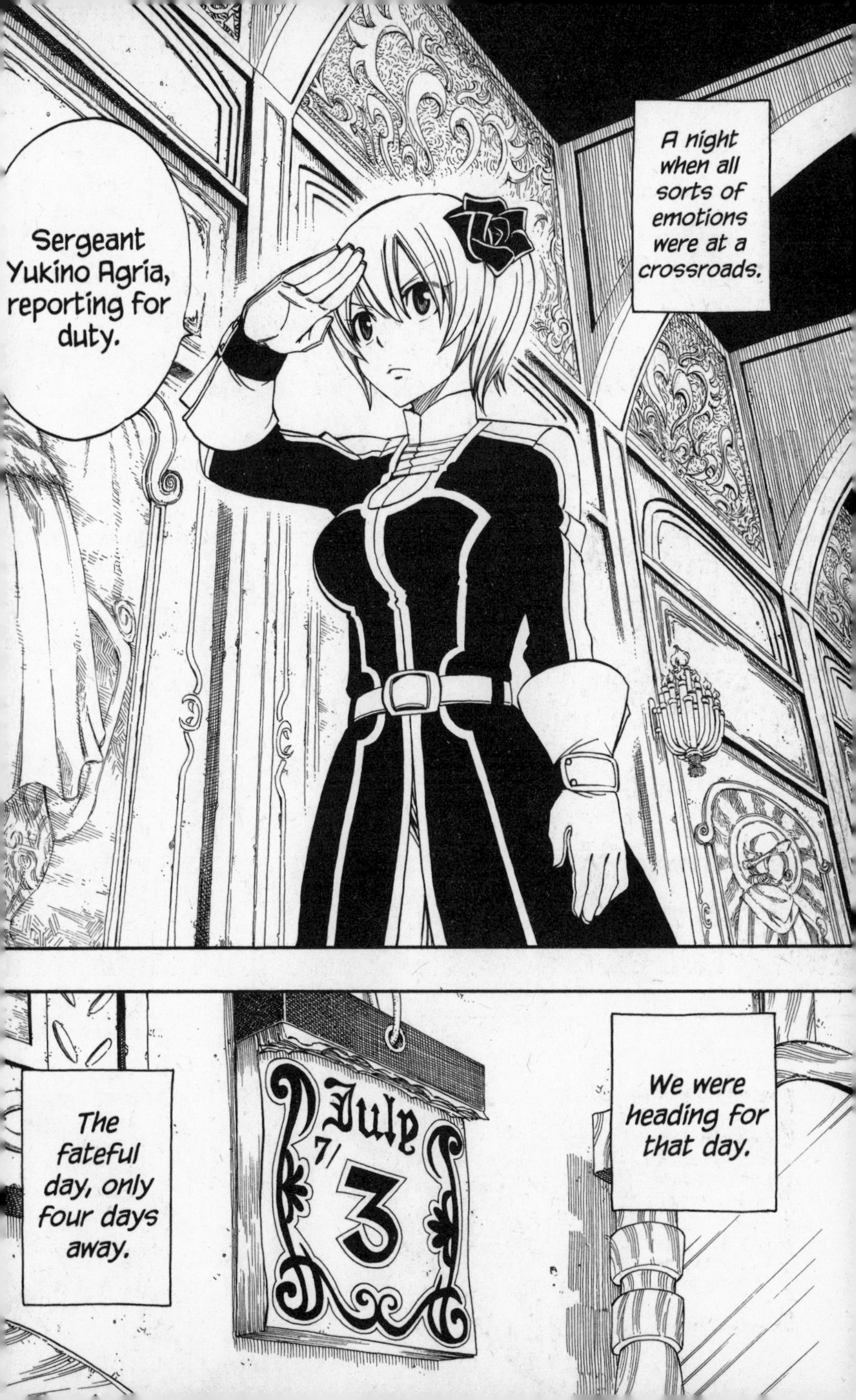
A night when all sorts of emotions were at a crossroads.
Sergeant Yukino Agria, reporting for duty.
We were heading for that day.
July
7/
3
The fateful day, only four days away.

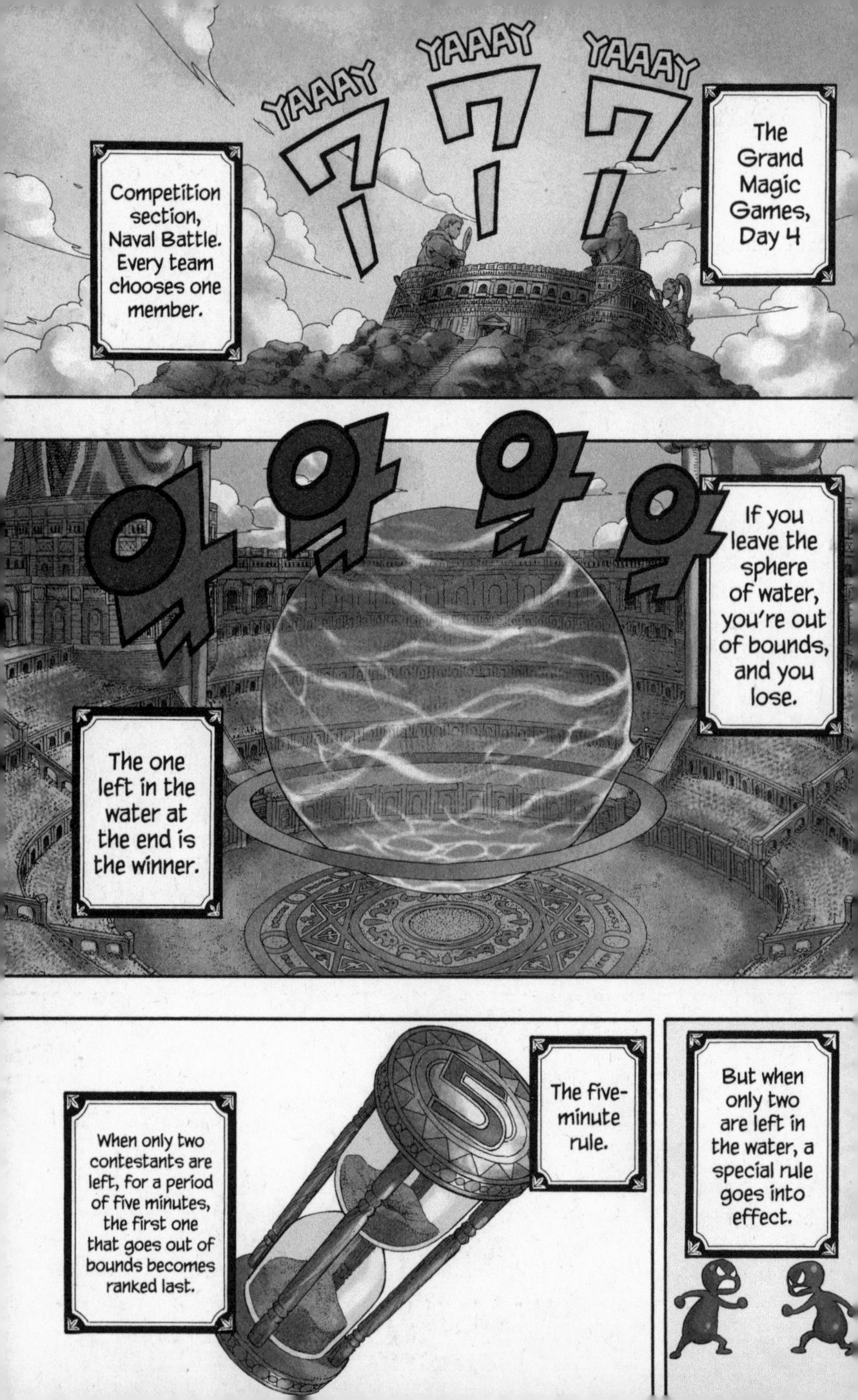
YAAAY
YAAAY
YAAAY
The Grand Magic Games, Day 4
Competition section, Naval Battle. Every team chooses one member.
If you leave the sphere of water, you're out of bounds, and you lose.
The one left in the water at the end is the winner.
But when only two are left in the water, a special rule goes into effect.
The five-minute rule.
When only two contestants are left, for a period of five minutes, the first one that goes out of bounds becomes ranked last.

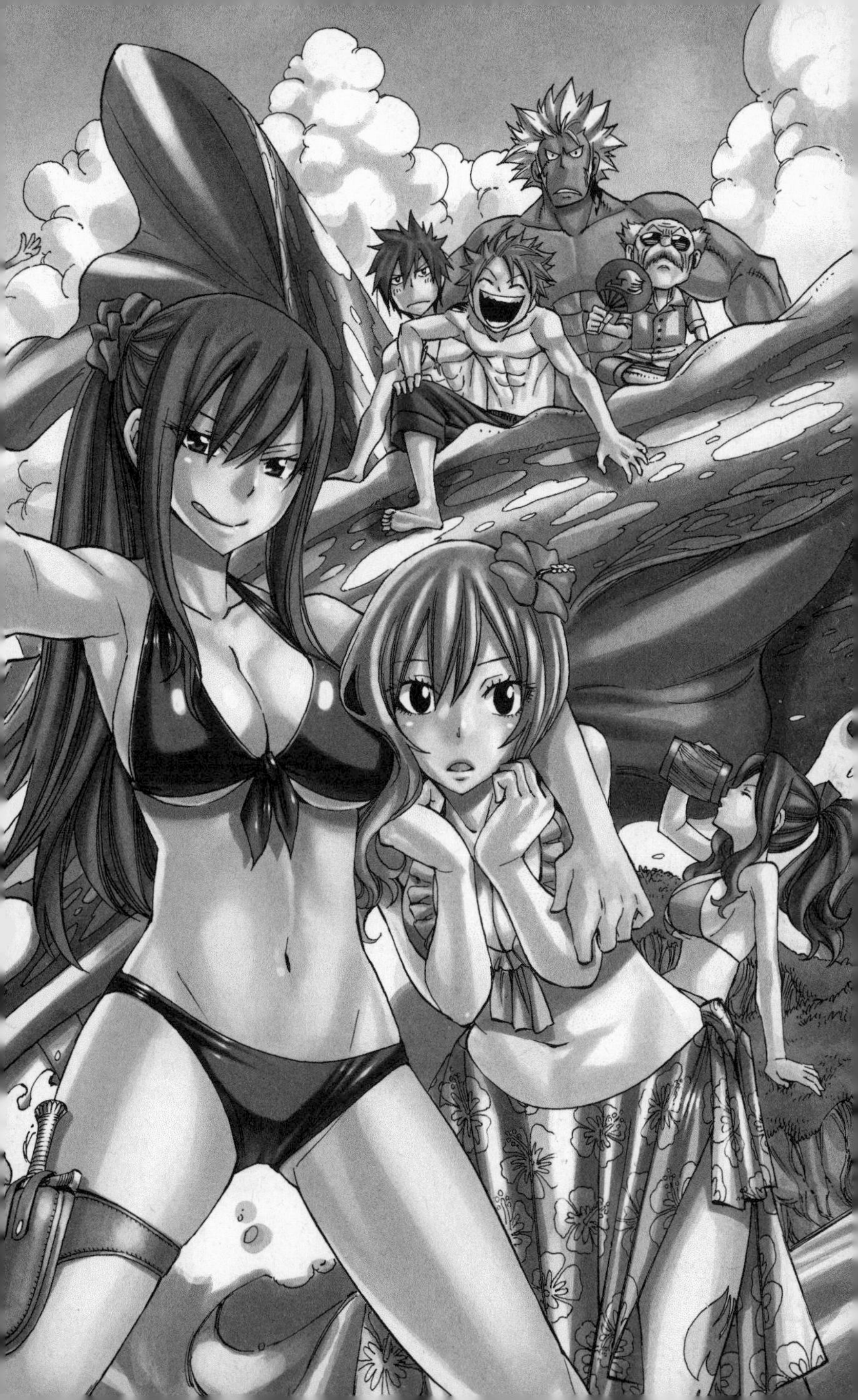

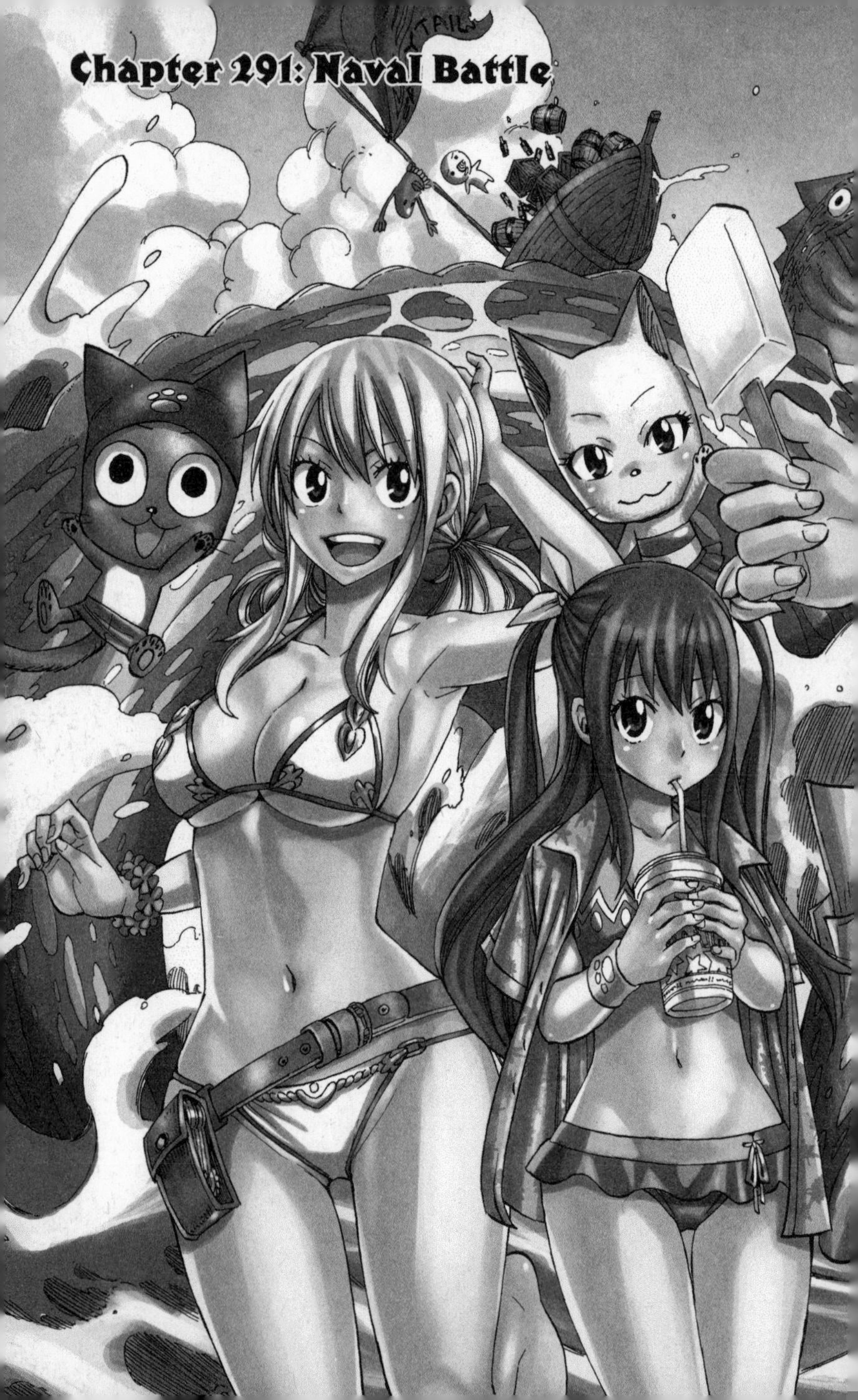
Chapter 291: Naval Battle

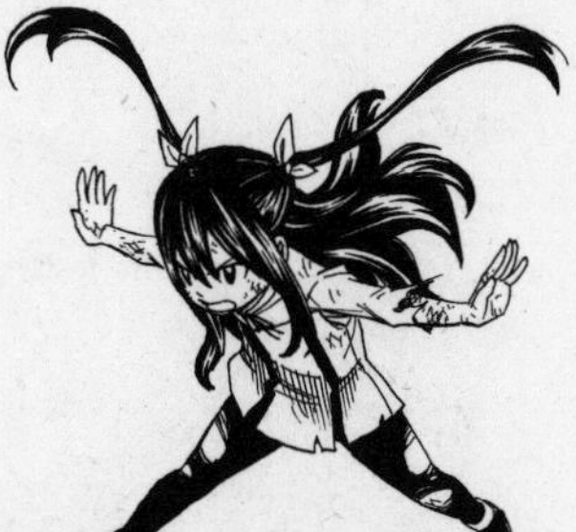

FAIRY TAIL

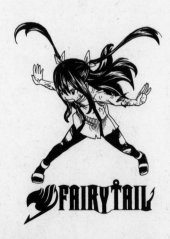

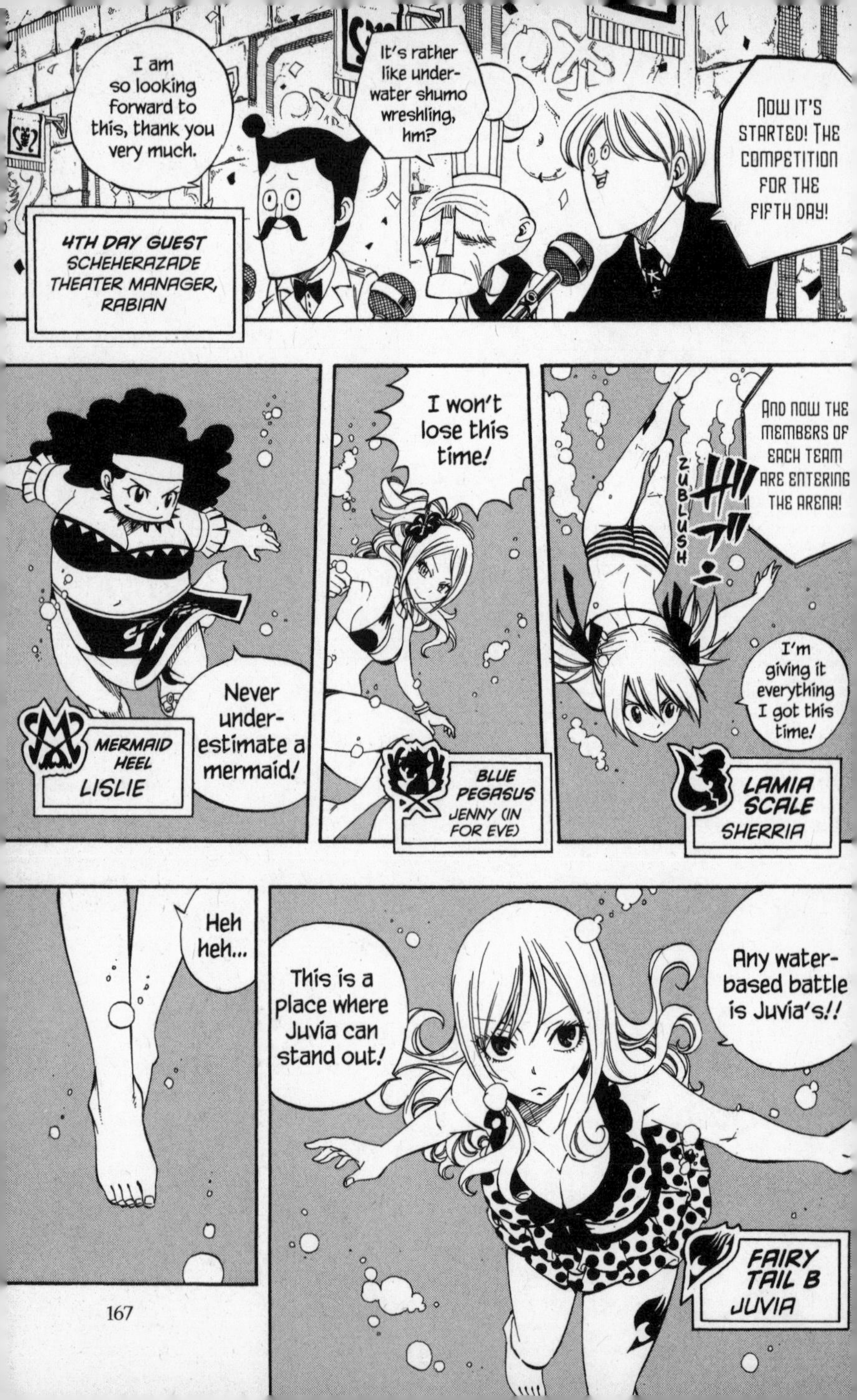
NOW IT'S STARTED! THE COMPETITION FOR THE FIFTH DAY!
It's rather like underwater shumo wreshling, hm?
I am so looking forward to this, thank you very much.
4TH DAY GUEST SCHEHERAZADE THEATER MANAGER, RABIAN
AND NOW THE MEMBERS OF EACH TEAM ARE ENTERING THE ARENA!
ZUBLUSH
I'm giving it everything I got this time!
LAMIA SCALE SHERRIA
I won't lose this time!
BLUE PEGASUS JENNY (IN FOR EVE)
Never underestimate a mermaid!
MERMAID HEEL LISLIE
Any water-based battle is Juvia's!!
This is a place where Juvia can stand out!
FAIRY TAIL B JUVIA
Heh heh...

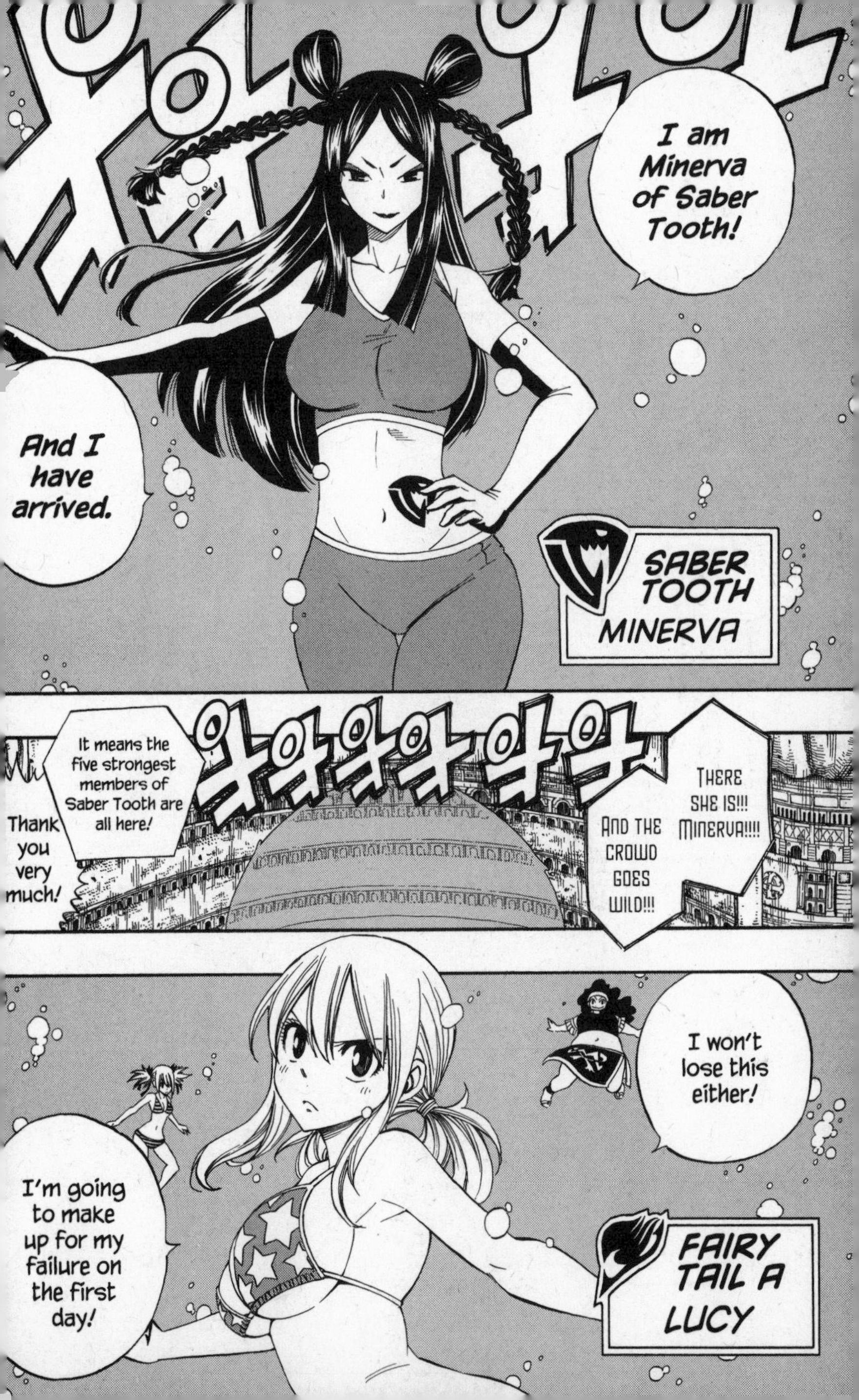
I am Minerva of Saber Tooth!
And I have arrived.
SABER TOOTH MINERVA
THERE SHE IS!!! MINERVA!!!!
AND THE CROWD GOES WILD!!!
와와와와와와
It means the five strongest members of Saber Tooth are all here!
Thank you very much!
I won't lose this either!
FAIRY TAIL A LUCY
I'm going to make up for my failure on the first day!

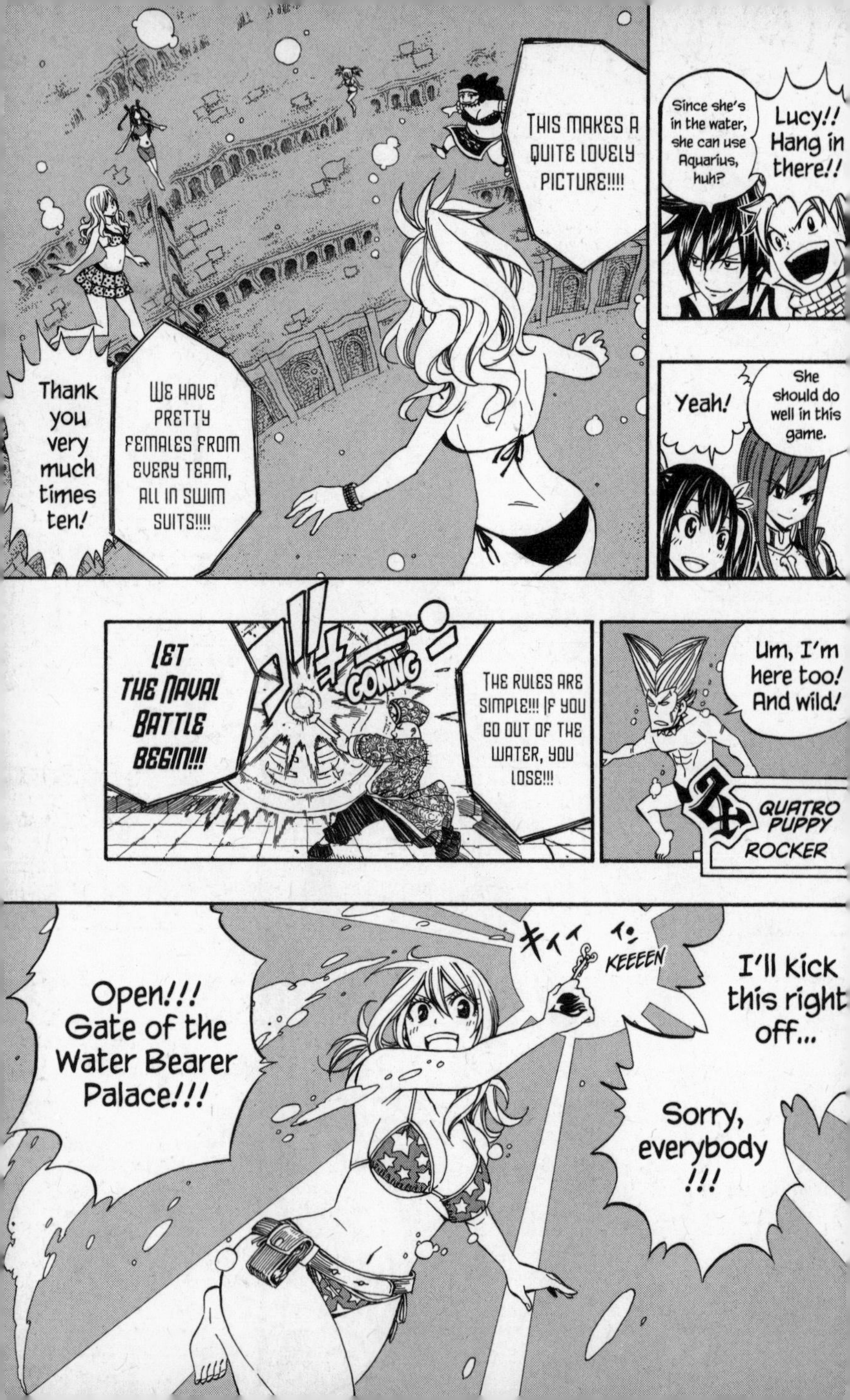
Lucy!! Hang in there!!
Since she's in the water, she can use Aquarius, huh?
She should do well in this game.
Yeah!
THIS MAKES A QUITE LOVELY PICTURE!!!!
WE HAVE PRETTY FEMALES FROM EVERY TEAM, ALL IN SWIM SUITS!!!!
Thank you very much times ten!
Um, I'm here too! And wild!
QUATRO PUPPY ROCKER
THE RULES ARE SIMPLE!!! IF YOU GO OUT OF THE WATER, YOU LOSE!!!
GONNG
LET THE NAVAL BATTLE BEGIN!!!
I'll kick this right off...
KEEEEN
Sorry, everybody!!!
Open!!! Gate of the Water Bearer Palace!!!

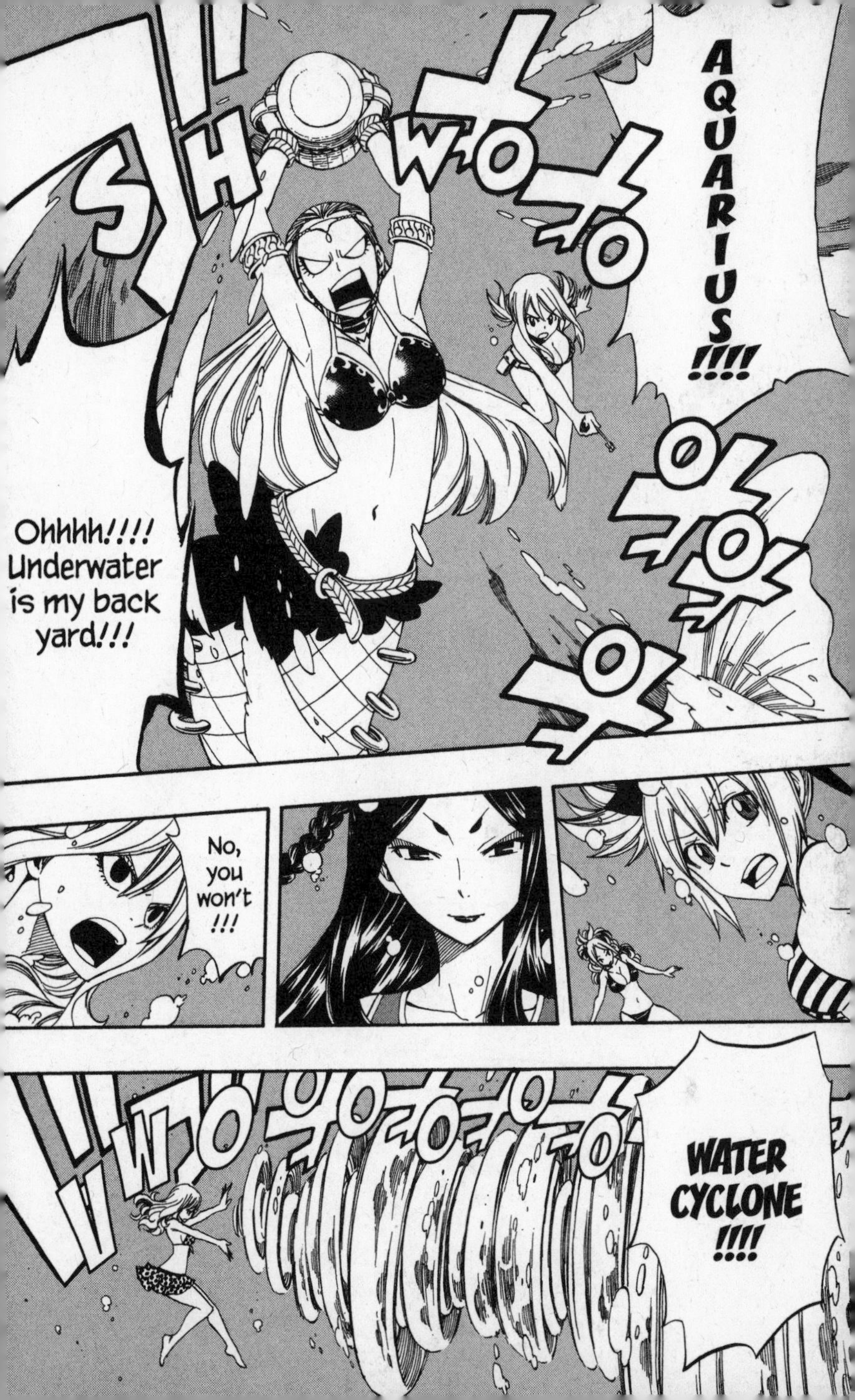
AQUARIUS!!!!
Ohhhh!!!! Underwater is my back yard!!!
No, you won't !!!
WATER CYCLONE !!!!

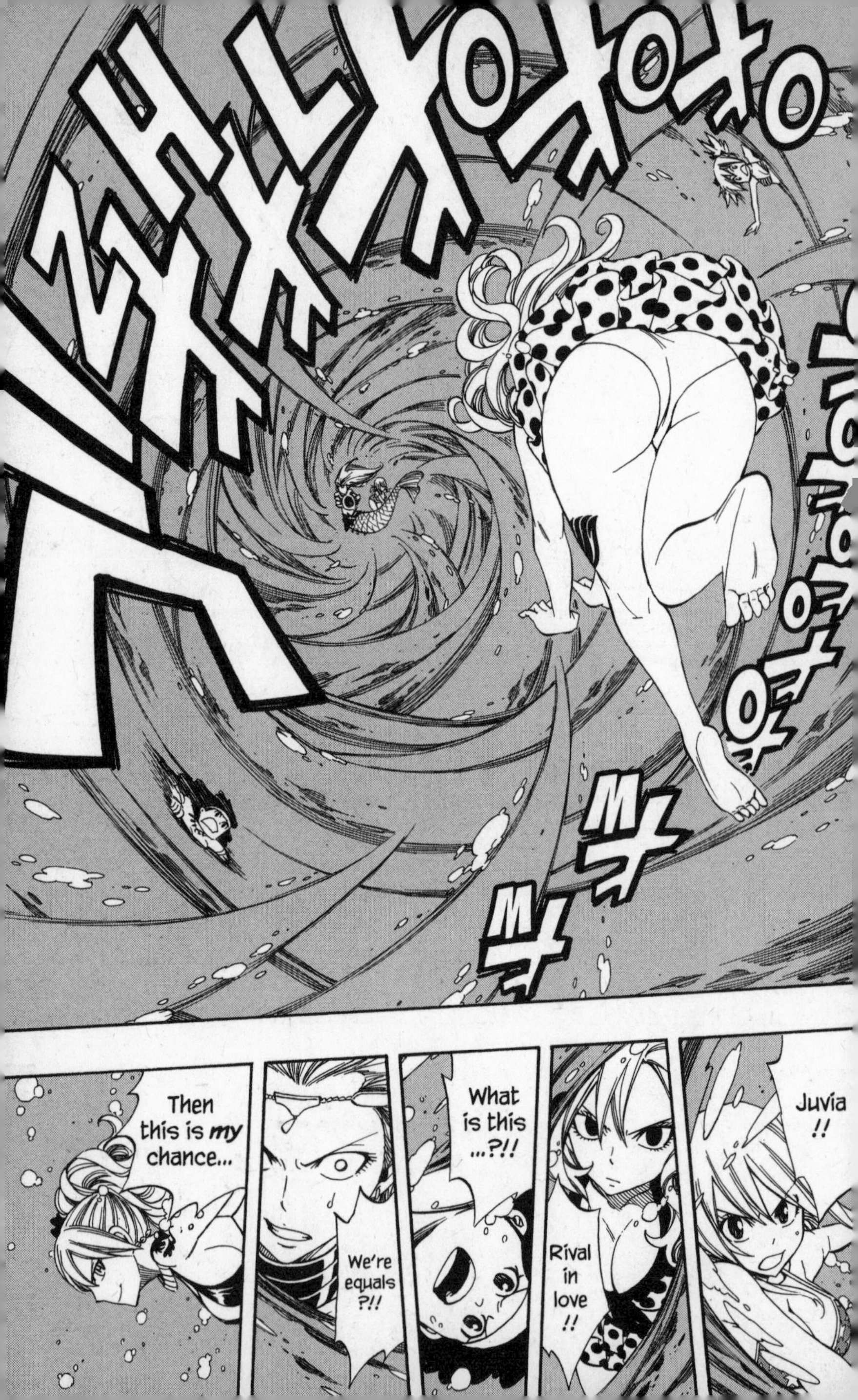
Juvia !!
Rival in love !!
What is this ...?!!
We're equals ?!!
Then this is *my* chance...

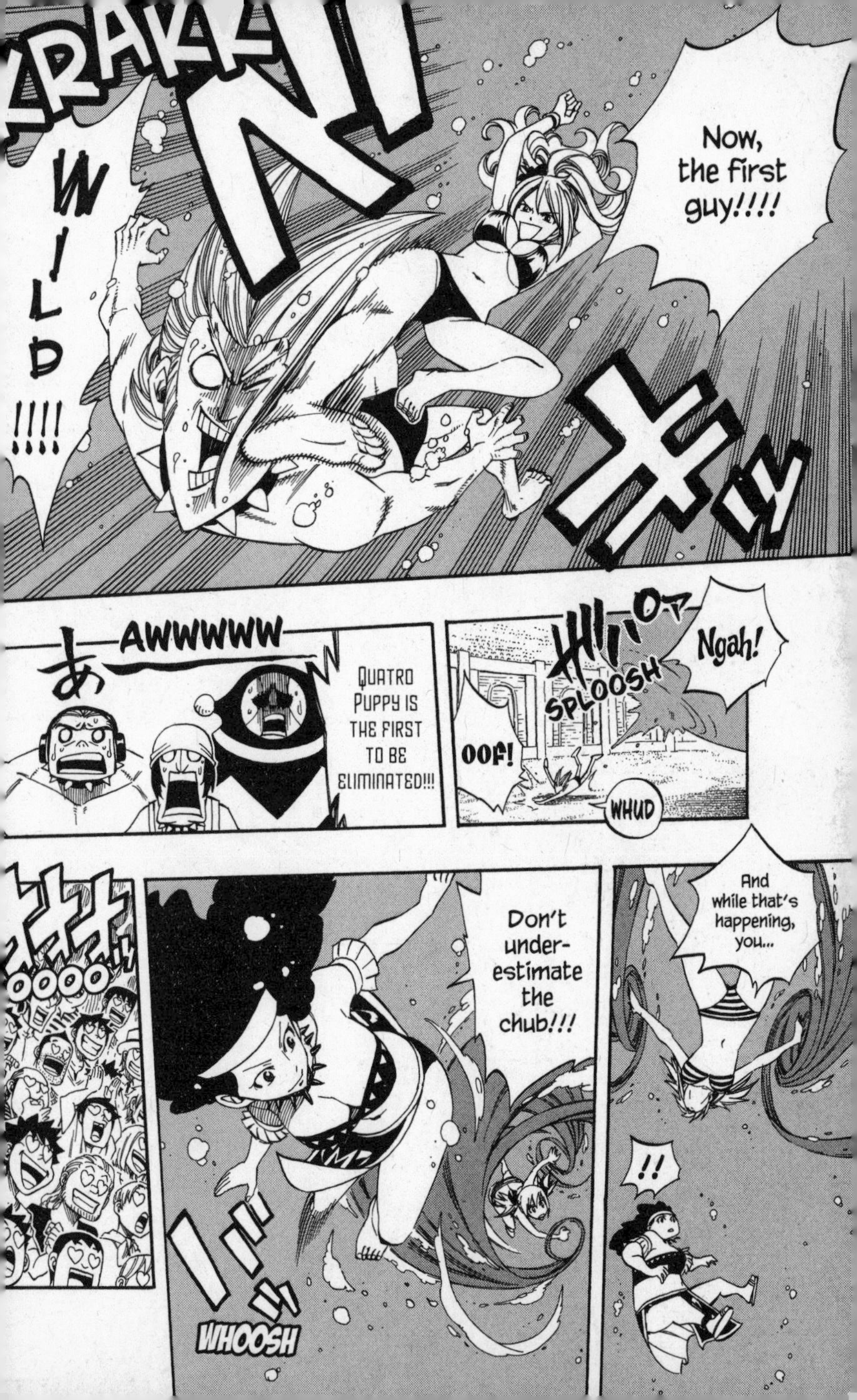

Now, the first guy!!!!
WILD!!!!!
Ngah!
SPLOOSH
OOF!
WHUD
QUATRO PUPPY IS THE FIRST TO BE ELIMINATED!!!
AWWWWW
あ
And while that's happening, you...
!!
Don't under-estimate the chub!!!
WHOOSH
OOOO

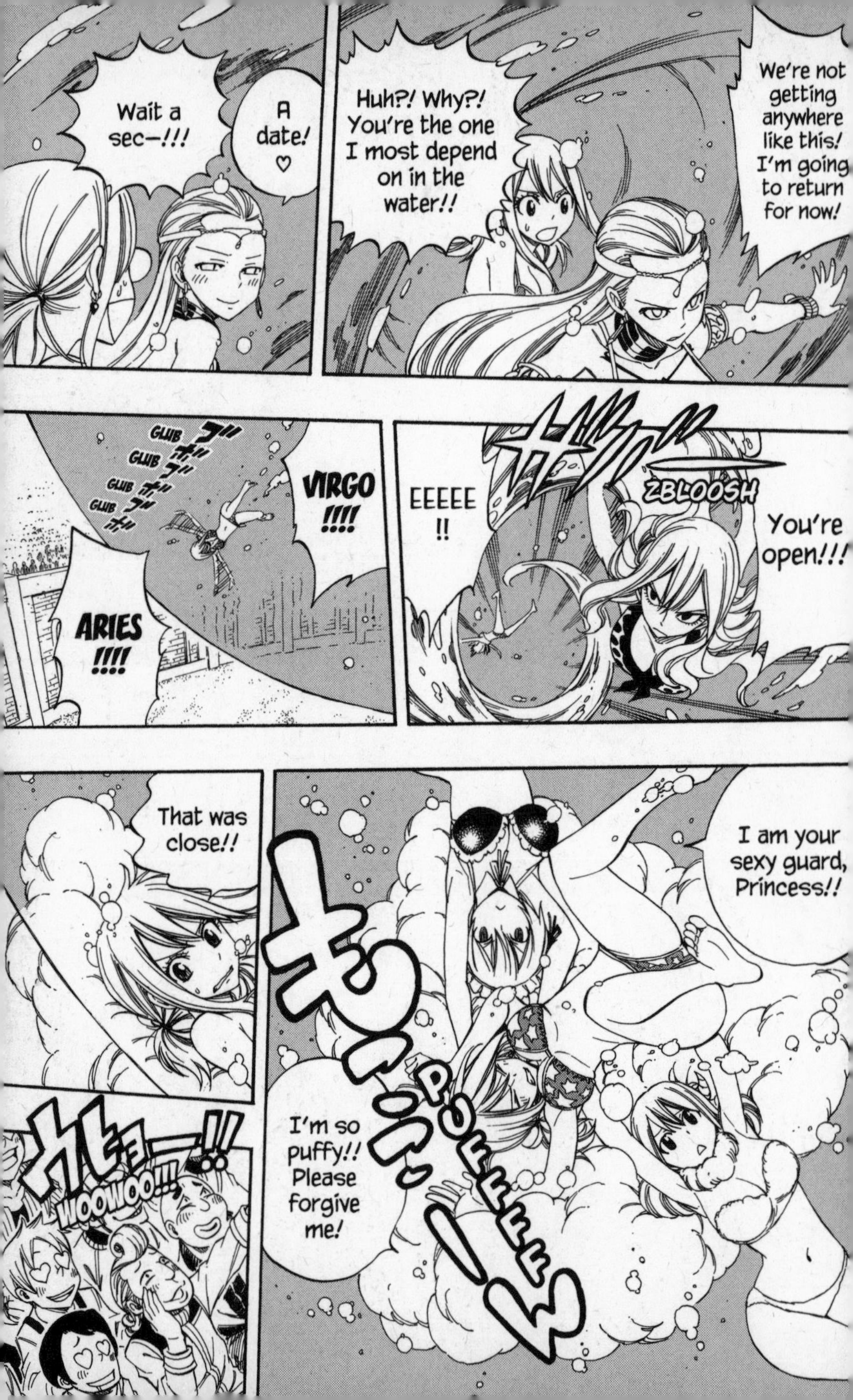
We're not getting anywhere like this! I'm going to return for now!
Huh?! Why?! You're the one I most depend on in the water!!
A date! ♡
Wait a sec—!!!
ZBLOOSH
You're open!!!
EEEEE !!
VIRGO !!!!
GLUB
GLUB
GLUB
GLUB
ARIES !!!!
I am your sexy guard, Princess!!
PUFFFFF
I'm so puffy!! Please forgive me!
That was close!!
WOOWOO!!!

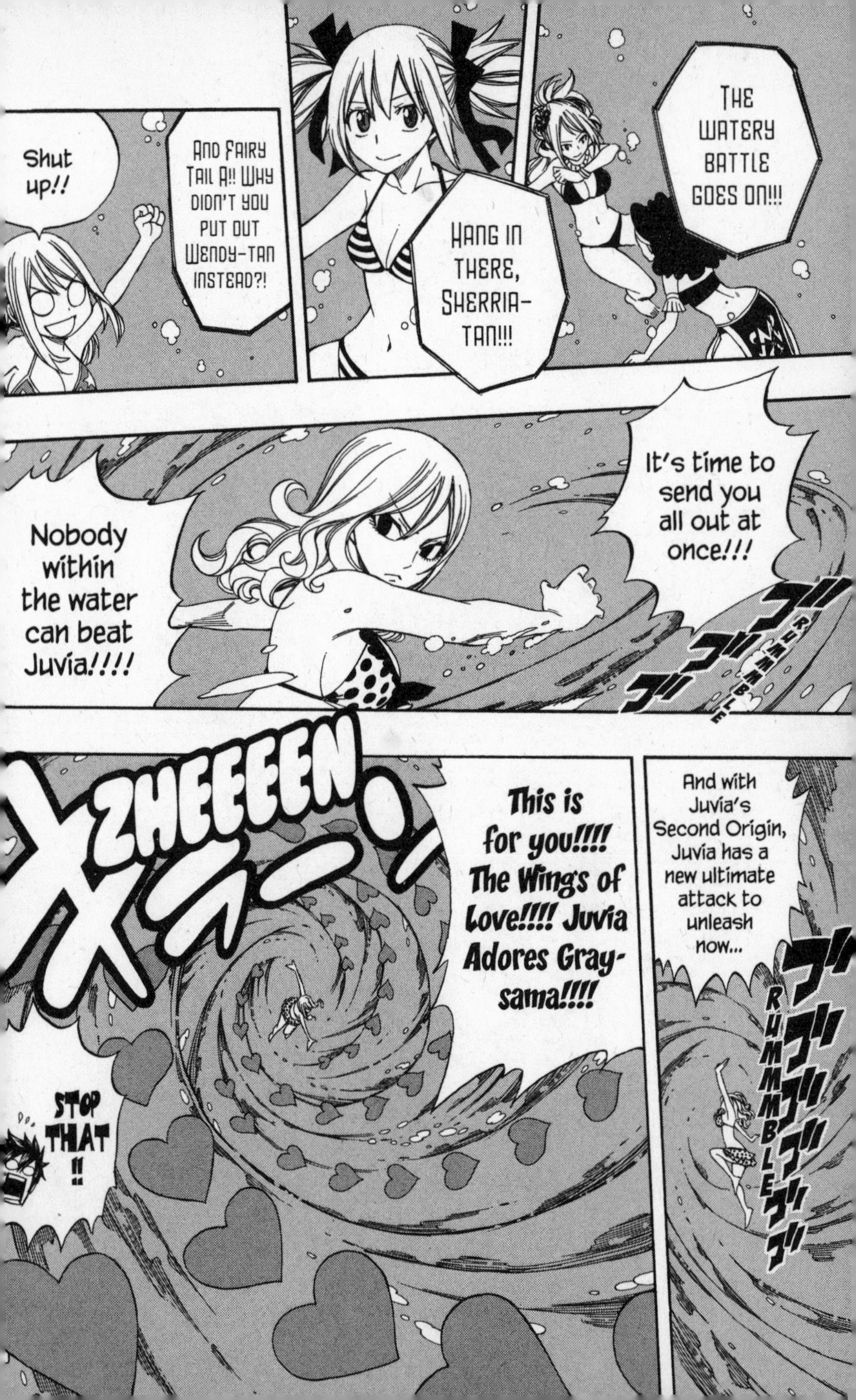

THE WATERY BATTLE GOES ON!!!
HANG IN THERE, SHERRIA-TAN!!!
AND FAIRY TAIL A!! WHY DIDN'T YOU PUT OUT WENDY-TAN INSTEAD?!
Shut up!!
It's time to send you all out at once!!!
Nobody within the water can beat Juvia!!!!
RUMMMBLE
And with Juvia's Second Origin, Juvia has a new ultimate attack to unleash now...
RUMMMBLE
ZHEEEEN
This is for you!!!! The Wings of Love!!!! Juvia Adores Gray-sama!!!!
STOP THAT!!

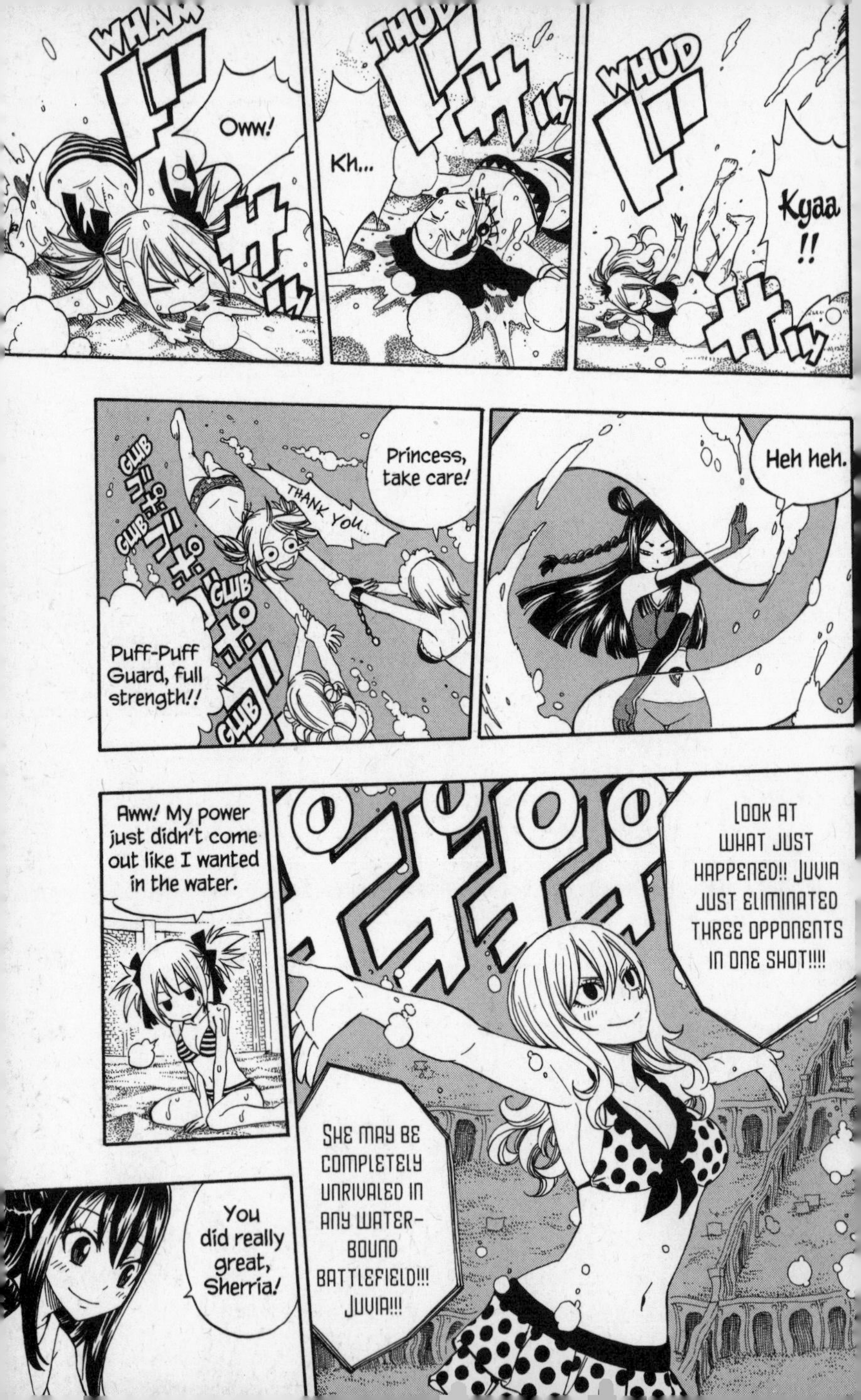
WHUD
Kyaa!!
THUD
Kh...
WHAM
Oww!
Heh heh.
Princess, take care!
THANK YOU...
GLUB
GLUB
GLUB
GLUB
Puff-Puff Guard, full strength!!
LOOK AT WHAT JUST HAPPENED!! JUVIA JUST ELIMINATED THREE OPPONENTS IN ONE SHOT!!!!
SHE MAY BE COMPLETELY UNRIVALED IN ANY WATER-BOUND BATTLEFIELD!!! JUVIA!!!
Aww! My power just didn't come out like I wanted in the water.
You did really great, Sherria!

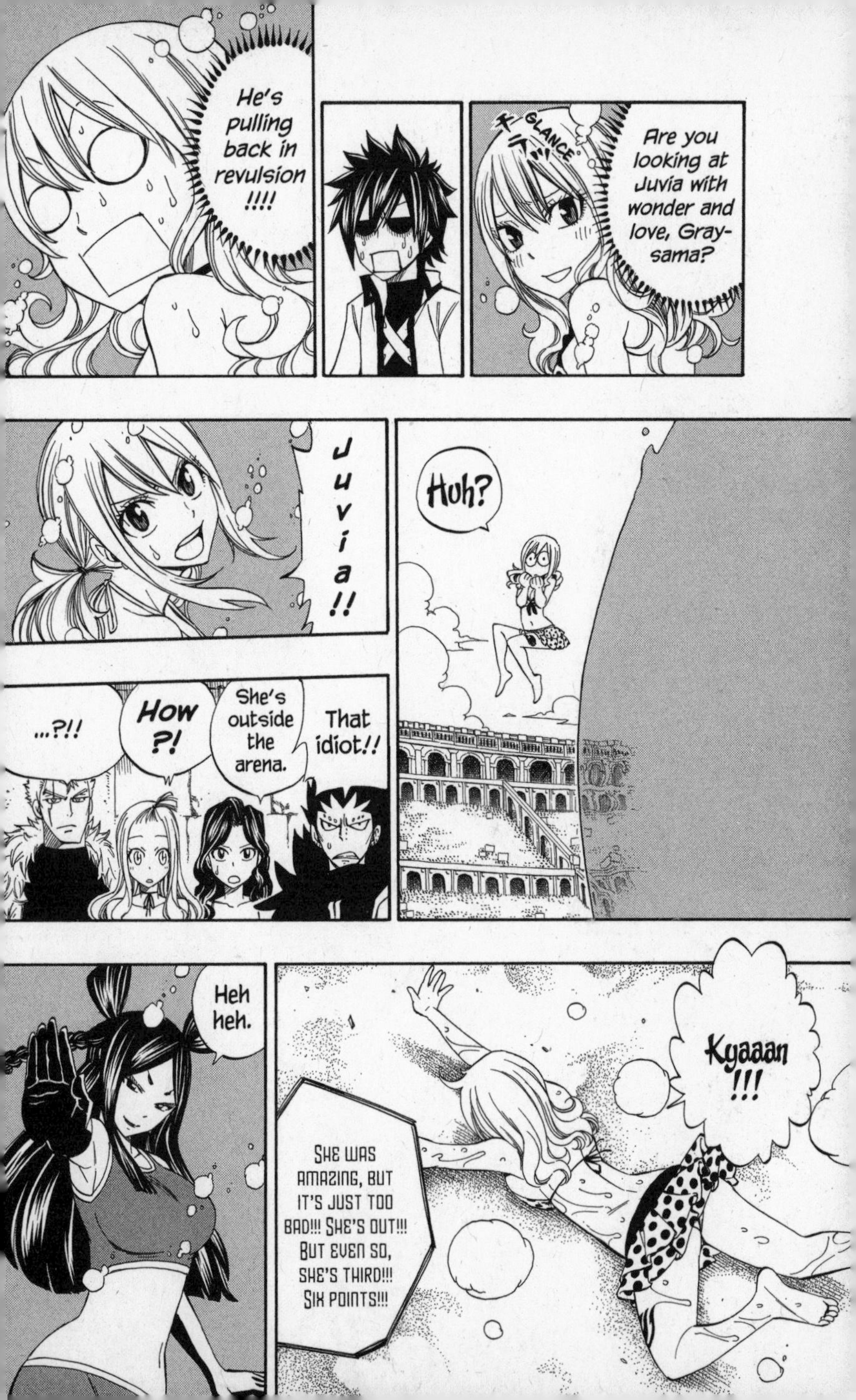
GLANCE
Are you looking at Juvia with wonder and love, Gray-sama?
He's pulling back in revulsion!!!!
Huh?
Juvia!!
That idiot!!
She's outside the arena.
How?!
...?!!
Kyaaan!!!
SHE WAS AMAZING, BUT IT'S JUST TOO BAD!!! SHE'S OUT!!! BUT EVEN SO, SHE'S THIRD!!! SIX POINTS!!!
Heh heh.

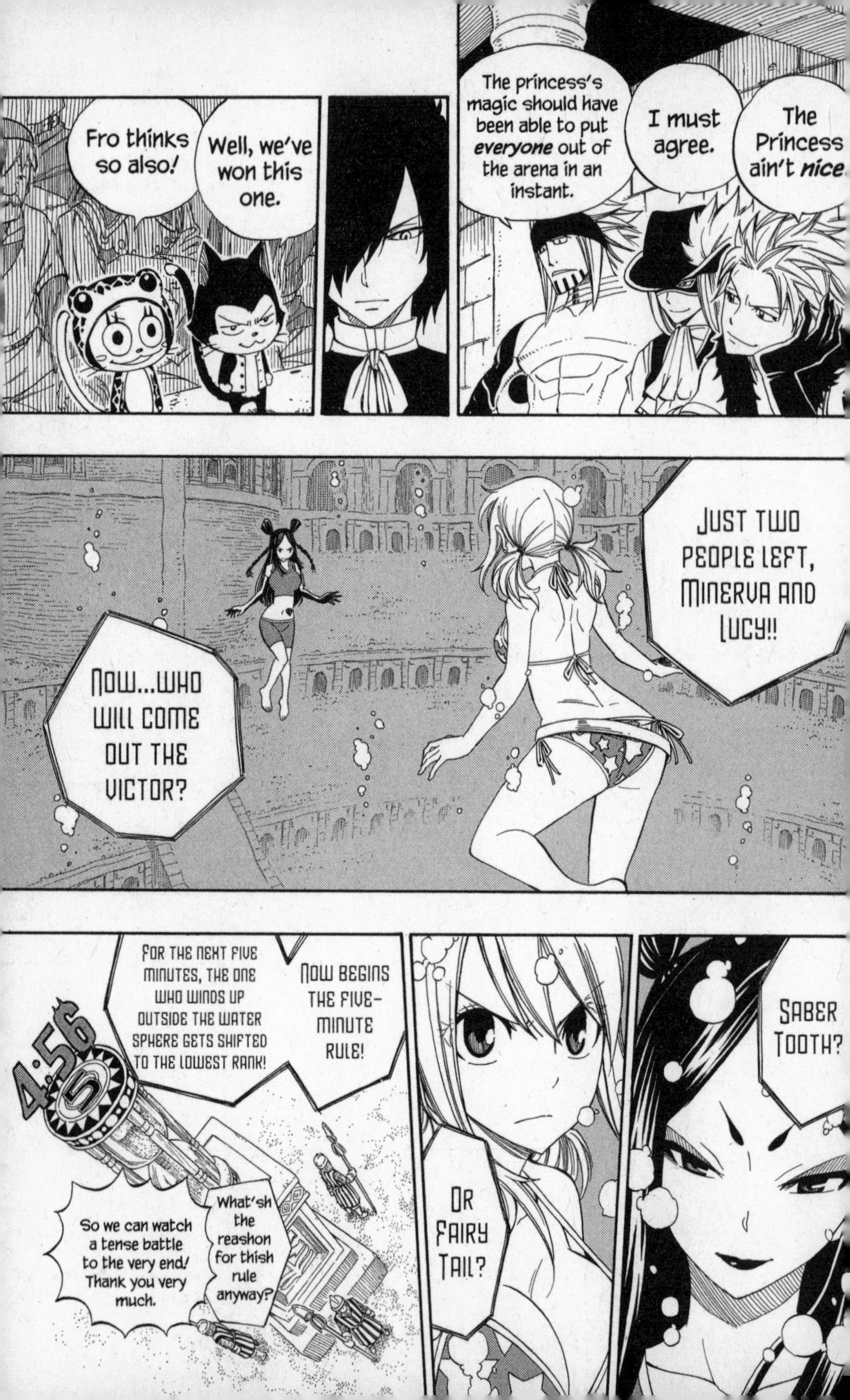
The Princess ain't *nice*.
I must agree.
The princess's magic should have been able to put *everyone* out of the arena in an instant.
Well, we've won this one.
Fro thinks so also!
JUST TWO PEOPLE LEFT, MINERVA AND LUCY!!
NOW...WHO WILL COME OUT THE VICTOR?
SABER TOOTH?
OR FAIRY TAIL?
NOW BEGINS THE FIVE-MINUTE RULE!
FOR THE NEXT FIVE MINUTES, THE ONE WHO WINDS UP OUTSIDE THE WATER SPHERE GETS SHIFTED TO THE LOWEST RANK!
4:56
5
What'sh the reashon for thish rule anyway?
So we can watch a tense battle to the very end! Thank you very much.

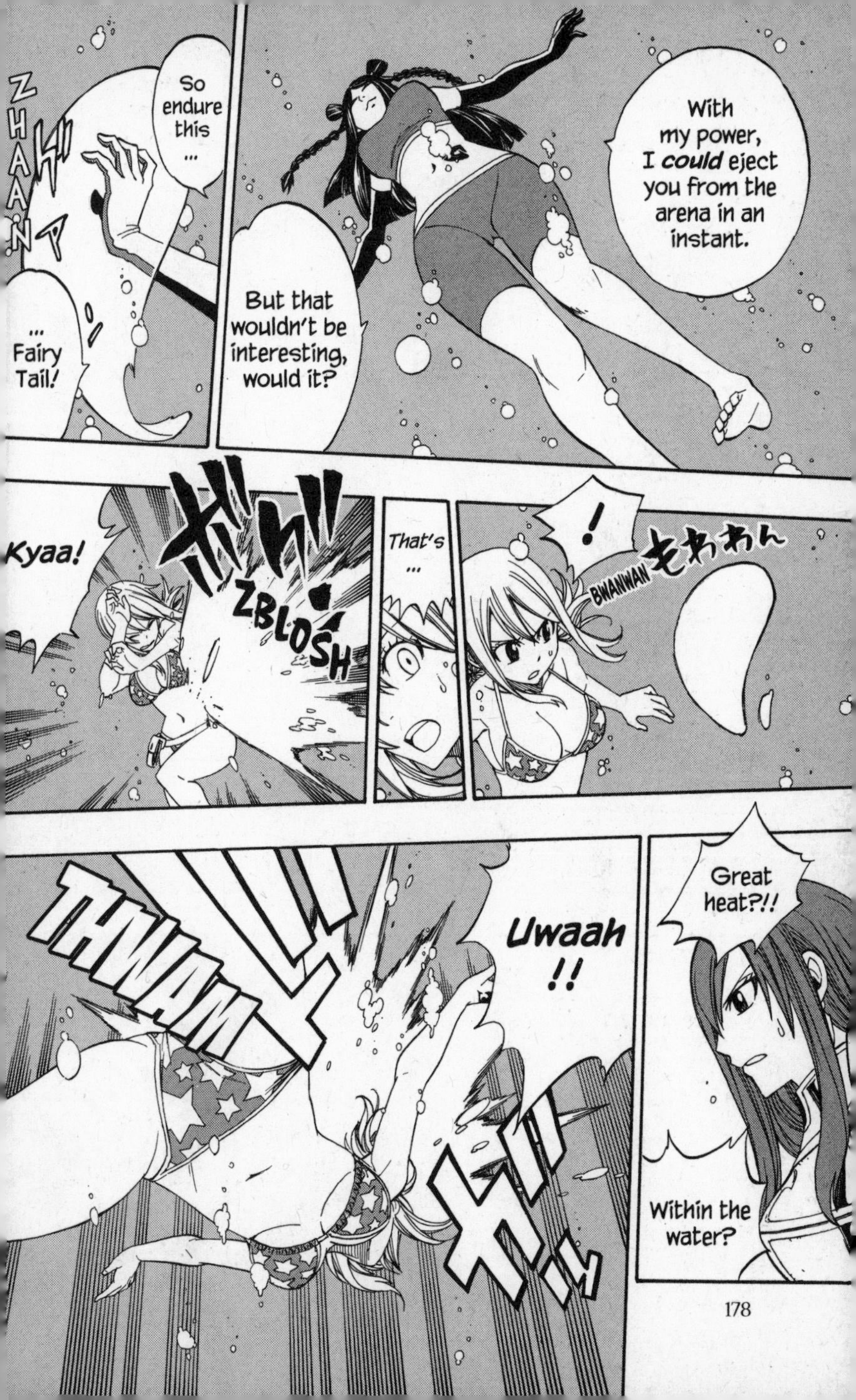
With my power, I could eject you from the arena in an instant.
But that wouldn't be interesting, would it?
So endure this ...
ZHAAAN
... Fairy Tail!
!
BWANWAN
That's ...
Kyaa!
ZBLOSH
Great heat?!!
Within the water?
Uwaah !!
THWAM

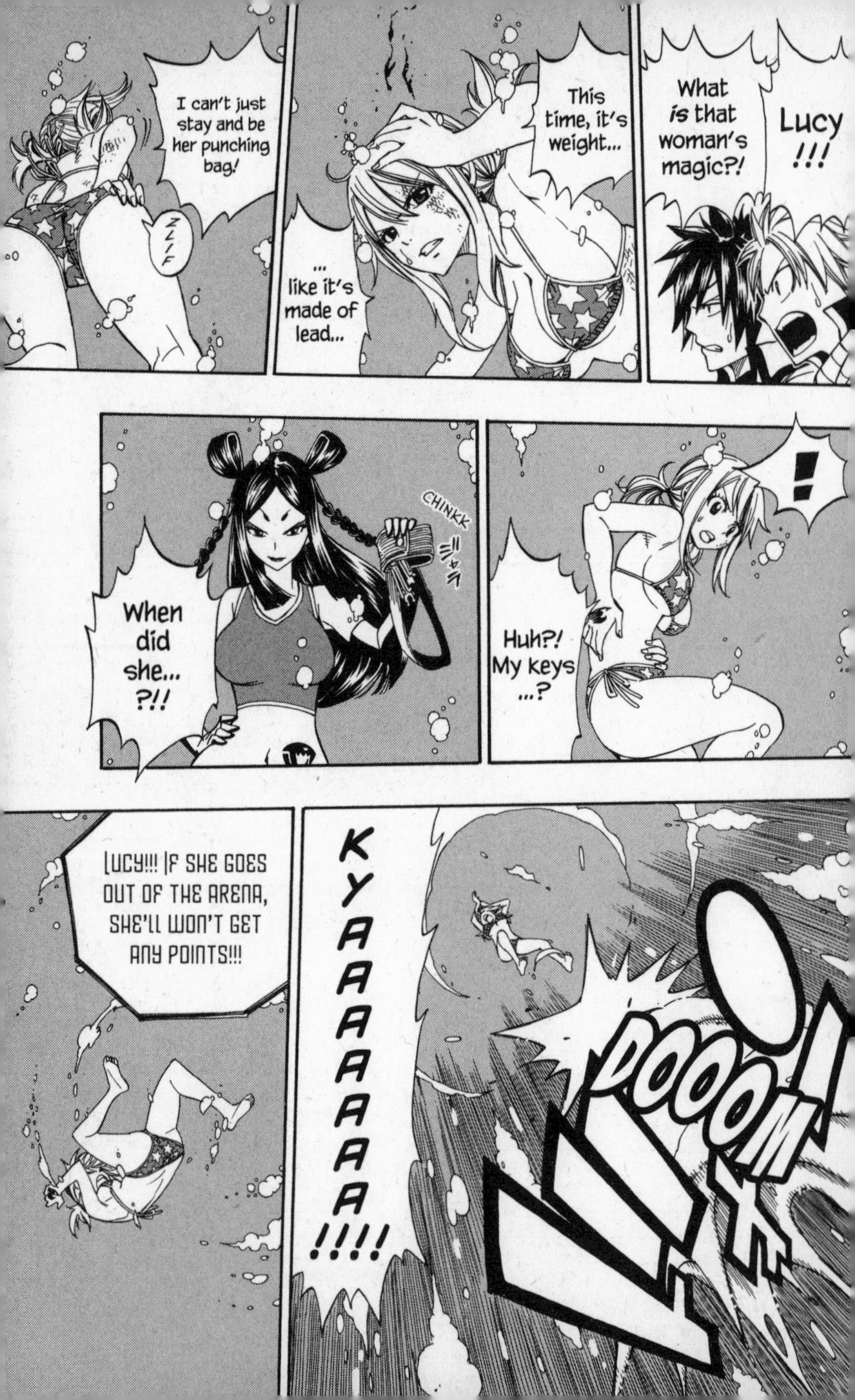
Lucy !!!
What is that woman's magic?!
This time, it's weight...
... like it's made of lead...
I can't just stay and be her punching bag!
ZZIF
!
Huh?! My keys ...?
CHINKK
ジャラ
When did she... ?!!
KYAAAAAAA!!!!
DOOOM
LUCY!!! IF SHE GOES OUT OF THE ARENA, SHE'LL WON'T GET ANY POINTS!!!

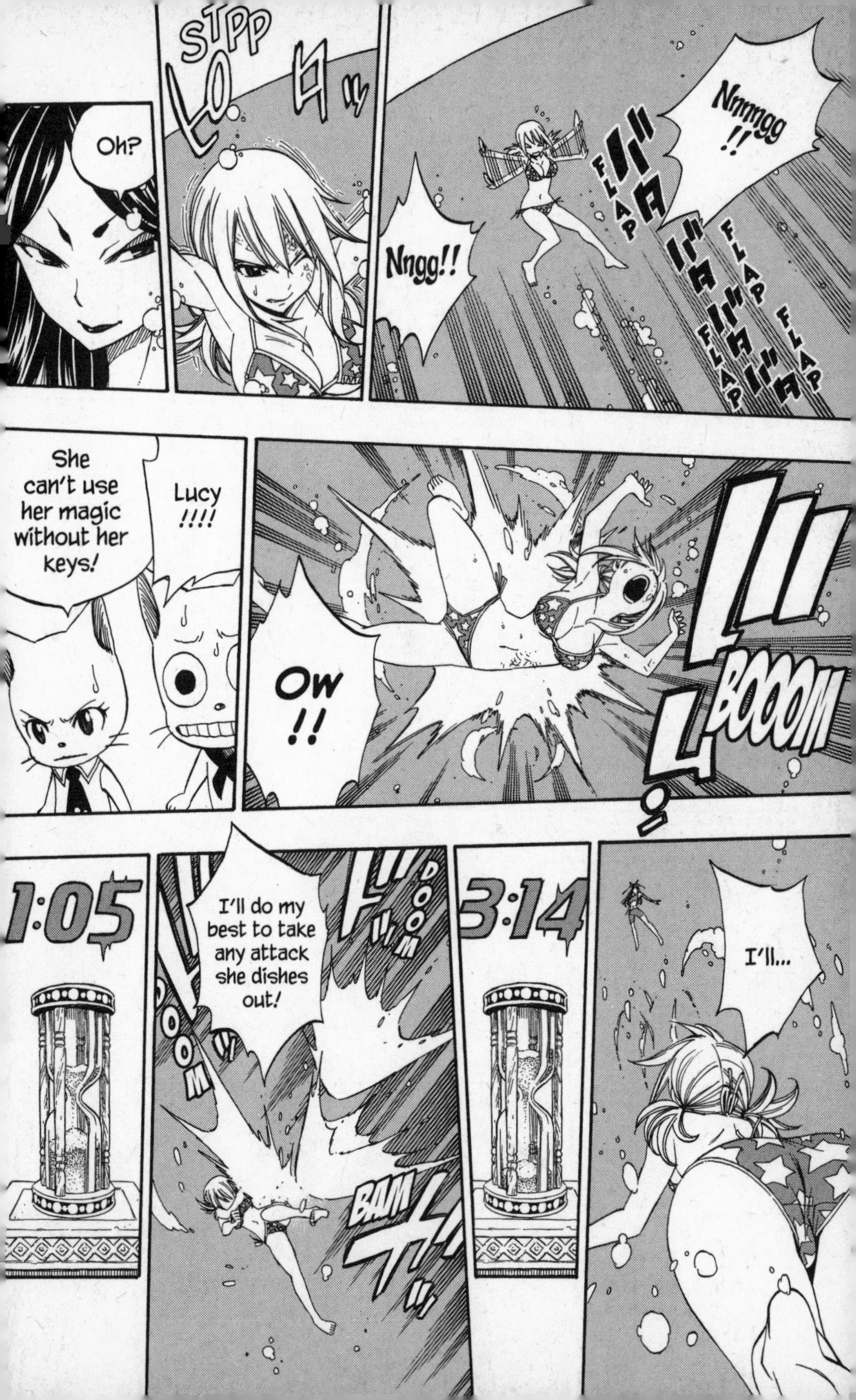
Nnnngg!!
FLAP FLAP FLAP FLAP
Nngg!!
STPP
Oh?
BOOOM
Ow!!
Lucy!!!!
She can't use her magic without her keys!
I'll...
3:14
DOOM
I'll do my best to take any attack she dishes out!
DOOM
BAM
1:05

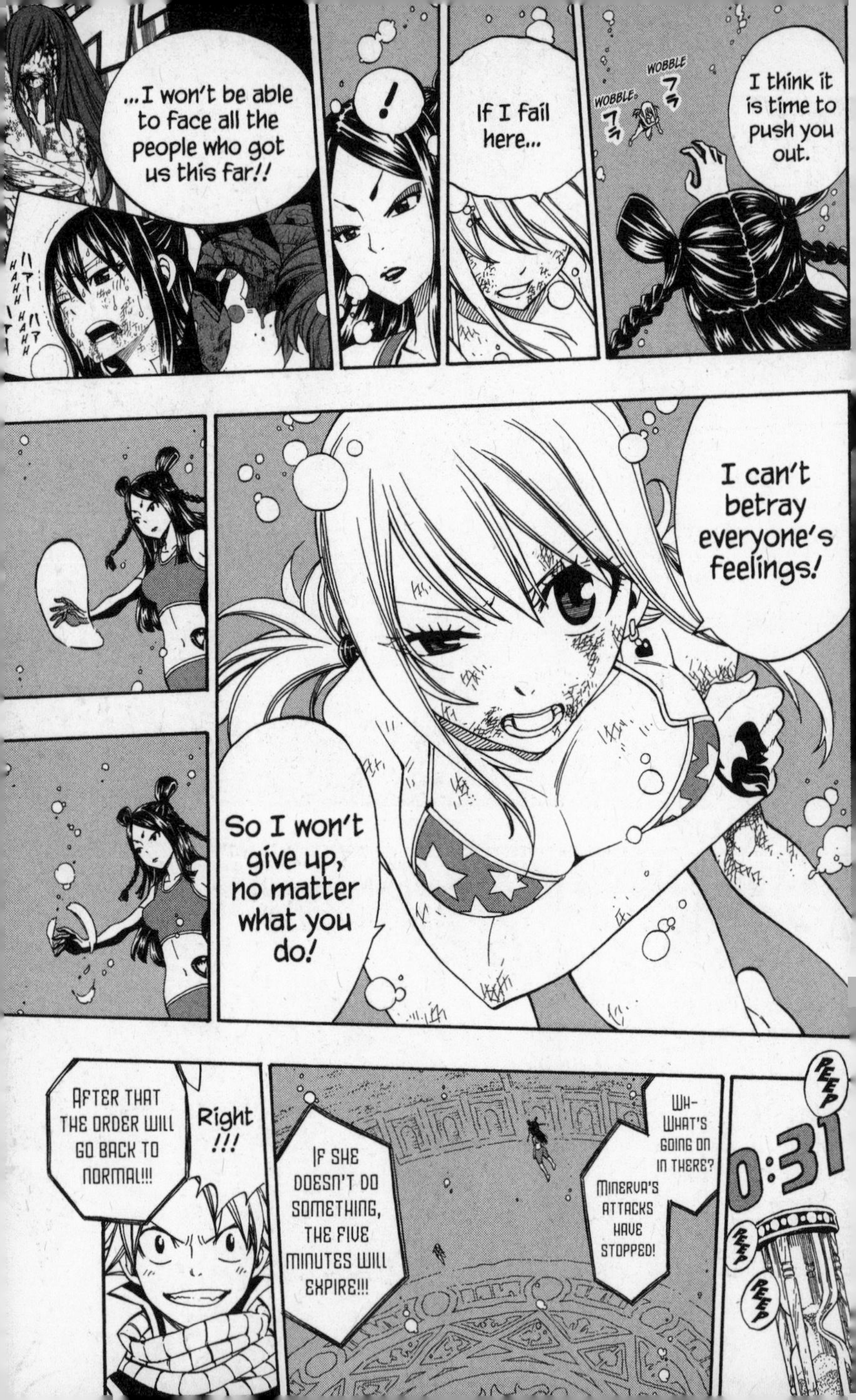
WOBBLE
WOBBLE
I think it is time to push you out.
If I fail here...
!
...I won't be able to face all the people who got us this far!!
HAHH HAHH
I can't betray everyone's feelings!
So I won't give up, no matter what you do!
BEEP
0:31
BEEP
BEEP
Wh- What's going on in there?
Minerva's attacks have stopped!
If she doesn't do something, the five minutes will expire!!!
Right!!!
After that the order will go back to normal!!!

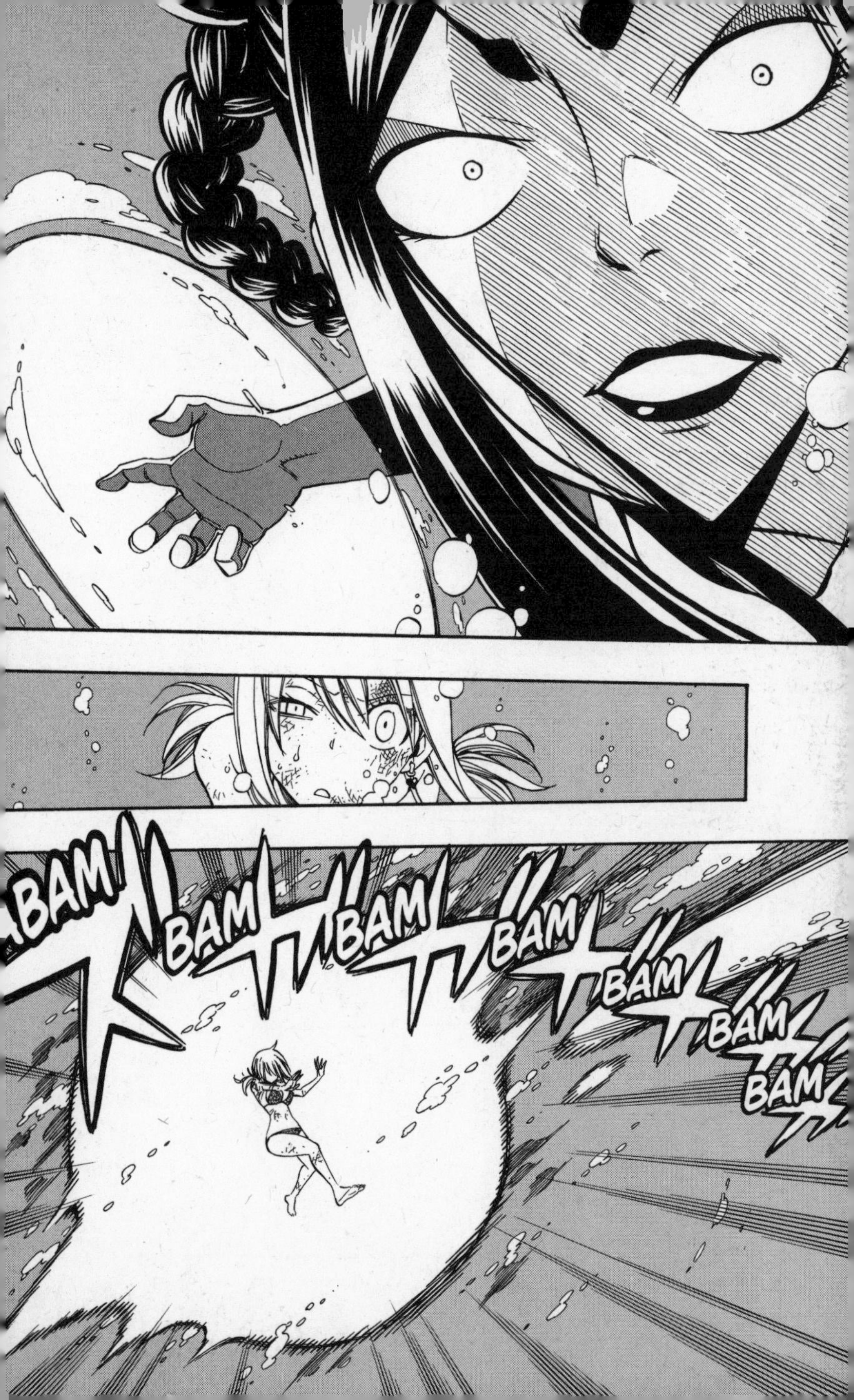
BAM
BAM
BAM
BAM
BAM
BAM
BAM

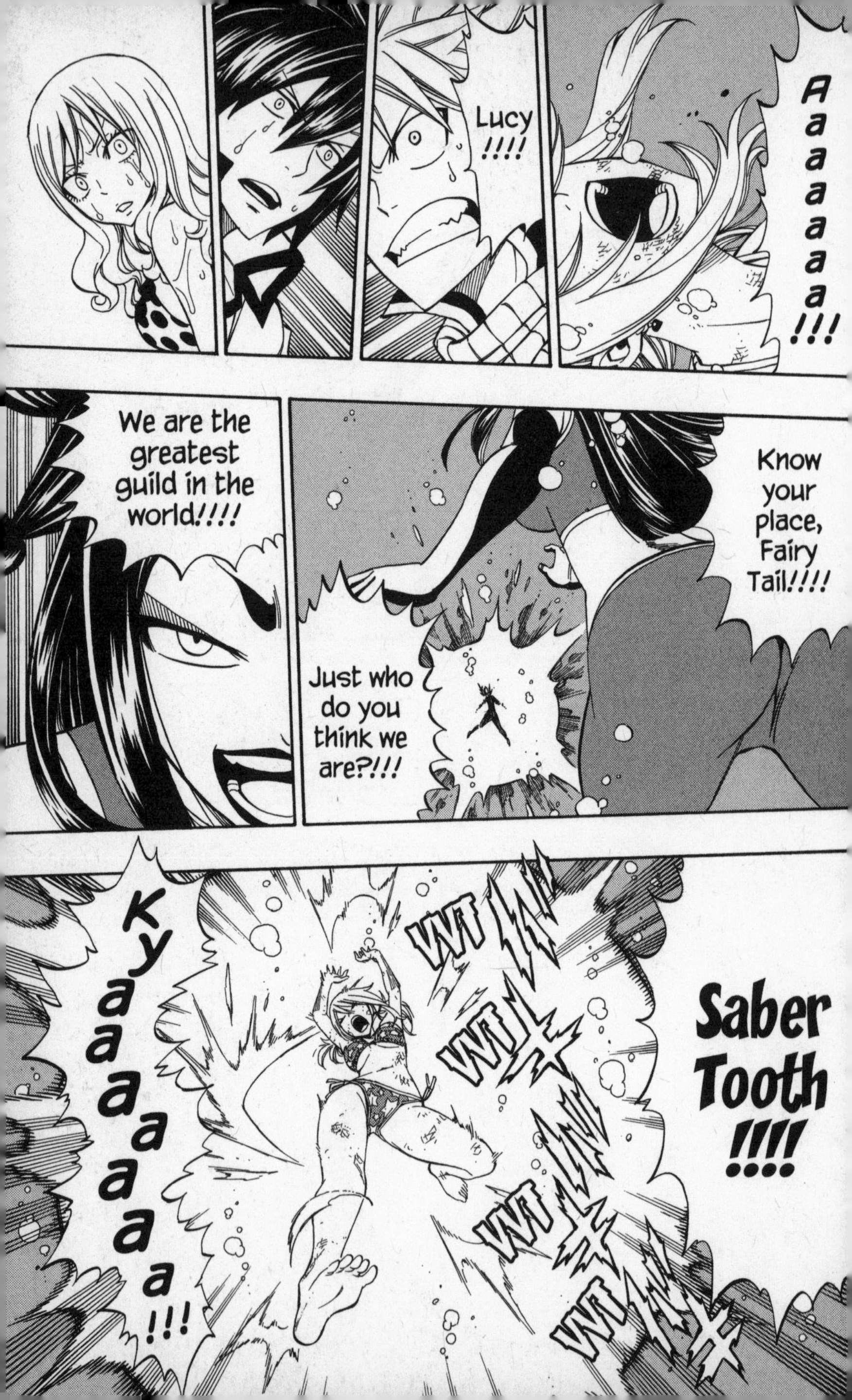
Aaaaaaaa!!!
Lucy!!!!
Know your place, Fairy Tail!!!!
Just who do you think we are?!!!
We are the greatest guild in the world!!!!
Saber Tooth!!!!
VVT
VVT
VVT
VVT
Kyaaaaaaaaaa!!!

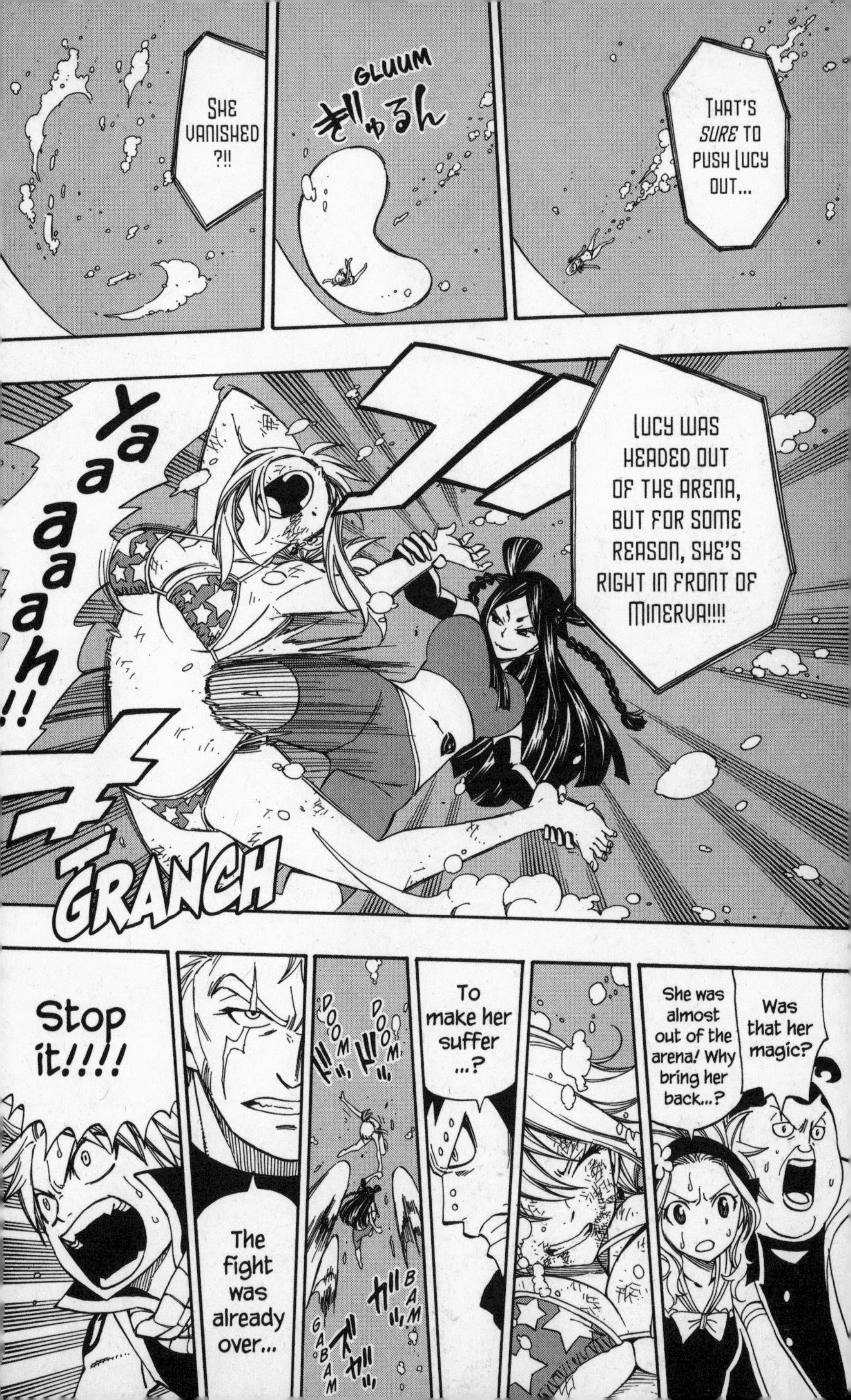
That's *sure* to push Lucy out...
GLUUM
ぎゅるん
She vanished?!!
Lucy was headed out of the arena, but for some reason, she's right in front of Minerva!!!!
Yaaaaaah!!
GRANCH
Was that her magic?
She was almost out of the arena! Why bring her back...?
To make her suffer ...?
DOOM
DOOM
BAM
GABAM
The fight was already over...
Stop it!!!!!

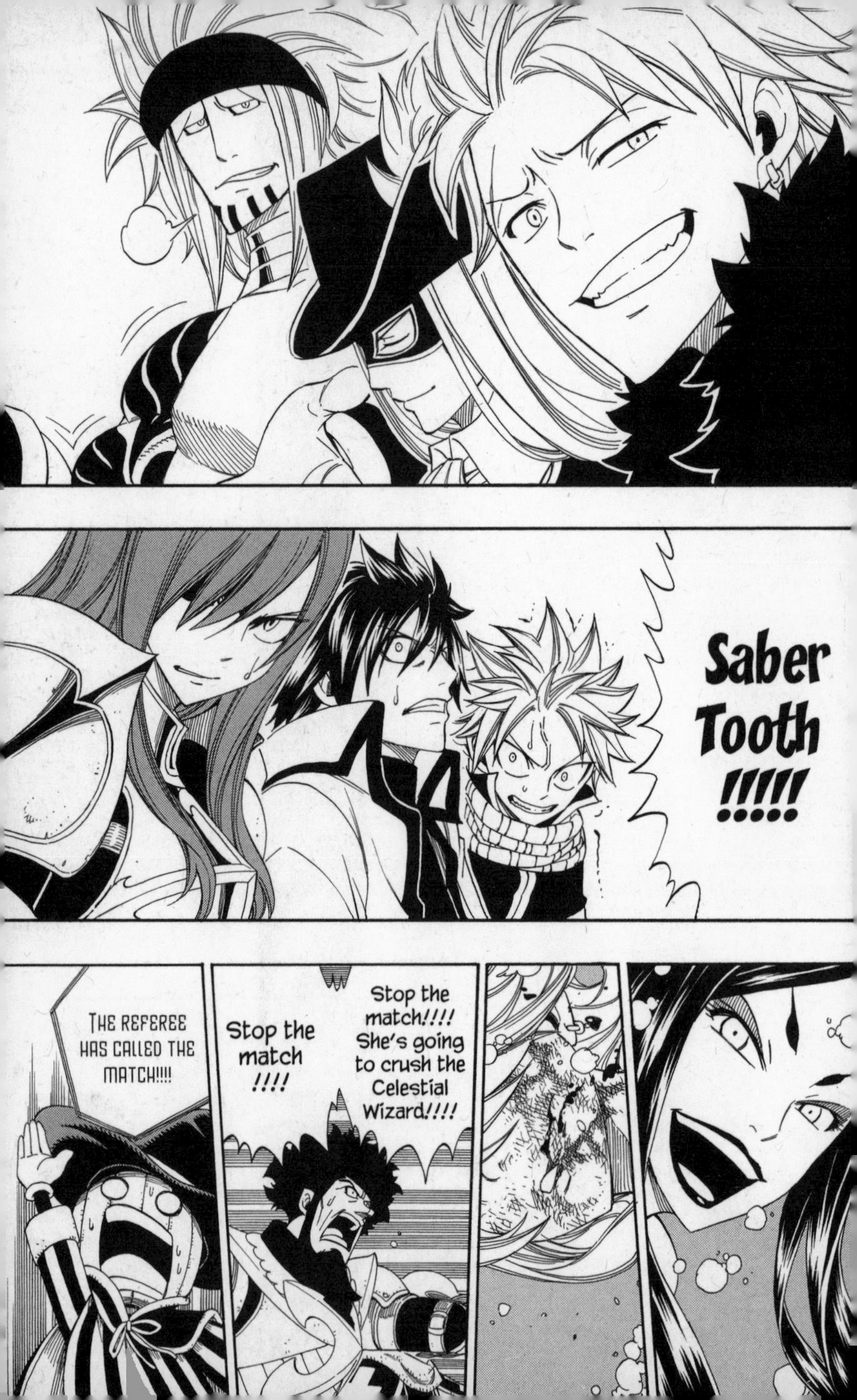
Saber Tooth!!!!!
Stop the match!!!! She's going to crush the Celestial Wizard!!!!
Stop the match!!!!
THE REFEREE HAS CALLED THE MATCH!!!!

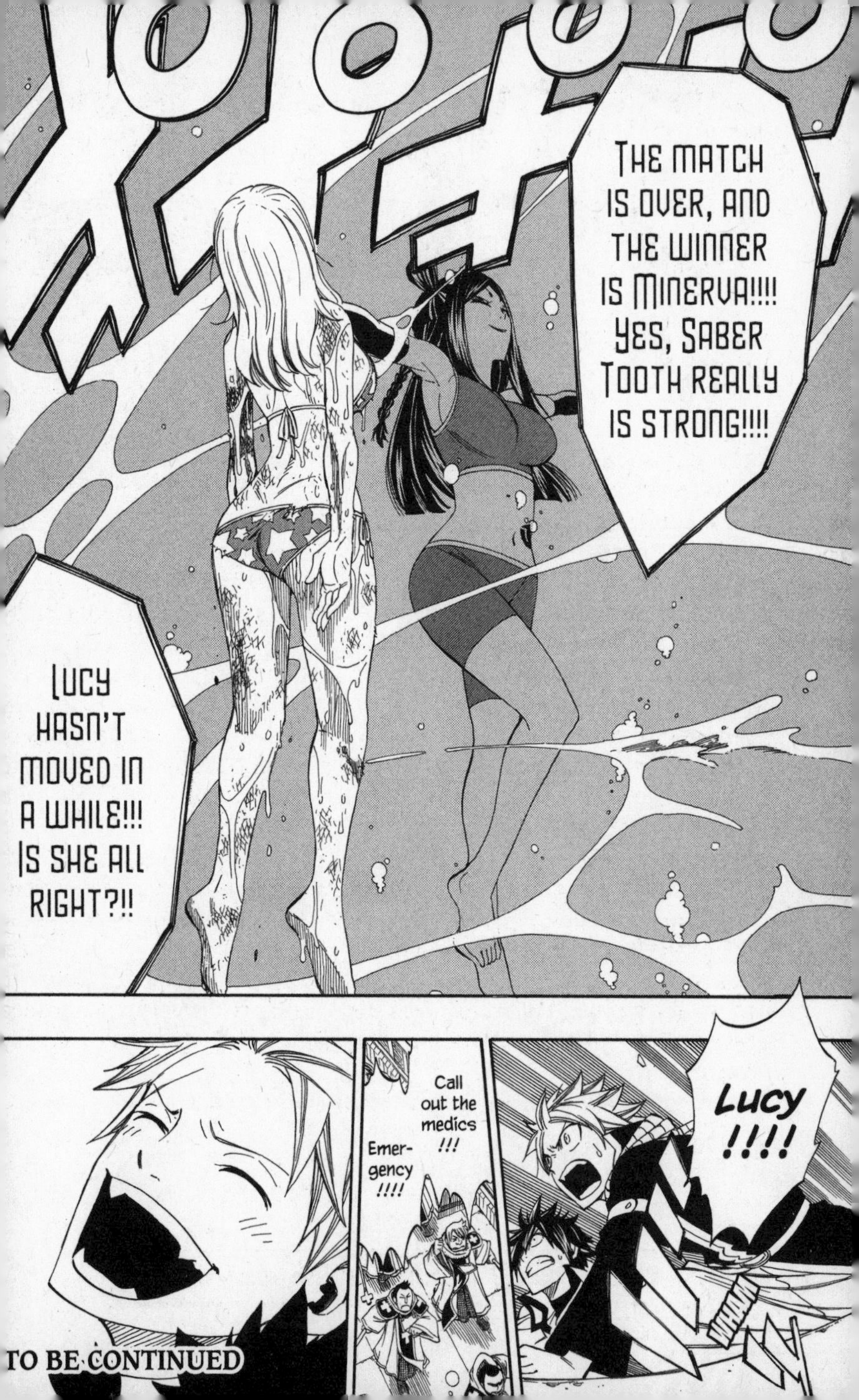
THE MATCH IS OVER, AND THE WINNER IS MINERVA!!!! YES, SABER TOOTH REALLY IS STRONG!!!!
LUCY HASN'T MOVED IN A WHILE!!! IS SHE ALL RIGHT?!!
Lucy!!!!
Call out the medics!!!
Emergency!!!!
TO BE CONTINUED

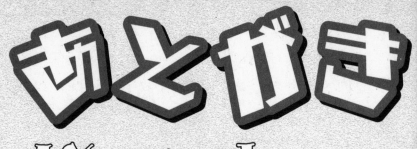

Afterword

This may seem sudden, but I started a Twitter account. I've had the itch to do it for a while, but I thought that I'd have to quit it quickly, so I never tried. But thanks to a friend's recommendation, I went ahead and started it anyway. And it's really fun! I found myself in conversations with all sorts of people, including famous people, and I really started to enjoy it. My original intentions were to use it for fan service and advertisement, but it's really hard to get the timing right on big announcements. So in the end, it just became an outlet for my sketches.

I often get the question, "Can I use your sketches as wallpaper for my screens?" You can save them, use them as wallpaper, use them as icons or for any personal reasons. I don't mind any of that. However, if you want to use them for commercial purposes, it seems there are many problems with that, so please don't use them that way.

Also one more important thing: I say you can "use sketches for your own personal use," but that is only for my sketches that I put out there personally. That doesn't mean other artists or any publishing companies feel the same way. Please be careful about that. Really, just about everything I tweet has nothing in it of any importance, but if you want to, you're welcome to follow my account. I'll happily read impressions of my work from manga fans on Twitter, but I also treasure the fan letters that I get from everybody too!

Anyway, I hope we can communicate, however you do it.

Twitter Account: @hiro_mashima

*Most tweets in Japanese.

Continued from the left-hand page.

Mira: We get that question a lot!

Lucy: But I wonder what they're doing now?

Mira: According to Millianna, they're out on a journey across the continent.

Lucy: Continuously for seven years?

Mira: A little behind-the-scenes talk, they were originally supposed to be mixed up in the Grand Magic Games too.

Lucy: But that was rejected...

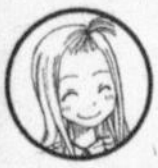
:I mean, the number of people that show up in this story is just shocking!

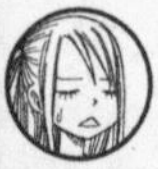
: Rejected...

Mira: Now, the next question.

Did Mira-chan and Jenny know each other a long time ago?

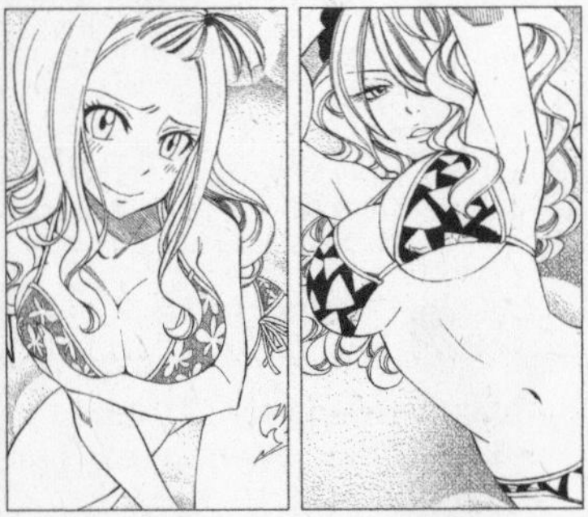

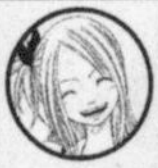
:Everyone who reads Sorcerer knows about that!

Mira: True. We've been friends for a long time!♡

Lucy: Come to think of it, a lot of readers may not know about other guild members who are friends with members of a different guild.

Mira: Well, I think everyone knows this already, but Erza and Ichiya (Blue Pegasus) know each other from somewhere.

Lucy: The master and Jura-san (Lamia Scale) are connected in that they're both wizard saints.

Mira: And while we're on Lamia, there's Gray and Lyon.

Lucy: Yeah, but... Those are all things that have been drawn in the main story. Are there any combinations we don't suspect?

Mira: Well...there's Droy and Araña (Mermaid Heel).

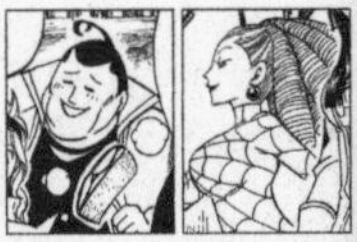

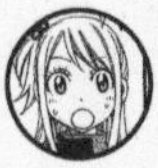
:Whoa!! I didn't know about that! What's their relationship?

Mira: They just came across each other by coincidence during the seven years we were gone.

Lucy: Really?

Mira: And Droy fell in love at first sight!

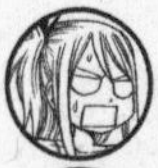
: ***Whaa?!***

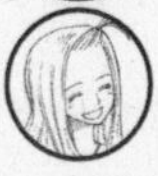
:And I hear that she rejected him big time!

Lucy: Oh, no...

Mira: There are others too! Let's see... A long time ago, Max...

Lucy: If we go on, it'll just make people feel sorry for them, so let's call it a day right here!

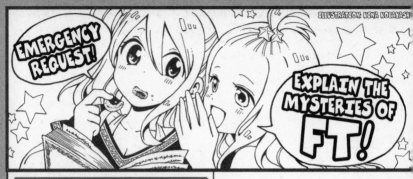

EMERGENCY REQUEST!

EXPLAIN THE MYSTERIES OF FT!

At an outdoor café in Crocus...

Mira: Hello!

Lucy: And hellhi!

: Okay! Welcome to the question corner where Lucy makes lame jokes!!

: It wasn't that lame!

Mira: Let's have the first question!

Are "Ancient Spells" and "Lost Magic" the same thing?

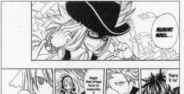

Lucy: It does seem like a hard distinction to understand.

Mira: But to be precise, they're completely different things.

Lucy: Ancient Spells are, just like the words say, magic from a long time ago.

Mira: "Lost Magic" is only one type of Ancient Spells.

: In other words, it comes out looking like this.

Ancient Spells

Lost Magic	Nirvana
Dragon Slayer Magic	
Arc of Time	Zeref's Magic
etc.	

Mira: The various types of magic are all pretty complicated, so it's probably very difficult to remember.

Lucy: Next question!

Millianna showed up, but are Shô and Wally ever going to appear again?

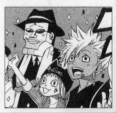

Continued on the right-hand page.

TAIL

d'ART

The Fairy Tail Guild is looking for illustrations! Please send in your art on a postcard or at postcard size, and do it in black pen, okay? Those chosen to be published will get a signed mini poster! ♪ Make sure you write your real name and address on the back of your illustration!

hizuoka Prefecture, Ayana Suzuki

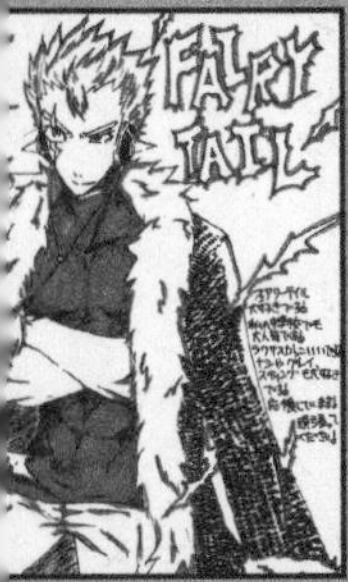
FAIRY TAIL

Laxus had a really big
rt this time!!

Gunma Prefecture, Kurumi Tamura

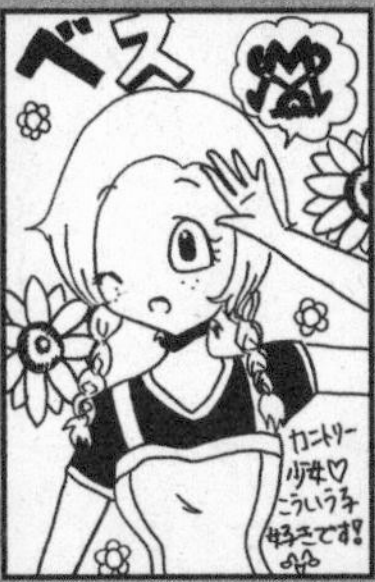
ベス

▲A girl with way too little to do in the story. Maybe she'll have a part soon?

Yamanashi Prefecture, Saki Mitsui

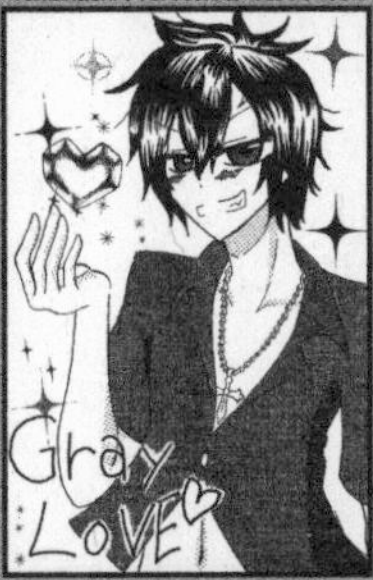
Gray
LOVE

▲A glittering Gray! Beautiful!

Okayama Prefecture, Akane

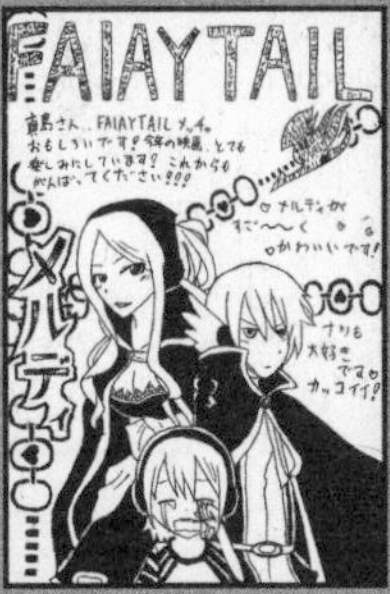
FAIAY TAIL

▲Merudy! In three versions.

Chiba Prefecture, Momoka Ishii

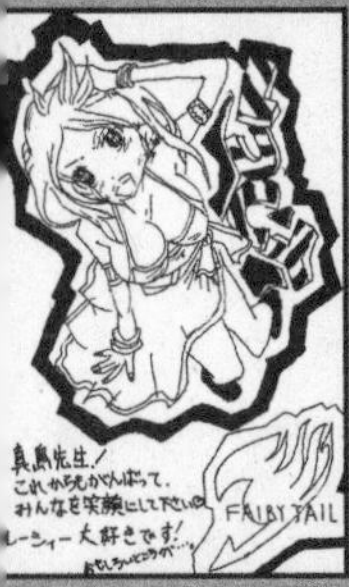
FAIRY TAIL

I wonder if Lucy is our
ost interesting character?

Hyogo Prefecture, Mayu Uchida

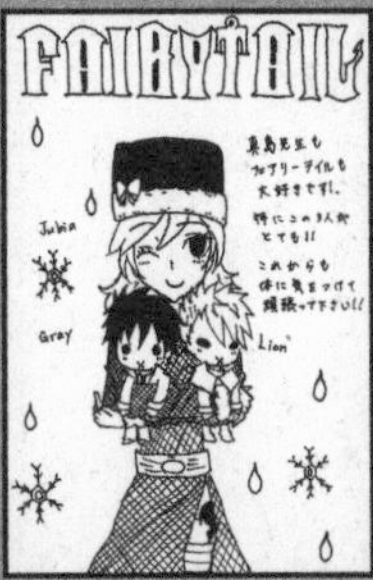
FAIRYTAIL
Juvia
Gray
Lion

▲Really! What's going to happen with these three?

I won-der if the boy will always hold Natsu in respect? ▶

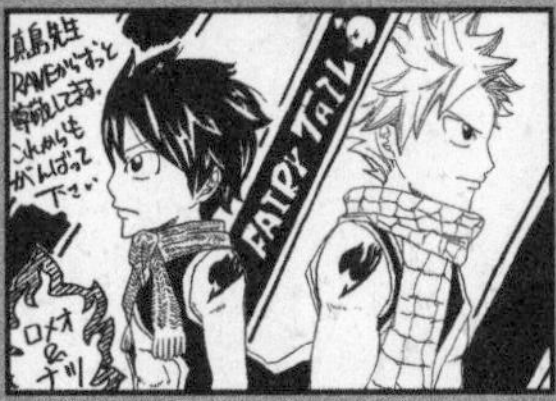
FAIRY TAIL

Shimane Prefecture, Hirotada.

Happy's being a little mean. Poor Lily! ▶

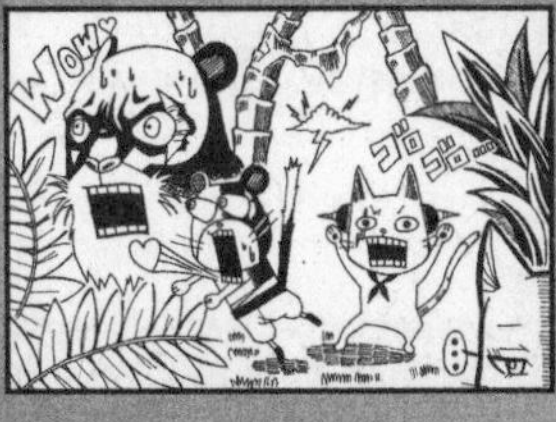
WOW

Chiba Prefecture, Tomoko Sasaki

Send to Hiro Mashima, Kodansha Comics
451 Park Ave. South, 7th Floor New York, NY 10016

FAIRY GUILD

Chiba Prefecture, Shiori Koike

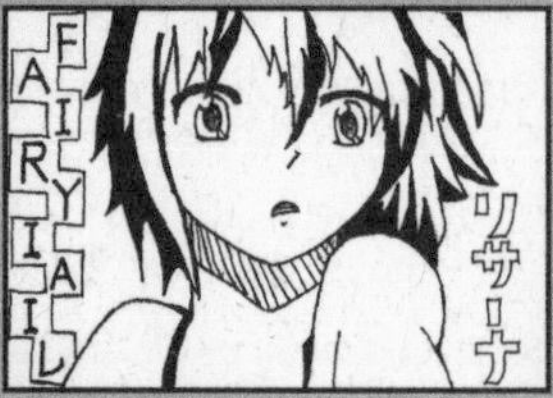
FAIRY TAIL
リサーナ

This ▶ one looks as if she's been surprised by something, right?

By sending in letters or postcards, you give us permission to give your name, address, postal code, and any other information you include to the artist as-is. Please keep that in mind.

REJECTION CORNER

Ibaraki Prefecture, Tomoharu Terakado

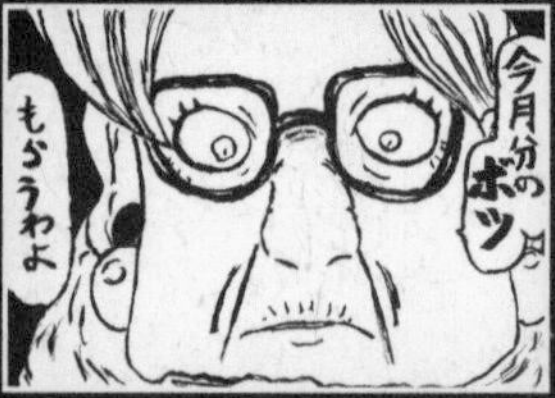
今月分のボツ
もらうわよ

▲U-Urk... Yes, it's yours...

Ibaraki Prefecture, Rind6

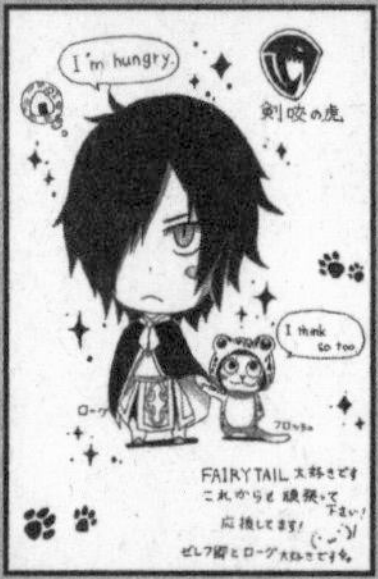
I'm hungry.
剣咬の虎
I think so too.
FAIRY TAIL

▲That's so cute! They're holding hands!

Yamaguchi Prefectur
Honoka Yoshim

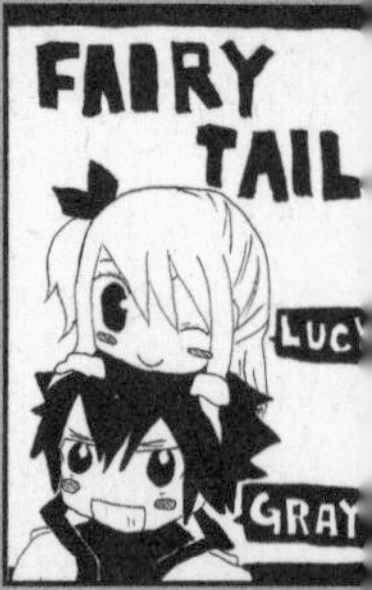
FAIRY TAIL
GRAY

▲The Lucy glomming onto Gray is so cute!

Hyogo Prefecture, Kasutiin

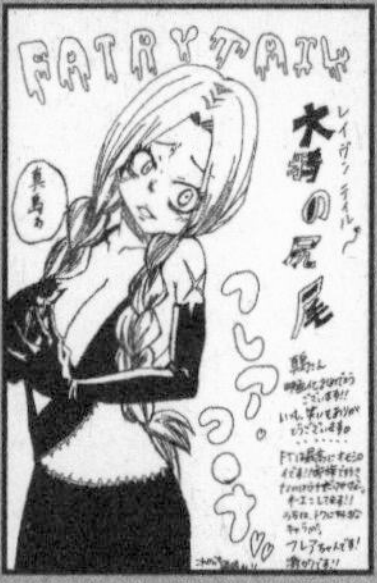
FAIRY TAIL
妖精の尻尾
フレア

▲Flare-san's following is borderline but there.

Yamanashi Prefecture, Ayane Naka

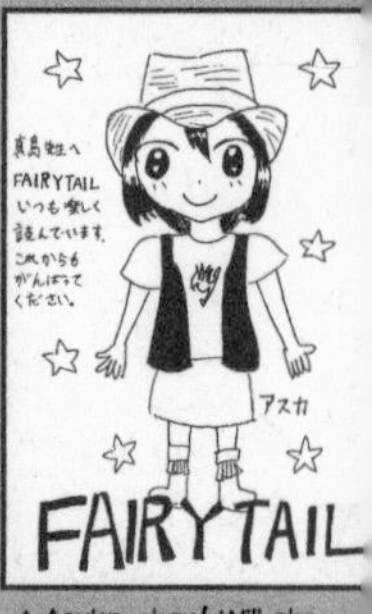
FAIRY TAIL
アスカ
FAIRY TAIL

▲Asuka-chan! Will she be a wizard when she grows up?

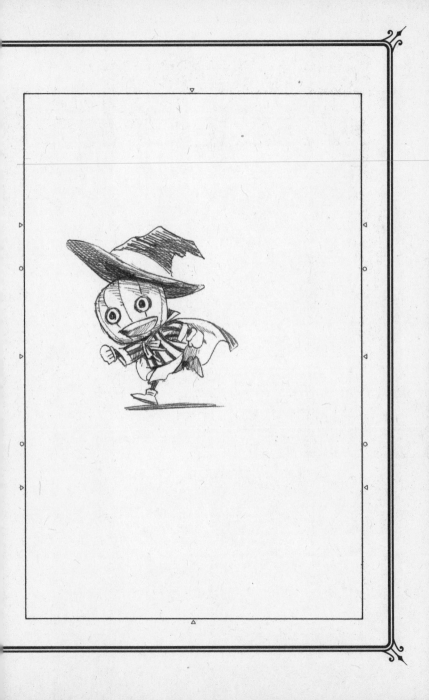

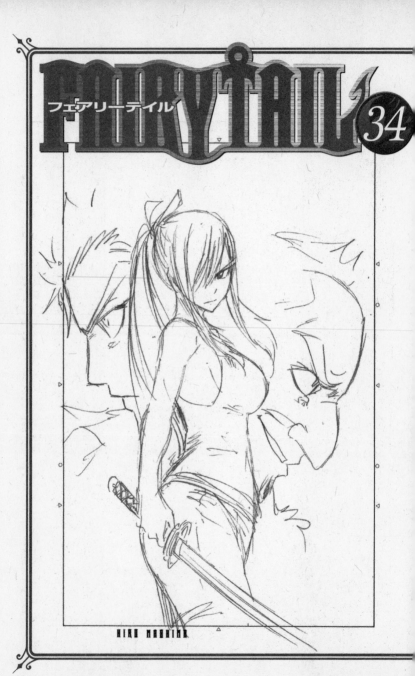

FAIRY TAIL
フェアリーテイル

34

HIRO MASHIMA

FROM HIRO MASHIMA

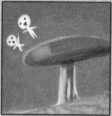

Volume 34!! In one more volume, this will match the entire run of my previous series. Huh? When I began Fairy Tail, I distinctly remember saying, "I plan on ending this at about ten volumes…" But when I wasn't looking, it got to a point where it's going to easily outdistance my previous work. Hmm… What'll I do? There are so many things I still want to do with Fairy Tail.

Original Jacket Design: Hisao Ogawa

Translation Notes:

Japanese is a tricky language for most Westerners, and translation is often more art than science. For your edification and reading pleasure, here are notes on some of the places where we could have gone in a different direction with our translation of the work, or where a Japanese cultural reference is used.

Page 33, Numbers games

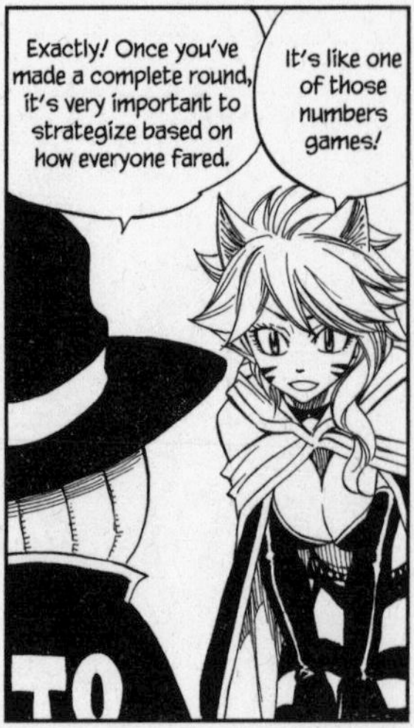

It's like one of those numbers games!
Exactly! Once you've made a complete round, it's very important to strategize based on how everyone fared.
TO

There is a type of game played in Japan where two or more people take turns to count up to a particular number. They can count all or some of the numbers within a limited range, then pass off their turn to the next person. When someone is forced to count the target number, that person loses. For example, were the rules to say that the target number is "30," and the players have a range of three numbers, the first player would count, either one, two, or three. Let's say the first player counts to two. Then the next player would start at "three" and count, "three," "three, four," or "three, four, five." Assuming the second player stopped at "five," the next player would start at "six" and so on. When the counting approaches the mid-twenties, one must strategize how many numbers to state so one is not put in a position to say the number "thirty." Pandemonium is similar to a numbers game because one chooses a number of monsters to fight, and then passes the turn on to the next player.

Page 35, Lottery stick

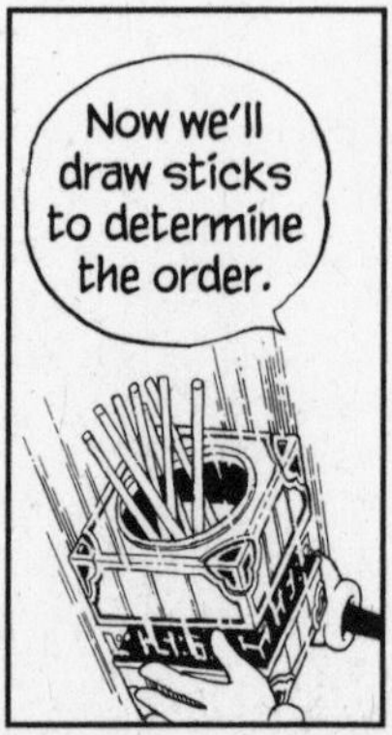

Now we'll draw sticks to determine the order.

This is a common way of "drawing straws" in Japan, although the sticks have a wider variety of outcomes than the single broken straw that the game has in the west. It is usually done with a large number of sticks, all inside a wooden box that is completely closed off except for a single hole just big enough to allow a single stick through. The sticks are shaken and mixed, and then one is allowed to drop through the hole. Each stick has a number or code on it, and the code correlates to some prize or outcome. This version of lottery is most commonly used in temples and shrines for drawing fortunes. When the stick is drawn, the person who runs the lottery checks the numbers or codes and retrieves a printed fortune that corresponds to what is written on the stick.

Page 114, -tan

This is basically a mispronunciation of the honorific, "-chan," that is normally used by young girls of about high-school or middle-school age to refer to each other or to their friends. However, it has also been used by idols who call themselves by that honorific because it is considered cute, and that has been picked up by the fans of those idols. Since then the honorific has spread until it is now fairly commonly heard in conversation and in the media. However, it still contains the nuance that it should be used by girl of high-school or middle-school age, so when a middle-aged man like Chapati uses, "-tan," a more "normal" person like Yajima or Lahar might be taken aback by the usage.

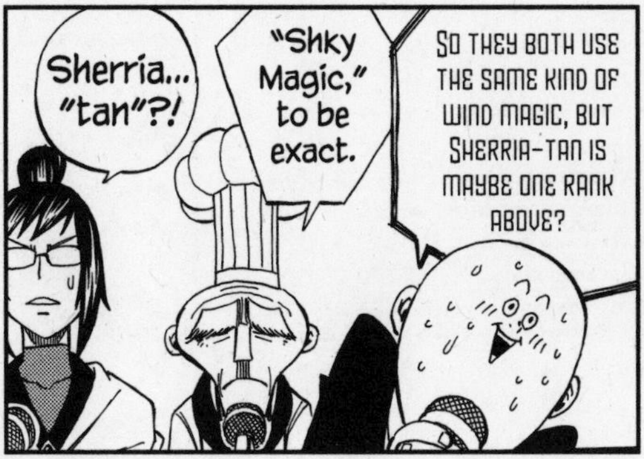
So they both use the same kind of wind magic, but Sherria-tan is maybe one rank above?
"Shky Magic," to be exact.
Sherria... "tan"?!

Preview of *Fairy Tail*, volume 35

We're pleased to present you with a preview from Fairy Tail, volume 35. Please check our Web site (www.kodanshacomics.com) to see when this volume will be available.

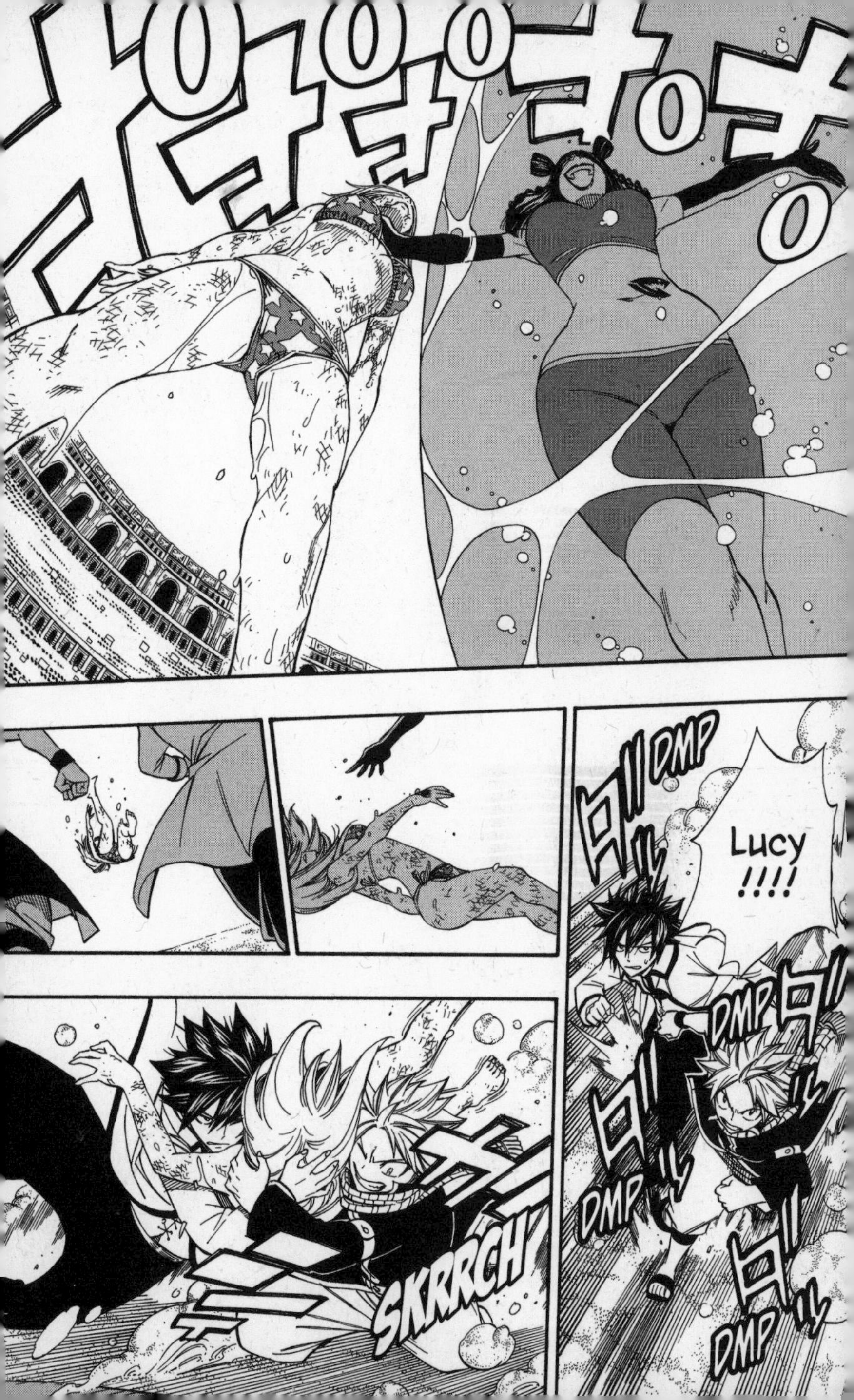
DMP
Lucy !!!!
DMP
DMP
DMP
SKRRCH

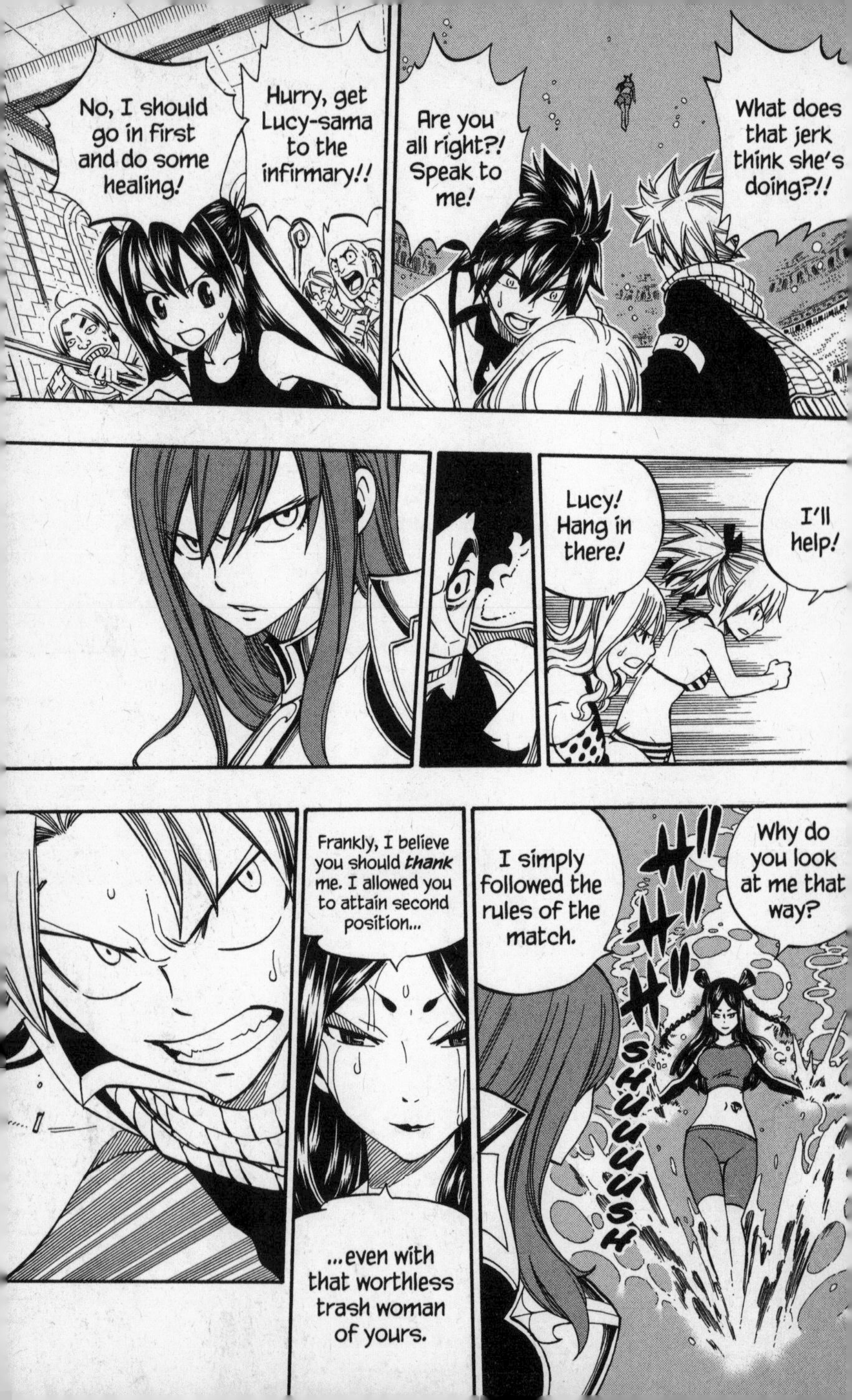
What does that jerk think she's doing?!!
Are you all right?! Speak to me!
Hurry, get Lucy-sama to the infirmary!!
No, I should go in first and do some healing!
I'll help!
Lucy! Hang in there!
Why do you look at me that way?
SHUUUUSH
I simply followed the rules of the match.
Frankly, I believe you should *thank* me. I allowed you to attain second position...
...even with that worthless trash woman of yours.

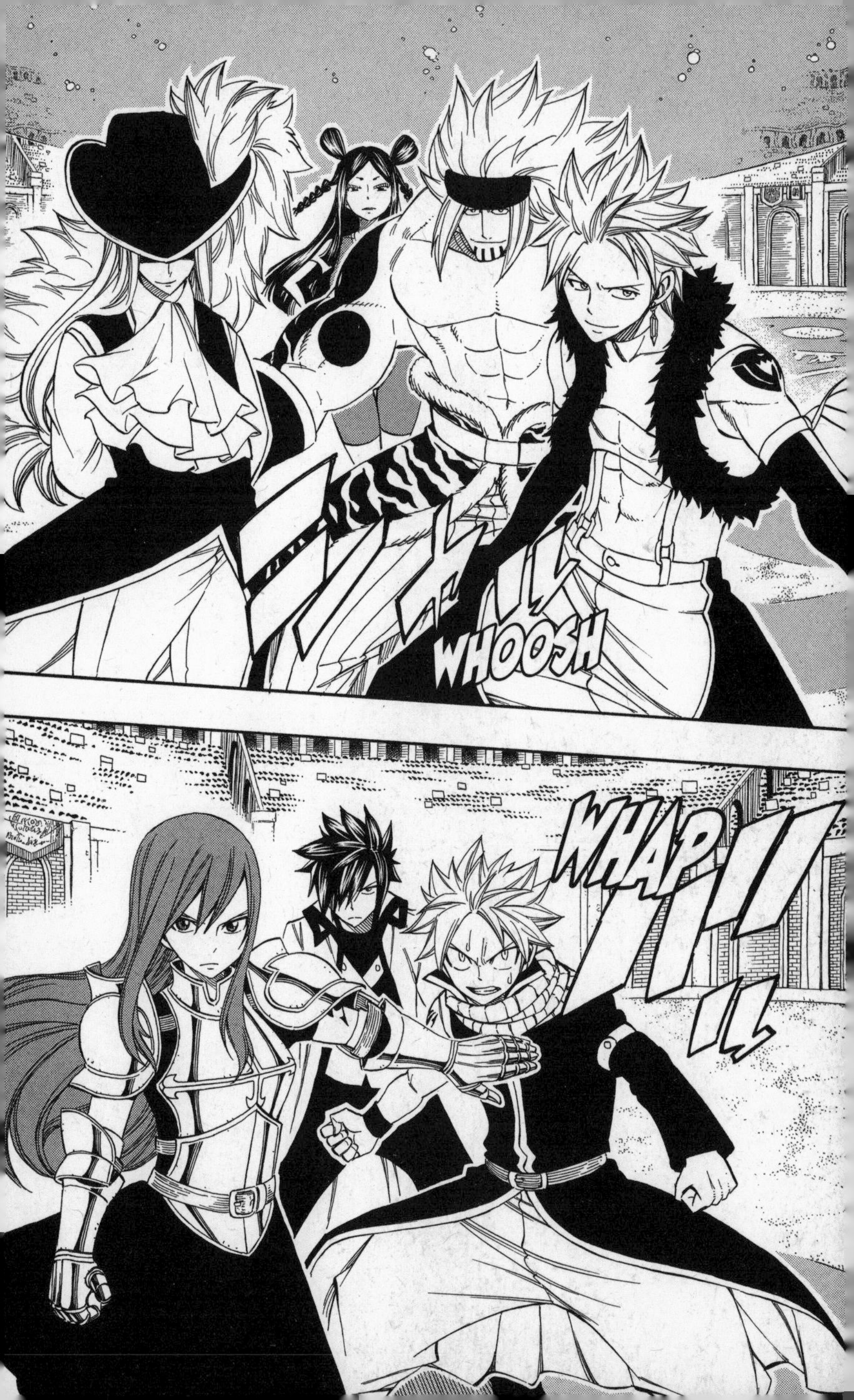
WHOOSH
WHAP!!

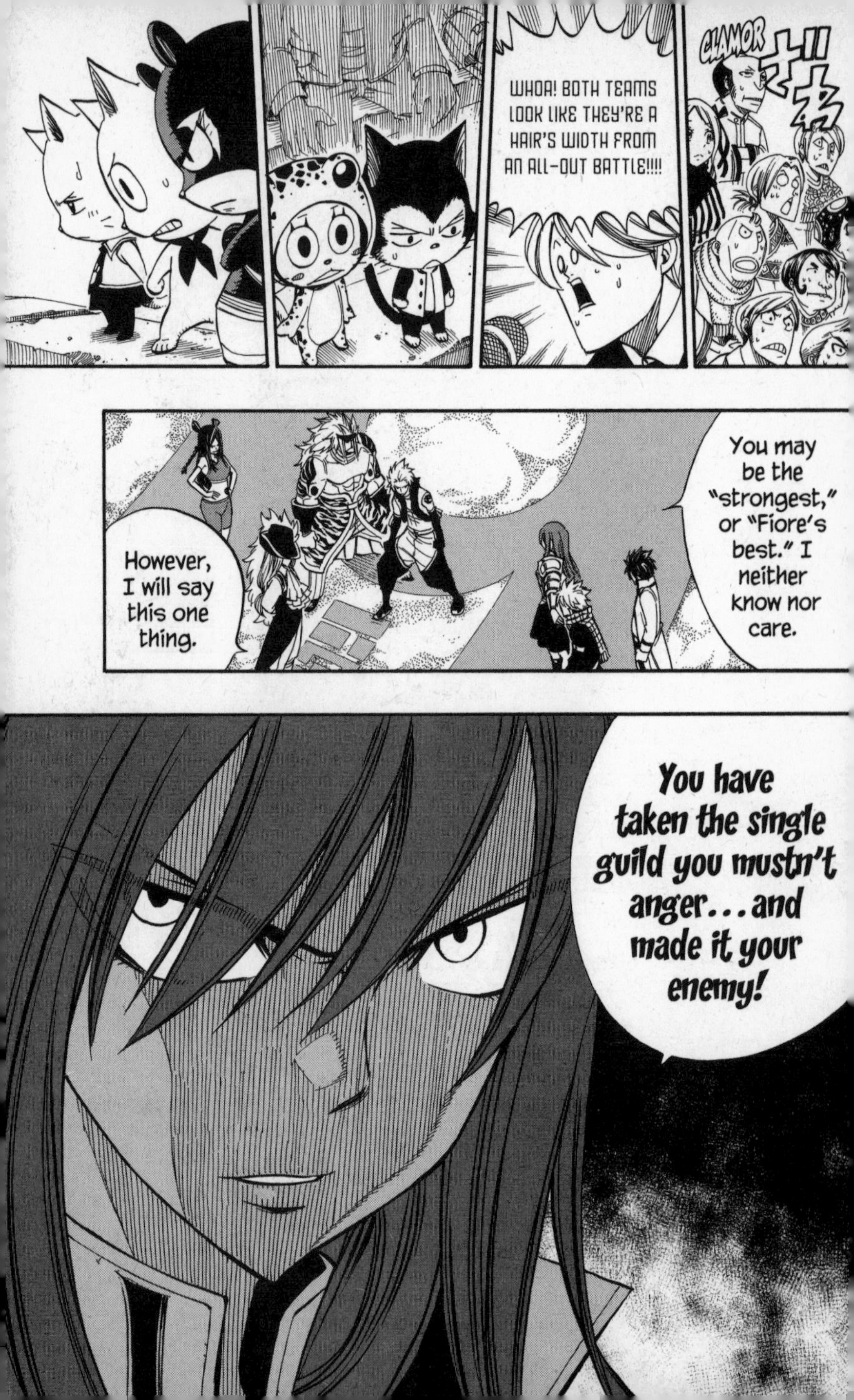
CLAMOR
WHOA! BOTH TEAMS LOOK LIKE THEY'RE A HAIR'S WIDTH FROM AN ALL-OUT BATTLE!!!!
You may be the "strongest," or "Fiore's best." I neither know nor care.
However, I will say this one thing.
You have taken the single guild you mustn't anger...and made it your enemy!

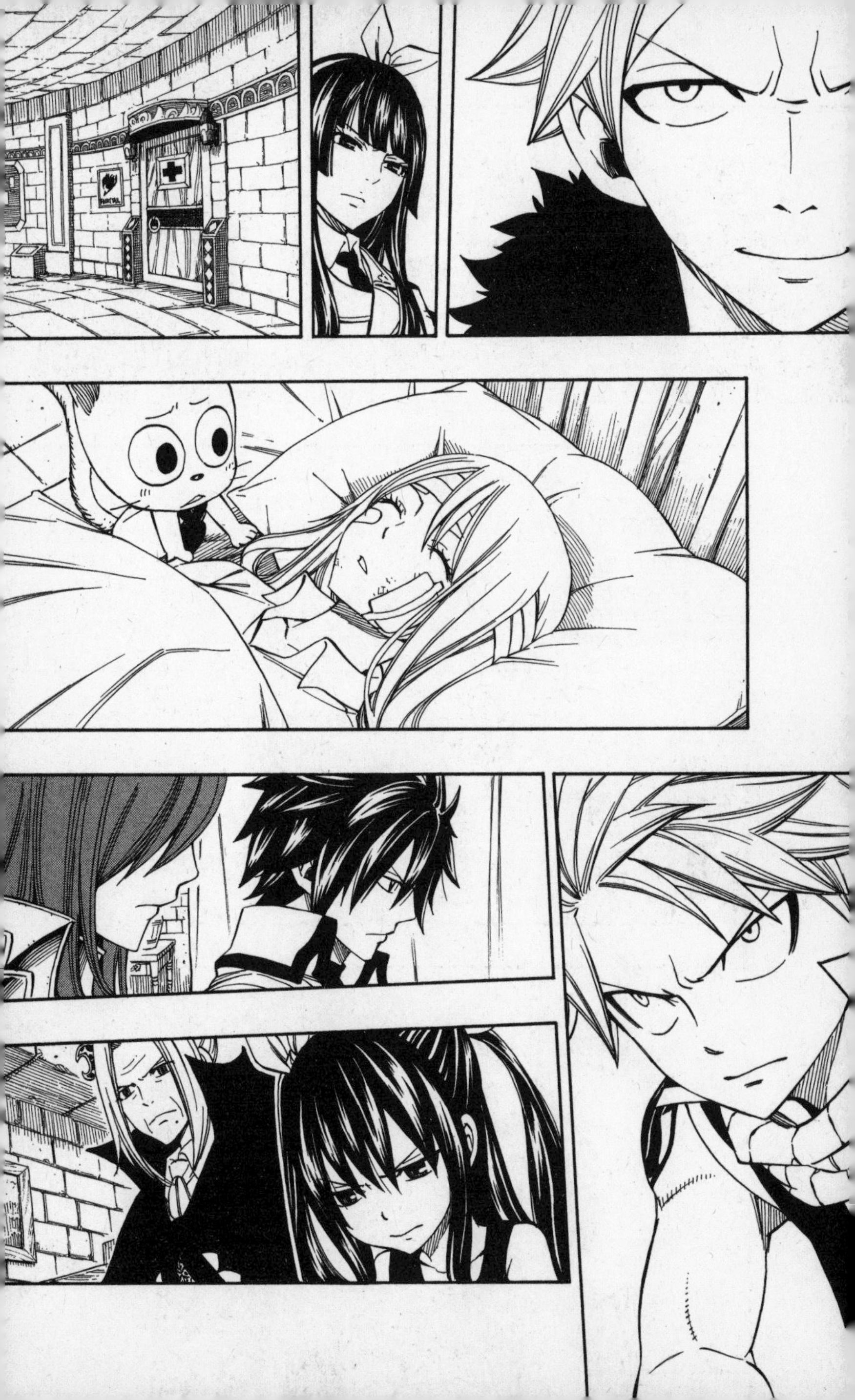

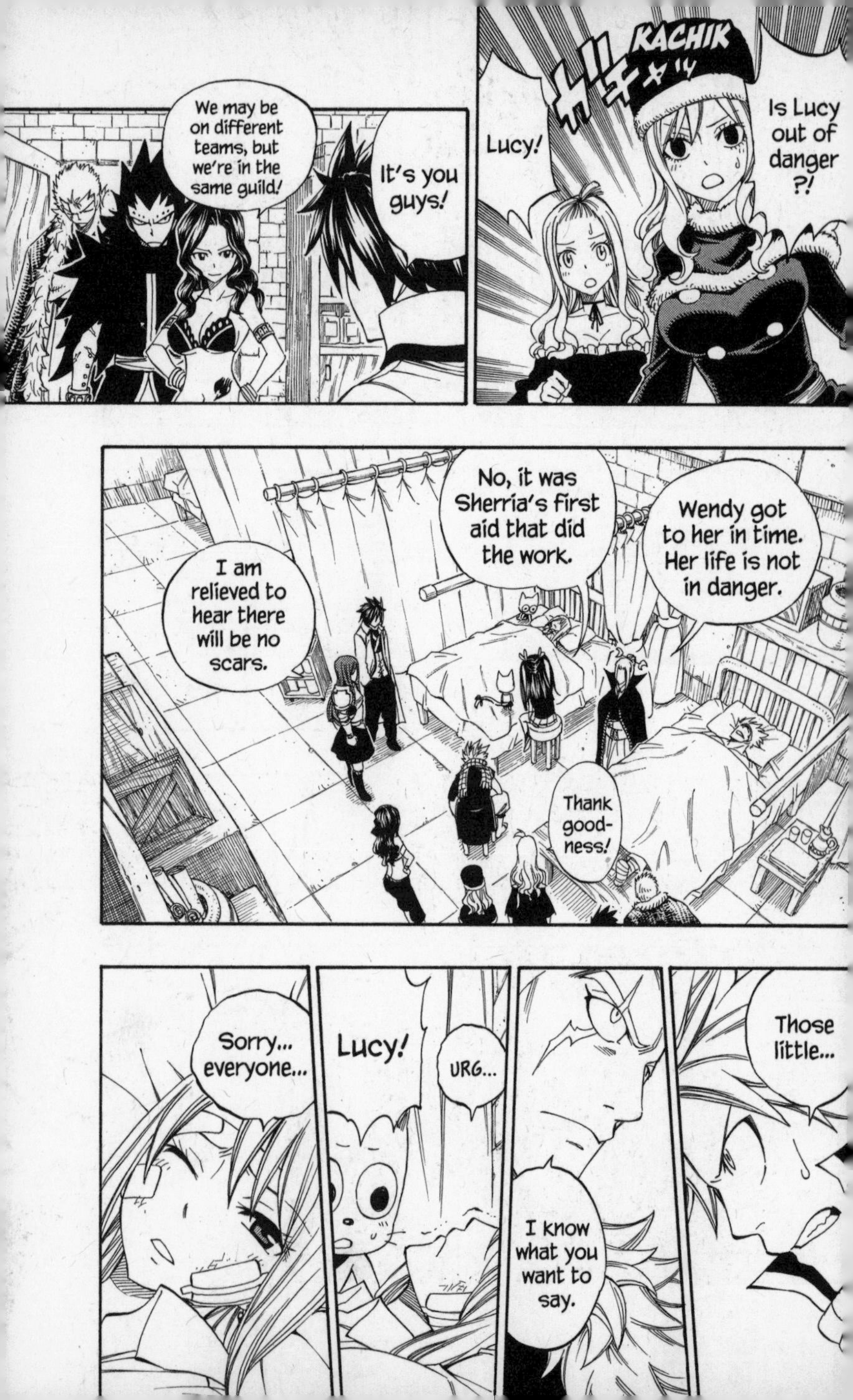
KACHIK
Is Lucy out of danger?!
Lucy!
It's you guys!
We may be on different teams, but we're in the same guild!
Wendy got to her in time. Her life is not in danger.
No, it was Sherria's first aid that did the work.
I am relieved to hear there will be no scars.
Thank goodness!
Those little...
I know what you want to say.
Lucy!
URG...
Sorry... everyone...

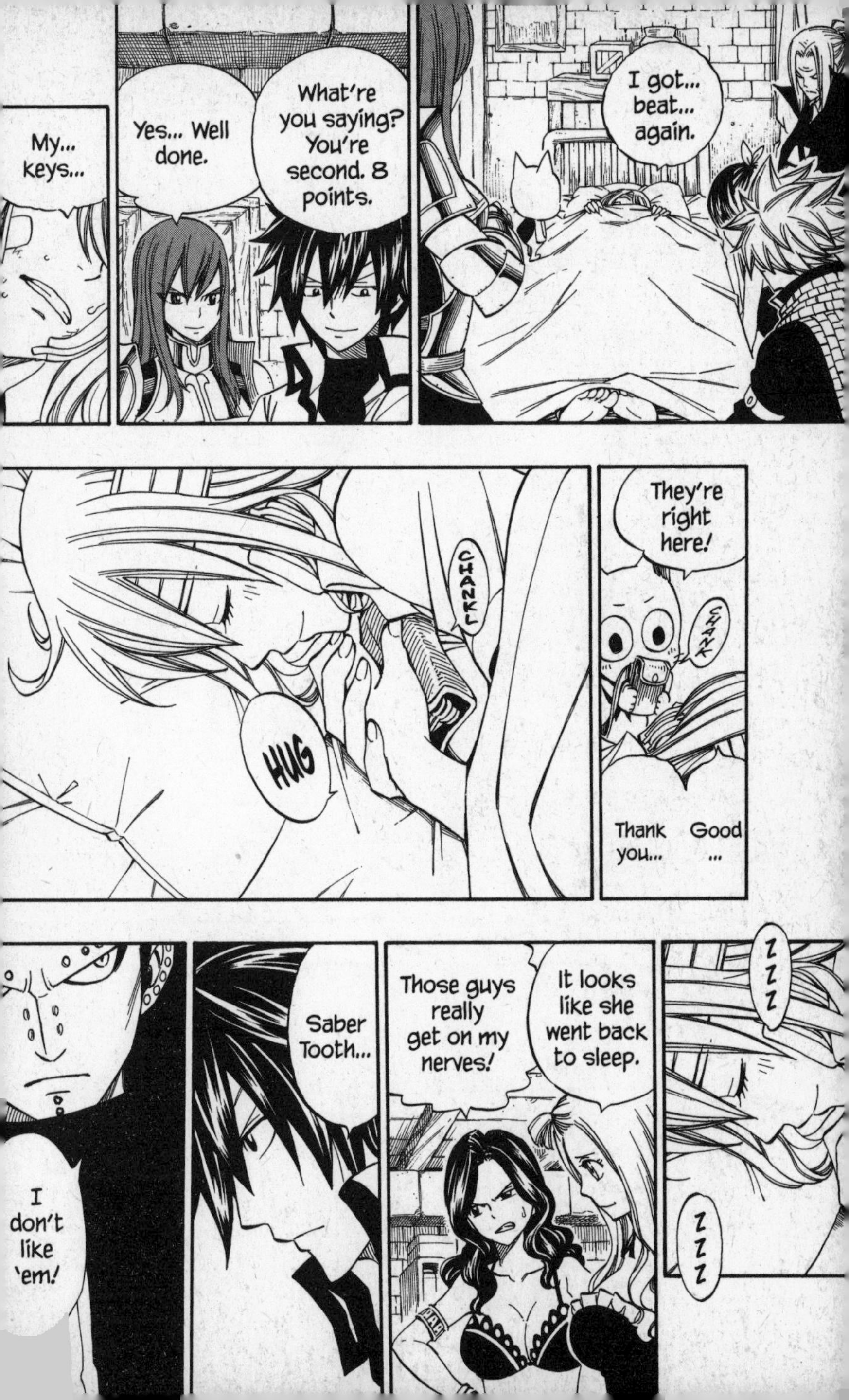
I got... beat... again.
What're you saying? You're second. 8 points.
Yes... Well done.
My... keys...
They're right here!
CHANK
Good...
Thank you...
CHANKL
HUG
ZZZ
ZZZ
It looks like she went back to sleep.
Those guys really get on my nerves!
Saber Tooth...
I don't like 'em!

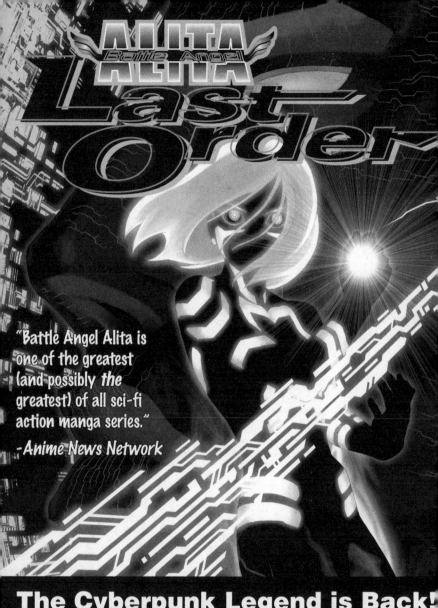

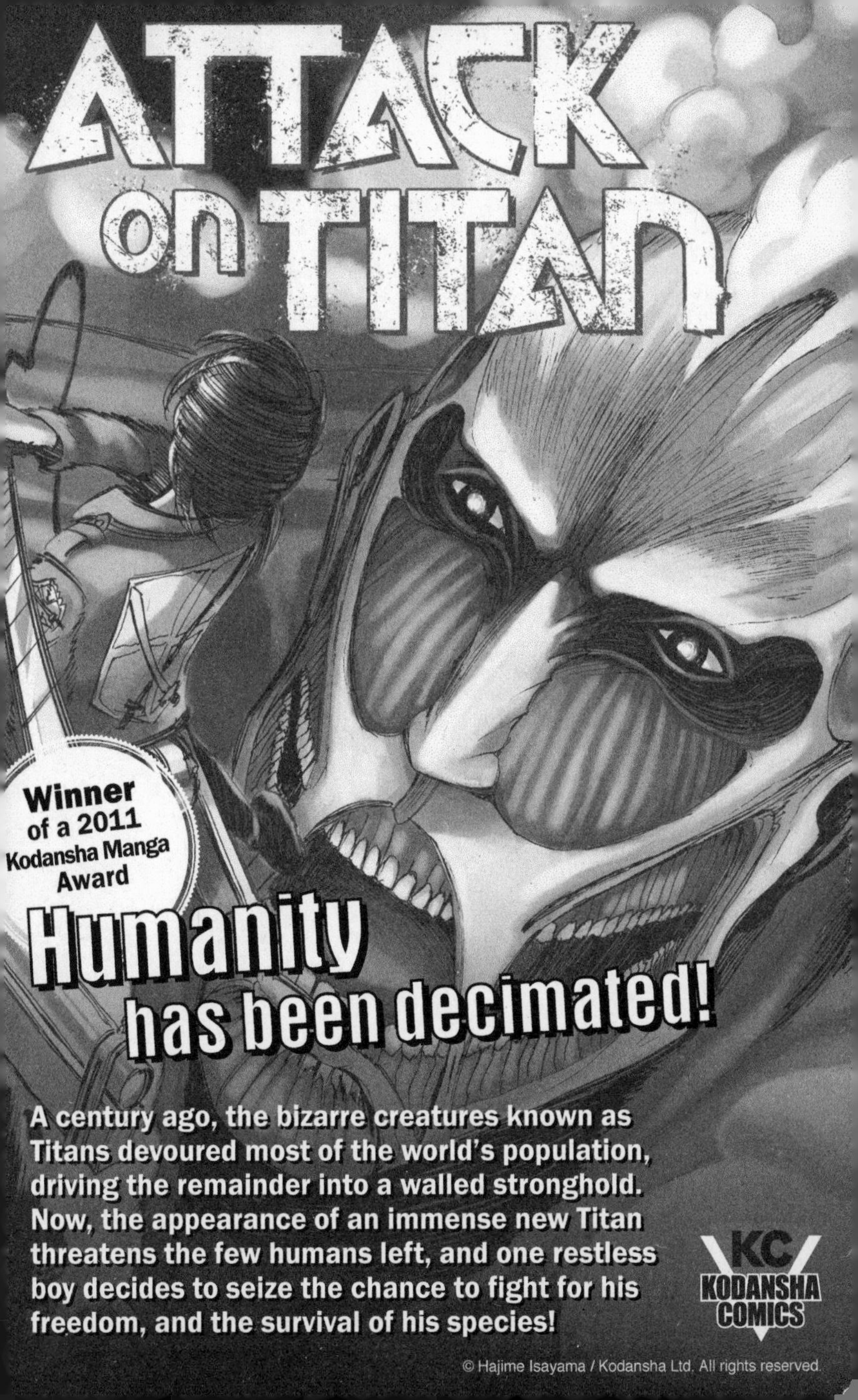
ATTACK on TITAN
Winner of a 2011 Kodansha Manga Award
Humanity has been decimated!
A century ago, the bizarre creatures known as Titans devoured most of the world's population, driving the remainder into a walled stronghold. Now, the appearance of an immense new Titan threatens the few humans left, and one restless boy decides to seize the chance to fight for his freedom, and the survival of his species!
KC KODANSHA COMICS
© Hajime Isayama / Kodansha Ltd. All rights reserved.

Fairy Tail volume 34 is a work of fiction. Names, characters, places, and incidents are the products of the author's imagination or are used fictitiously. Any resemblance to actual events, locales, or persons, living or dead, is entirely coincidental.

A Kodansha Comics Trade Paperback Original.

Published in the United States by Kodansha Comics, an imprint of Kodansha USA Publishing, LLC, New York.

Publication rights for this English edition arranged through Kodansha Ltd., Tokyo.

First published in Japan in 2012 by Kodansha Ltd., Tokyo
ISBN 978-1-61262-411-2

Printed in the United States of America.

www.kodanshacomics.com

9 8 7 6 5 4 3 2 1

Translation: William Flanagan
Lettering: AndWorld Design
Editing: Ben Applegate

TOM

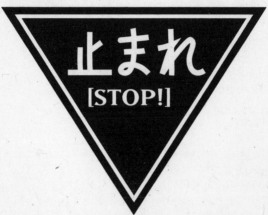

You're going the wrong way!

Manga is a completely different type of reading experience.

To start at the *beginning*, go to the *end*!

hat's right! Authentic manga is read the traditional Japanese way—
om right to left, exactly the *opposite* of how American books are
ead. It's easy to follow: Just go to the other end of the book and read
ach page—and each panel—from right side to left side, starting at
e top right. Now you're experiencing manga as it was meant to be!